Practical Public Affairs in an Era of Change

Practical Public Affairs in an Era of Change

A Communications Guide for Business, Government, and College

Edited by

Lloyd B. Dennis

Public Relations Society of America
and
University Press of America, Inc.
Lanham • New York • London

Published by
University Press of America,® Inc.
4720 Boston Way
Lanham, Maryland 20706

3 Henrietta Street
London, WC2E 8LU England

Library of Congress Cataloging-in-Publication Data

Practical public affairs in an era of change : a cutting-edge
communications guide for government, business, and college / Lloyd
B. Dennis, editor.
p.   cm.
Includes bibliographical references and index.
1. Public relations.   2. Publicity.   I. Dennis, Lloyd B. (Lloyd
Burton),
II. Public Relations Society of America.
HD59.P68   1995   659 --dc20   95-31940 CIP

ISBN 0-7618-0085-9 (cloth : alk: ppr.)
ISBN 0-7618-0086-7 (pbk: alk: ppr.)

Contents

ISSUES IN PUBLIC AFFAIRS MANAGEMENT

CHALLENGES ON THE HORIZON

Introduction

Practical Public Affairs in an Era of Change: A Communications Guide for Business, Government, and College aims to provide a comprehensive review of what is currently and largely known about the subject of public affairs in the context of the public relations profession. Given that the professional activity and inquiry on this subject has evolved in rather diverse and often seemingly unrelated disciplines, the task of bringing together a wide spectrum of qualified specialists capable of covering the multiple nuances of the public affairs experience—past, present, and future—has been an exciting and arduous challenge.

The rules of business and government are constantly changing, thus imposing the need for flexibility in the public affairs practice. This book is designed to provide you with information you will need to manage the increasingly complex world in which we all try to operate, often responding to issues and problems and less often given the opportunity to proactively prepare for or head off those problems. In either case, however, the skills needing to be brought forth require a delicate balance between maintaining excellent working relationships with a host of external stakeholders—a company's or institution's constituents—while seeing to it that the interests of the master, i.e., the managers of the institution, are reasonably and effectively represented. The public affairs issues the practitioner has to deal with often have public policy impact. This, in reality, is oftentimes in the public interest, however defined, and is thus the public affairs professional's overriding obligation and concern.

Practical Public Affairs is sponsored entirely by the Public Relations Society of America, the world's oldest, largest, and most prominent society for public relations professionals. The genesis of the book can be traced to the 1982 publication of the *Public Affairs Handbook* by the American Management Association. Sensing the need, after more than a decade, for a follow-up edition, and com-

mitted to producing a volume which was contemporaneously definitive and simultaneously forward-looking, the sponsors of the PRSA
volume recruited a cadre of nationally-prominent authors. Viewed
as a whole, their work has produced a volume which is at once
comprehensive and coherent. Its central focus grows out of the last
decade itself, a time of profound, unrelenting and transformational
change in American business and government. (Given PRSA's leadership in bringing this project to completion, it is understandable
that a commentary identifying public affairs as a discipline within
the larger purview of public relations, authored by John L. Paluszek,
appears nearby.)

This volume contains 30 chapters, divided into five sections,
addressing a broad range of specific changes, problems, and issues
facing business and government. Contributors include well-known
practitioners in the field, academics who are esteemed in their particular discipline of teaching, and other experts whose insights often help determine how an issue or problem is handled for many
years. The authors hail from every region of the country.

The communications revolution is the chief dynamic underlying
all the practical material presented in this book. Just as the technology of the communications revolution has rendered time-honored
boundaries of time and space largely irrelevant, so, too, has it transformed the way professional communicators ply their craft. In the
end, the best benefit of *Practical Public Affairs* rests in the contribution it makes to help turn theory about various communications-
related disciplines into more definitive ways to provide both wisdom
and direction for public affairs and public relations professionals in
the future.

Finally, in his much-praised book *The Age of Extremes*, British
scholar Eric Hobsbawm strives to make sense of the tumultuous 20th
century. He writes:

> By the century's end large numbers of citizens were withdrawing from
> politics, leaving the affairs of state to the "political class" who read
> each other's speeches and editorials—a special interest group of pro-
> fessional politicians, journalists, lobbyists and others whose occupa-
> tions ranked at the bottom of the scale of trustworthiness in
> sociological enterprises.

While there is much that is valid in this statement, I hope Hobsbawm is wrong in the long run. After more than thirty years work-

ing as a public affairs professional in one or another incarnation, I know he is wrong about public affairs in America. Certainly there is growing despair and anger at politicians and deep disenchantment with seemingly unresponsive governmental institutions. But at the same time, growing numbers of ordinary Americans are becoming involved in public policy making. And this is good. But we need more people to do that.

Given its interest in civic commitment and political participation, the profession of public affairs has the potential of being the catalyst which, as the 21st century approaches, rejuvenates American democracy.

— Lloyd B. Dennis
Editor
September, 1995

Acknowledgments

Practical Public Affairs is the proud achievement of a group of public affairs, public relations and communications professionals who came together as members of the Public Affairs and Government Section, under the umbrella of the world's oldest, largest and most prominent professional organization for public relations professionals, the Public Relations Society of America.

As we all know, books like this are not accomplished without the help of many people. And in the course of four years—from inception to publication—there were a great number who helped in many ways. I have been greatly impressed at the high level of commitment and dedication of so many who so graciously and unselfishly volunteered their time and expertise to help make this enterprise a success. I hope I've identified all of them, but if not, please accept my apologies.

In late 1991, some then active in the Section began considering the possibility of revisiting the earlier pioneering *Public Affairs Handbook*, published in 1982 by the American Management Association. More than a decade after its publication, the *Handbook*, though dated, continued to be widely used. But we thought it needed shoring up in some areas. Those who had this initial discussion, in addition to myself, were William E. Duke, Joseph R. Cerrell, William J. Koch, Lloyd N. Newman, and the Section Chair at the time, Robert A. Burns. After a spirited debate about the merits and arduous road ahead, we agreed to move forward.

By mid-1992, the Section took its first cautious steps down the road which ends in the volume before you now. A management consultant, Gary D. Avery, was commissioned to do a feasibility study, first developing a vision statement and timeline, then assessing likely content, and finally evaluating financial and marketing variables. Later, a preliminary survey of potential financial supporters was undertaken by Suzanne Campi, a philanthropic consultant.

She polled several large corporations and her findings were heart-
ening. By mid-1993, ever faithful to its commitment to give back
something to the profession which had given each of us so much,
the Section reaffirmed its intent to pursue publication of what by
now had the working title of *Practical Public Affairs in an Era of
Change*. During this period the Boards of both PRSA and its Foundation affirmed the Section's intent and officially supported our goal.

During this same period of development, an Editorial Advisory
Board was established and a Table of Contents was crafted. Though
modified again and again, I cannot help but observe that both the
scope and character of our earliest drafts remained largely intact to
the end. At the same time, contacts were initiated with a number of
prospective publishers and a list of prospective Partners were identified and later contacted about their possible support. Lastly, with
the assistance of a few outside the Section, a list of prospective
authors was created. Subsequently, the writing process began in the
late summer of 1994. All of these vital housekeeping-related matters took about a year-and-a-half to accomplish.

From the outset, Section Executive Committee members have
been extraordinarily supportive. Encouragement has come in all sorts
of ways, from ideas about financial and marketing approaches, to
publishing, to prospective authors as well as dealing with the myriad organizational needs in such a large voluntary membership organization. In addition to those already named, we also owe a big
"thank you" to the following Executive Committee members of recent years: Alison Knowlton Thomas, B. J. Altshul, Cheryl L. Budd,
Sidney J. Frigand, Charles A. Russell, Wayne R. Hill, and William
J. Brown.

Four Section chairs in particular deserve special mention. In 1992,
Bill Koch provided a strong and steady hand in helping manage the
thicket of all those housekeeping chores essential in order to get
started; in 1993, Bill Duke presided over what was in essence the
formal "takeoff" with a "can-do" attitude that proved vital; and in
1994, Sylvia J. Brucchi's steadfast enthusiasm and deft management
oversight proved critical at several points when it would have been
much easier to take another road. Over this past year—*the* year of
getting it all done—John L. Paluszek deserves special commenda-
tion for his strong leadership in seeing this project to completion.
At the same time, there was a considerable amount of very
hard work from the rest of the current Executive Committee: Gary
Koch, Anna L. West, James E. Lukaszewski, Katherine R. Hutt,

Susan B. Hess, William E. Duke, Sunny David and Janet M. Bedrosian. It has been an honor to have worked with all these truly dedicated professionals.

It is a personal privilege for me to have been chosen to serve throughout this entire period as Chairman of the Book Subcommittee of our Section. My partners on the Subcommittee, William E. Duke and James E. Lukaszewski, each contributed immeasurably to the effort. From the very beginning, Bill Duke has been a great source of strength and support to me and the Section in this major undertaking.

At PRSA headquarters, Ellen Gerber and Jill Weiner provided ongoing staff support that was invaluable, especially dealing with the follow-through resulting from all the transcontinental phone meetings held through the project's life. Very importantly, both Ray Gaulke, Chief Operating Officer, and Joe Cussick, Chief Financial Officer, working closely with the Board as a team, collectively provided the necessary support which significantly helped bring the project to fruition.

Special thanks are also in order to a handful of non-Section individuals consulted along the road for a number of important publishing-related needs: Lucia Staniels, a book agent based in New York provided great insight to the difficult task of shopping a book idea to prospective publishers; Bert Gader, a retired advertising executive in Los Angeles, whose knowledge of word-processing needs for book publishing was most valuable; Kathy and Mark Bloomfield, close personal friends in book publishing, provided an early education about the complexities of that world, along with encouragement to proceed because they, too, saw the need for such a volume; and Judy Hilsinger, a well-respected literary publicist based in Los Angeles, who helped shape our marketing plans.

Special thanks are certainly in order for our distinguished Editorial Advisory Board, chaired by William C. Adams. Bill and his colleagues have provided able, imaginative counsel, from honing a Table of Contents, identifying potential authors, and finally, in reviewing chapters submitted for inclusion in the book. There are also those working "behind-the-scenes" of the book who helped produce it: Maureen Muncaster, assisting the editorial project director; Mary Brighthaupt of Chesapeake Booksmith; and Michelle Harris, Acquisitions Editor and Jonathan Sisk, Editor-in-Chief, of University Press of America.

A special tip of the hat to our Partners. The generous support of these organizations, earmarked for enhanced marketing and distribution, will serve to bring the book to an ever-widening audience of practitioners, academicians and students, policymakers, opinion leaders, libraries, book clubs and meeting and convention locations across the country. No hyperbole involved here: many who benefit from this book owe a debt of gratitude to our Partners.

Both the Partners Program and the quality of the book are a testament to the involvement of a key public affairs professional, Raymond L. Hoewing, President of the Public Affairs Council. As a member of the Editorial Advisory Board, a contributing author and leader in the Partners Program outreach effort, Ray's contribution has been enormous. This partnership between PRSA and the PAC may, in essence, be a metaphor for both professions as we prepare for the next century.

Finally, a special word about two others: Gary D. Avery, who as editorial project director was tenacious and steadfast in helping us keep the focus and getting the work done. This is not easy, since there have been many occasions when it has been necessary to dance delicately between the many egos that are part and parcel of any large national membership organization which changes leadership every year. And Sada Izumi, my faithful assistant now for nearly 10 years, has provided calm administrative support since the start, often preventing storm warnings from easily turning into hurricanes.

In summary, this major undertaking has been the product of a lot of hard work by a very large number of truly dedicated professionals who have volunteered a considerable amount of their valuable time. We also acknowledge with great gratitude all of those whose originality and expertise appear throughout these pages—our authors. The profession can take great pride in this successful collaboration.

On a more personal closing note, it has been both a challenging and maturing process. All of us involved in this exciting enterprise share, I know, my fervent hope that this effort will bear living fruit in thousands of public affairs and public relations careers. And we look forward to that future time when the foundation laid here is built upon once again by those who follow.

—Lloyd B. Dennis
September, 1995

Practial Public Affairs in an Era of Change
Editorial Advisory Board

William C. Adams (Chairman)
Florida International University, North Miami, Florida

Teresa Yancey Crane
Issues Action Publications, Inc., Leesburg, Virginia

Lloyd B. Dennis
Dennis & Associates, Los Angeles, California

William E. Duke
Pacific Visions Communications, Los Angeles, California

Raymond L. Hoewing
Public Affairs Council, Washington, D.C.

Dr. James F. Keane
Winston Strawn, Chicago, Illinois

James E. Lukaszewski
The Lukaszewski Group, White Plains, New York

John L. Paluszek
Ketchum Communications, New York, New York

Dr. James E. Post
Boston University, Boston, Massachusetts

Dan Young
GTE, Irving, Texas

Dr. David Vogel
University of California, Berkeley, California

Practical Public Affairs in an Era of Change
PARTNERS PROGRAM

Early on, the Section determined that the financial support of PART-NERS would be needed to assure the widest possible marketing and distribution of this book.

We gratefully acknowledge the generosity of these prominent organizations who shared our vision and responded to our call:

Air Products and Chemicals, Inc.
American Council of Life Insurance
APCO Associates
ARCO
Lockheed Martin
Panhandle Eastern Corporation
Philip Morris
Public Affairs Council
Rockwell International
Shell Oil Company

EDITORIAL NOTE:
DEFINING TERMS

A Brief Statement Concerning
Public Relations and Public Affairs:
Let a Hundred Flowers Bloom!

In recent years, many valiant attempts have been made to reconcile the terms—and the management functions—"public relations" and "public affairs."

Perhaps surprisingly, this volume will not attempt to achieve such reconciliation. The reason is quite simple: The paths to public relations and public affairs practice are many and varied, so the approaches to defining those terms, and to describing an inter-relationship are equally varied.

We prefer to "let a hundred flowers bloom." So you will find at least several such "flowers" in this 400-plus page "garden."

Nevertheless, because this book is published under the auspices of the Public Relations Society of America, it seems appropriate to offer one such "flower" here at the outset, a standard against which others can be compared and one which reflects the PRSA structure.

That structure is one in which the general professional needs and interests of public relations practitioners are largely satisfied by membership in the national society; the more specific needs of a given professional practice are addressed by a PRSA Section— such as the Public Affairs and Government Section.

This approach to member service generates the following suggested description-distinction:

Public relations helps an organization develop and maintain quality relationships with the various groups of people ("publics") who can influence its future.

Public affairs is the public relations practice that addresses public policy and the publics who influence such policy.

Welcome to our garden.

—John L. Paluszek, Chairman
PRSA Public Affairs and Government Section
1995

Overview

Chapter 1

Public Affairs: From Understudy to Center Stage

W. E. Duke and
Mark A. Hart

> Public opinion is everything. With public sentiment, nothing can fail. Without it, nothing can succeed. Consequently, he who molds public opinion goes deeper than he who enacts statutes or pronounces decisions.
>
> — Abraham Lincoln

If the first half of the 1990s is any guide, the practice of public affairs will be one of the fastest growing and most closely scrutinized communications professions long into the next century. The reason: proponents and detractors alike no longer consider public affairs as a frill. It has come of age as a vital tool in the formation of public policy at all levels of government.

Once considered essential only in election campaigns or as a helpful communications adjunct to lobbying, public affairs expertise is now deemed essential to the success of any important legislative or regulatory battle in most state capitals and certainly in Washington, D.C.

What's more, practitioners who have long pleaded unsuccessfully with management or clients for adequate funding for their programs are now being authorized to use the best and the most modern

research techniques, constituency-development strategies and communications tactics to impact the process of making or derailing
legislation.

Such a scenario, with its promise of more meaningful work, prestige, funding and profitability for practitioners, sounds ideal for the
growth of the profession. But like much else in the real world, there
is a down side to this rosy prospect.

There is a genuine concern that message research focusing on
negative communications—and the single-issue, in-and-out grassroots
organizing now common in political campaigns—will be used to
undermine policy debates, adding to public confusion and cynicism.
This view holds that it's one thing to produce negative 30-second
sound bites to attack an electoral opponent for a few months, but
quite another to use the same tactics to alter the terms of debate
when complex legislation is being written.

The rapid growth in the number and profitability of specialized
agencies, the less-than-forthcoming tactics employed by some, and
the amounts of money spent in such controversies as the 1994 health
care reform debate in Washington have raised caution flags among
the media, government officials, and industry groups such as the
Public Relations Society of America (PRSA).

One such yellow flag was raised in California during the 1995
legislative session. Impressed by the new ability of public affairs
to influence legislation and encouraged by some public relations
practitioners, state Sen. Quentin L. Kopp (I-San Francisco) introduced a bill to require public relations firms to reveal their clients
and their compensation when working on grassroots lobbying campaigns.

The idea was suggested by Dennis Revell, a public affairs professional who voluntarily registers as a lobbyist, and endorsed "in
concept" by the PRSA California Capital Chapter. The rationale
given for this initiative is that successful lobbying now requires
integrating government relations with the sophisticated research,
communications, grassroots organizing, and coalition-building provided by public affairs firms.

Sen. Kopp told the *Sacramento Bee:*

> . . . contrived, manufactured (grassroots) campaigns (and) . . . those
> who run them should be subject to the same rules as other lobbyists.
> Otherwise, they are shadowy figures operating to influence public
> policy.

The imagery of such rhetoric is reminiscent of the "shadow government" described by William Greider in the 1992 best-seller, *Who Will Tell The People?* A stinging indictment of public affairs, the book's thesis is that government is run in league with powerful economic interests, represented by lobbyists, who ignore or actively work against the public good.

That such issues are now being raised in the bellwether state of California suggests that professional ethics will play an increasingly important role in the management of public affairs nationally. But as with any topic that is becoming controversial, definitions and a historical perspective are needed to fully understand how public affairs will evolve in this era of change.

A Question of Semantics

Public affairs is a term commonly used in public administration, journalism and public relations. In public relations, it has different meanings within corporate, government and agency settings.

Lesly's Handbook of Public Relations and Communications strictly defines public affairs as "a company's activities in political action and government relations." Public relations is defined in this context as "all other corporate affairs and communications in most companies."

Such definitions imply that public affairs mainly involves the exercise of influence with politicians and government officials, while public relations entails the development of a positive corporate image.

But such historical and traditional meanings have become blurred in the public sector. Public relations practices are called public affairs in government settings because of the unfortunate, but all too real, baggage that the term public relations carries with public officials.

Meanwhile, public affairs in an agency setting is most often thought of as the public relations practice that applies to public policy issues and election campaigns. Indeed, as *Lesly's Handbook of Public Relations and Communications* further notes:

> The artificial—but all too real demarcation between public affairs
> . . . and public relations is waning. The complexity of dealing with
> many external constituencies has led some companies to effectively
> integrate *all* communications . . .

Semantics aside, it is clear that traditional public affairs and public relations practices have become integrated to varying degrees. Perhaps less obvious is that such integration has occurred because public affairs owes a debt to labor unions and some of the hundreds of policy activist groups in the United States. They have long known how to influence public opinion to shape public policy.

From Understudy to Center Stage

What is now the 500-company Public Affairs Council in Washington, D.C. was founded in 1954 to counter organized labor's growing grassroots strength by training business executives to become active and effective in lobbying and politics. A handful of major corporations followed suit by establishing similar in-house programs of their own.

During that era, success in public affairs was partially based on thorough knowledge of a given business and of the key public policy issues affecting that business. However, the most important prerequisite for success was personal familiarity with key public policy makers.

So corporate public affairs specialists were generally drawn from the ranks of government "insiders"—congressional staffs, key administrative departments, Washington law and lobbying firms, and industry associations. Congress was then governed by a strong seniority system, which enabled lobbyists to concentrate on developing one-on-one relationships with a mere handful of key decision makers.

In addition, political reporting was relatively unaggressive by today's standards, and public watchdog groups were virtually nonexistent. As a result of such factors, lobbying was an activity that generally could be conducted behind a few closed doors and out of the public spotlight.

But things changed in the 1960s. Social unrest fostered by the anti-Vietnam War and civil rights movements spawned environmentalism, consumerism and, later, feminism. Protestors blamed the "military-industrial complex" for escalating the Vietnam War, and the other "rights" movements were decidedly anti-Establishment in nature. As a result, big business was indirectly indicted as being among the root causes of American society's woes.

Among responses by business to the tenor of the times was the establishment of political participation policies, which were considered a litmus test of whether a company had a true public affairs program in the 1960s. The policies, which are in place today at such concerns as Honeywell and Reynolds Metals, generally define a firm's role in politics. They encourage employees to be knowledgeable and active in the political process, whether as voters, campaign volunteers, poll watchers, candidates, and elected or appointed public officials.

But such innovative practices were insufficient to stem the tide of negative public opinion directed toward business interests that was generated in the 1970s. The Arab oil embargo and Three Mile Island nuclear accident occurred, the Love Canal hazardous waste site was discovered, and there were seemingly endless cycles of recession and double-digit inflation.

The result was greater public support for more government regulation of industry. Major corporations started relying heavily on community relations and philanthropy to demonstrate the company's sense of social responsibility. The term "issues management" began appearing regularly in the business press for the first time.

Negative public perceptions of big business abated somewhat in the 1980s. Deregulation under the Reagan administration contributed to an increasingly robust economy. Meanwhile, government cutbacks led to expansion of the volunteer movement and to even greater prominence for corporate community involvement activities.

Strange Bedfellows No More

Nonetheless, the social trends and issues impacting business and government remained complex. As a result, public affairs and public relations were, by the early 1990s, "strange bedfellows no more," in the words of Burson-Marsteller's then-President and Chief Executive Officer James H. Dowling.

"The integration of public relations and public affairs resources [is] the key to effective work in the public policy arena. We are really talking about the relevance of public opinion to public policy," Dowling said in a 1990 speech to the Public Affairs Council in Washington.

Lobbying must now be supplemented with a variety of techniques—coalition-building, media contact, constituent mobilization, even advertising—to convince government officials to support a point of view," Dowling said. "Successful public affairs demands strategically designed and individually tailored communications and lobbying efforts so that targeted decision-makers are educated to the logic of your point of view *and* the political power behind it." Raymond L. Hoewing, Public Affairs Council president, struck a similar note in the council's 1993 annual report:

> Economic success would seem to depend in significant part on such public affairs tools as *government relations* to interact with unpredictable and activist federal and state governments, *issues management* to provide foresight on sociopolitical trends, *public relations* to educate leader and citizen on the nexus of public interest and business, and *community relations and philanthropy* to delineate the company's social responsibility.

Power to the People

No less an authority than consumer activist Ralph Nader acknowledged the growing power of public affairs in the foreword to *Public Interest Profiles, 1992-93.*

"The 1980s witnesses a further convergence of business and government agendas, more vigorous PACs, a more pro-business federal judiciary, and more tailored public relations acumen in the corporate sector," Nader wrote.

Yet there are striking similarities between public affairs programs and the approaches used by activist groups to, in Nader's words, "achieve social improvement." Grassroots programs and coalition building provide the best case in point.

University of Chicago sociologist Saul Alinsky pioneered grassroots organizing in the Back-Of-The-Yards slums of Depression-era Chicago. He was attempting to empower the urban poor in their struggles with exploitive slumlords, corrupt politicians and an indifferent City Hall.

As applied by Alinsky, the term grassroots meant "from the bottom up." His basic principles are set forth in *Reveille For Radicals*, a manifesto for the social activists of the 1960s who were the forerunners of the activist groups of today.

However, the meaning of grassroots has evolved over the years to mean something closer to "on the local level," or "the groundwork or fundamental source" of something. Such expressions are ideal working definitions for the term as applied to modern public affairs where disagreements flourish over what is legitimately an expression of popular opinion and what is "manufactured" opinion.

Basic grassroots programs are in place today at most large corporations, such as International Paper, ARCO and Union Carbide. They traditionally involve local plant managers and other employees developing personal relationships with key state and federal legislators and thereby communicating their companies' positions on legislative matters.

In other cases, public affairs taps into a pre-existing wellspring of grassroots backing for an issue. For example, the Southwest Florida Water Management District used extensive public opinion research to identify widespread support among environmentalists, news media and residents of the Kissimmee River area for restoring the channelized waterway to its original banks.

A small group known as Residents Opposing Alleged Restoration (ROAR) was also identified, and their concerns about the project were addressed in a series of meetings with district officials.

Such activities, coupled with extensive lobbying and communications programs, led ultimately to the district securing $380 million in state and federal funding for the restoration. "An early grassroots campaign . . . (that) crystallized into a very focused effort" was credited when the district won a 1992 Public Relations Society Of America Silver Anvil for the overall public affairs program. Striking a balance between apparently competing interests is another means of tapping into grassroots support. A prime example is Arkla, Inc.'s pursuit of a permit for its natural gas pipeline from Oklahoma to cross the Cossatot River in Arkansas in the early 1990s.

The project was expected to encounter overwhelming opposition from environmentalists. So the *Fortune* 500 concern consulted with the Arkansas Nature Conservancy, decided to purchase a prime piece of property along the riverfront, and donate it to the organization.

The Nature Conservancy then gave the land to the state for a park and Arkla, in return, got the group's blessing to cross the river. Arkla combined the crossing with an attractive, handicapped-accessible pedestrian walkway. In recognition of such initiatives, Arkla won the U.S. Fish and Wildlife Service's first national "Corporate Wildlife Citizenship Award."

Grassroots or Astro-turf

But as *Wise Use* movement leader Ron Arnold has noted: "Citizens groups have credibility and industries don't." That perspective, confirmed by public opinion research, manifests itself in grassroots programs and coalition building in a variety of ways. For example:

- Members of the National Association of Home Builders arriving in 1995 at the Houston Astrodome for their annual trade show were greeted by two banks of word processors. Each of the 20 terminals was equipped with a modified software package and staffed with specially-trained personnel.

  The word processors generated form letters to Congress supporting a balanced federal budget amendment and property rights legislation. Upon inputting the home address of a participating NAHB member, the software instantly personalized the letter into versions for all of the members' Congressmen.

  More than 3,500 association members participated, generating approximately 10,000 letters to Congress supporting the two issues. The letters, sent on plain white paper, made no reference to the NAHB.

- Texaco Inc. and a coalition of oil companies announced plans in 1989 to build a storage tank farm for various liquid fuels in the rural community of Lloyd in the Florida Panhandle.

  Local environmentalists organized in opposition to the project, forming the "Friends of Lloyd." They accepted thousands of dollars from a lobbying arm of the maritime industry, which feared added competition from the tank farm.

  In response, Texaco organized local supporters of the project into "Citizens For Progress." The group produced a pro-tank farm newsletter and made charitable contributions to the Lloyd chapters of the American Legion and National Association for the Advancement of Colored People, according to the *Wall Street Journal.*

Such examples illustrate that communications tools are an essential element of grassroots programs and coalition building in this era, even if consisting of only face-to-face meetings as in the case of Arkla's pipeline project. Indeed, using communications vehicles to advance policy positions is a capability shared by public affairs practitioners and activist groups alike. Publicity and media relations have long been used by each to motivate and mobilize constituents. But mass communications has inherent limitations when attempting to influence targeted audiences with specialized interests.

Other techniques have evolved for more directly reaching potential supporters. They cover the communications spectrum and include but are not limited to: issues-oriented manuals, videotapes, briefing papers, newsletters, direct mailings, advertising and legislative guides; issuing "calls to action" to constituents; use of 1-800 numbers and information "hot lines"; letter writing campaigns; and conducting civic/political events.

The importance of communications to conducting effective grassroots programs and building coalitions cannot be overestimated. It was alluded to in a grudging tribute to activist groups paid by James Dowling during his comments to the Public Affairs Council about integrating public affairs and public relations.

"With all due respect to Ronald Reagan, the truly great communicators of today are *against* global warming, *for* the spotted owl, *for* choice and *against* abortion, and abhor smoking, drinking and anything that smacks of pornography, including some of the greatest classics of all times," Dowling said. "And they enjoy the advantage of being totally focused on their single cause. They are formidable adversaries in the battle for public opinion."

Role of the States . . .
and the State of the Art

In the constant ebb and flow of American national politics in the early 1990s, one trend of major importance to public affairs has been obvious: the shift of more power and responsibility to state and local government.

Whether it is under the rubric of the Clinton administration's program of "reinventing government," or the Republican "Contract With America," the federal establishment seems determined to delegate social problem-solving closer to the people. Understandably, public affairs firms as well as public interest groups have been quick to follow.

In California, generally considered a leading indicator of political trends, legislative term limits and sophisticated public affairs technology have been credited with powering the growth of public affairs firms. "With term limits and [member] turnover, grassroots efforts and coalition building are becoming more important," Bobbie Metzger, a partner in the firm of Stoorza, Ziegaus, Metzger & Hunt told the *California Journal*.

"Issues previously considered the sole domain of the federal government are now being decided by state legislatures. Everything from advertising and insurance to solid waste and AIDS is being legislated in the states—with some truly frightening results," James Dowling has observed.

Ralph Nader has similarly noted that public interest groups are working more on the local level because of increasing frustration with a federal government "bent on deregulation and dismantling or diminishing social programs." For example, the Citizens Clearinghouse for Hazardous Wastes, a national umbrella organization for grassroots environmentalists, boasts membership by more than 6,000 affiliated organizations on the local level.

The shift of public affairs activities away from "within the Beltway" is being accompanied by dramatic technological advances. One such advance is illustrated by a visionary model for an integrated public affairs database that was advanced in late 1992 by Stuart Z. Goldstein of the National Securities Clearing Corporation. It included the following capabilities to enhance public affairs activity:

- Tracking by Congressional district, reporters who have written positive articles about a particular issue, or seem predisposed to an organization;

- Tracking philanthropic grants and philanthropic group members by congressional or state legislative districts;

- Comparing biographical data of elected officials with the backgrounds of "grass-tops" employees involved in local political contact programs;

- Providing public relations people with direct, on-line access to information about the location, by legislative district, of philanthropic contributions;

- Providing senior management with a detailed breakdown of all public affairs involvements and a list of supporters, media contacts and stakeholders in a key congressional district—within 15 minutes.

Activist groups are already leading the way in the use of new technology. Organizations ranging from the Pesticide Action Network to the NRA are now using e-mail to mobilize up to 200,000 members at a time. In addition, a national computer bulletin board/subscription service known as "HandsNet" has been established for grassroots and news organizations to post and share information about the world of non-profit advocacy.

"Citizens who are not organized with huge budgets and . . . huge political campaign contributions can actually begin to level the political playing field by mobilizing through new technologies," former Federal Trade Commission Chairman Mike Pertschuk told "NBC Nightly News" in January 1995.

Pertschuk is now co-director of the Advocacy Institute, which plugs special interest groups into computer networks. Since the Internet will connect an estimated 100 million computer users by 2001, business will certainly use the medium for grassroots activities as well.

Meanwhile, old public affairs standbys are being updated for 1990s applications. For example, the National Association of Realtors announced in 1994 that it would reduce its direct PAC contributions over two years from $5 million to $3.5 million, according to the *Wall Street Journal*. Among the association's planned uses for the difference is organizing members to join the campaigns of candidates it favors—a new spin on the corporate political participation policies of the 1960s.

And the days of charitable giving by businesses purely to demonstrate a sense of social responsibility is increasingly a thing of the past. Corporate giving budgets increasingly are becoming based more on "perceived benefit to business objectives" than on a "fair share" giving figure, according to Craig Smith of Corporate Citizen, a philanthropic think tank.

Practicing the Art of the Possible—Ethically

Nonetheless, demonstrating a sense of social responsibility is a challenge facing individual public affairs professionals, regardless of whether they work for corporations or other organizations. Practitioners need to provide some level of assurance that, in "the battle for public opinion," they do not use their sophisticated techniques to add to the cynicism and alienation of the public.

After all, even the best-intentioned campaigns can produce casualties. That fact was dramatically underscored by the efforts of petroleum and maritime interests to organize grassroots supporters and opponents respectively of the Texaco-backed fuel depot in Lloyd, Florida.

Texaco and its investors abandoned the effort in 1995 after spending six years and $27 million in public relations and legal fees without even breaking ground. The rural community was left bitterly divided, but not before a storefront office owned by an environmentalist opposed to the project was destroyed in a 1993 fire blamed on arson.

"People got so hot and passionate about things so quick," depot backer Sandy Helton told the *Wall Street Journal*. "You could really see people drawing their lines."

Such individual failures are fodder for critics of public affairs such as author William Greider. Perhaps, as Greider asserts, business and government are the biggest special interests of all.

But a less extreme view is that everyone in a democratic society is entitled to organize into a "special interest." Indeed, the same First Amendment to the U.S. Constitution that protects the press freedoms enjoyed by journalists like Greider also ensures "the right of the people . . . to petition the Government for a redress of grievances."

Public Affairs Comes of Age

Like a rite of passage, the debate about professional ethics should be taken as a sign that public affairs has truly come of age. Born of a marriage between lobbying and communications and schooled in the techniques of community organizing, public affairs has grown up to be a credible participant in the formation of public policy.

Integrating the effective message development and communications techniques of public relations with political organizing ability has made public affairs a vital tool in the legislative arena. The increasing pace of change in the power relationships between the political parties, and among federal and local governments, has only expanded the need for professional public affairs.

The challenge to public affairs professionals now is to continue to prosper and to grow while upholding the integrity of open and honest communications essential to the formation of public policy in a free society. As an ideal, the techniques professional public affairs offers are designed to illuminate all points of view and bring more people actively into the public policy process.

But meeting the challenge of this ideal will not be easy. The line between issue education and propaganda can be exceedingly fine in some instances. So can the line between genuine grassroots activism and "false-front" coalitions.

Given the newly-recognized influence of the field, the increasing pace of political change and the complexity of legislation, the challenge may require action by practitioners to fashion a realistic code of conduct for public affairs as it relates to the formation of public policy. As Dennis Revell, the professional who is supporting California's public affairs disclosure legislation, has noted:

> If the industry doesn't set some guidelines for itself, we are going to have an instance when somebody really crosses the line. This is enlightened self-interest. If we don't do it, someone else will do it for us.

Chapter 2

Historical Antecedents: Public Affairs in Full Flower—1975-1985

Lloyd B. Dennis and
John M. Holcomb

Introduction

In a century of unprecedented tumult, upheaval and profound change—social, political, economic and especially technological—the decade of the 1960s is a standout. It is also seminal for the material to be discussed in this chapter.

Much of the impetus for the gathering consensus, in both the public and private sectors, which eventuated in the "full flowering" of the public affairs movement in the years between roughly 1975 and 1985 can, in fact, be traced to roots buried deeply in the 1960s.

It is more than happenstance that Earth Day I came near the end of the 1960s, when in 1962, Rachel Carson's *Silent Spring* heightened environmental awareness as few works—before or since—had. Likewise it was more than happenstance that the mid-decade 89th Congress (1965-1966) produced an unprecedented array of consumer protection legislation including hitherto unheard-of laws regulating automobile safety. The latter laws instigated massive "recalls" for defects in America's most celebrated manufacturing triumph, the assembly-line-built automobile. They emanated from an articulate activist and critic of governmental regulation of industry, Ralph Nader. His *Unsafe at Any Speed*, indicted General Motor's Corvair as a "one-car accident" whose faulty design was known to industry insiders prior to production. Despite this information, the car was sold aggressively to unwary consumers. Publication of the book led to an ugly confrontation between Nader and GM spanning nearly three decades.

Similarly, the triumph of the civil rights movement in the wake of the tragic murder of Dr. Martin Luther King in 1968, carried with it the impetus for government to redress racism in employment as well as in purchasing goods and services from minorities. This affirmative action movement at first applied narrowly to African Americans. Over time, however, it came to be applied to women and other ethnic minorities. Eventually, even such considerations as age, marital status, sexual orientation and disabilities were incorporated into the affirmative action schema.

These and a host of other public policy initiatives, especially in combination, resulted in unprecedented governmental intrusion into and oversight of the nation's business sector. Costs were incurred, as well. Even businesses long absent from the public policy arena, except as individual members of active trade groups, now began counting the costs and confronting the reality presented to their companies and industries as the late 1960s turned into the 1970s. Both to implement many new socially-directed mandates, comply with new reporting requirements inherent in them and to contain the contagion of confrontation, bad publicity and harsh new regulation, companies in every sector began gearing up. However varied and creative the nomenclature, business' response to this challenge was met in its time-honored customary way: It institutionalized and centralized the personnel and procedures needed to address these often traumatic external relations challenges.

In this chapter we will describe and analyze, using a broad-brush approach, the stimulus and response which produced a virtual explosion of organizational activity on the interface between the private sector and government in roughly a two-decade period bracketed by 1965 and 1985. Understandably the response portion of the equation lagged stimulus somewhat, which accounts for the official focus of this chapter being limited to primarily one decade, 1975-1985. A "golden age" overview of this sort necessarily requires the reader to look elsewhere in this book for a more complete discussion of the individual elements of the then-emergent and now institutionalized public affairs practice.

While today's practitioners experience a profession different from that reviewed here, past is always prologue. Like the economy itself, or the social life of change-oriented multicultural Information Age America, there are to all venues distinct periods of ebb and flow, of up-building and downsizing. The most important lesson the past holds: Mastering change requires a sense of history.

The Rise of Corporate Social Responsibility

As the 1960s wore on, accompanied by an unprecedented period of economic growth, attitudes in boardrooms and executive suites about what would soon come to be called "corporate social responsibility" were at best embryonic. Only a relative handful of American business leaders sensed that expectations of American business were, along with the passage of the decade, rising rapidly and on many divergent fronts at once, including investor relations, pensioner relations, employee relations and especially community relations.

As one of this chapter's authors observed in 1974: "Some profound changes have occurred in the way the public expects business to operate. . . . this questioning of business will only intensify, and we had better be prepared to deal with it. I submit that we . . . are not prepared now—and that failing some changes in the way we think and operate, the public franchise under which we operate could be revoked or profoundly narrowed."[1]

In truth, were it not for the civil rights protests, urban riots, and the antiwar protests, followed shortly by the consumer, environmental and women's rights movements, the vast majority of corporations would likely not have taken social initiatives. The convergence of these contentious issues raised the specter of the preservation of the existing commercial system. As a consequence, there were more references to moral obligation and preservation of the system in chief executive speeches between the late 1960s and the mid-1970s than during any similar time period in the century.

Corporations did not respond simply with chief executive rhetoric; many established corporate social responsibility departments and programs. Moreover, companies did not respond solely at the firm level, but also in a joint and cooperative fashion. The National Alliance of Business was formed, at the instigation of President Lyndon Johnson and Henry Ford, and sponsored a JOBS program to target the hiring of the hard-core unemployed. The National Urban

Coalition was formed under the initial leadership of John Gardner and later Carl Holman, to coordinate corporate, union and government efforts to attack urban problems. The Urban Coalition had a corporate urban affairs advisory council, composed of urban affairs specialists from leading companies and business associations. Local coalitions, such as New Detroit, were also formed in troubled metropolitan areas.

Major business associations also hired urban affairs staff specialists and formed urban affairs committees with interested Board members. The U.S. Chamber of Commerce, National Association of Manufacturers and the American Bankers Association all developed urban affairs components. In an organizational sense, the insurance industry was the most responsive, forming a clearinghouse on Corporate Social Responsibility in 1971 at the American Council of Life Insurance. The Clearinghouse was later renamed the Council for Corporate Public Involvement.

The Public Affairs Council, an association of over 400 corporations, added an urban affairs staff specialist in 1969 and sponsored urban affairs training seminars for new corporate staff in such positions. In the peak years, new staff from as many as a hundred different large companies were being trained annually. Consultation and information were provided corporate staff by many national organizations and business groups. Two such organizations were the National Urban League and the National Center for Urban Ethnic Affairs, founded by Msgr. Geno Baroni.

The Committee for Economic Development (CED), a progressive business organization in existence since 1941, produced a major document in 1971 on the *Social Responsibilities of Business Corporations*. It urged management to develop a broader social role for the corporation and called for the "release of the full productive and organizational capacities of the corporation for the benefit of society." The CED said it was in the enlightened self-interest of business to defend and help rebuild the system, since the firm cannot "hope to operate effectively in a society which is not functioning well."

The statements, positions and activities of business groups came during a short-lived era, but were unparalleled in American business history. During the heyday of corporate public affairs, the CED published other reports on urban affairs. Thirteen years elapsed, however, before its next release of a report on urban issues, *Re-*

building Inner-City Communities: An Emerging National Strategy Against Urban Decay (1995).

In 1981, the then-new Reagan Administration formed a Task Force on Private Sector Initiatives which quickly won cooperation from many companies and business groups. However, its mission emanated not from a spirit of tackling social problems collectively but from a belief in limited government. Its pragmatic goal: Getting the private sector to fill the large breach left by substantial government cutbacks. The Administration tried to encourage business to get more involved in helping fix many intractable community issues. Several corporations responded with some modest increase in philanthropic contributions and a resurgence in some of their community relations activities, including volunteerism. But the cresting wave of mergers and takeovers, competitive pressures in many industries, and the impact of the 1986 Tax Reform Act brought a slowing and, eventually, a reversal of corporate social initiatives.

Rise of Volunteerism

In response, business developed a program and activity agenda that some considered peripheral to the core activities of the firm. Employee volunteer programs became a common tool used to meet external and internal expectations of socially responsible behavior. One of the most extensive and ambitious employee volunteer programs was sponsored by Levi Strauss, which organized Community Involvement Teams (CITs). CITs are groups of employees who donate their time and work addressing local community programs. As of 1983 there were 106 teams worldwide, at least one in every plant. They choose projects which may range from building a baseball diamond to supporting battered womens' shelters. The Levi Strauss effort subsequently became a model for other corporate volunteer programs.

Other important volunteerism models are the social service leave programs sponsored by Xerox and IBM which permitted "sabbaticals" with up to a full year's pay for work in a community, social service or civil rights organization. IBM and other companies also have executive-faculty exchange programs.

Still other companies and business groups pioneered innovative twists in such volunteer programming. Some New York-based companies loan executives to the Economic Development Council which has extended management assistance to the city government. In California, United California Bank (later named First Interstate Bank) launched a small cities project to assist communities with great needs and few technical resources to address strategic planning and economic development issues.

Alternative Socially Responsible Practices

Beyond employee volunteer programs, some companies explored how they might conduct traditional business functions in a more socially responsible manner. Amoco, for instance, was one of the early pioneers in developing a minority purchasing program; by 1976, the National Minority Purchasing Council had about 850 corporate members. Chemical Bank launched a street banker program to be more responsive to the needs of New York neighborhoods and also pioneered the hiring of former drug addicts. Other banks and insurance companies launched urban investment or "greenlining" strategies in response to criticism of their alleged policies of "redlining" in minority neighborhoods, denying them needed resources. Shorebank Corporation, based on Chicago's south side, became a model of community banking even through the 1990s. Meanwhile, Control Data, with the guiding philosophy that it intended "to do well by doing good," launched industry daycare, education, and urban revitalization programs as a way of making a profit.

Beyond the Urban Coalition movement, some local business communities joined hands with local governments to attack social problems and even to advance governmental reform. The Hartford Process, Philadelphia Partnership, and Detroit Renaissance were three examples of such efforts in this era, precursors of more contemporary efforts such as the Atlanta Project and Rebuild L.A.

Firms in the 1970s also sometimes pursued a policy of social lobbying, advocating public policies to address social and urban problems. AT&T, for example, lobbied for government financing of daycare programs. IBM, before agreeing to build a facility in Louisville, promoted open housing laws in order that its own minority executives would have realistic, unrestricted real estate choices.

Finally, the social impact of corporate relocation decisions became salient concerns during the late 1970s. Through the prodding of the Suburban Action Institute, companies in the northeast often reconsidered or delayed their decision to leave central cities for more pristine environments. The Mead Corporation reaffirmed its commitment to the downtown of Dayton, Ohio while Kellogg did the same in Battle Creek, Michigan. In the early 1980s, Pfizer elected to keep its oldest plant operating in a section of Brooklyn and to help rebuild the surrounding community.

Conclusion: Conceptual Ambiguity

Before, during and after the heyday of corporate social responsibility, a debate raged over the usefulness of the concept. Preston and Post (1978) observe that the major problem with the concept is that its boundaries are vague and ill-defined. Conservatives like economist Milton Friedman believe that business is sufficiently responsible when it fulfills its primary functions of producing goods and services and providing jobs while abiding by basic societal rules of the game.

Others might more realistically contend that business is only responsible when its behavior rises to another level—making sure all its core activities are conducted responsibly: that its hiring and promotion policies are fair; that its advertising manifests laudable values; that its products and services have quality, integrity and value while contributing to social well being; that it treats its employees, customers and suppliers with fairness; and that it safeguards surrounding communities from any of its activities. Advocates of this second version of social responsibility contend that it is in the long-term self-interest of business to be responsible, that concerning itself with this secondary level of activity will inevitably have a positive impact on the firm's bottom line.

Other advocates of corporate social responsibility contend that firms must go beyond the bottom line to a tertiary level of activity to be truly responsible. They believe that business must proceed beyond core functions to tertiary or peripheral activities, for example, hunger, crime, housing *et alia*, to be truly responsible. If a cereal company is located in a community with a housing problem, this viewpoint holds that the company should address that problem, perhaps developing a new division that builds affordable housing. Others, meanwhile, might argue that a company should not tackle a social problem when it lacks the expertise to do so or is not accountable—primarily to its shareholders—for it. Such problems, in this view, are best left to government.

With such a wide range of approaches to corporate social responsibility, it is obvious that there is no uniform definition of the concept that provides an adequate guide for corporate action. It is also obvious that the debate will continue.

Media Relations

If one familiar element of the emerging public affairs paradigm of the 1970s existed, it must surely have been media relations. For decades, American managers in companies of every size and kind had used the relatively direct tool of publicity to help shape mass opinion. In its barest form media relations meant press releases concerning either a firm's product(s) or service(s) or company personnel. The activity, as the full-flowering of public affairs era opened, was routine, circumscribed by time-honored canons of practice despite a decade of assassinations, urban riots, space spectaculars, antiwar protests, political change and more.

If change in the corporate media relations strategy was evident anywhere, it was displayed in two areas. The rapidly increasing technological component and growing willingness on the part of at least some CEOs to talk not just about company interests but also about larger public policy priorities.

With respect to the impact of technology, there can be no doubt that the saturation by television, and in particular by satellite and other space-program spinoffs, transformed the shape and means of media relations during this era. One sensed as the decade of the 1960s came to a close, a growing acceleration in the news business itself. This quickened pace fed on itself as 24-hour news-radio formats proliferated in major markets, and then smaller ones, along with the beginnings of interactive talk radio which would itself come to full flower a quarter century later in the congressional elections of 1994.

As for the changing role of CEOs, the appearance of new business organizations, such as the Business Roundtable and various state versions of such elite groups, dominated by CEOs and giving for the first time names and faces to the "leaders of commerce and industry" cutline, was part defensive and part egoistic. A few visible, vocal CEOs—Irving Shapiro at Dupont, David Rockefeller at Chase Manhattan Bank, William Norris of Control Data, and a handful of others—had long since emerged as spokespersons for business. They were accessible to media and willing to explore larger questions than stock prices, management changes or new product introductions. For Norris, as for others, this leadership ultimately proved hazardous.

One stand-out action in this period altered the way the media viewed business and vice versa: the early 1970s advocacy advertising by Mobil Oil Corporation. The nexus between media and business was never really the same again. The fact that a very large commercial institution took an advocacy position in the media at a time when government was increasingly imposing greater regulatory burdens and as business was attempting to deal with social upheaval, all seemed to come together in the media. Indeed, after the Watergate scandal, the media seemed to move to a new level of aggressive, investigative and crusading journalism sometimes bordering on confrontation. Media posturing by very accessible politicians, community activists and others seeking instant celebrity and notoriety and who could speak in soundbites, resulted in misleading stories and headlines. These nonetheless captured public attention and formed hard and fast public perceptions. Media-related activities thus moved to a new level—more confrontational than reasoned, often seen as contentious bordering on demagogic.

As a final irony in the evolution of the media relations function during this period, the full glare of the media spotlight would soon be turned on business itself, giving rise to publications and television and radio programming riveted intensively and exclusively on the nitty gritty of America's financial and commercial sectors at home and overseas. Yet despite a decade and half of such specialized business programming, and despite the growth in openness and recognition of the power and value of media not just for publicity but for public affairs programming, an uneasy relationship remains. Research in the mid-1990s disclosed that while 7 of 10 CEOs considered media skills the best resource for their communications deputies, most executives still continue to hold the media at a distance, harboring feelings of fear, distrust and misunderstanding.[2]

Government Relations: Overview

Arguably the oldest public affairs function, *government relations* involves the interface between organizations with interests and the institutions of power in society, namely the government.

To be sure, literature about government relations is extensive. Indeed, entire books have been published which focus solely on a single key element of the function, for example, lobbying.[3]

The extraordinary convergence of stimulus and response which produced contemporary government relations practice was formed from the confluence of several key elements noted earlier: the civil rights movement, the rise of consumerism, and the emergence of the environmental movement. The free market, which Ronald Reagan would extol in the 1980s, was hobbled in this period by government intervention into the everyday affairs of business. Long familiar with government's alphabet soup, business' lexicon suddenly was adjusted to include a host of new entries such as EEOC, MBE/WBE, OSHA, EPA, and CRA, to name only a few.

CEOs seeing wave upon wave of ever-larger governmental interventions, responded by recruiting public affairs officers from within the government, the media, and even academe. Business hoped that marshaling such expertise could redirect, deflect or minimize the impact of newly activist government.

In the course of this awakening serious public affairs structures were created. Trade associations covering Washington initially bridled at the proliferation of proprietary offices dealing with Capitol Hill and the bureaucracy. By the mid-1970s, however, the wariness remained but working alliances had been crafted on a large scale. In fact, trade groups and Washington representatives for individual companies often became two sides of the same spear. The surfeit of problems confronting businesses of every shape and size provided more than enough working space for all who wished to become players.

Toward the end of the 1970s, attention began to turn toward newly revitalized state legislatures, as their long period of self-distraction and heavy-handed reliance on growth-swollen taxation crashed to an end with California's trend-setting Proposition 13. Over time, larger companies began to develop the sort of state (and even local) public affairs mechanisms that had begun to function well in Washington.

Then came the new decade of the 1980s and a new public attitude. The battle cry of the Reagan Revolution—"government is the problem, not the answer"—became dominant. Exhausted from the prior period of confrontation, preoccupied by stockholder concerns and rising globalization, many CEOs simply withdrew, believing that the heat was now off. Even the once-crusading media aided this self-delusional somnolence by suddenly seeming less interested in public policy issues. In another irony, the media began to view *business itself*—including management theories, P/E ratios, LBOs,—

as news. Hard-hitting pieces were replaced by weekly (even nightly) business shows on radio and television (a theme developed in
depth in Chapter 4).

Key Studies: Charting the Growth
of Government Relations

The earliest date cited for the creation of corporate public affairs
departments is 1914. An additional 19.2% were created by 1959.
Between 1960 and 1980, according to this same analysis, another
80% of then-existing public affairs structures were added. In these
operations, fully 84.2% included government relations practitioners.[4]

The same study reported that respondents believed professional
staff in such units had increased in a single five-year period—1975
to 1980—by 62.5%. More than seventy-three percent asserted that
their company maintained a significant involvement or presence in
Washington, D.C. "albeit trade associations and traveling executives
. . . still constitute business's most significant Washington presence."[5]

As to when companies opened Washington offices, the study reported the first "in 1901, a second . . . in 1924, and a third in 1937.
The period of steady growth began in 1940. . . ." There was a virtual explosion of such openings, some 96 in all, between 1965 and
1980.[6]

Surprisingly, while most top executives accepted the idea that the
advent of Ronald Reagan meant it was once again safe for business
in Washington, facts proved that this was not so: "In fact, four out
of five . . . surveyed firms reported . . . the number and importance of federal issues affecting their firms increased after January,
1981."[7]

This study concluded that "all in all, 44% of the surveyed companies increased the size of their federal relations staff since 1980,
and an additional 8% added to their resources. . ."[8]

State Government Relations

During the same timeframe, significant developments were
registered in other noteworthy aspects of the government relations
function including focus on state (and local) levels of governance,
political contributions and "grassroots" efforts.

While businesses generally have long enjoyed good relationships with state governments, many of the faultlines which produced heightened awareness and involvement in the federal arena produced like effects in many state legislatures. One analysis noted that, in 1981, the run-of-the-mill state government relations apparatus would have a staff "of five or fewer and have an annual budget smaller than $500,000."[9]

Two years later, another study concluded that more than 75% of companies reported "that they engage in efforts to influence public policy in one or more states."[10] The study also observed that "seven . . . of ten companies with state-relations specialists have had them in their employ only since 1970; almost half, since 1975."[11]

Several factors converged during this period to cause intensified involvement with state governments. Many businesses operating nationwide were suddenly faced with gathering storm clouds in multiple locations. Just as the social legislation of the Great Society had an impact at the state level, so too, did the budgetary cutbacks of the Reagan years. By 1992 "an overwhelming majority of companies (85.9%) have a formalized state government relations function."[12] Indeed, *more companies reported having a formalized state government relations function in 1992 than had a community relations function, an ironic twist underscoring the return to defensive ball-playing by business.*

Political Contributions

Another aspect of government relations which experienced sharp growth involved mechanisms facilitating political fundraising. Some government relations practitioners in states such as California, which permitted corporate funds for state and local candidates and ballot measure campaigns, were experienced in the political money game prior to 1965. It was, after all, California's colorful Assembly Speaker Jesse Unruh who once referred to money as "the mother's milk of politics."

But with such key Supreme Court cases as *Bellotti v. First National Bank of Boston* and the *Sun Oil Company* decision, government relations became unmistakably entangled with campaign finance.

By 1979, 65% of all companies with annual sales exceeding $2.5 billion had established and were operating PACs. Just 12 years later, 79.8% of companies had PACs (77.3% federal, 54% state).[13]

Issues Management

Assessing origins of contemporary public affairs emanating from the 1965 to 1985 period necessarily requires some attention to the issues management activity which first gained a foothold in the late 1970s. One 1982 survey found that 91% of Fortune 500 companies had established issues management efforts and almost 70% saw it as a function of growing importance. Some saw issues management as a way to assist the corporation in anticipating social and political change while at the same time strengthening strategic planning. Others saw it as merely a way to make government relations more sophisticated. The Public Affairs Council defined it, in 1978, as "a program which a company uses to increase its knowledge of the public policy process and enhance the sophistication and effectiveness of its involvement in that process." In 1984, Arrington and Sawaya, public affairs executives at Atlantic Richfield Company, defined issues management as "a process to organize a company's expertise to enable it to participate effectively in the shaping and resolution of public issues that critically impinge on its operations."

Organizationally, issues management most often started in public affairs units, and even today commonly resides there. Some experts believe it is more effective when organized as a cross-functional task force and integrated into line management. Some believe it must be more closely tied to the corporate operational and strategic planning process and, importantly, that it can be (see Chapter 17).

There are major differences between an issues management approach to managing the public affairs function and other more traditional policy-oriented approaches. First, it takes a proactive as well as interactive approach to forces in the business environment, rather than a reactive one. It is not as aggressive as a traditional public policy or government relations approach and requires more flexibility in dealing directly with groups critical of the corporation. At the same time, a firm with an issues management approach will not accommodate as readily as it might with a social responsibility approach and will keep a closer eye on its own self-interest.

Second, an issues management approach would be more anticipatory than any of the other management styles, forecasting future pressures and opportunities and focusing on emerging issues. A company interacting with important groups in its environment is more likely to accurately monitor the external environment and anticipate new trends while, by contrast, a public policy approach emphasizes political fire-fighting. Even a social responsibility approach emphasizes responding to momentary crises rather than truly momentous developments.

A third attribute of the issues management approach is that it is more systematic than any of the other approaches. It identifies issues and interest groups on the horizon and distinguishes between the more important and less vital, thereby helping establish priorities for the firm.

To be systematic requires a high level of expertise, the fourth attribute of an issues management process. Insider connections, often the foundation of a public policy approach to public affairs management, are undeniably valuable but expertise in public policy including forecasting, strategy development and evaluation are even more important if a firm is to have a bona fide issues management process in place.

Fifth, an issues management process broadens the arena of interaction between the company and its stockholders. The public policy approach deals with issues and political forces only within the formal institutions of government.

Finally, an issues management approach involves top management and line management in corporate responses to outside forces to a much greater extent than any of the other approaches. Issues management practitioners often have frequent contact with the president or chairman of the company and it is to be hoped, connections with the strategic planning department, too. Even more importantly, they involve senior staff and divisional executives in the issues management process, often from the earliest stages. They bring valuable information to such managers, elevate them internally and, in turn, build in-company support for public affairs.

Notes

1. Dennis, Lloyd B., "Warning to Businessmen: Public Wants Reform," *Los Angeles Times*, October 6, 1964.

2. "Media Relations and Community Relations Most Highly Valued by CEOs," *Public Relations News*, vol. 50, no. 42.

3. For example, Mack, Charles S., *Lobbying and Government Relations*, (Quorum Books, 1989).

4. Public Affairs Research Group, Boston University, "Public Affairs Offices and their Functions," March 1981, p. 3.

5. Op. Cit., p. 4.

6. Op Cit., p. 7.

7. The Conference Board, "Managing Federal Government Relations," Report No. 905, 1981, p. 21.

8. Op. Cit., p. 22.

9. Public Affairs Research Group, Boston University, Op. Cit., p. 16.

10. The Conference Board, "Managing Business-State Government Relations," Report No. 905, 1981, p. 21.

11. Ibid.

12. Foundation for Public Affairs, "Survey on the State of Corporate Public Affairs," 1992, p. 5. (The authors acknowledge with gratitude the assistance of Ms. Leslie Swift-Rosenzweig, Executive Director of the Foundation, for facilitating this chapter's research.)

13. Sorauf, Frank. *Inside Campaign Finance*, (Yale University Press, 1992), p. 103.

Chapter 3

The State of Public Affairs:
A Profession Reinventing Itself

Raymond L. Hoewing

This chapter develops three loosely-related propositions:

- That by many measures the corporate public affairs field has made significant advances in the past decade;

- That public affairs officers (PAOs) today confront a mixed bag of opportunities and threats; and

- That the most significant trend today may be the reinvention of how the public affairs function is managed.

But first an attempt at definition—what does this author mean by "public affairs?" In the real world one finds public affairs used variously as synonymous with "public relations," as another name for "government relations," as a variant of "community relations" and, of course, as the name for the integrated department combining all, or virtually all, external non-commercial activities of the business world.

It is the latter definition that comes closest to the author's concept—or, more accurately, how most members of the Public Affairs Council use the public affairs terminology. Here are the functional breakdowns of their departments as reported by PAO respondents in a Foundation for Public Affairs study in 1992:[1]

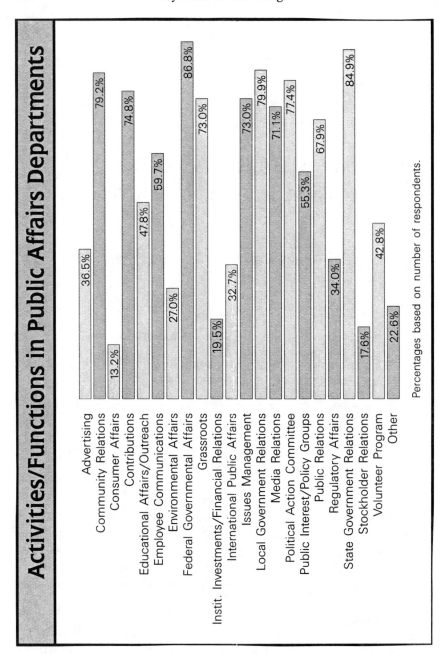

Activities/Functions in Public Affairs Departments

Activity/Function	Percentage
Advertising	36.5%
Community Relations	79.2%
Consumer Affairs	13.2%
Contributions	74.8%
Educational Affairs/Outreach	47.8%
Employee Communications	59.7%
Environmental Affairs	27.0%
Federal Governmental Affairs	86.8%
Grassroots	73.0%
Instit. Investments/Financial Relations	19.5%
International Public Affairs	32.7%
Issues Management	73.0%
Local Government Relations	79.9%
Media Relations	71.1%
Political Action Committee	77.4%
Public Interest/Policy Groups	55.3%
Public Relations	67.9%
Regulatory Affairs	34.0%
State Government Relations	84.9%
Stockholder Relations	17.6%
Volunteer Program	42.8%
Other	22.6%

Percentages based on number of respondents.

Chart I

As Chart I demonstrates, government relations is the prototypical function in the 163 corporate programs profiled in the Foundation's study. It should also be noted that for a variety of reasons the Council's services and programs relate predominantly to the political/government relations/public policy-oriented program areas as opposed to external communications/public relations/media relations. Therefore, it is only fair to caution that the purview of the Council—and thus the knowledge base on which this chapter is based and the various implications, conclusions and examples drawn—are heavily weighted toward the political/government relations/public policy-connected parts of the "public affairs" field.

Progress in Public Affairs

Corporate public affairs, though experiencing both internal and external stress, is by and large continuing its maturation into a valued and strategic entity.

It is also a corporate activity qualitatively different from the mid-'80s, particularly when one considers the addition of important new programmatic responsibilities to the PAOs' portfolios, the growing vertical and horizontal linkages of public affairs within the company and the new management tools being utilized in day-to-day public affairs work.

Those are two ways of summarizing the most recent comprehensive survey of corporate public affairs by the Foundation for Public Affairs (see above). This 1992 study was the first comprehensive examination of the field since the Conference Board's 1987 undertaking, "The Organization and Staffing of Corporate Public Affairs."

One section of the Foundation survey deals with nomenclature—something which has been confusing about the public affairs field from the onset, considering the wide variety of names by which the function is known from company to company. The most popular appellation today is *public affairs* (43 percent), and if one adds the term's three "first cousins"—*corporate affairs, corporate relations* and *external affairs*—more than 62 percent of the department titles are accounted for. (This represents a small increase from the Conference Board's sample in 1987, in which comparable figures were 40 percent for public affairs alone and 57 percent when all four titles were combined.)

More important than nomenclature is where public affairs resides

in the corporate pecking order. While the ranking on the corporate
ladder is fairly impressive, the overall picture has remained relatively static since 1987. The Foundation survey shows that in 1992
51 percent of the responding senior PAOs reported to the CEO, 8
percent to the chairman and president (not the CEO), 14 percent to
an executive vice president, 4 percent to a vice chairman, 4 percent to the chief counsel or legal officer, and the remaining 19
percent to other executives.

Key New Program Areas

In terms of programmatic trends, the "top three" program areas
which had been added to the public affairs department portfolio in
the Foundation survey's 1989-1992 time frame were environmental
affairs (17 percent of the cases), grassroots (16 percent), and educational affairs (15 percent). It is interesting that none of these
functions even surfaces in the Conference Board compilation of
public affairs program areas.

The growing integration of the public affairs function is clearly
reflected in a key question which probed how corporations were
attempting to coordinate "political/ government/public policy functions and public relations/communications functions." Of the 158
responding to this Foundation query, 55 percent reported that these
functions were already part of a single department while another
33 percent reported that the functions were coordinated informally.
Perhaps more important, when asked whether these two areas were
more coordinated or less coordinated than three years earlier (156
respondents), 49 percent reported that they were more coordinated,
46 percent reported no change and only 5 percent reported that they
were less coordinated.

Staffing Issues

Turning to staffing questions, the median number of professional
staff was seven. Confounding conventional wisdom that most public affairs departments had been cut, the Foundation study showed
that professional staff had increased during the previous three years
in 34 percent of the companies, remained the same in 31 percent,

and decreased in 33 percent. (The comparable numbers were not all that different in the Conference Board study—35 percent, 37 percent and 38 percent, respectively.)

There was better news on the budget front—45 percent surveyed by the Foundation reported increases, 28 had stayed even and only 27 percent reported decreases. Only 10 percent said they thought public affairs had been cut more drastically than other departments— a lament heard frequently in the public affairs community.

The data on government relations staffing yielded some mild surprises. Many familiar with the federal government relations scene would have predicted a greater percentage of companies reporting decreases in their Washington office staffing over the preceding three years, but the figure emerging from the Foundation survey—23 percent—was relatively low, and 32 percent reported increases. On the other hand, some might have thought that a greater percentage of respondents would have reported increases in their state government relations staffs over that same period than the 29 percent who did (56 percent reported no change). Less surprising were responses on local government relations, where considerably more departments—24 percent—reported increases in staffing the three-year period as opposed to decreases (15 percent).

Other Program Areas

Clearly, and unsurprisingly, a significant "growth area" for public affairs has been regulatory work. Respondents to the Foundation survey described the roles in regulatory affairs as "major" in 29 percent of the cases and "moderate" in 41 percent. Furthermore, one-third reported that additional resources had been committed to regulatory affairs during the previous three years. (It is instructive to note that regulatory affairs did not surface as a significant public affairs activity in the 1987 Conference Board study.)

Public affairs began four decades ago as essentially political involvement activities. High proportions of companies in the Foundation study did enumerate one or more political activities— for example, 80 percent had political action committees, 84 percent scheduled facility visits for elected officials, 58 percent conducted voter registration programs, and an impressive 43 percent communicated on issues with "third parties." But their involvement in another respect was surprising low:

- Fifty-six percent had no formal policy to encourage employees to volunteer for political campaigns;

- Fifty-one percent had no formal policy to encourage employees to run for public office;

- Sixty-four percent had no formal policy to provide time off for employees to run for political office.

It has long been recognized that—compared to companies' relative stakes in overseas trade and investment—international public affairs is undernourished in most firms. The Foundation study shows that international public affairs remains, in the grand scheme, a secondary function. Only about a third of the respondents—54 had accountability for international public affairs (the comparable figure in the earlier Conference Board study was much higher), and among those 54 companies, only 34 categorized their international programs as "highly" or "moderately" developed. Moreover, international staffs were small, with a mean number of full-time employees at U.S. headquarters amounting only to 1.4 persons.

Relations within the Company

Turning to relations with other parts of the company, public affairs organization was fairly complex for half of the Foundation respondents. The complexity derives from the multiple-division-nature of more than three-fourths of the companies. Among the interesting data reported:

- More than two out of three had full-time public affairs personnel at operating-unit level;

- Many of these unit-level people had solid line reporting relationships to operating management (approximately 60 percent);

- Part-time public affairs people were also frequently domiciled at non-headquarters locations (66 percent of respondents).

In this milieu of scattered public affairs personnel, the corporate public affairs staff performed one or more of several predictable functions—for example, fostering coordination of public affairs activities among operating units, reviewing and evaluating public affairs plans of operating units, participating in the strategic planning processes of operating units, etc. And, quite apart from whether public affairs personnel were located at subheadquarters sites, more than a third of the respondents charged expenses for services rendered back to their "customers" in other departments.

Other Trends

The Foundation study contains much other relevant data. Here are some examples:

- The "extension" of public affairs by assigning non-public affairs executives to part-time public affairs chores seems to have reached heretofore-unrecognized proportions;

- Washington offices reported to the senior public affairs executive in much higher proportions than reflected in a 1988 Conference Board survey on federal government relations;

- Issues management apparently continues to grow in importance: 46 percent of the respondents described their issues management as "more important" than three years previously;

- Although two-thirds of the public affairs departments identified or prioritized public issues for input into business, only one-fourth were actually represented formally in the planning process;

- Thirty-three percent of the companies thought their public affairs function had become more centralized within the preceding three years, compared to the 12 percent who thought the activity had become more decentralized.

PAOs: Threats and Opportunities

Never before has success depended so much on knowing the "business," whatever it may be for the individual public affairs officer.

In the simpler past, it sufficed in public affairs to be technically proficient—writing press releases, handling government relations problems, initiating a community relations program.

PAOs were viewed, and viewed themselves, as specialists. They could ply their craft relatively unknowledgeable about, and often uninterested in, the sum and substance of the operations, whatever they were, of their employer.

That often self-declared insulation was at one time not a serious impediment. It is today!

The constituencies to which PAOs speak, the complexity of the issues with which they deal, and the expectations of their seniors today demand that they become steeped in the details of the operations of their employer. To be effective operationally, to successfully communicate externally and to be credible internally, they have to know, feel and smell what truly defines their institution. Failure to grasp this reality explains why top managements—to the chagrin of some of us in the field—have moved operations people into senior position in the public affairs field with the comment, "It's much easier to train a person in public affairs than it is to educate a person about our company."

Failure to develop this knowledge is likely to explain what our professional periodicals so frequently bemoan—that the role too many PAOs play is that of technician or implementer, rather than that of strategist and adviser to senior management.

Considering the nature of the external environment, the often bifurcated public relations/government relations function must be viewed and implemented as a strategically unified, integrated, coordinated function.

The Chinese Wall in both conceptualization and programming that has separated government and political affairs from the so-called public relations functions has inflicted a severe penalty on effectiveness.

Events are driving home a hard lesson. What is required to energize and optimize the various activities lumped under the public affairs or communications umbrella is unification and coordination (though "organization chart integration" per se may not be necessary).

In the past in all too many organizations the functions were separated either organizationally or de jure—and the executives often

were contemptuous of their peers, whether they were public relations people who tended to view their government relations partners
as involved in some kind of seamy activity or government relations
executives who viewed their public relations associates as "flacks."

The synergism of integrating these activities has been proven. For
example:

• Linking government relations and community relations;

• Using sophisticated communication messages to design
  grassroots or legislative support programs; and

• Seeking to use philanthropic outlays for public policy
  purposes.

All those who labor in external affairs are about the business of
communications and each has something to bring to the table.

**PAOs will be wise to implement already developed, already
known tools to "harden" the function they manage.**

Parameters and expectations need to be developed relating to
performance aligning PAOs with the parameters and expectations
of managers in other corporate functions. In short, the functions must
be managed in such a way that PAOs are seen as using the same
tools and processes, and being as bottom-line oriented, as business-
related, as peers in other departments.

There are many dimensions to this. But one is particularly worthy of comment—the need to subject public affairs work and
performance to tougher standards of measurement. For all too long
PAOs have argued that there is little at the end of the day that can
be measured.

That line won't work in most organizations, given the prevalent
competitive environment and the internal financial stringencies faced
by most PAOs. Most PAOs *will* be measured and PAOs should seize
the initiative. The point to be remembered: if PAOs don't establish
the basis on which their performance is measured, others will.

Whether the yardstick is put to what might be called process
(i.e., input) audit, or whether it is an attempt to quantify results (i.e.,
output), or whether it is comparative analysis with public affairs
practices in other firms (i.e., benchmarking) the effort has to be

made. To be sure, whatever the measurements are they will not be as precise as counting widgets, but they will represent a big step forward from where most PAOs are now.

There is another point here worth commenting on. In many organizations the so-called Quality Process has been introduced in recent years and has resulted in reappraisal and redesign in many parts of the operation. Too many public affairs departments have viewed the Quality Process as inapplicable and irrelevant. That is a mistake.

PAOs have to improve their management skills.

This point can be put this way. In many instances those in the public affairs field have seen their role as one of administering certain programs or functions—the essential job was to carry on "activities."

As a whole, PAOs have attached sufficient significance to *how* they managed their time, their human resources, their financial resources. Consciously or unconsciously, they have not given enough attention to what our friends in public administration sometimes call POSCRIB—Planning, Organizing, Structuring, Communicating and Coordinating, Resources, Implementing, and Budgeting.

PAOs need to understand and speak the language and be able to employ the management methodologies and technologies of their corporate brothers and sisters, who are often schooled in (and comfortable with) the latest business-school buzzwords on managing people and resources. The public affairs manager has no choice but to seek to develop tools and techniques to better measure productivity, to subject optional strategies to cost-effectiveness tests, and to relate the work of public affairs to corporate strategies and objectives.

The Public Affairs Work Environment

The public affairs "workplace" is no longer what it once was. "Working harder and enjoying it less" would surely be the inevitable summation of any poll of PAOs honestly answered. In fact, no PAO needs a study to prove that, measured by almost any standard— workload, stress, hours worked, job security—the average PAO's workplace is a less friendly place as we near the beginning of a new century than in it was in previous years. And there is nothing, absolutely nothing, to suggest abatement, much less reversal of these trends in the near future. Indeed, a 1994 study by the American Management Association suggested that downsizing is now the cultural norm in corporate America—a "systematic, ongoing corporate activity," in the words of the study director.

Beyond that, PA staffs—*all* staffs in fact—are under particular scrutiny. The extreme of top management thinking was perhaps most colorfully (if inelegantly) expressed by the CEO of Scott Paper who in an interview in the *Wall Street Journal* in March, 1995, had this to say about headquarters staff: "The success of a corporation is inversely proportionate to the size of the headquarters. Large headquarters are just there to stroke the ego of chief executives."

So the "churning"—my term for the unprecedented combination of cutbacks, turnovers, job insecurity, stress and frequent dissatisfaction with the overall working environment—will apparently continue in public affairs.

Reinventing the Management of Public Affairs

In the face of all this change, managers of the public affairs function have not stood still. In fact, change is very much the order of the day. Those frequently-used descriptors of corporate America—restructuring and re-engineering—can legitimately be applied to the practices of public affairs management. An examination of trends suggests that the transformation in the tools and processes of public affairs management is advancing rapidly. Some of the trends are organizational. The thinning of headquarters staff in larger companies, for example, is usually accompanied by decentralization to operating units of accountability for public affairs.

But the trends that are most important have to do with the fundamentals of day-in, day-out management: How do we improve the tools and processes by which we manage time, people and other resources? How do we measure efficiency and effectiveness? How do we quantify our contributions to business strategies?

Three inter-related processes have figured significantly in the management of public affairs in recent years:

- Total Quality Management came late to public affairs, as it did to most other staff departments in the typical corporation.

But come it did, at least in a significant number of companies, and PAOs now find themselves struggling with such
tools of TQM as "customer" surveys, process mapping, and
benchmarking. To be sure, the experience, to say nothing of
the receptivity, of public affairs departments has been un-
even. But there are more than a few PAOs who credit TQM
with dramatic improvements in their departments' efficiency—and effectiveness.

• Public affairs benchmarking—measuring a public affairs
  department's processes, methods and programs against those
  employed in a competitor corporation's public affairs office
  —has become a fixture, often mandated by top management
  to prove public affairs proficiency. A variety of mechanisms
  —one-on-one interviews with peers, written surveys of practices in other firms, analyses of relevant data collected by
  the Foundation for Public Affairs—have been used to benchmark virtually every public affairs program area.

• Quantification—the bromide, "you can't manage it if you
  can't measure it," has driven the search for numbers to answer such questions as: What do government relations activities contribute to the bottom line? What is the comparative
  corporate benefit in funding Organization A versus Organization B in our philanthropic program? What are the demon-
  strable benefits of the cost of dues paid to Association X?

It need hardly be said that cost-benefit accounting for public affairs processes is less precise than that for assembly line processes,
for example. But in the current milieu, that is no defense—in public affairs work "soft" numbers and subjective evaluations are
analogous to crawling before we learn to walk.

Two other trends deserve comment. The first relates to the self-
perception of cutting-edge public affairs departments. Their view
clearly is that they will not be viewed as strategic unless they relate directly and organically to business strategies. Take the language
of these public affairs mission statements:

Chevron: "Our mission is to maximize the company's ability to
conduct its worldwide business in the best interests of its stockholders."

ABB: "Support ABB's mission, goals and business objectives by developing programs . . ."

Hewlett Packard: ". . . shape public policy to foster an environment that allows HP to achieve its business objectives."

Olin: "Support Olin's business objectives of market leadership and profitability."

Household Finance: ". . . creating and maintaining the legislative and regulatory environment necessary for the Household International companies to implement their business plans."

Rhetoric is of course one thing, implementation is quite another. But the evidence from the 1992 survey by the Foundation for Public Affairs suggests that PAOs are using a variety of tools to link themselves more closely with corporate objectives [See Chart II].

A closely related trend is a much more organic tie-in between public affairs staffs and peer departments. Giving "ownership" for certain public affairs responsibilities to colleagues in other departments may be a near-necessity for under-staffed public affairs units. Hence, the use of cross-departmental teams for issues management work, the establishment of multi-departmental committees to make philanthropic decisions, the empowerment of lower-level employees to manage volunteer programs.

But the push to connect to other departments is not always driven solely by financial considerations. It is also a practical way to insure alignment of public affairs with strategies driving the firm.

The epitome of redefined internal relationships is a new definition by public affairs of its accountability for performance. For example, many public affairs departments view other departments as "clients" to be serviced, in much the same sense that a good salesman "takes care" of his or her customers. In some companies, this tendency has gone so far as the development of written contracts spelling out the mutual obligations of the public affairs department and its "client" or "customer" in realizing an objective (say, achieving a legislative goal). Two other recent trends represent even further attenuation of this new approach to public affairs operations:

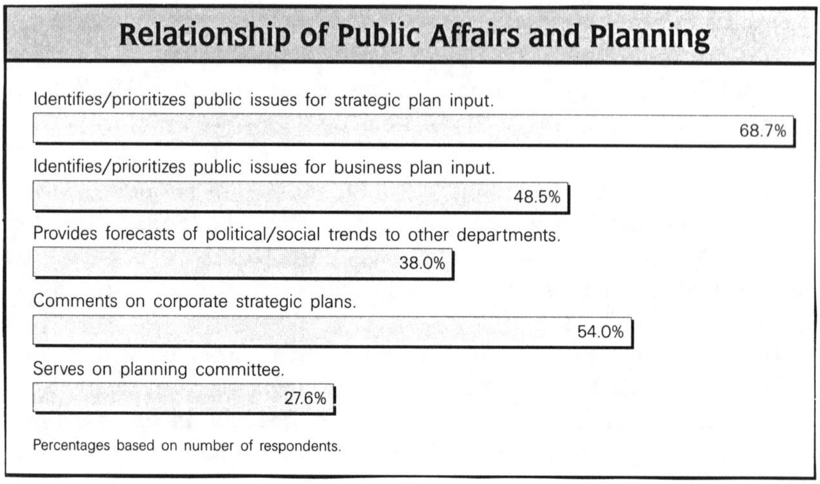

Relationship of Public Affairs and Planning

Identifies/prioritizes public issues for strategic plan input.

| | 68.7% |

Identifies/prioritizes public issues for business plan input.

| 48.5% |

Provides forecasts of political/social trends to other departments.

| 38.0% |

Comments on corporate strategic plans.

| 54.0% |

Serves on planning committee.

| 27.6% |

Percentages based on number of respondents.

Chart II

1. In some companies, would-be "client" departments have the power to "contract out" their needs externally if they are not satisfied with service the public affairs unit can provide. (Similarly, public affairs departments may have to find funding for some or all non-corporate-level programs from internal "users.")

2. In some companies internal "clients" play formal roles in assessing the performance of PAOs (sometimes including a say on awards of bonuses).

This, then, is one man's snapshot of corporate public affairs. Because it is by its very nature dynamic, we cannot predict what public affairs will look like even in the near future—only that it will almost certainly be very different.

Note

1. The Foundation for Public Affairs is the 501(c)(3) affiliate of the Public Affairs Council.

CONTEMPORARY PUBLIC AFFAIRS

Chapter 4

Impact of the Communications Revolution on Public Affairs: Pervasiveness of Public Affairs Messages Today

Herb B. Berkowitz and
Edwin J. Feulner, Jr.

For those of us involved in public affairs, the current communications revolution is a two-edged sword. The good news is that a handful of elite news organizations no longer controls the agenda and defines the terms of the debate. The coming of age of mainstream talk radio, cable and direct-satellite television, new computer technologies, and alternative newspapers and periodicals has broken the hold of the *Washington Post, New York Times, Newsweek, Time, U.S. News and World Report* and big three television networks. Today, if you have an important story to tell, you have the opportunity to tell it effectively even if the big media choose to ignore you.

The flip side, however, is that there are now so many different ways of communicating to both niche and mass-market audiences—and so many individuals and interests clamoring for attention—it is increasingly difficult to be heard above the din. In the "old" days, you could devote virtually all of your resources to a relative handful of target news organizations and individual journalists and commentators. Taken as a whole, they alone determined what was news and which opinions would be considered legitimate and worth including in the national conversation known as U.S. politics.

The landscape today is dramatically different. Most major daily newspapers in the United States—the *Los Angeles Times, New York Times, Wall Street Journal* and *Washington Post* among them—have been losing readers, according to the Audit Bureau of Circulations. The overall number of daily newspapers continues to decline. United Press International is no longer seriously involved in the large-scale gathering and dissemination of news. Network television's market share has declined significantly. And the newsweeklies no longer ignite sparks the way they once were able to do.

But for every contraction there has been a significant expansion. Rather than greater concentration of power among even fewer news organizations, the marketplace has exploded, resulting in a dramatic dispersion of power. For those who often felt frozen out by the self-designated "mainstream" media, the opportunity now exists to ignore, or even end-run, them.

Such opportunities also create new challenges, however, because it is now necessary to deal with more news organizations than ever and greater-than-ever competition for their attention.

The Changing Face of the Media

The old lineup of powerful and important media was easy to follow: If you had a story of national importance to tell, you told it to the Associated Press, United Press International, the *New York Times, Washington Post, Wall Street Journal, Time, Newsweek, U.S. News & World Report*, and the three national television networks: ABC, CBS and NBC. Stories involving issues, ideas and policy also might be fodder for a handful of powerful national columnists and political journals such as the *Nation, New Republic* and *Progressive* on the left, and *Commentary* (after its dramatic ideological shift under former Editor Norman Podhoretz) and *National Review* on the right.

The new lineup—considerably larger and more complicated—includes the following key players.

News Services

The Associated Press is omnipresent. Reuters, the British news agency, also now has a significant U.S. presence. The biggest change has been the expanded, competitive role now played by the supplemental news wires, including Scripps-Howard, Knight-Ridder/Tribune, New York Times, Los Angeles Times-Washington Post, Gannett, Newhouse, Copley, Cox and the newer and more specialized Bloomberg Business News. While most of these supplemental news services existed in one form or another in the past, they played second fiddle to AP and UPI, frequently serving only company-owned papers, as Gannett News Service does even now. The collapse of UPI created a major void, however, which the supplemental news services aggressively have filled. Now a story of national interest written for the *Los Angeles Times* or Cox's *Atlanta Constitution* might appear in hundreds of newspapers around the country. Indeed, stories originated by several dozen individual newspapers—the *Arizona Republic, Boston Globe, Baltimore Sun, Dallas Morning News* and *Providence Journal*, to name just a few—also may be distributed by one of the supplementals. Thus, a *Providence Journal* story or op-ed page column, moving on the Knight-Ridder/Tribune News Service wire, might reach just as large a national audience as an AP, *New York Times* or *Washington Post* story.

National Dailies

The *Washington Post, New York Times* and *Wall Street Journal*—still, arguably, the three most influential newspapers in the United States—now have competition. *USA Today,* Gannett's flagship, is widely read and less politically correct on its news pages than the *Post, Times,* or even the *Journal.* The *Washington Times* is a must-read in the nation's capital, and is much more closely tuned in and sympathetic to the conservative mood of the country and Congress than the *Post, Times, Journal* (news pages), or *USA Today.* The *Christian Science Monitor,* once a very influential international daily, was financially drained by the church's failed television venture and has become a slim and almost irrelevant imitation of its former self. *Investor's Business Daily,* conservative like the *Washington Times* and *Wall Street Journal* editorial page, is the growing new kid on the block.

In addition to the national dailies, several major "regional" dailies have significant national impact: the *Boston Globe, Chicago Tribune, Los Angeles Times, Miami Herald,* and *Newsday,* to name a few. They are especially important because all of them originate stories—in Washington, their home states, and occasionally overseas—that move on the national supplemental wires. The *Globe* is now owned by the *New York Times*, so many *Globe* stories are distributed by the New York Times News Service. *Newsday* is owned by the Times Mirror Company, co-owner with the *Washington Post* of the Los Angeles Times-Washington Post News Service. The *Miami Herald* is Knight-Ridder's third-largest newspaper, which is a partner with Chicago's Tribune Company in the Knight-Ridder/Tribune News Service.

Opinion Writers

For public affairs executives involved in the development and marketing of policy, having their ideas and views validated by the media in editorials and opinion columns can be critical to success. That is why many public-affairs "campaigns" include meetings with the editorial boards (or individual editorial writers) of major daily newspapers and smaller papers in the districts of key members of Congress. Though they may not really care what the *New York Times* or *Washington Post* say editorially, unless, of course, the *Times* or *Post* agree with them, members of Congress *do* care what the newspapers in their states and districts have to say about an issue.

Interestingly, editorial pages are read not only by the people who are the most politically involved in a community, but by most newspaper readers. According to a 1993 "Study of Media & Markets" by Simmons Market Research Bureau, based on interviews with more than 22,400 adults, of 10 sections found in most newspapers, the editorial pages have the second-highest average daily readership (79 percent), trailing only general news (95 percent). The opinion pages did better than entertainment (78 percent), sports (75 percent), even comics (74 percent). Among young people in the 18-to-34-year-old cohort, thought by many to be less serious readers, editorials also are remarkably well read (74 percent), trailing only general news (92 percent) and entertainment (77 percent). The high readership cuts across virtually all demographic categories. As Susan Albright, editorial page editor of the *Minneapolis Star-Tribune*, wrote in a September 1994 task-force report to the National Conference of Editorial Writers, ". . . whether you break out readers by income, gender, age, whatever, editorial pages, like general news, attract readers in high numbers—higher numbers than most other sections/pages of the newspaper."

The editorial pages of America's largest 100 daily newspapers remain overwhelmingly left-of-center—"socialist," in the opinion of Rep. Newt Gingrich, R-Ga., the Speaker of the House. Our own informal survey, conducted with Hugh Newton, president of the Alexandria, Virginia-based public affairs firm, Hugh C. Newton & Associates, found fewer than 30 of the 100 largest-circulation dailies provide their readers with a fairly consistent conservative editorial-page voice. We would define such a voice as favoring limited government intervention in our lives and the national economy, a firm commitment to U.S. national defenses, and strong, traditional family values. This small, exclusive club includes the *Boston Herald, Wall Street Journal, New York Post, Washington Times, Richmond Times-Dispatch, Cincinnati Enquirer, Greensburg/Pittsburgh Tribune-Review, Detroit News, Indianapolis Star, Tampa Tribune, Florida Times-Union* (Jacksonville), *Arkansas Democrat-Gazette* (Little Rock), *Rocky Mountain News* (Denver), *Daily Oklahoman* (Oklahoma City), *Arizona Republic* (Phoenix), *Orange County Register, San Diego Union-Tribune* and perhaps a dozen others.

Editorial pages remain important, not because they are active crusaders, as many were in the past, but because members of Congress pay attention to what appears on the editorial pages of the papers in their districts.

By contrast, the impact of nationally syndicated columnists appears to have waned somewhat. Opinion-writing these days is a field dominated by conservatives. Yet, there are now so many national columnists that no one has the influence of the giants of the past, when a handful of well-known pundits—Joseph Alsop, David Lawrence, Walter Lippmann, Drew Pearson, George Sokolsky and William S. White, for example—helped set the agenda and define the terms and tone of the political debate. As important as David Broder, Maureen Dowd, William Raspberry, William Safire, Tony Snow, Cal Thomas, and George Will may be, the market is more diffused than in the past. Thus, even today's most influential columnists must vie for attention with a large and constantly expanding universe of competitors.

Op-Ed Pages

Newspaper op-ed pages—traditionally, the page "opposite" the editorial page—underwent a major transformation in the late 1970s and early 1980s. Today, those of us with an axe to grind have the opportunity to make our own best case, in our own words, without going through the usual journalistic filtering process.

Historically, op-ed pages were the place in the newspaper where political columnists—the newspaper's own and syndicated columnists—were featured. Many newspapers have added something new to this mix since the 1970s: guest columns by outside contributors. This has been an extraordinarily useful and healthy development, resulting in a vigorous clash of competing visions and ideas on a daily basis. For anyone who has ever felt short-changed, slighted, or misunderstood by the mainstream media, op-ed pages have been a godsend.

The development of this new forum has not gone unnoticed. The competition for space on the op-ed page is as keen as the competition for everything else. The editor of the *Wall Street Journal's* editorial features (op-ed) page told us in May 1995 that the *Journal* received, on average, some 900 unsolicited manuscripts *every* week. Of the 900 fewer than 10, about one percent, typically will make it into print. The *New York Times* in a typical week receives an average of 1000 unsolicited manuscripts, some 200 a day.

By most measures, the *Washington Times* "Commentary" section, edited by Pulitzer Prize-winner Mary Lou Forbes, and the *Wall Street Journal* editorial features page, and the *New York Times* and *Washington Post* op-ed pages are the most influential platforms in the country. The *Washington Times* provides the most space for the clash of ideas day in and day out, both in "Commentary" and on the op-ed page. The op-ed pages of *USA Today* and, to a lesser degree, the *Los Angeles Times* also have considerable national impact.

The supplemental news wires play an important role here as well. Op-ed page articles that appear in the *New York Times, Washington Post* and *Los Angeles Times* are distributed nationally by their respective news services. Scripps-Howard News Service and Knight-Ridder/Tribune News Service also distribute op-ed page features to subscribing newspapers.

Political Journals

As with the nationally syndicated political columnists, the number and variety of opinion journals also have proliferated in recent years. In addition to *National Review, Commentary* and the *New Republic*, and the now-almost-irrelevant *Nation* and *Progressive*, we have R. Emmett Tyrrell's sprightly *American Spectator, American*

Enterprise, Reason, American Prospect, Public Interest, National Interest, the Heritage Foundation's *Policy Review,* and the newest of the group, the Rupert Murdoch-financed *Weekly Standard,* edited by conservative stalwarts Fred Barnes (formerly of the *New Republic*), William Kristol (former chief of staff to then Education Secretary William Bennett and later to Vice President Dan Quayle), and John Podhoretz (son of former *Commentary* Editor Norman Podhoretz), and Hachette Filipacchi Magazines' political journal, *George,* edited by John F. Kennedy Jr. (son of the former president).

For detailed information on the activities of government and those trying to influence it, you can't beat *National Journal. Congressional Quarterly* (owned by the *St. Petersburg Times*) is *National Journal's* leading competitor, while the more gossipy *Roll Call* and *The Hill* focus almost solely on Congress. For a hard-edged conservative spin on the issues, in tune with the GOP-controlled Congress, don't forget *Human Events,* the influential weekly, now owned by Phillips Publishing International, a highly successful specialty publisher.

Talk Radio

Talk radio is not new; what is new is its "interactive" format, its pervasiveness, and its expanded and redefined role as an alternative source of *news,* as well as opinion, for millions of Americans alienated by the traditional media. Since the late 1980s, Rush Limbaugh has been the undeniable "800-pound gorilla" of talk radio. But he is by no means alone: Ken Hamblin, G. Gordon Liddy, Oliver North, and Michael Reagan, on the right, and Alan Colmes and Tom Leykis, on the left, all have significant followings and substantial impact, as do a number of local and regional "talkers," including Dallas's David Gold, Denver's Mike Rosen, New York's Bob Grant, and Seattle's Mike Siegel. All told, at mid-year 1995, some 1,200 radio stations (mostly AM) had talk or news-talk formats, according to the trade journal, *Radio & Records.* Talk radio has the unique ability among the grassroots media to light up Congress's telephone switchboard and tie up congressional fax machines. Such power was first demonstrated in the 1970s by George Putnam on his popular "Talk Back" show, on KIEV radio in suburban Los Angeles, which helped spearhead the drive for the state's revolutionary tax-limitation initiative, Proposition 13.

Television

A decade ago, the three major television networks—ABC, CBS and NBC—controlled virtually the entire broadcast marketplace. Americans viewed only what network (and PBS) programming executives wanted us to view. Today, 65 percent of American households are wired for cable (June 1995), the phone companies are entering the business, and direct-satellite television is available to everyone, everywhere. Thanks to these innovations, plus the miniaturization of satellite dishes, most television viewers can select from a virtual smorgasbord of offerings in each timeslot during the day, from network sitcoms, to re-runs of network sitcoms, current and "classic" movies, sports, talk shows, news and public affairs, and even the televised proceedings of Congress.

The big three still control a large share of the market. ABC's "Good Morning America," for example, had a Nielsen-rated audience of 4.7 million in March 1995, while "The 700 Club," syndicated via The Family Channel, had a Nielsen audience of 127,000 and CNN Headline News, during the same timeslot as "Good Morning America," had a Nielsen audience of 227,000. Still, the networks no longer have the monopoly they did just a few years ago.

Meanwhile, the choices available to television viewers continue to expand. In addition to ABC, CBS, NBC, and PBS news and public-affairs programs, television viewers—and public-affairs executives with a story to tell—can turn to: 24-hour-a-day news programming on Cable News Network (CNN), CNN Headline News, and a number of local and regional all-news stations, such as News Channel 8, in the Washington, D.C. area; the televised proceedings of Congress and various public policy organizations on the Cable Satellite Public Affairs Network (C-SPAN); and public affairs talk shows—many of them involving "interaction" between the host, guests and viewers—on a number of networks, including America's Talking, NET/Political Newstalk Network, CNBC, and NewsTalk Television.

More such networks are in various start-up stages, including the American Political Channel, Conservative Television Network, The Ecology Channel, Global Village Network, The History Channel, and the Military Channel.

Cyberspace

When we purchased our first PCs in the early 1980s, little did we anticipate that a little more than a decade later we'd have our own "home page" on the Heritage Foundation/National Review "Town Hall" forum on Internet's World Wide Web. Indeed, such talk a decade ago probably would have met with considerable bewilderment.

Dramatic advances in computer technology not only have changed the way many of us communicate—with Congress and the traditional media, as well as other audiences—but also have changed the way we gather and assimilate information. With the Internet and available CD ROMs, the challenge is no longer to get enough data, but to avoid getting swamped.

Computers, modems, and a growing number of databases and interactive networks have combined to create what is commonly called the "information superhighway." The Internet alone not only provides a venue for political chat, as do such commercial ventures as CompuServe, Prodigy and America Online, but also provides access to Federal Election Commission records, Library of Congress databases, and government documents and reports, including Census Bureau data. The Library of Congress' World Wide Web site, called "Thomas," accesses the *Congressional Record* and information on legislation. A separate House of Representatives site includes the text of legislation and amendments, the House schedule, and recent floor action. Many special-interest groups also have sites on the Internet, ranging from the National Rifle Association to the National Organization for Women. Several useful directories of political resources also can be accessed on the Internet. The number of organizations and directories and "home page" sites continues to expand so rapidly it is virtually impossible to keep up. Stanford University's "Yahoo" directory provides a good guide to the political databases available on the Internet.

A Multitude of Voices

Just as the communications revolution has ended the near-monopoly that the networks and New York/Washington print media giants had on the public policy debate, it also has enabled and encouraged many new voices to enter the public arena.

On any given day in Washington, for example, you are competing for attention with the White House, the various cabinet-level departments of government, the Environmental Protection Agency and other independent agencies, the majority and minority leaderships of the House and Senate, House and Senate committees and subcommittees, 535 individual Senators and Members of Congress, the 50 state governors, think tanks such as The Heritage Foundation and Brookings Institution, the Chamber of Commerce, National Federation of Independent Business (NFIB) and AFL-CIO, dozens of other Washington-based academic, trade and professional associations, the AFL-CIO's affiliate unions, and dozens of lobby groups and activist organizations. You're also competing with external events beyond your control, ranging from state visits by foreign dignitaries to natural disasters, terrorist attacks and the District of Columbia's latest fiscal crisis.

Without the media—through various editing and production processes—channeling and filtering this deluge of data and cacophony of voices, the entire enterprise would devolve into Communications Age static, not unlike the noise you pick up on your car radio when driving near certain overhead electric lines.

The challenge for public affairs professionals responsible for getting their firms' messages across is to break away from the pack and use all appropriate media—both new and old—to tell their stories to their target audiences, whether the broad grassroots public, the nationwide community of opinion-leaders and policymakers, or other target audiences.

To accomplish this goal it is important to remember that the new technology and new media are merely transmission devices. The medium—whether a newspaper op-ed page or a leading radio talk show—should not be confused with the message.

The Medium is Not the Message

Because they have confused the two, many communications professionals have found themselves "lost in cyberspace," generating messages for an audience they cannot define or locate, other than to note that millions of "them" are "out there."

Remember, however, that our job is communications, not satellite engineering or software design. Such technologies are merely tools that may (or may not) enable us to deliver our messages to our target audiences with more precision—ideally, reducing the static created by competing or conflicting messages. Public-affairs executives no more have to be technology experts than they have to be experts in the internal combustion engine in order to turn on and drive their cars.

While computer technology and the Internet and compressed digital narrowcasting and other changing technologies may help us accomplish our goals, they are really little more than contemporary versions of the Medieval courier: ways of getting our message from here to there. The major difference: we are now privy in many cases to immediate feedback.

The basic communications process, however—whether dealing with traditional print media, television, or the computer screen—still involves the organization of words and thoughts into a coherent, convincing and passionate message, which may be accompanied and enhanced by sound and visuals, depending on the medium. If you can't put your thoughts and arguments into words and organize them in a coherent and convincing fashion, all the new technologies in the world won't help you. We have seen such technological advances before: the printing press, the telegraph, the telephone, radio, television, global satellites, and fiber-optic cable. As policy communicators, we may or may not be able to use the new technologies to our advantage; it depends what we are trying to communicate and to whom.

A decade-and-a-half ago the new technology of the hour was the video news release. For several thousand dollars, you could create a video news release and bounce it off a satellite to television stations around the country. Public relations agencies and corporate PR offices were hooked, and the industry grew. Then somebody started to ask the unthinkable: Whom are we trying to reach and is this the best way to reach them? As we contemplate cyberspace and new television technologies—narrowcasting, rather than broadcasting—we need to ask these same questions: Whom are we trying to reach with our message and what is the best way to reach them?

Selling a Point of View

The public-affairs profession is engaged in the development, creation, packaging and marketing of ideas and opinions, rather than products or services. While selling a point of view may be similar to selling soap in some respects, the marketplace generally is different. Producers of consumer goods intend their products for the general public or for relatively large demographic segments of the broad general public: teenagers, Generation Xers, Baby Boomers, the elderly, African-Americans, Latinos, people who keep Kosher homes, families with incomes above (or below) a certain level, dog or personal computer owners, lovers of classical music, and so forth. The job of the marketing department is to craft a message that will appeal to the target audiences and select the mix of print, broadcast and direct marketing that will provide the highest degree of market "penetration" at the most   reasonable price.

Mass marketers, of course, look for large numbers—audited circulation figures, Nielsen ratings and the local radio "books." Specialty marketers, on the other hand, seek niche audiences and the publications, cable channels and other media that reach them.

Rallying public support for an idea or cause may involve both. Former *New York Times* Washington Bureau Chief Hedrick Smith, in his 1988 best-seller, *The Power Game*, described the process as "widening the circle." Smith noted that "spreading information to summon political allies . . . or to rally public opinion" can be essential to success in the political arena. It "is the regular stuff of the power game. Everyone does it, from presidents on down, when they want to change the balance of power on some issue . . . [or] stir up public opinion and use public pressure to influence" the debate.

Yet, not all public-affairs programs depend upon the large-scale "manipulation" of public opinion. Public affairs professionals frequently deal with technical issues about which the general public knows little and cares even less. In these cases, communications objectives may be far more modest, involving carefully selected "influentials" who can be reached—by telephone, letter, fax, e-mail, or by visiting with them personally—without any public notice on the political radar screen.

The communications revolution has increased the number of options available to those of us involved in the national policy debate and has brought many new voices into the public arena. In doing so, it has neither provided a solution to our problems, nor has it created any insurmountable new obstacles. Changes in communications technology have revolutionized everything but the basic building blocks of strategic communications: the written and spoken word.

Chapter 5

Research Designed for Public Release: A Powerful Tool for Public Affairs and Public Relations

Kathleen O'Neil

Introduction

In recent years, the public release of survey research results has been recognized as an important tool in public affairs. Surveys that are prepared for public release offer a way to generate news, to focus attention on an issue, or to position a topic or client in a unique way. These surveys can create news events, serve as the basis of ongoing media campaigns, or enhance grassroots organizing. Because survey research provides information that is both new and newsworthy, it can attract the attention of journalists, policy makers, and other key opinion leaders. Such studies can also be very helpful in attaining specific marketing objectives, such as introducing new products or repositioning products and services. Properly done, a publicly released study (PRS) can be a powerful addition to the repertoire of the public affairs and public relations professional.

This chapter explores the elements of an effective PRS, examining the opportunities that this kind of research offers. Like other tools in this business, the PRS is not a foolproof vehicle to success, so we also examine the pitfalls that one may encounter without

careful planning. At Roper Starch Worldwide, we have conducted
many PRSs for a wide variety of clients. This experience has enabled us to identify seven essential elements that underlie the
successful PRS. Below we address these seven essential elements
in turn.

Clearly Define the Objectives of the PRS

The PRS can be used to accomplish many different objectives.
Perhaps first and foremost, the PRS can be used to inform and educate people about a public affairs issue. Owing to its ability to
attract news coverage and provide solid facts about public attitudes,
the PRS is an excellent tool for focusing attention on a topic.

The National Geographic Society's campaign on the nation's water
supply provides a notable example. To help focus attention on the
threats that jeopardize fresh water, the Society—along with the
Conservation Fund, and the U.S. Geological Survey—undertook a
broad initiative that included publishing an unprecedented thirteenth
issue of the magazine and conducting a series of educational forums. As part of this initiative, National Geographic commissioned
a national opinion survey covering public perceptions of the quality and availability of fresh water. The study also examined attitudes
toward possible solutions to water problems and knowledge of water issues. The survey brought the issue of water to people's attention
in a variety of ways. The study was released at the National Press
Club in Washington in a major media event that generated television and newspaper coverage, and was carried live on national radio.
Informational packets containing the survey results were distributed to every member of Congress, and copies were provided to
scientists working on the water issue. Through such efforts, the
National Geographic survey helped focus attention on water's im-
periled status.

Public affairs professionals have also found the PRS to be effective when lobbying for legislation. Public opinion research about
pending legislation, and the subsequent release of the findings, can
often help an organization influence the outcome of political debates. The Dehere Foundation study on gun control is a case in
point. Key questions in the survey concerned the so-called Brady
Bill, which called for a five-day waiting period prior to purchasing
a handgun. The survey showed that the public overwhelmingly sup-

ported the bill and wanted Congress to pass it; in fact, many people did not believe that the bill went far enough.

The news coverage of the survey was enhanced by joining its release to the announcement of the Dehere Foundation "death clock." This clock, constructed in Times Square, would keep a running tally of the number of Americans killed by guns. The survey also attracted attention on Capitol Hill and was praised by the Senate Majority Leader.

Beyond focusing attention on an issue or topic, the PRS can be used to publicize a corporate name or product by generating attention for the company or organization that commissioned the survey. Consider the Virginia Slims surveys of American women, a series of seven studies conducted over the last 25 years that assess how women perceive their role and status in American society. The first Virginia Slims survey was undertaken in 1970, a period when women's attitudes were undergoing significant and rapid change. The surveys have helped position Virginia Slims as a brand that understands and supports the continuing evolution of women's roles in society. This goal is also consistent with its tag line "You've come a long way, baby."

Each survey has generated a storm of publicity—in venues ranging from national news programs, to daytime television, to radio interviews, to articles in women's magazines. The results also continue to be cited by many journalists and academics long after their initial release. Indeed, many view the Virginia Slims survey data as the most comprehensive available on the attitudes and opinions of American women. The series represents an example of how a company can use the PRS to promote its name in a favorable light, and support its brand positioning.

These examples illustrate a few of the objectives that can be achieved with the PRS. But because the PRS is so versatile, one must be alert to the danger of it becoming too many things to too many people. Nothing is more important than getting a clear picture of what you are trying to accomplish with a campaign designed around a PRS.

As a practical matter, the professional in public affairs or public relations must make sure that the client has a clear sense of the objectives. The client may have only a vague notion of his or her objectives or may develop unrealistic expectations. In a large organization, different units may perceive the objectives differently. Unless the key players have signed on to a set of central objec-

tives, trouble may appear down the road. It is important to engage
the client in early discussions and follow-up with clearly written
memos, to help everyone involved reach a shared understanding of
the goals of a PRS campaign.

Develop and Focus the Research Topic

Formulating an overall objective, like generating favorable publicity, is only the first step in developing a PRS. Finding a research
topic that matches the client and its objectives is equally important.
Developing a research topic will usually be an evolutionary process. The best advice is to start out broad, consider many
possibilities, and avoid getting locked into one idea too early. Talk
through a number of approaches—with the client and with an outside research firm (if you hire one)—and then begin to define and
refine the topics the survey will cover.

Think about what key publics you are trying to reach: the general public, journalists, specific types of consumers, the trade, policy
makers. Always be thinking about how the survey will be received
by these key publics, and what topics and lines of inquiry will interest them most. Keep in mind that for the PRS to be taken
seriously, the topic of the survey must be consistent with the goals,
image, and positioning strategy of the campaign and the client. If
the client makes outrageous-looking wrist watches, it might be appropriate to release a "fun" survey around daylight savings time
on time travel. (Where would you like to go if you could travel in
time?) But if the client is a supplier of financial services who seeks
to influence tax legislation, "fun" may not be the appropriate approach. A survey targeted for coverage in the business press, on
how different generations are planning for retirement might better
fit the company's image and goals.

Insist on Objectivity

The cardinal rule of a successful PRS is remembering that
survey research gains its credibility from its use of objective research methods. A commitment to objectivity on the part of all the
participants—client, public relations firm, and research firm—is es-

sential. The client often will have a point of view, but the survey—as an objective piece of research—can not. The survey must be reliable and believable. If it does not look like an objective piece of research, it will not be reported, as no journalist wants to be an unwitting mouthpiece for biased results.

Anyone with any experience with questionnaire construction knows that the way you word a question can affect the responses. The use of heavily loaded, biased words and phrasing can affect responses, as can wording which is in any way confusing or vague. It is imperative that the question wording be as objective and as clear as possible.

But designing an objective study involves much more than simply getting the question wording right. Bias can result, for example, from the failure to ask certain questions: the questions that are not included are in some ways as important as those questions which are. The point is that a survey should cover a topic fully, and not look like it avoided the questions that might have been potentially unfavorable for the client. Bias can also result from the selection of the sample of people to be interviewed, from the methods used by the interviewers, and from the compilation of the data.

At first glance, some may be tempted by the vision of a survey that would produce responses that from the client's point of view are "perfect." However, objectivity is the watchword of the PRS. By their very nature, these studies are scrutinized heavily. To be credible, the client must be willing to cover a topic in its entirety, and to report both the favorable and not-so-favorable results.

Consider the case of a company, which will go nameless, that wanted to do a detailed study on how people felt about the products and services of its industry. Suspecting consumers were angry about prices and problems with service, the company commissioning the study did not want to include any questions that might reflect badly on the industry. When told that this wasn't possible, the client wanted to be guaranteed that the answers would come out favorably. When told that this wasn't possible, the client suggested what is known among survey research professionals as "cherry picking"—publicly releasing the results of only some of the questions that were included in the survey. Under no circumstances is cherry picking considered ethical, and when the client was told this, she decided to cancel the study. This was not the only course of action open to the client, however. Clients always have the option of choos-

ing not to release an entire survey if they are uncomfortable with
its results. The point is, a client should never selectively release
results from a survey.

To uphold objectivity in opinion polling, the Council of American Survey Research Organizations (CASRO), an industry trade
association, has established a set of rules and standards that apply
to PRSs. Most reputable research firms strictly uphold the CASRO
standards. These state that:

1. Clients have to release all of the results of a survey if they
   release any of the results;

2. Once the survey is released publicly, people have a right to
   review the questionnaire and the full data tabulations;

3. Any public release of the data, as a minimum, must include
   the dates that the interviewing was conducted, the sponsor
   of the survey, a description of its purposes, sample description and size, name of the research company, exact wording
   of questions, and any other information that a lay person
   would need to make a reasonable assessment of the reported
   findings.

Pick a Qualified Research Firm

While some organizations have the in-house expertise to conduct
survey research for their own internal use, in the case of the PRS
it is wise to invest in hiring an outside research firm. The most
important reason for this can be expressed in one word: credibility.
Why should anyone believe a survey which finds that most people
think that widgets are great if the survey were conducted by a widget manufacturer? But the same survey would be taken seriously if
it were conducted by Gallup, Harris, Roper, Yankelovich or any
other well-known research firm. These firms have no involvement
in the widget industry, and are known for their objectivity. Journalists, especially, will generally ascribe more credibility to a PRS if
an outside research firm has been involved.

From the public affairs professional's point of view, several other factors make it desirable to hire an outside firm, rather than

conduct a PRS in-house. Time constraints are one factor, as most public affairs professionals work on a number of projects simultaneously. Moreover, few firms maintain fully-staffed research departments, so even those with a seasoned research staff may still need help. Managing a survey—from questionnaire design, through sampling, data collection, and survey analysis—is often a full-time job. Finally, an outside research firm can be an important ally for the public affairs professional in dealing with the client on issues such as objectivity and balance. In fact, it is best to get a research firm involved early in the formation of a campaign, even as its overall objectives are still being developed.

Use Appropriate Study Design

When it comes to designing a PRS, there are a multitude of possibilities, as the above examples suggest. Experts in survey research pepper their discussions with what seems like impenetrable jargon—phrases like probability sampling, multivariate analysis, margin of error. The public affairs professional need not master all this terminology. However, it is essential to be familiar with several issues of survey research design.

The first issue involves defining the population of people from which a representative group, or sample, will be chosen to be interviewed. Given the topic of the study, whose opinions are you most interested in and why? Is the most relevant population the general public? Is it consumers of a specific product? Owners of small businesses? Children from disadvantaged neighborhoods? Sometimes there is more than one population whose opinions are pertinent. For example, when H. J. Heinz decided to undertake a major PRS as part of an initiative on the American family, interesting findings resulted from including the views of children and adults. Parents and kids are two very different populations, and each had to be surveyed separately, necessitating that two different samples be drawn, two questionnaires be written, and so on.

A related question concerns the appropriate size of the sample. The reliability of the data depends on having a large enough sample to accommodate your analysis. Many research designs call for examining the views of various sub-groups of the population studied. For example, one might want to compare employed women with children living in the East versus employed women with children living in the Midwest. The smaller the subgroups you want to analyze, the larger the sample you will need. What an adequate sample size is depends on the type of analysis you plan to do. The research firm you hire will be able to tell you what sample size is appropriate given your objectives, and your budget. Often there is a need to balance what is ideal and what is affordable—without sacrificing the basic quality which is the bedrock upon which everything else is built.

Above, we noted the importance of writing a balanced, unbiased questionnaire, but there are several other factors related to the questionnaire that are useful to keep in mind. For example, before the questionnaire is actually constructed it is often quite helpful to conduct several focus group sessions. Focus groups discussions often spark new ideas, help develop concepts, and provide a way to explore topics with a group of people who are reflective of the population to be surveyed. Another helpful step is to make sure that the questionnaire topics are interesting to the audience that you are trying to reach with your PRS campaign, so it is useful to talk with a few opinion leaders from your target audience early on. For example, in advance of a survey on American youth commissioned by a confectionery division of Warner Lambert, Roper spoke with a variety of experts on children's issues to ask them, "What one thing would you most want to learn from a survey of American youth?"

Similarly, once the questionnaire has been written, it is useful to pretest it among a few people who represent your sample in order to be sure that the questions are clearly understood, that the questionnaire flows well, and so forth. Pre-testing a questionnaire often provides invaluable feedback, and allows one to refine and improve the questionnaire before it is administered to the full sample.

Other study design and methodological issues will also need to be decided: How long will the interview be? Will it be administered in person or by telephone? The question of how the sample will be drawn can also be tricky, especially if the study is examining a specialized sample, such as corporate executives or computer professionals. Through discussions with the research firm, you will agree on a basic design. Once you and your client have approved the basic elements of the study, don't try to micro-manage the process. Step back and let the research firm do its work. After all, that is what you hired it for.

Present Results Cogently,
Carefully, and Accurately

The results of PRSs are usually written up in a report, which is almost always accompanied by press packets, news releases, and other supporting materials. If you hire an outside research firm, most likely it will provide you with a report. PRSs need to be presented in reports that are well-written, easy to understand, and make good use of graphics and layout to provide an effective communication vehicle. Usually the news releases and press packets are handled by the public relations firm working closely with the research firm to make sure technical errors do not creep into the reporting of the data. As in other types of journalism, the ABC rule applies: accuracy, brevity, clarity. It is absolutely essential that the data remain consistent throughout, with the survey interpretation and analysis being echoed in the report, news releases, press conference materials, speeches etc.

Results also should be presented in accordance with the CASRO standards that were outlined above. It is especially important to provide access to the full questionnaire and complete tabulations of data. A PRS should also provide information on the dates interviews were conducted, the sponsors of the study, the purposes of the study, the sample and sample size, the name of the research company, exact wording of questions and any other information that a critical observer would need to assess the reported findings.

Many research firms insist on reviewing news releases and reserve the right to correct any misstatements or erroneous analysis that a client may put forth. This review process protects both the client and the research firm. No one wants to be in the position of having to backpedal when a reporter questions the interpretation of the findings.

Plan an Appropriate Release Strategy

The public affairs professional can utilize the PRS in a variety of creative ways. Sometimes the PRS is the star of the show, the centerpiece of a news conference or media event. Consider a recent study on attitudes toward the environment among children from disadvantaged neighborhoods. Commissioned by the National Environmental Education and Training Foundation (NEETF), an organization concerned with environmental education, the study was released at a news conference featuring the head of the U.S. Environmental Protection Agency. A PRS can also be a supporting character in a larger campaign. The *Wall Street Journal* commissioned two studies of the experiences of business owners from minority groups. These studies were part of the paper's effort to generate discussion among business leaders, policy makers, and academics about the obstacles that minorities who own small businesses face. Released in conjunction with a national conference on Black Entrepreneurs in America, the survey was featured in a series of articles in the newspaper, and was the subject of a panel discussion at the conference.

It is important to remember that media publicity is the beginning of a campaign, and it need not be the end. The creative professional can often use a single PRS in a whole range of activities. Consider what one company might do with a single piece of research aimed at, say, finding out what consumers, and potential consumers, want most from its product.

With these results in hand, the company would have powerful marketing and public relations data. It could package the results in a pamphlet directed at consumers in order to demonstrate that the company wants to hear from consumers and is responding to their needs. The results also might be presented at a news conference for the general media and trade press. The press clippings can be nicely packaged and mailed to key constituencies, e.g. the trade, legislators, etc., with a cover note that, once again, reinforces the company's message. Advertising and marketing materials might highlight the survey results, for example: "We're undertaking this important initiative because survey results told us. . . ." Representatives of the company could incorporate survey results into their speeches, showing—among constituencies and competitors alike—that the company was responsive to the needs of the market. In fact, the survey itself also could become a "hook" to get executives of the company speaking invitations at key conferences and venues.

In these ways, the company could use a single PRS to improve its understanding of the needs of the market, to reach out to consumers, to position itself as caring and responsive, and to convey the impression of being an industry leader.

Conclusion

The public affairs professional of the 1990s cannot neglect the PRS. It has become an established technique, which when properly conducted, offers unique opportunities. Professionals in public affairs and public relations who are familiar with the seven essential elements of the PRS will be well-equipped to take advantage of this increasingly important tool.

Chapter 6

The Importance of Media Relations in Public Affairs Planning

William C. Adams

> If companies do not inform the public on public policy issues, someone else will.
>
> Robert L. Heath,
> *Strategic Issues Management*

> Public issues thrive on media exposure or die from the lack of it. . . .
>
> Ernest & Elizabeth Wittenberg,
> *How to Win in Washington*

> If you don't exist in the media, for all practical purposes you don't exist.
>
> Daniel Schorr,
> National Public Radio

From late 1993 to mid-1994, a middle-aged couple did something that professional lobbyists could only dream about: They visited all 535 members of Congress without an appointment, and without ever leaving home.

"Harry and Louise" may have been only actors in a widely watched series of television ads portraying a couple concerned about President Bill Clinton's proposed health care program, but their impact on reform debate in Congress and elsewhere was no act.

Created by the Health Insurance Association of America (HIAA), the ads "skewered" the Clinton Administration's proposed program, with spots airing even before the plan had been presented to Congress in September, 1993.[1]

But it wasn't even the ads per se that turned the tide against the Clinton program. According to at least one observer, it was the overall *media attention* resulting from Hillary Clinton's "frequent and biting attacks" which gave the ads "recognition that no amount of money could buy." That, along with a carefully orchestrated multi-million dollar public relations effort, "turned a popular idea into a political millstone."

One reporter even named "Harry and Louise" the "political couple of the year," beating out Bill and Hillary.[2] The fictional twosome contributed as much to the health debate of 1994 as "Murphy Brown" and Dan Quayle did to the "family values" controversy the news media had fun with in 1992.[3]

The HIAA's campaign goal was to make certain the spots were seen by "those who will shape the debate."[4] Thus, the campaign's impact was not on the citizenry at large, but "on the people who make the decisions."[5] The HIAA had a definite target market in mind: Congress. And the organization went about a decidedly "traditional" public affairs program—to influence pending legislation—in a decidedly "new breed" fashion: The news media played as crucial a role in the program as "old breed" lobbying tactics, which often involve only face-to-face Congressional visits and backroom machinations.

Granted, the "old breed" style is not to be dismissed, but as longtime Washington lobbyist Tom Korologos points out, "new breed" lobbying definitely includes public relations and the news media. The role of media relations in a professionally-organized grass roots lobbying program is not only *smart* in an era when Congressional representatives are "more publicity prone and more responsive to (their) district," but *essential.*[6]

Media Crucial to Program Success

While it still may be true that "nothing beats a personal visit" with your legislator, Victor Kamber cautions that "to win in Washington, you must increasingly fight public affairs battles as if they were political campaigns," including utilizing the news media.[7] If today's public affairs officers don't think the news media play a crucial role in the success of their programs, they'd need only be reminded of numerous cases where companies either misunderstood or underestimated the media's importance or simply didn't care, whether because of corporate culture or a total reliance on "old breed" lobbying methods.

"High visibility can have a wildfire effect on legislation," whether it be a media plan utilizing *controlled* communications such as the advocacy advertising Mobil has placed on op-ed pages since the early 1970s, or *uncontrolled* methods such as news releases and talk-show appearances.[8] However, before embarking on a media relations effort, public affairs managers must also be aware that while the media impact on sensitive issues can be vital to a public policy program, "negative (media) coverage, especially coming from an undecided legislator's district, can significantly weaken your ability to gain that legislator's vote."[9]

But it's clear the rewards of including a media relations component in your public affairs program far outweighs the risks. In effect, it's being sure your organization has "married public affairs with public relations," something Richard Armstrong, former head of the Public Affairs Council, called for back in 1982.[10] Substantiating this view, James Post wrote that "as firms seek to influence the public . . . they place the media responsibility in the public affairs unit."[11] And in the same era, Ray Ewing counseled public affairs executives that the media must "play a role in issues development," offering a public policy process "flow chart" in which the media play a prominent role throughout a given program's various stages.[12]

A decade later, Washington public affairs counselor Peter Hannaford told of the need to consummate the public affairs/public relations marriage, and outlined how crucial it is to include a "media element" in public affairs planning. Most public affairs strategies, he wrote, "benefit from close coordination between the public affairs staff and those who deal in the art of strategic communications." At the very least, he noted, working with the news media will result in "an increased exposure of the merits of your case."[13]

Some ten years after Armstrong's prediction, his successor at the Public Affairs Council had embraced the concept, calling the link between public affairs and public relations the "new trend," naming "media relations" one of the five elements of a typical modern public affairs department.[14] And in their seminal text, Grunig and

Hunt indicate the value of "media relations specialists whose job it is to publicize a company's positions on policy issues."[15]

Borrowing from conclusions found in Grunig's research showing that "excellent organizations practice excellent public relations," one could speculate that excellent public affairs programs feature an excellent media relations component.[16] Certainly, the literature is rife with examples—ranging from the American Iron & Steel Institute's "rolling petition" campaign to build support for legislative action, to the footwear industry's "Save Our Soles" program and Frito-Lay's successful efforts to generate grass-roots support for workman's compensation reform—all involving the news media to help "heighten public awareness. . . ."[17]

In one of the many retrospectives of the American Bankers Association's campaign to repeal withholding-tax legislation, Fritz Elmendorf cites the campaign's media relations effort for "keeping the issue alive and further (fueling) the grass-roots movement."[18]

Media's Power Can Influence Attitudes

Today, the power of the news media in the public policy arena is unquestioned, whether one believes the media actually do "set the agenda," or as Bernard Cohen wrote in 1963: The media don't tell us *what* to think, but they tell us what to think *about*.[19] From the pioneering underpinnings of Lazarsfeld and Merton's 1948 research into the mass media and its ability to "confer status on public issues"[20] to Ehling and Dozier's work more than four decades later revealing that publicity "can change deeply rooted and complex patterns of mass behavior,"[21] it's clear "the power of the press to set the agenda for public debate . . . is unmistakable."

Legendary educator, Scott Cutlip, always wary of potential overreliance on media relations by public relations professionals, nonetheless has written that "media coverage can effect the agenda priorities of some specific and important publics, such as legislators, regulators and other policy makers."[22]

Just ask Newt Gingrich, current Speaker of the House of Representatives, cited by the *National Journal* as being in the vanguard of those on the Hill using the latest media technologies to disseminate their views: C-Span and talk radio have become staples in not only the Speaker's public policy campaigns, but in virtually all of the "5 per cent of Congress who make 50 per cent of the news."[23]

Or check in with Bob McIntyre, head of the Washington-based public interest group, Citizens for Tax Justice, who allegedly never went near a Congressperson during his campaign to influence the Tax Reform Act in 1986. He worked exclusively through the news media, making himself available, establishing his credibility and cultivating journalists, who are always on the lookout for sources who can turn difficult public policy issues into English. While most of his corporate opponents weren't pleased with the outcome, observers credit McIntyre's orchestrating of the Tax Reform issue with plugging loopholes in the new law.[24]

McIntyre knew what most savvy players in the Washington public policy game know: "An editorial, a news story, or an interesting op-ed piece in one of the major papers will have the Hill talking about it from breakfast through lunch."[25] To amplify the effectiveness of traditional one-on-one lobbying, there must be a news media component in the public affairs program.

And the program can't be provincial in nature; it needs to be widened beyond the Beltway. In fact, a grassroots public affairs communication effort can be even more effective than one concentrating solely on Washington.

Hedrick Smith, former *New York Times* Washington bureau chief, referred to this expansion beyond the Beltway as "widening the circle" of influence.[26] Echoing this, Newton and Berkowitz found that in order to win public support, public affairs programs must give attention to the hometown media. "Members of the legislature are equally or more concerned with what editors of their local newspapers say about an issue."[27] After all, the folks back home reading those local editorials, news stories and op-eds are the people those legislators have to deal with at re-election time. Even though a majority of Congressional staffers say the best way to gain their attention is through personal contact, "an editorial in the (legislator's) local paper is almost twice as likely to get attention from the Congressional office as a similar piece in a national publication. . . ."[28] A grassroots public policy campaign, Mario Cooper wrote in *Public Relations Quarterly*, must have a media relations plan as an "essential building block."[29] In a grassroots program, the media can help arouse public opinion and overcome what has been termed the "information gap," when your constituencies don't have enough information about your issue to make an informed decision.[30]

While it's equally clear that "it is almost impossible to reverse a trend of public opinion through communications efforts alone,"[31] and that "publicity" itself is never the solution to a public policy problem or opportunity, a media relations strategy should have a "place at the management table" and be effectively combined with overall decision-making.[32] With apologies to George Santayana: Those who fail to consider the role of media in public affairs planning are bound to repeat their mistakes.

Optimizing Media Relations in Public Affairs Programming

As public affairs managers, we must educate CEOs and other top executives to the benefits (as well as the dangers) of media relations as an integral component to the public policy campaign. Even though a 1994 study discovered some 70 per cent of CEOs surveyed named "media relations" as a qualification "most valued" in their communications officers,[33] research indicates most business executives continue to fear, distrust and misunderstand the news media.[34] An analysis of this top-executive attitude and an in-depth look at whether or not the media actually *do* "set the agenda" go far beyond the scope of this chapter. But with the discussion above in mind, we offer the following guidelines to help ensure that media relations plays a successful part in your public affairs program.[35]

1. Assess your organizational culture/structure.

Is public relations linked to public affairs? Where does media relations fit in the overall communications program? A communications audit can answer these questions and more. Determine if pro-active media relations is supported by top management as well as the public affairs unit. Then seek to make the organization even more open to the media as well as other constituencies. Organizational culture will play a crucial role in the success or failure of these efforts as you seek to adapt your campaigns to fit the organization's philosophy and mission.[36]

2. Assess and understand the news media.

Know what constitutes *news* (local angle, timeliness, human interest, etc.). Some reporters say up to 90 per cent of information they receive isn't news; it goes right into the circular file.[37] Understand what the media think about your organization (regular contact, feedback); and cultivate beat journalists and others who cover your business and its issues. Good media relations involves a two-way relationship, established long *before* your campaign (or crisis) begins.[38]

3. Train your management and other spokespeople.

Whether by in-house communications professionals or an outside firm specializing in media relations training, it's imperative that those expecting to be on the front lines of contact with newspeople be given instruction in how to successfully conduct themselves when doing interviews with print or broadcast journalists. While some larger corporations and trade associations have the luxury of in-house video studios and staff communications professionals, smaller organizations can take advantage of the many specialists who have created a cottage industry in media training in recent years. Many are former print and broadcast journalists who bring a "real-world" view into the training sessions. There are also a number of excellent books on how to prepare and conduct media interviews. Having such a text on hand for management referral might be a good investment.[39]

4. Establish your organization's source credibility by developing informative and relevant background materials.

Frame your materials in understandable terms; clarify confusing jargon. Don't provide only self-serving propaganda and information that doesn't allow constituencies to make an "informed decision"— a doctrine David Martinson refers to as "substantial completeness."[40] Remember, journalists are on the lookout for fresh new sources. The *Washington Post*, for example, has gone on the record as seeking to avoid "dependence on the same academics or public figures" for its stories.[41]

5. Establish accessibility and visibility of management and other spokespersons.

Assuming organizational culture will permit it, take a *pro-active* stance in your media relations activities. Offer your management as experts in those subjects crucial to the media's understanding of your public policy issues. While research has shown that journalists will often seek out third-party sources before going to your organization for information on issues of importance to you, you can stay in the loop by giving signs of your availability, knowledge of the subject and willingness to cooperate.[42]

In the "Harry and Louise" situation, one observer faulted the Clinton administration for its late start in the health-care communications effort, noting an earlier appointment of a White House spokesperson as media focus would have helped "solidify the message."[43]

6. Establish feedback for your program.

Effective communication is a two-way proposition. It's not enough simply to send your messages and assume they're being heard, let alone understood. And don't let the ease of today's technology in allowing you to get out the message lull you into false security about the *effectiveness* of your communication.[44] Make sure you have resources in place to measure your program's effectiveness. The best public affairs programs involve not only clear, concise messages, but a willingness to listen and react to information feedback. Even feedback from the media can help modify a company's program, initiate a policy change or head off a problem.[45]

Although the very nature of public affairs programming puts your organization in an advocacy position with the news media and other important constituencies, its important to recognize that compromise and flexibility are crucial aspects of the public policy game.[46]

Keep in mind that classic public policy issue campaigns such as the one mounted by the American Bankers Association to repeal legislation which would have allowed withholding from individual savings accounts are often successful largely because a media relations component was built into the program from the beginning.[47] And, conversely, companies ignoring the news media—or underestimating its power to help "set the agenda" on public issues—have lost their cases on Capitol Hill as well as in the court of public opinion.

In sum, the above examples, suggestions and guidelines can help your organization effectively utilize media relations in your public affairs programs. But the guidelines will only work if management is convinced the public relations/public affairs "marriage" is built on a sound relationship. It's your challenge to consummate that relationship.

Notes

1. See, for example, *Chicago Tribune*, January 15, 1995 (Associated Press), "Ex-Lobbyists Now Working on the Inside"; *Business Insurance*, De-

cember 26, 1994, "The Newsmakers in '94"; and Kolbert, Elizabeth, "New Arena for Campaign Ads: Health Care," *New York Times*, October 21, 1993, Sec A, p. 1, col. 2.

2. *Business Insurance*, ibid.; *Political Finance & Lobby Reporter*, December 16, 1994, "Harry and Louise Were Democrats".

3. Roberts, Cokie and Steven, "Viewpoints." *Dallas Morning News*, September 11, 1994, p. 5J (United Features Syndicate).

4. Kolbert, op. cit.

5. Kolbert, ibid. (quoting Kathleen Hall Jamieson, dean of the Annenberg School for Communications).

6. Smith, Hedrick, *The Power Game*. (Ballantine, New York, 1989), p. 237; telephone interview with Korologos, May 25, 1995; also see Aduss, Edward L. and Ross, Matthew C., "Integrating Efforts of Advertising Agencies and Public Information Organizations," in Robert L. Heath, *Strategic Issues Management*, (Jossey-Bass, San Francisco 1988). Chapter 11, pp. 287-304.

7. Kamber, Victor, "How to Win and Really Lose in Washington". *Public Relations Quarterly*, Winter 1993-94, pp. 5-7; Schmertz, Herb, "Reaching the Opinion Makers," in Heath, *Strategic Issues Management*, op cit. pp. 199-237.

8. References to successful ABA campaign include Elmendorf, Fritz M., "Generating Grassroots Campaigns and Public Involvement," in Heath, *Strategic Issues Management*, op cit. Chapter 12, pp. 304-320; Hendrix, Jerry A., *Public Relations Cases* (Wadsworth, Inc. 1988), "Ten Percent Withholding on Savings: Help Repeal a Bad Law," pp. 236-243; Heath, Robert L. and Nelson, Richard Alan. *Issues Management*, (Sage: Newbury Park, 1989), "The Withholding Tax Battle: Grassroots at Its Best," pp. 101-103.

9. Volkening, Ronnie. "Case Study: Frito-Lay Generates Grassroots Support for Workers' Compensation Reform in Texas," in *Leveraging State Government Relations*. (Public Affairs Council, Washington, DC, 1990), ed. Hal Warner, pp. 105-109.

10. Armstrong, Richard A. "What is Public Affairs?" in Nagelschmidt, Joseph S., ed., *The Public Affairs Handbook* (AMACOM, Washington, DC, 1982), pp. 3-7.

11. Post, James. "Public Affairs: Its Role" in Nagelschmidt, op cit. pp. 28-36.

12. Ewing, Raymond P. "Modeling the Process" in Nagelschmidt, op cit, pp. 47-56.

13. Hannaford, Peter. "Snow White Revisited," remarks to Bay Area Public Affairs Council, San Francisco, May 29, 1991.

14. Hoewing, Ray. "Dynamics and Role of Public Affairs," in Lesly, Philip, *Handbook of Public Relations and Communications* (4th ed., 1991), pp. 66-67.

15. Grunig, James and Hunt, Todd. *Managing Public Relations*. (Holt Rinehart & Winston 1984), p. 295.

16. Grunig, James (ed.). *Excellence in Public Relations and Communica-*

tion Management (Erlbaum, Hillsdale, NJ 1992).

17. See, for example, Cook, Steven K. "How to Turn the Microphone on Your Members," PRSA *TACTICS*, November 1994, p. 10; "Save Our Soles" and "The Road Information Program," cases in Hendrix, op. cit.

18. Elmendorf, op. cit.

19. Cohen, Bernard. *The Press and Foreign Policy* (Princeton University Press, 1963), cited in Grunig and Hunt, op. cit., p. 63.

20. Lazarsfeld, Paul and Robert Merton, "Mass Communication, Popular Taste and Organized Social Action, quoted in Lesly, op. cit., Chapter 48, "Other Functions, Principles and Trends."

21. Ehling, William P. and Dozier, David M., "Public Relations Management and Operations Research," Chapter 10 in Grunig, ed., op. cit., pp. 251-284.

22. Cutlip, Scott M., Center, Allen H. and Broom, Glen. *Effective Public Relations*. (Prentice-Hall, 1995), 7th ed., p. 482.

23. Starobin, Paul, "Is the 'Elite' Press Out to Get Newt?" *National Journal*, November 26, 1994, p. 2788-9; also see Harwood, Richard, "Sources Who Supply the News," *Washington Post*, January 7, 1995, A21.

24. Wittenberg, Ernest and Wittenberg, Elizabeth. *How to Win in Washington*. (Blackwell, 1990; 2nd ed.), p. 126; also see Harwood, op. cit., on "news sources."

25. Wittenbergs, op. cit.

26. Smith, op. cit., p. 80.

27. Newton, Hugh C. and Berkowitz, Herb B. "Winning Public Support for an Idea or Cause," in Lesly, op. cit., Chapter 10, pp. 152-163.

28. "Local Press Grabs Congress' Attention," *Public Relations Journal*, October, 1992, p. 34 (reports on survey of senior House and Senate staffers, cites Peter D. Hart Research Associates, "Communicating With Congress 1992").

29. Cooper, Mario, "Winning in Washington: From Grasstops to Grassroots," *Public Relations Quarterly*, Winter 1993-94, pp. 13-15.

30. Adams, William C., "Helping Your Organization Triumph Over Negatives," *Public Relations Quarterly*, Spring 1992, pp. 12-16.

31. Newton and Berkowitz, op. cit., p. 157.

32. Ehling and Dozier, op. cit., p. 257 (quotes Harold Burson on public affairs' "place at the table").

33. *Public Relations News*, "Media Relations and Community Relations Most Highly Valued by CEOs," October 24, 1994, Vol. 50, No. 42 (cites Florida Public Relations Association study).

34. Lehrer, Adrienne, "Between Quotation Marks," *Journalism Quarterly*, 66(4), Winter 1989, pp. 902-906; Mapes, Judith A., "Top Management and the Press - The Uneasy Relationship Revisited, *Corporate Issues Monitor*, 11(1) 1987, pp. 1, 3; Spitzer, Carlton, "Fear of the Media," *Public Relations Journal*, November 1981, pp. 58-63.

35. A number of excellent sources for "effective media relations" are available, both in texts and as stand-alone books. Among sources consulted in

preparing the guidelines for "optimizing media relations" include: Lesly, op. cit., especially Chapter 21, "Relations With Publicity Media"; Adams, William C. and Rodgers, Joann Ellison. *Media Guide for Academics*, Foundation for American Communications, Los Angeles, 1994; Howard, Carole, "Media Relations: Public Relations' Basic Activity," in Cantor, Bill (ed.), *Experts in Action* (Longman, 1989), Chapter 24, pp. 258-267; Adams, William C., "Helping Your Organization Overcome Negatives," op. cit.; Hunt, Todd and Grunig, James E. *Public Relations Techniques*. (Holt, Rinehart and Winston, Inc. 1994); Evans, Fred J. *Managing the Media: Proactive Strategy For Better Business-Press Relations*. (Greenwood 1987); *Media Resources Guide*, Foundation for American Communications, Los Angeles, 1983; Wittenbergs, op. cit., especially Chapter 9, "Working With the Media."

36. Kendall, Robert. *Public Relations Campaign Strategies*. (Harper Collins 1992), Chapter 6, "Adapt the Campaign to the Organizational Culture," pp. 165-188.

37. Wittenbergs, op. cit., p. 136; Reisinger, Sue (former Deputy Managing Editor, *Miami Herald*), presentation to Florida International University School of Journalism and Mass Communication students, February 1995 (and subsequently quoted in a number of professional public relations journals).

38. A good overview of what makes news in a public affairs campaign may be found in Wittenbergs, op. cit.; also see Lesly, "Relations With Publicity Media," op. cit.; Freedman, Michael, "Media Relations: How to win not just ink and air but media respect," in *IMPACT* (Public Affairs Council, Washington, July/August 1992), pp. 1, 4; Morton, Linda, "Producing Publishable Press Releases: A Research Perspective," *Public Relations Quarterly*, Winter 1992-93, pp. 9-11; Atkin, Charles K, "Mass Media Information Campaign Effectiveness," in *Public Communication Campaigns*, Ronald E. Rice and William Paisley, eds. (Sage, Beverly Hills 1981), p. 278.

39. See especially Howard, Carole and Wilma Mathews, *On Deadline: Managing Media Relations*. (Waveland Press, 1995); Hilton, Jack, *How to Meet the Press*. (Dodd, Mead & Co. 1987); Adams and Rodgers, op. cit.

40. Martinson, David L., "How Should the PR Practitioner Respond When Confronted With Unethical Journalistic Behavior?", *Public Relations Quarterly*, Summer 1991, pp. 20-21.

41. Harwood, op. cit.

42. A number of studies have shown that reporters often seek out other sources before going to the organization most likely to be affected by an issue; as examples, see Adams, William C., "The Role of Media Relations in Risk Communication," *Public Relations Quarterly*, Winter 1992-93, pp. 28-32; Howard, op. cit.; Adams and Rodgers, op. cit.

43. *Journal of Public Policy & Marketing*, October 1994; also see *The President's Health Security Plan*, The White House Domestic Policy Council (New York: Times Books, 1993).

44. Budd, John, quoted in Hunt and Grunig, op. cit., p. 404; also telephone conversation with Budd, May 1995.

45. For a review of how the "two-way symmetric model of communica-

tion" applies to media relations, see Grunig & Hunt, op. cit.; also Howard, op. cit.

46. Kamber, op. cit.; for additional references to the role of compromise and flexibility, also see Smith, op. cit.; Wittenbergs, op. cit.; Hahn, Bruce N. with Robert J. Horgan. *Winning at Public Affairs!* (National Association of Manufacturers, Washington, 1991).

47. Wittenbergs, op. cit., p. 126.

Additional References

Baxter, Tom, "New Breed of Ad Dares to Mix Politics, Drama," *Sacramento Bee*, September 13, 1994, p. B7.

Crain, Rance, "Politicians Respect Ads More Than CEOs," *Advertising Age*, September 5, 1994, p. 16.

Dennis, Everette E., "TV news brings more than sound bites to the party," *Communique* (Freedom Forum Media Studies Center, New York), Vol. 9, No. 9, May 1995, p. 2.

Dilenschneider, Robert L. *Power and Influence: Mastering the Art of Persuasion.* (Prentice Hall, New York 1990).

Faucheaux, Ron, "The Grassroots Explosion," *Campaigns & Elections*, December-January 1995, pp. 20-30.

Gardels, Nathan, "A serious talk about the American press," *New Perspectives Quarterly.* (Distributed by the Los Angeles Times Syndicate, 1995).

Hanson, Janice and Alexander, Alison. *Taking Sides: Clashing Views on Controversial Issues in Mass Media and Society.* (The Dushkin Publishing Group, Inc., Sluice Dock, Guilford, CT, 1991).

"Harry and Louise Were Democrats," *Political Finance and Lobby Reporter*, December 16, 1994.

"Headlines and Sound Bites: Is That the Way It Is?" Freedom Forum Media Studies Center (New York, 1995).

Jackson, Brooks. *Honest Graft.* (Knopf, 1988).

Lacopo, John D., "Making Public Affairs a Strategic Function," in *Adding Value to the Public Affairs Function*, Peter Schaefer, ed., (Public Affairs Council, Washington, 1994), pp. 143-147.

Lesher, Stephen. *Media Unbound.* (Houghton Mifflin Co., Boston, 1982).

Levy, Ronald N., "Public Policy Publicity: How to Do It," *Public Relations Journal*, June 1975, pp. 19-21, 35-36.

McCombs, Maxwell, Edna Einsiedel and David Weaver. *Contemporary Public Opinion: Issues and the News.* (Erlbaum, Hillsdale NJ, 1991).

MacKuen, Michael B. and Coombs, Steven L. *More Than News: Media Power in Public Affairs.* (Sage, Beverly Hills, 1981).

Matlack, Carol, "Home, Home on the Washington Range," *National Journal*, November 9, 1991, p. 2749.

Patterson, Thomas and McClure, Robert D. *The Unseeing Eye: The Myth of Television in National Elections.* (G.P. Putnam's Sons, 1976).

Robinson, Michael J. and Clancy, Maura E., "Network News, 15 Years After Agnew," *Channels*, January-February 1985.

Rusher, William A. *The Coming Battle for the Media: Curbing the Power of the Media Elite.* (William Morrow 1988).

Salmon. Charles, "God Understands When the Cause is Noble," *Gannett Center Journal*, Spring 1990, Vol. 4, No. 2, pp. 23-34.

Sethi, S. Prakash, "Corporate Political Activism," *Public Relations Journal*, November 1980, pp. 14-16.

Sethi, S. Prakash. *Advocacy Advertising and the Large Corporation.* (Lexington, MA: Lexington Books, 1977).

Straubhaar, Joseph and LaRose, Robert. *Communication Media in the Information Society.* (Wadsworth 1996).

Tate, Sheila, "Prescriptions to Avoid Disaster in Washington," *Public Relations Quarterly*, Spring 1992, Vol. 37, No. 1, pp. 24-26.

Tisinger, Russell, "Health Care Reform's Hidden Persuader," *National Journal*, October 30, 1993, p. 2604.

Van Leuven, James K. and Slater, Michael D., "How Publics, Public Relations and the Media Shape the Public Opinion Process," *Public Relations Research Annual.* James A. Grunig and Larissa A. Grunig, eds. Vol. 3 (Erlbaum 1991).

Wilcox, Dennis, Phillip H. Ault and Warren K. Agee, "Public Affairs and Government," *Public Relations Strategies and Tactics,* 3rd ed., (Harper Collins 1992), pp. 370-408.

Wilson, James Q., "Capital Power Struggle; Don't Bemoan Gridlock—The Constitution Likes It," *Los Angeles Times*, November 20, 1994, M1, Col. 4.

Chapter 7

Government Relations in the 90s and Beyond

Margery Kraus

Introduction

Americans have always had a love/hate relationship with their government. It can be the worst of enemies or the best of friends. Americans who actively seek government intervention one day are the same Americans who condemn government as intrusive the next. Nearly all Americans belong to what is defined as a "special interest group" of one kind or another. Most of those groups are professionally represented in Washington, yet no other broadly defined entity suffers more public disdain in opinion polls than special interests and the government relations professionals who represent them.

It is the great conundrum of American politics. One person's pork is another's bread and butter. Is an individual's access to government a sign of political corruption or, as defined by the Constitution, a protected right to petition the government for redress of grievances?

More than any other political system, ours is based on the principle of open government—open to disagreement, deliberation, and dialogue; open to influence; open to information and persuasion; and open to the active, voluntary participation of the body politic, whether that participation is by individuals, organizations or their hired representation. Ours is an open government and, because it is open, it is enlightened, constantly invigorated and enduring.

In an open and participatory democracy where sound principles apply, so do cliches like the "squeaky wheel." Government is so large, and the bureaucracy so cumbersome, those who complain the loudest usually get served the quickest. It is a fact of political life that citizen access under our system of government places the burden on the citizen to know how to get attention, by whom and what to do with it once gotten. Today, however, American citizens have more knowledge and more means of access than ever before. Nonetheless, this has not obviated the need for representation and government relations professionals, whose job it is to make the best use of public and private resources to further corporate and client objectives.

Over 7,400 national associations with headquarters in Washington represent the interests of a vast majority of Americans, from Boy Scouts to farmers to pharmacists. If employed, a member of a community group, a volunteer, or even a lobbyist, then you are probably represented in Washington. This citizen/government interaction is further expanded when you consider how technology continues to impact government relations through "on line" services and "talk radio" and the transparency through which government is forced to operate, due to strict media scrutiny. These factors only begin to illustrate how the manner in which government operates has been permanently changed by the way organizations and individuals interact with their leaders. No longer are a few well-placed lobbyists the primary intermediaries, managing issues, access, and information. Our leaders, at all levels, are exposed to constant interactions with many "publics." Thus, controlling issues in the 1990s poses a significant challenge to managers responsible for government relations in their organizations, as well as those of us who conduct government relations activities on behalf of others.

Where Are We and
How Did We Get There?

The First Amendment to the Constitution guarantees citizens the right to "petition the government for a redress of grievances." This is the foundation for government relations. At its most basic level, government relations is knowing what government is doing and letting people in government know how their actions affect you.

Whether people think of themselves as lobbyists or not, attempting to influence the outcome of government action is lobbying. While the right to lobby was guaranteed in the First Amendment, the actual term "lobbying" did not come into existence until the 1860s. The story goes that after Ulysses S. Grant became president in 1869, he began a routine of strolling to the Willard Hotel, just a few blocks from the Executive Mansion, for a drink and a cigar. When the practice became known, people would gather in the ornate lobby of the swank hotel hoping to have a word with the President. Thus, the moniker "lobbyist" entered the language and the world of government relations.

Whatever the terminology or its origins, government at all levels in the United States—and, increasingly, in other countries—is more open, accessible and accountable today than any time in history. Paradoxically, it is this openness that is creating unprecedented opportunities for government relations practitioners.

In 1990 Bruce C. Wolpe, author of *Lobbying Congress*, wrote that in Washington "an explosion of representation, from the largest corporations in the United States (and many from abroad) to the smallest conceivable constituencies, is reverberating."

But the explosion had been touched off well before then. James Deaking, who wrote *The Lobbyists* in 1966, described the government relations landscape in Washington then:

> There is an association, union, society, league, conference, institute, organization, federation, chamber, foundation, congress, order, brotherhood, company, corporation, bureau, mutual cooperative, committee, council, plan, trusteeship, movement, district, assembly, club, board, service or tribe for every human need, desire, motive, ambition, goal, aim, drive, affiliation, occupation, industry, interest, incentive, fear, anxiety, greed, compulsion, frustration, hate, spirit, reform and cussedness in the United States.

Nearly thirty years later, there is all of that, and more.

To be sure, there are people who still view government relations as little more than the contemporary version of whispering in the ear of the President, or a Member of Congress, governor, mayor or county commissioner. More and more they may end up the people who find themselves on the losing end of the issue.

In the new environment of change and competing interests, the winners are those who realize that relying solely on "who you know" is not as effective as what you know and what you can do with what you know. The most effective government relations efforts are those that incorporate a broad range of creative, coordinated messages, messengers and tactics, which, in the right circumstances and at the right time come together with experience, judgement, and yes, access to win the issue.

What is Today's Environment for the Government Relations Professional?

The Government Relations Environment of the 90s

Today's environment for government relations poses new challenges and opportunities. There are less experienced policy makers at all levels of government at a time when issues are more complex. For instance, over 50% of the U.S. House of Representatives has been in office less than four years. Term limits (or the threat of them), more stringent ethics rules, more media scrutiny, negative campaigning, the cost of campaigning and a general dissatisfaction with those in power have caused a turnover of epic proportions which will affect politics at all levels for years to come. At the same time, the information explosion, the use of issue advertising, and citizen referenda have involved the public in partisan advocacy as never before. Some of the factors affecting today's government relations practitioners are discussed below.

1. Turnover. Whether term limits remain a legal constraint or not, the issue has caused many officials to "take a pledge" of self-limitation. To the extent this "opens up" opportunities for higher office, state and local officials will focus their sights on running for higher office and measuring their actions accordingly. Also, to the extent that a professional staff remains an important part of our political process, these staff members could become even more powerful since they are likely to outlast the Members they serve.

2. Ethics Rules. A heightened awareness of ethics issues and a shift in what is considered ethical behavior has increased the sensitivity of legislators and regulators about their actions, especially if it is perceived that their actions favor "special interests." Thus, it is not only important to know the rules in working with elected officials (discussed below), but it is also important to build support for your issues in a way that shields the elected official from unfair and unfounded criticism.

3. Heightened Media. The degree to which the media is now reporting on all aspects of a candidate's or politician's life affects both the quality and quantity of those willing to run for office. It also causes both the government official and the government relations professional to consider how the action or proposed action would look on the front page of the *New York Times*. Thus, the appearance of an action needs to be considered almost as carefully as the action itself.

4. Instantaneous Information. Today's communications allow the debate on issues to move faster and involve more people than ever before. With 24-hour news channels, C-SPAN, satellite communication, the Internet and other forms of instant communication, people not only have been given unprecedented access to national and global events, but also can be a part of these events as they occur. News is reported in real time. Those who do not react quickly can be overtaken by events.

5. Nationalization and Globalization of Issues. A result of our increased access to information is that local issues no longer remain local issues. If not managed, they can become regional, national or even international issues overnight.

6. Increasing Importance of the States. As the Federal government looks to trim the budget and cut back in programs, the states are assuming a greater role in the political process. For the government relations professional, this decentralization may cause a proliferation of state rules and regulations that need to be monitored. It is possible that having programs operate under different rules and regulations from state to state will make doing business harder and create a nightmare for the government relations professional, especially as organizations are streamlining their staffs.

7. A More Complex Regulatory Environment for Conducting Government Relations. As government, and particularly this Administration, seeks to demonstrate that it is appropriately regulating the lobbying industry, the myriad of rules and regulations that have to be followed is growing. Consider the following:

— *Federal Regulation of Lobbying Act (FRLA).* This requires all persons who engage in lobbying of the U.S. Congress to report their activities and expenditures.

— *Foreign Agents Registration Act (FARA).* Lobbyists who represent a foreign entity must file reports with the U.S. Department of Justice if they are attempting to influence any segment of the U.S. population concerning U.S. foreign policy.

— *Byrd Amendment.* This law requires potential recipients of government funds to disclose to the applicable government agency all lobbying activities and third-party payments provided in attempting to secure a Federal contract or grant.

— *Political Contributions and Gifts.* There are many statutory and regulatory limitations and reporting requirements affecting the amount and type of political contributions that organizations and individuals can give to political candidates. There are even recent and conflicting rules on gifts, travel and entertainment.

And the rules are constantly changing. Changes include limiting access to the Capitol, total bans on congressional gifts, registration requirements for lobbying the Executive Branch, campaign finance reform and tightening of definitions that define lobbying and lobbyists. Any professional government relations practitioner should be familiar with these rules and regulations and any impending changes. Again, the importance is not only the rule itself, but its interpretation and its coverage by the press which helps shape public opinion.

How Does This Affect
the Practitioner Today?

In this environment of change, the successful government relations professional will have to learn to use all the tools available. Lobbying will consist of more than one-on-one contact. Government relations programs need to be reinforced by the tools available throughout the government relations professional's business environment. Successful issue campaigns will be those that integrate public relations and government relations skills and tactics. Effective programs will maximize organizational advantages, issues management, employee action and intelligence on future developments.

While knowing the right people will always play an important role in any effective government relations program, the smart practitioners have learned to reinforce their efforts by finding ways to give their issues the broadest support among many segments of the public and especially with those constituents "back home." Hubert Humphrey once said that "political popularity is but a deposit in the bank to be used for noble purposes." Given today's climate, elected officials do not have the tenure or experience to build up those deposits of popularity. The effective government relations program must help fill the gap.

The steps that government relations professionals should take to conduct an effective government relations program in the 1990s include:

1. **Inventory your Assets**. The best government relations programs make use of the various parts of their organization. This can include public relations, corporate philanthropy, employee interest and contacts, well-placed vendors and advertising. Understanding the value of an integrated approach and educating your fellow workers about the need for their input and involvement can help develop a mutual reinforcement that is useful in any political battle. For instance, a government relations professional with knowledge about key corporate grants can act to involve policy makers in the activities surrounding the awarding of a grant. This lets the organization take advantage of an opportunity to work with the elected official, and it gives the elected official a chance to be part of a project that benefits the community.

2. **Conduct an Affirmative Government Relations Program**. Some government relations practitioners see themselves as fire fighters, going from one problem to another. While crises are inevitable, formalizing an issues management program can improve the effectiveness of a government relations team and promote proactive action.

   The organization should have an annual, formal planning session to identify primary and secondary issues. Decisions should be made about how to handle each issue and the organization's desired outcome. This should not just include the things you oppose. At a time when fundamental decisions are being made in major policy areas, smart organizations will decide on issues they can support—not just those they oppose.

Decisions should be made about how to handle each issue and what action can be taken to keep issues from becoming ripe. For instance, early action could preempt or delay government action. With planning, many issues can be anticipated.

3. **Encourage Employee Action/Develop Allies.** Third-party advocacy is an essential part of today's government relations efforts. Encouraging and mobilizing constituents to contact their legislators is a critical element of any issue campaign. This is commonly referred to as "grassroots." However, it is important that these efforts are genuine and that the people engaged are properly educated about the issue. Where there have been large-scale campaigns, smart legislators will randomly call to see if there is genuine interest or if the grassroots is really "astroturf"—names that have been generated artificially. Recently the term grasstops has become popular. Grasstops programs are more targeted efforts, engaging opinion leaders or key contacts in approaching policymakers, rather than emphasizing volume of contacts. Though more focused, the same caveats about being educated on the issue apply.

To effectively conduct grassroots campaigns, an organization should not have to wait for a crisis to organize employees or allies. Having an internal network that is informed on issues saves time and can be a lot more effective in supporting major issues of the organization. An effective internal program will track levels of interest on issues, determine who knows whom, arrange for elected officials to have meetings on a more regular basis with local plant officials or representatives of district chapters of an organization and generally keep allies and employees knowledgeable about the issues of concern to the organization. Training should also be a major component of a well-organized grassroots program.

A grassroots campaign can be effective in crafting strategies that match messages to audiences; profiling legislative targets to ensure that they are hearing from the right constituents; preparing materials and systems that make it easy to contact legislators; analyzing the opposition in order to anticipate their arguments and to counter their influence; and measuring the results and impact of grassroots tactics.

4. **Explore the Latest Technology.** The new technologies pose both a challenge and an opportunity. Real time access to information is creating a shorter response time. New technologies (teleconferencing, videoconferencing, the Internet) are creating direct interactions between government officials and constituents that were virtually impossible in the past. Today, teleconferencing allows constituents and Members to discuss hot legislation with minimal effort and time restrictions, even from great distances. While this is not a substitute for meeting face to face, it allows for an easier access to information and informed opinions. The advent of government on-line services will help bridge an information gap. It will increase direct access to government in ways never before possible via electronic town-hall meetings and other vehicles soliciting feedback on policy decisions.

   The government relations professional must learn to use these tools. Government officials are already making plans for participation in hearings via these new technologies, while others are soliciting their constituents on issues of interest and having them respond by e-mail. What is the role of the government relations professional in a system that is moving more toward "direct democracy" through these technologies? The choice will be either to be at the front end building contact programs that make sense or grabbing onto the tail and catching the horse after the barn door is open.

5. **Don't Underestimate the Power of the Media.** Media relations is an important part of any government relations program, as is detailed further in chapter six. Popularizing your cause through talk radio and engaging the public through a variety of media actions have never been more useful tools for the government relations professional. The integration of government relations and media relations functions can be very powerful. Surprisingly, most firms (both private contractors and corporations) are not organized to take full advantage of the synergies of the two disciplines working together. Having a seamless team will take training and mutual effort, but the re-

sults can be rewarding for both and success can be greatly
enhanced.

6. **Plan Globally, Act Locally.** Public affairs in the 21st century
will be increasingly global. It is already difficult to tell a domestic industry from a foreign one. More American products
and more American jobs are dependent upon foreign markets
and foreign marketing. The relationship between government
and business in Europe, Asia, and South America is a relationship that affects products, services and the bottom line in this
country. Doing business in the international community requires
a sensitivity to social, cultural, political and religious patterns
of behavior different from ours. However, it is surprising how
many tools of public affairs are as applicable in other countries as they are in our own. It is important to have access to
professionals indigenous to the foreign locality, but it is equally important that they are partnered with professionals here at
home who specialize in international business and government
relations. These two distinct perspectives produce a full picture with the broadest possible application and the greatest prospects for success.

7. **Remember the Basics.** While government relations is changing, some aspects remain the same, one being the need for
good, solid, experienced professionals with good political judgement who know politics, process and policy. Today professionals need to be active within the political community,
knowledgeable about the issues, respected, trusted and willing
to do the work and take pride in it.

Going Outside

Those of us who practice government relations in a consulting
environment are probably not the most objective advisors on outside consultancies. However, given the varied needs of the 1990s
and the general trend of companies and organizations to downsize,
there is no doubt about the role for the outside practitioner.

Given the multifaceted needs of clients, government relations
firms are diversifying their professional staffs, building a broader
range of practice areas and even increasing their international reach
through the establishment of alliances or offices in key international cities.

Here are some ideas for the best use of outside resources:

1. Hire people whose skills, experiences and contacts add value to your own. With the many changes in government and among elected officials, outside firms can add to your contact base.

2. Ideally, use a firm that can both strategize and implement. This means you need to base your selection on senior experience and the ability to validate your own thinking on a given strategy or issue as well as tactical execution to supplement the "arms and legs" when needed.

3. Given the changes taking place, select a firm that has experience being involved with the variety of tools and tactics that affect a modern issue campaign. Whether the firm has the capability to deliver all elements of an integrated program is not as critical as familiarity with how the pieces work together and how to get the most and best use of each part of the program.

4. To the extent that your needs are global, it is worth exploring the international capability of a given firm. The resources of a firm with global connections can be useful for both entering new markets and working within a market on regulatory or governmental impediments. A firm's ability often varies from market to market and it is useful to check on capabilities for all the markets of interest to your company or organization.

A Final Challenge

The ability to be a successful government relations professional, whether in a corporation or in a consulting firm, is challenged by the low regard in which the profession is held. It is clear that this profession has an image problem. There is skepticism and even scorn about the work we do. We need to do a better job of demonstrating how we contribute to both the public good and the corporate bottom line.

We need to conduct a major education effort within our organizations to assure that our contribution is better understood throughout the companies and organizations we serve. For years, the government relations professional has tended to operate independently, communicating only up the organizational chain. Today's government relations professional should work as broadly within the company as possible.

Solid representation programs have to be built with managers throughout the organization who share both the success and failure of governmental relations programs. Government relations professionals need to be considered as vital to the welfare of the organization as is the CFO or divisional manager.

The challenge is to show how we add value—in the ideas we present, the resources we secure and the savings we cause. The imagery of the Washington insider in smoke-filled rooms needs to be replaced by the consummate professional who knows how to win in an increasingly complex environment.

With the changes occurring in the nature of lobbying and access to information and the practice of government, the value of the government relations professional may come to be recognized by government officials, the public, and our own organizations to a much greater extent than is the case today.

Chapter 8

Lobbying and Political Action

Charles S. Mack

For all the controversies surrounding them, lobbying and political action are expressions of free speech, protected by the First Amendment to the U. S. Constitution. They are critical to the preservation of liberty in our democratic society. Let's define our terms.

Lobbying means the advocacy of a point of view on a matter of public policy. Individuals lobby, but so do interest groups. Lobbying is widespread on legislative issues, but people and organizations commonly lobby government agencies as well. State and local governments lobby each other and the federal government as well. Lobbying also occurs between governments of different countries, through the process of diplomacy. Private-sector organizations often lobby other organizations, and they frequently ask their own members to contact lawmakers and public officials on particular issues—a process called *grassroots lobbying. Direct lobbying*, the best known form, refers to direct communications with legislators or officials to affect a pending vote or a decision.

Lobbyists work with whomever happens to be in office. *Political action*, on the other hand, tries to affect who the lawmakers will be. In a sense, political action ends on election night; lobbying begins the next morning.

Lobbying

Interest groups lobby for any of several reasons.

- **For benefits or relief they cannot gain in the private sector.** Labor unions, for example, have sought advantages over employers they were unable to win in collective bargaining. Automobile and textile manufacturers have looked for help relative to competition in other countries.
- **For economic advantage.** Banks have pursued legal changes that would permit them to get into other financial businesses. Farm groups want agricultural support programs that will maximize farmers' incomes. Senior citizens lobby to retain or extend retirement income and medical payment programs.
- **For new, beneficial programs.** Defense contractors urge approval of new weapons systems. Labor unions and contractors want new public works and infrastructure investments. Cultural conservatives and the religious right want new legislation that will advance their social objectives.
- **For actions that only government can take.** Groups representing AIDS victims believe that government-sponsored research is essential to finding a cure for the disease. Both pro-life and pro-choice movements call on government to act in support of their goals. Civil rights organizations relied on government to adopt affirmative action and other minority programs, and now call on government to minimize changes in the light of recent Supreme Court decisions.

Some of these interest groups treat government as the court of last resort, others as the first, but all act on the reality that, even in a climate of government retrenchment and slimmer expenditures, the public sector remains a prime arena for the achievement of private-sector objectives. The tactics and techniques of lobbying are the means by which they work to persuade government decision-makers to adopt or support their objectives.

Those techniques fall into different categories, some of which are discussed in further detail in this chapter or elsewhere in this book.

- **Direct lobbying:** The best known of the lobbyist's tools, direct lobbying typically (though not invariably) involves person-to-person communications, orally and in writing. The lobbying may occur with a lawmaker or other public official, with a staff or committee aide, or through a third party known to be personally or politically influential with the decision-maker.

- **Indirect lobbying:** More commonly known as *grass-roots lobbying*, this technique promotes large numbers of communications with the government decision-maker, usually from legislative constituents. Another version is *grass-tops lobbying*, which stimulates communications from prominent individuals and organizations known to be particularly influential with the legislator. The emphasis of grass-roots tends to be on quantity, that of grass-tops on quality.

- **Alliances and coalitions:** Many organizations make common cause with others to advance joint legislative or regulatory objectives. Some are long-term (alliances), often extending a number of years until the goal or goals have been achieved. Others are usually short-term (coalitions), dealing with perhaps a single issue. Coalitions are frequently more diverse in their composition. For example, coalitions comprised of labor unions, protectionist companies, consumer advocates, and environmental groups were formed in attempts to defeat ratification of the North American Free Trade Area treaty and the General Agreement on Tariffs and Trade.

- **Associations:** Associations are really permanent alliances. Companies in the same industries or with other shared purposes form business and trade associations to advance their economic objectives. Individual members in similar careers, trades, or lines of work come together in professional associations or in labor unions. Thousands of other associations exist to advance every conceivable economic or social interest. Many, perhaps most, of these groups lobby government in behalf of their members, and indeed lobbying is the most significant function of a very large number of associations. For the vast majority of their members, whether organizational or individual, associations are the principal means by which they seek to affect governmental policies and programs.

- **Public relations and advocacy advertising:** Because public opinion has a major impact on governmental policy decisions, interest groups frequently engage in mass or selective communications of various kinds in an attempt to broaden

the audience for their messages. These include the many
tools of public relations including, but certainly not limited
to, techniques to influence the treatment of their issues by
the mass media. Sometimes, these interest groups purchase
advertising space to take their message directly to the public,
unfiltered by journalists' interpretations.
- **Political action:** This term describes a range of activities,
discussed in detail later in this chapter, by which individuals
and interest groups work to elect or retain in office public
officials favorable to their cause. There are two distinct, if
often overlapping, forms of political action. One involves
personal participation in politics to help nominate or elect
specific candidates, or perhaps all the candidates of one
political party. The other is the promotion of *financial
contributions* to those candidates or that party.

Government relations, government affairs or *public affairs* are the
terms usually used to describe in the aggregate these different means
and modes of affecting public policies.

The Forms and Functions of Direct Lobbying

Lobbying to affect the outcome of legislation is the best-known
form, but lobbying is widespread in other arenas of public policy
as well. Lobbyists work to affect policies and proposals of executive departments and agencies. They try to shape regulatory proposals and, often, the enforcement of regulations. They may speak
up concerning proposed appointments of particular individuals to
various public offices. They seek an impact on governmental pro-
curement decisions, frequently lobbying, first, the legislative body
in behalf of a new or expanded program, and then particular agencies for a substantial piece of the action for themselves. Even the
judicial branch is susceptible to lobbying through so-called "friend
of the court" briefs and arguments.

Interest groups lobby not only governments within the United
States, but sometimes those of other countries as well where they
have a significant stake. International organizations, ranging from
the United Nations and those under its umbrella, to the European
Union and other regional bodies, are frequent recipients of private-
sector lobbying communications—and the entire field of international

diplomacy is not much more than the campaigns of national governments to shape the public policies and actions of other countries.

Virtually every one of these forms of lobbying actually has two functions: not only communications intended to shape governmental decision-making, but also the collection of information and intelligence about those decisions while they are still in formative stages. Indeed, lobbyists spend substantially more time collecting information from government than they do communicating to it, since sound lobbying strategies, tactics, and positions are highly dependent on a strong base of information.

Regulation of Lobbying

Lobbying in the United States is regulated in at least 51 different and varied ways by the states and the federal government; some local governments also regulate different aspects of lobbying. Lobbying is typically regulated in two ways: registration, and reporting of finances and activities.

The federal government and all 50 states require paid lobbyists to register with some government agency or official under certain circumstances. Those circumstances vary widely, however.

Federal regulation. In the case of the federal government, paid lobbyists must register and file periodic financial reports with officials of Congress. Organizations must register only if lobbying is their "principal purpose;" many groups claim that their activities are primarily informational or educational, even though they focus on legislative matters, and therefore need not register. Furthermore, legislative lobbying is defined as communications only with members of Congress themselves; even contacts with their staffs are exempt. The law is widely regarded as toothless and unenforceable. Congress did pass a fairly comprehensive lobbying regulation law in 1946, but most of its provisions were declared unconstitutional by the Supreme Court in 1954 (*U.S. v. Harriss*) as violations of the First Amendment. There are tighter restrictions on lobbying in behalf of foreign governments.

Officials of the executive branch are theoretically barred from lobbying Congress, but this restriction is completely ignored by both the executive and legislative branches. Certain former executive branch officials are restricted in their abilities to lobby Congress or their former agencies, at least for a period of time, and this law has been vigorously enforced. It does not apply, however, to former members of Congress.

The 104th Congress failed in an attempt to regulate gift-giving to members of Congress. At mid-1995, there was discussion of resurrecting this legislation in the 105th Congress.

Washington does restrict federal lobbying through the tax code. Expenses for direct and grass-roots lobbying are not tax-deductible. A portion of dues paid associations that lobby is similarly non-deductible unless the association pays a proxy tax on the group's lobbying activities. The constitutionality of these provisions is being challenged in federal court.

State regulation. Every state has a different set of lobbying registration and reporting requirements. Every state requires registration if lobbyists are in communication with legislators, and a majority also applies this to executive and regulatory agency lobbying. All but a handful of states also require periodic reports from registered lobbyists, but the information, comprehensiveness, and frequency of these reports vary quite widely.

As a generality, most of these state laws are more stringent than the federal law. Oddly, however, the U.S. Supreme Court has declined opportunities to review the constitutionality of these state statutes. Logically, few of these laws seem likely to withstand a court test under the First Amendment if only an innocuous federal statute can stand up under scrutiny, but they will be fully enforced until and unless the Supreme Court takes and rules on a test case.

Political Action

Lobbyists who work with elected officials must deal with whomever the election produces. *Political action* tries to affect the outcome of elections to produce public decision-makers favorably inclined to the views of particular interest groups—either by involving their members directly in the political process or by providing financial support to friendly candidates.

Personal Political Participation

Lobbying is undoubtedly as old as government itself, but political action, at least in the United States, is a comparatively recent development. Among major interest groups, political activity on the part of labor unions probably has the most venerable tradition, dating back at least to the early decades of the 20th century. Farm groups also have a long history of support for pro-farmer candidates. Political activity by business groups, the professions, and other interest groups is more recent.

Organized political activity by the labor movement dates back to 1936 when unions worked actively for the reelection of Franklin Roosevelt. The old Congress of Industrial Organizations (CIO) formed a political action committee in 1943, as later did its rival, the American Federation of Labor (AFL). When the two groups merged in 1953, they merged their political arms into COPE—the Committee on Political Education. COPE has long and vigorously promoted action at the precinct level by the members of the AFL-CIO's constituent unions, and achieved considerable electoral success for a number of years. COPE's activities have been almost exclusively in behalf of Democratic candidates, and it remains to this day a major (though lessening) force within the Democratic Party. From Roosevelt through at least Walter Mondale in 1984, no Democrat won the presidential nomination without COPE support. In many industrial states, it virtually dictated the Democratic nominees for governor, for members of Congress, and for many state and local offices. COPE's financial support, but also the armies of precinct workers and campaign aides it mobilized for its endorsed candidates, made it one of the most powerful political forces in America during its heyday. In many parts of the Northeast, the Midwest, and areas of California and Texas, it is still a power, though it has declined nationally as labor's influence has overall. The AFL-CIO is now making major efforts to revive its political and lobbying effectiveness, though with uncertain prospects. The lesson, however, is that for six decades the effectiveness of union lobbyists in persuading local, state, and federal lawmakers to enact labor's agenda has been directly related to COPE's success in electing pro-labor candidates.

Business groups came later to this process, and have never matched labor's success in mobilizing business people to personal political activity. In the 1950s, the U. S. Chamber of Commerce sought to train business people in the political process, and the Effective Citizens Organization—now the Public Affairs Council—was formed to promote business political participation. In 1963, the Business-Industry Political Action Committee (BIPAC) was created to be the counterforce to COPE. Although there have been many notable instances of business executives getting involved in grass-roots politics and in successfully running for public office, as a whole business people have shied away from personal political involvement.

Among the professions, lawyers have long been active political participants and it is only in recent years that most legislatures ceased to be completely dominated by attorneys. This was rarely an organized professional activity, however, until the rise of the trial lawyers' association and its active promotion of political and lobbying activity among its members. The American Medical Association has long encouraged political participation among physicians and they have been joined in recent years by other health professionals as well. Teachers have become more active in grass-roots politics over the years, as their organizations have behaved less and less like professional societies, and more and more like labor unions. Public employees have followed in their wake as legal restrictions on their political activity have been repealed.

Among other major interest groups, senior citizens and environmental organizations have had some limited success in promoting political participation among their members. Both have been much more effective with grass-roots lobbying programs.

Campaign Finance

"Money is the mother's milk of politics," said Jesse Unruh, long a powerhouse in California politics. As the focus of political campaigns for at least major offices has moved away from precinct organization to television, campaigns have become progressively more expensive. It was not that many years ago that a successful congressional district campaign could be waged for $50,000. By 1994, some House campaigns in competitive districts spent as much as $2.5 million, and there is no reason to believe the ceiling has been reached. Campaigns for Senate seats and governorships in major states cost many multiples of that number.

Critics of the steady escalation of campaign spending, particularly advocates of public financing, bemoan the impact on the integrity of public officials. Certainly, no one can applaud these progressively higher costs, nor the increased time candidates must spend in raising money. Still, it is worth putting campaign finance in perspective. The hundreds of millions of dollars spent in all congressional campaigns in 1994, and those likely to be spent in campaigns for Congress and President in 1996, are only a fraction of the cost of a single B-2 bomber—less than the price of the nation's agricultural subsidies—and infinitesimal compared to the total appropriations which Congress will pass and the President will sign in any single year of even this fiscally retrenched decade. Relative to the cost of the nation's government, the expense of electing America's lawmakers and its chief executive is quite small. It is part of the price we pay for democratic government.

With the exception of some parts of the presidential campaign, the costs of running for federal public office, and most state and local offices, are funded solely through the voluntary contributions of private citizens and organizations. (A few state and municipal elections are publicly financed.)

There are at least half a dozen legal techniques by which private contributions are funneled to political candidates and parties. Let's examine each of them.

Individual contributions. Donations from individuals are the solitary source of all funds for congressional campaigns, for a portion of presidential campaigns, and for contests in about half the states. State election limits on individual contributions vary widely. At the federal level, individuals can give up to $1,000 to a candidate in each of primary, runoff, and general elections, up to $5,000 a year to a political action committee or state or local committee supporting federal candidates, and up to $20,000 to a national party committee. However, the total of all of these individual donations may not exceed $25,000 annually. A number of techniques exist for raising this money: direct mail or telemarketing solicitations, dinners or similar events, and the like. Funds raised from individuals are sometimes called *hard dollars*.

Bundling. Some interest groups choose to deliver a group of individual contributions as a means of demonstrating the size of their support for particular candidates. There is no legal limit on the number of individual contributions that can be so delivered, although the practice has been criticized as an attempt to skirt the ceilings on political action committee contributions.

Corporate and union donations. Though prohibited in federal elections, corporate contributions are permitted in varying degrees in over 30 states, including most of the large states. Direct union contributions are permitted in about 40 states. *Soft money* is the term used for corporate and union donations to state party committees, which thereby free up other funds that can be used to help congressional and presidential candidates. *In-kind contributions* are donations, similar to soft dollars, of merchandise and services, often at a lower cost to the donor than to the party committee.

Political action committees. Second today only to lobbying as the beneficiary of criticisms and public opprobrium, pacs were seen as a post-Watergate political reform barely two decades ago. Political action committees are voluntary associations of classes of individuals who choose to aggregate their political contributions for maximum impact. Pacs give to candidates, to political party committees, or make *independent expenditures.*

Most political action committees are organized under federal law, but there are many single-state pacs and a few multi-state pacs (regulated by state laws if they don't give to federal candidates). The comments that follow relate to federal pacs only.

COPE began giving money to candidates in 1943, and had the field to itself for 20 years. BIPAC was created in 1963. Both are considered "leadership pacs," their endorsements widely influencing the contributions of other labor or business pacs.

The swell of corporate pacs came after a 1975 decision by the Federal Election Commission (FEC) that legitimized them. Several thousand corporate pacs exist today, although the majority of them collect a fairly small sum of money; a few hundred give most of the corporate pac dollar total. Virtually all of the largest pacs contributing to federal candidates are run by labor unions. Teachers, trial lawyers, health professionals, environmental groups, gun owners, and women's organizations all have pacs of considerable size. Among the 50 largest pacs in 1994, 14 are affiliated with companies or business associations, 22 with labor unions. In the 1994 election cycle, corporate pacs spent $117 million, labor pacs $88 million. (The business pac total is undoubtedly larger, but spending by association pacs is lumped with health and other pacs by the FEC.)

Pacs organized by corporations, unions and other groups have a considerable financial advantage. The sponsoring organization can finance all the fund-raising and administrative costs of the pac. So-called *unconnected pacs*, like BIPAC and many ideological pacs, on the other hand, must pay all their costs out of the hard dollars they raise, limited by the $5,000 ceiling on individual donations to them. Pacs can give up to $5,000 per candidate per election, with no limit on aggregate contributions. They can also donate $5,000 a year to another pac, and up to $15,000 to party committees. These limits have never been raised since they were first established 20 years ago. In inflation-adjusted dollars, they are worth today perhaps a third of their original value.

Criticisms of pacs stem largely from their motivation for giving. There are two prime rationales for pac contributions (and other types of political donations as well).

Access giving. The pacs of many interest groups give primarily to gain or retain political access to incumbent lawmakers, particularly leaders and committee or subcommittee chairmen, plus others with notable legislative influence. Such pacs give preponderantly to incumbents.

Ideological giving. The other principal motivation for contributions is to elect lawmakers sympathetic to the views of the interest group sponsoring the pac. Ideological pacs give to both incumbents and non-incumbents, according to whether their friends are in or out, but all try to maximize the number of like-minded lawmakers they can elect. COPE, for example, over the years has given to pro-labor candidates (almost all of them Democrats), whether or not they are incumbents. BIPAC contributes to pro-business candidates in competitive races; through 1994, most of its beneficiaries, largely Republicans, were non-incumbents because pro-business incumbents were in the minority. (BIPAC is virtually unique among pacs in that it does not lobby.)

The access pacs are the ones that receive the brunt of the criticisms and that have generated the calls for new restrictions on pacs. Yet, even access pacs are protected by constitutional rights of association and free speech, with every right to advance the interests of their sponsors and members. These attacks came from self-styled reformers, but also from many Republicans who have resented the large share of corporate pac dollars going to Democrats who largely ran Congress for 40 years. Since the 1994 elections when Republicans won control of both houses of Congress, contributions from both access pacs and corporate pacs of an ideological bent have been flowing more in the Republican direction. It remains to be seen how much this mutes Republican criticisms, but to the extent it does, attacks from Democrats can be expected to rise.

Independent expenditures. In a 1976 decision (*Buckley v. Valeo*), the Supreme Court held that any group may make unlimited expenditures in any election so long as its efforts are not coordinated with the candidates or party they benefit. Although this form of expenditure still accounts for a small percentage of all political dollars, it is potentially a weapon of enormous impact. A few groups, notably the National Rifle Association, have been instrumental in defeating candidates they oppose through independent expenditures.

Public financing. The use of taxpayer dollars (derived from the check-off on tax returns) finances matching funds for presidential candidates in the pre-nominating convention period, subsidizing the national party conventions, and the post-convention presidential campaign. Its use in congressional elections has also been long urged by reformers who argue that it would clearly separate lobbying and influence building from campaign funding—so far to no avail. Public financing for congressional races has been strongly opposed in most opinion polls as "welfare for politicians." Moreover, taxpayer participation in the presidential campaign fund has steadily declined year after year, most recently to a low of 14 percent. By 1996, it may be below 12 percent. Rather than yield to a clear trend of citizen opinion, in 1994 Congress opted to increase the check-off from $1 per taxpayer to $3 so that the presidential campaign fund would not be bankrupted.

Money and Politics

Jesse Unruh's maxim remains as true today as it was the day he expressed it. So long as the citizenry continues to oppose public financing with its present vehemence, congressional elections will be funded with privately-derived money. And money, like water, will always find its own level. Whatever restrictions lawmakers may choose to impose on campaign finance, motivated givers will find a way to participate in the process in behalf of the candidates they choose to elect—or to defeat.

The law is imperfect. A principal imperfection was imposed by the Supreme Court which said that contributions to others may be limited but not on behalf of one's own candidacy. The effect has been to draw wealthy, often wholly unqualified candidates into congressional politics, in the knowledge that they are free to pour unlimited sums into their own campaigns. If campaign contributions are an expression of free speech, as the Court has held, what is the logic of limiting contributions to others without limit for oneself? Congressional action to remove limits on individual contributions would end this inequity.

Another liability of the present system is its bias towards incumbents, who meet their challengers on a playing field anything but even. Even in elections like 1994 when the former minority party in Congress finally seized control, over 90 percent of incumbents seeking reelection won. Given the enormous advantages incumbency provides, a fair system of campaign finance would allow challengers to spend more than incumbents, perhaps by a formula tied to the incumbent's previous margins of victory.

A further desirable change would not only retain political action committees as a legitimate expression of free speech, but would recognize two decades of inflation by increasing the donation and expenditure ceilings and by indexing them to future inflation. Pac operations can be democratized by requiring annual disclosure of contributions to pac donors and allowing them the final say in contributions. Registered lobbyists should be barred from serving on pac decision-making bodies.

The worst campaign finance offenses are often committed by incumbents. They should be restricted to raising funds outside their districts to the 12 months preceding the next election—and in the case of Senators—to *any* fund-raising prior to 24 months before their next election. Incumbents should not be allowed to solicit lobbyists for contributions.

It makes little sense to have two separate systems of federal campaign funding. The public takes an increasingly dim view of public financing for congressional campaigns. Why retain it at the presidential level? A rational system of private financing, with no public funds and with full disclosure of contributions and expenditures, should be reinstituted for presidential campaigns.

In June 1995, President Clinton and House Speaker Gingrich publicly agreed to establish a commission to develop major changes to the federal laws regulating campaign finance and lobbying. They also agreed that Congress would have the power only to accept or reject the commission's proposals, but not to amend them. At mid-year, it remains to be seen whether this idea will come to life and achieve genuine reforms in the funding of America's elections and in lobbying regulation.

Chapter 9

"Shadow Constituencies" and Silver Anvil Case Study Models: Synergistic Public Affairs Management

Richard R. Mau

This chapter proposes that no one is more capable than communications professionals when it comes to scanning the far margins of the organization's external environment; identifying, following, interacting with, allying with, neutralizing when possible, mitigating as necessary, and diverting from confrontation when essential, the ever-present plethora of cause groups being generated by our complex, diverse society.

Introduction

Some 65 million Americans, according to an early-1990s study, belong to special interest or cause groups of one kind or another.[1] This single fact speaks volumes about the growth and potential impact of these groups in our society in recent decades. It underscores as little else can the reality that in this mixed-agenda society businesses must never for a moment presume they can operate autonomously. It has become increasingly imperative today for businesses to be attentive not only to competitors but also to the goals, objectives and tactics of myriad other entities as well, many of them non-commercial, who share geography, time and space if nothing else.

I have come, in recent years, to dub these self-proclaimed business partners "shadow constituencies," however ad hoc their appearances and abrupt their departures may be.[2] In this chapter we will explore the nature, rise, impact and prudent management of this stakeholder phenomenon, not because it may be intellectually interesting to do so, but because experience teaches—as do the case studies in synergistic public affairs examined later in the chapter—that coping with shadow constituencies begins long before their presence is felt or known and continues long after as well.

The Function's Role: Counseling

Among the most discriminating observations I have read in recent years is this trenchant comment by legendary public relations practitioner, Harold Burson:

> Public relations (call it corporate or public affairs or communications or whatever) now has a seat at the management table. Public relations, in many if not most of the Fortune 500 companies I know, now is part of the decision-making process.[3]

The goal of every senior corporate public relations officer must surely be to participate in management at the top of one's organization, the capstone of a long and productive career. Never before has this corporate function faced such complex and compelling challenges. None is more essential than earning an integral role in councils at the very top of the organization. Additionally, understanding clearly the content and intent of business strategies is fundamental to anticipating and communicating with those constituencies that are probable advocates or adversaries in our public arenas.

The simple truth is that the basics of corporate public affairs are more complex and the environment more dynamic than ever before. To aspire to be the senior public communications officer in any large organization today is to aspire to be consulted at the table when organizational policy and strategy are decided—not via the telephone after crucial choices have been made.

Another sagacious professional, Ed Block, concludes "that the principal role—the primary value added—of the public relations function can be expressed in a single word: Counseling."[4] Based on his own long experience at AT&T, Block identified these attributes of a good counselor:

1. An intimate understanding of the business, its culture, its goals, or, as we used to phrase it, the Big Picture;
2. A confident understanding of what a company's various publics are thinking or may think about the company's policies and actions; and
3. The assertiveness to make certain these perspectives are heard, understood and heeded when management seeks to solve problems that exist or head off problems that may emerge.[5]

Understanding Shadow Constituencies

In today's highly complex, global milieu, "corporate strategy cannot be framed as only economic or competitive in character. . . . The globalization of modern commerce ensures that managers in firms everywhere will have to attend actively to relationships of business, government and society."[6]

This is precisely the portfolio the senior public communications officer brings to the management table. Others understand marketing dilemmas, resource imperatives, labor constraints, capitalization quandaries and the many other factors involved in shaping corporate strategy. It is the senior public communications officer who must counsel the CEO on effective corporate decision making in the nexus where business, government and society intersect. This kaleidoscopic setting is usually beyond the focus of others at the managerial table. It requires understanding the agendas of a host of stakeholder groups when weighing the pros and cons determining strategic decisions.

In business we have been handling difficult situations rather successfully and for a relatively long period of time with what I view as core, structural demands from government and, to a lesser extent, society. By this I mean that we customarily behave as responsible, law-abiding organizations. We have become more involved in the political and legislative tides as they affect our prerogatives. We conform to laws that emanate from the federal, state and local legislative process and regulations that flow from the administrative process and, of course, we obey the law as defined over time, through interpretation, by the judicial process. Similarly, we characteristically conform to general societal expectations concerning the obligations of "good corporate citizenship." International business people find the totality of American corporations' community-based involvement typically awe-inspiring. And, to the extent that American business today enjoys any credibility and popular confidence, it is because past generations of management saw fit to meet and sometimes exceed society's expectations.

Today's condition is a manifestation of the greatly increased expectations of business that arose from a variety of social movements in the 1960s and thereafter. Specifically, the apparent seedbed for the challenges senior public communications officers face today and will be facing for some time to come include: (a) the explosion in the African-American community of Watts, near downtown Los Angeles, in the mid-1960s, followed by intensification of the civil rights movement; (b) the flood of Great Society legislation; (c) the emergence of a full-blown and decidedly anti-business consumer movement shepherded by an unlikely Harvard-educated activist, Ralph Nader; and (d) the beginnings of an environmental movement that has yet to run its course even though it has now spread eco-consciousness to every corner of the world. Few if any would argue that the convergence of these broad and largely unrelated social movements transformed the business, government, society nexus as had little else in American history.

Today the challenges we face are derivatives of these movements but they are vastly different, too. I perceive the core challenges as artifacts of shadow constituencies. Unlike an organization's core constituencies, employees, investors, unions, etc., shadow constituencies are denizens of dimly perceived, now-you-see-them-now-you-don't flickerings on an organization's extreme periphery. These stakeholders have no institutionalized organization chart existence nor relationship to the organization's business. Nonetheless, shadowy and insubstantial as they may appear, all too often they possess the capability to affect—when sufficiently energized—an organization's operations in numerous ways. Their activation often causes abrupt and dire consequences for an organization's financial performance and can create adverse perceptions that may be difficult to neutralize, taking years and costing millions of dollars.

Describing them can be pointless since they can emerge only to recede into invisibility again with the fabled speed of UFOs. They sometimes display the transformational qualities of much-feared mutating viruses. Defining them is best approached by explaining why organizations now face frequent hit-and-run assaults from a variety of these shadow constituencies. In the main they are the product of increasing fragmentation in American society. How and why we have developed into a "hyperpluralistic" society is not the purpose of this chapter, but the topic is explored in Chapter 15.

Sufficient for our discussion are a few basic observations. The traditional sociological model of American society with a strong midsection of "mediating" institutions, such as schools, churches, fraternal groups, has long since yielded to a revised sociological model that is far more diverse and fragmented in character. Today's special interest or pressure groups (terms that have been around for decades) run the gamut from gangs to gays, from the homeless to health care activists. Others range from a group of neighbors concerned about electromagnetic fields near their elementary school playground to increasingly militant Western Americans who, as members of the Wise Use movement, demand compensation from government for losses from environmental protection enforcement and even termination of mining and logging on vast of tracts of federal lands.

The modus operandi of today's diverse special interest groups varies, too, from investor resolutions at annual meetings to abrasive, even intimidating encounters with such representatives of the federal government as national park service personnel or fish and wildlife officers. The point is that with today's communications opportunities any group can assure by its actions that its cause becomes a high priority for those it seeks to influence. However distant that concern may be from the corporation's priorities or mission statement, the cause may mushroom quickly from a shadowy, quirky, far-edge virtually intangible blip on the business' societal radar to a full-blown exigency replete with media firestorms, caustic confrontations and "fact-finding" legislative hearings. One further fact: few others in the organization share the senior communications officer's awareness of the emergence and potentially vexing existence of these elements on our corporate horizons. That can be an advantage. Accepting the assignment to monitor and engage such groups, hopefully to dull their more dangerous thrusts or even convert them to allies on occasion, can redound significantly to your credit and the function's contribution to the bottom line.

Case Studies

We now turn our attention to two case studies that elucidate the discussion to this point. Both of these examples of synergistic public affairs management received the Public Relations Society of America Silver Anvil award. But case studies need not be trophy winners to be instructive. The key lessons of each case will be identified at the end of each case.

Case Study Number One
"Hell on Earth: The Incident at Edison"

Case Facts

An energy utility's worst nightmare roared to life for Panhandle Eastern Corporation just before midnight on March 23, 1994. A portion of the natural gas utility's interstate pipeline had ruptured in Edison Township, New Jersey only 30 miles southwest of the nation's number one media market. The rupture and subsequent explosion and fireball occurred just 800 feet from the parking lot of a nearby apartment complex. Residents' cars began bursting into flame and melting.

The fireball provided an eerie, brightly lit midnight sky as 2,000 residents were evacuated and swarms of state and federal authorities, and media, descended on tiny Edison. Understandably, the first thing on everyone's mind within minutes after the incident was containing the disaster and shutting down the pipeline. How Panhandle Eastern and its operating subsidiary, Texas Eastern Transmission Corporation (TETCO), managed to address both the human concerns and operational requirements of the disaster is a prime example of synergistic communications management. Against all odds, they won popular and regulatory approval to reopen the pipeline at full pressure just 21 days after the incident

The gravity of the situation became clear with first light. The *New York Times* reported:

> The landscape resembled a battlefield with a crater—120 feet wide and 60 feet deep—shaped like a giant's footprint at the center. Deep in the crater, a stub of the exploded pipe protruded with jagged steel edges. . . . A line of utility poles stood upright, and others had fallen, burned and blackened like matchsticks. . . . Farther on, one could

see the flattened, blackened rectangles where eight apartment buildings had stood. . . . Oddly, sidewalks snaked along the complex leading to doors that no longer existed.[7]

But as desperate as the situation was, Panhandle Eastern later judged the incident to have produced a textbook example of how "employing the synergistic power of its combined public, community and government affairs efforts . . . turned this . . . nightmare . . . (to) actually improving the company's 'image' as well as achieving a nearly impossible corporate objective. . . ."[8]

Response

At 3:15 A.M. (CDT) as the flames were being extinguished, the corporation's Emergency Response Team's jet took off from Houston. Members represented Transmission, Legal, Safety, Risk Management, Security, Regulatory and Public Affairs departments. The team quickly established three objectives and priorities from which it never departed: First, address human needs; second, cooperate completely with the accident's investigation; and third, restore the pipeline to operating capacity as soon as possible.

All members of the team took care to repeatedly express concern about the people affected in all contacts with media, residents and government personnel. The primary goal was to let everyone know how to get help and to convince them that Panhandle Eastern truly wanted to help. Because *perceptions* are the dominant factor at times like this, the team's approach was particularly effective. Immediate cash relief to people affected with no strings attached was also enormously valuable in shaping those all-important perceptions of the company. Because the company immediately provided hotel rooms and food, clothing and other basic necessities to the affected residents, fewer than 100 spent the night at the American Red Cross shelter in the local high school gymnasium. Additionally, the company immediately disbursed up to $5,000 for people whose apartments or contents thereof had been severely damaged. In addition, displaced residents were paid $350 per week for living expenses. Cash distributions for basic expenses totaled more than $10 million. Local governments were reimbursed some $440,000, and the company also contributed some $80,000 to charities and 22 local governments involved in the relief effort.

Despite all of this, concurrent efforts to get the pipeline back in

service ran into local political problems involving the mayor of
Edison. Ultimately, after the company acceded to various demands
not in the mayor's jurisdiction, a final sign-off with the city was
negotiated. For the first time in Panhandle Eastern's history, this
agreement was negotiated not by attorneys but by the company's
public affairs officer.

Lessons

In this case, the company was also a victim. A third party had
caused damage to its pipeline that resulted in the calamitous rupture, explosion and fire. Still it was the *attitude* and the actual *behavior* of the company in the emergency's aftermath, including a
period of weeks thereafter, that turned the corner on winning both
credibility and local government and federal support for the company's priority objective: returning the TETCO pipeline to operation as soon as possible. In other words, focusing effort on the
actions of being a good corporate citizen generated much more
goodwill toward the company than merely pushing a story through
the media. Actions do speak louder than words. If one walks the
walk, someone else will talk the talk in your behalf, making it all
the more convincing.

A key shadow constituency dimension not readily apparent rests
in Panhandle Eastern's assiduous work in cultivating the goodwill
of such agencies as Red Cross and United Way. Dr. Judith Craven,
Houston-area United Way president, was instrumental in winning
acceptance of Panhandle's emergency team when local United Way
authorities required reassurance. Craven's characterization of Panhandle as a trustworthy partner in addressing human needs gained
acceptance from not only Middlesex County United Way but also
Catholic Charities, the Salvation Army and the Red Cross.

Case Study Number Two
"The Case For Space"

Case Facts

In mid-summer 1995 millions of theatergoers were enthralled by a
cinematic retelling of the near-calamitous moon journey of Apollo
13.[9] The incident came perilously close to losing three astronauts
to a drift through space or in-capsule incineration.

Twenty-five years later, the Apollo 13 story is being retold with the emphasis where it belongs—on engineering prowess, astronaut coolness and heroism—and, of course, with the requisite Hollywood happy ending. Yet in those 25 years, the National Aeronautics and Space Administration and the space program have traveled a difficult road. Surely the infamous Challenger disaster was the actual low-point on that road, though there were others.

Somewhere along the way America's love affair with the space effort as structured and interpreted by NASA faded. Despite the success of the Apollo program, which probably will be regarded by future historians as the unqualified best human achievement of the century, space programs following Apollo's moon-and-back-safely success simply failed to ignite public enthusiasm. That fact, coupled with the burgeoning deficits of the 1980s and 1990s, brought Congressional criticism, numerous redefinitions and repositionings by NASA and noteworthy budget contractions year after year. By the time the Soviet empire imploded, as manifest in the collapse of the Berlin Wall in 1989, even the secret military and defense dimensions of the space program, never well articulated in any event, could not shield the program from serious critical assaults and downsizing threats bordering on elimination.

Ruminating about the space program's earlier days and the fall from grace in recent years calls to mind the ancient ritual, used in the coronation of Roman Catholic pontiffs where a candle is extinguished three times accompanied by the words *sic semper gloria* [thus always with glory].

Response

By the early 1990s, officials at Rockwell International Corporation, based on dialogue with legislators and NASA policy makers, concluded that approval of both the NASA budget, already diminished significantly, and the next-step space station program, were in serious doubt. Audience research polling commissioned by Rockwell International for over a decade revealed, ironically, strong public support for the space program. The research also indicated that winning continued support from key publics hinged on highlighting space benefits and the positive impact on educational programs, particularly mathematics and science.

A program evolved over time, with two chief objectives:

1. Gain active enthusiasm for the program as part of an "American tradition" yielding jobs plus medical, scientific and
   technological benefits;
2. Channel this support, through quantitative messages directed
   at Congressional decision makers, to win Congressional
   approval of the NASA budget and space station.

The program was focused on locales in states with the largest
intrinsic concern about space activity. Among targeted publics were:

- 1,000 members of Congress, mayors and governors in key
  states;
- 15,000 Rockwell International employees and families;
- 2,500 outside vendors supporting Rockwell's space projects;
- 20 million members of the space-interested general public;
- 200 key officials of varied pro-space organizations, including
  NASA; and
- 150 educators.

Strategies involved a media program targeted to areas where
Rockwell International and other aerospace companies had a large
presence, particularly Southern California, Florida, Texas and Washington, D.C. Considering the scope of the issue, most traditional
communications methods were used, including print and broadcast
mass media, speeches, interviews, special events and opinion pieces. Theme lines incorporated into these various communications
included: "We Need Our Space," "I Need My Space," and "Space:
Our Presence Is Our Future."

Thousands of postcards featuring distinctive, mold-breaking graphics were created for use in conveying attitudes to Congress. Costs
of the program, including survey research, totaled some $120,000.
The program, once developed, was fully implemented replete with
informative and inspiring events crafted for specific target audiences, often timed to occur just before key Congressional votes. Decision makers were aggressively invited to participate in on-site visits
to get to know the "people behind the space program." Additionally, several programs aiding educators in teaching science and technology were implemented along with a new national survey gauging
American views on space. All of these efforts were undertaken with

a full awareness that some prior proposals with similar goals had scarcely achieved "lift-off." And one proposed tool, a space hot line, was never used due to lack of adequate staffing support needed to meet the expected strong public response.

Evaluating the program's success relied upon both quantitative efforts expended and, more saliently, results realized. Ultimately Congress did approve 1994 funding of the space program—and especially the space station. Some 75 million media impressions were recorded, including a key turnaround in coverage by the *Los Angeles Times*. One year earlier the paper had carried this synoptic headline: "Space Station . . . big science . . . big mess."[10] After the new effort, the *Times* demonstrated a dramatic change of heart, lauding the space station as a good investment.

Finally, and perhaps the most enduring, was the wide publication of the national space survey results carried throughout the United States by *Florida Today*, Reuters, United Press International and other wire services.

Lessons

Few cases that could be selected to exemplify the value of mobilizing shadow constituencies can be found that enjoy the amplitude of this one. After all, the ultimate in non-core constituencies, arguably, would be countless millions of fellow citizens.

The key to this extraordinary example of achieving organizational objectives by orchestrating a concerted campaign is far more subtle than one might think. It rests not with all the creative thinking and planning, but in accepting in the first place the potential value of shadow consistencies. If such groups share our viewpoint, once motivated they may help us even while expressing themselves. Contact with, motivation of and involvement by vast numbers of space activists or space enthusiasts created the program's success.

In this instance, too, shadow constituencies were neither antagonists nor adversaries but generally inert or untapped resources. This important point adds to understanding of the management of shadow constituencies precisely because it underscores the sometimes positive value even very peripheral interests can have. Not every contact with a non-core constituency need be abrasive, adversarial or antagonistic. Some, indeed, may be productive and even profitable.

Conclusion

Early in this chapter we noted Harold Burson's comments concerning the maturation of corporate communications as a business management discipline. He writes from personal experience about the evolution of the discipline from the source of news releases responding to a CEO's need for a "how-do-I-say-it?" to a "what-do-I-say?" Here the communications professional is a partner in the decision-making process. The management role remains incomplete, however, until the communications executive is not only a partner in organizational decision making but a full voice in discussions at the management table addressing the most vital query of all: "What do we do?"

Increasingly, it may take two rights to avoid being wrong in business today. As cogently advocated by a San Francisco banking executive, it behooves businesses to consider these questions in their 1990s decision making: "Is this the right thing to do and is this the smart thing to do?"[11] Equally important, these are not necessarily mutually exclusive.

The dynamic character of all businesses today demands that every functional discipline change continuously. Reaching maturity is important only so far as participation in the decision process is concerned. Understanding the infinite demands to adjust horizons, to apply judgment, common sense and strategic sensitivity to maximizing the organization's service to stakeholders will be central to holding one's seat at the table in the years ahead.

This chapter proposes that no one is more capable than communications professionals when it comes to scanning the far margins of the organization's external environment; identifying, following, interacting with, allying with, neutralizing when possible, mitigating as necessary, and diverting from confrontation, when essential, the ever-present plethora of cause groups being generated by our complex, diverse society.

Or, in the words of Burson: "Our challenge as professional public relations practitioners is to bring to our responsibility the experience, the talents and the accountability . . . expected of others in the corporate hierarchy."[12] Odd as it may seem at first, communications executives may well reach the apogee of their professional potential when managing through creative, sometimes premonitory and synergistic modes the relationships their organizations are ineluctably going to have anyway, whether good or ill, with their shadow constituencies.

Notes

1. "The Vocal Minority in American Politics," *Times Mirror Center for People and the Press*, (July, 1993): 82.

2. Richard R. Mau and Lloyd B. Dennis, "Companies Ignore shadow Constituencies at Their Peril," *Public Relations Journal* 50(5) (May 1994): 10-11.

3. Harold Burson, "Introduction: The Maturation of Public Relations," (V), (1994-95): 5.

4. Edward M. Block, "Changes in Corporate Public Relations," San Francisco Academy Seminar on "Leadership," San Francisco, 5 May 1995.

5. Ibid.

6. James E. Post, "The Corporation and Public Policy in the 1990s," J ournal of Organizational Change Management, (I) (1991): 9.

7. *New York Times*, (March 24, 1994): 1.

8. James W. Hart, "The 21 Days of Edison," PRSA Public Affairs and Government Section Monograph, (1995), Abstract: 1.

9. James Lo;vell and Jeffrey Kluger, "Lost Moon: The Perilous Voyage of Apollo 13," Houghton-Mifflin, New York, New York, (1994).

10. Donald Mullane, address, San Francisco Academy Seminar on "Stakeholder Relations," San Francisco, 9 Dec. 1994.

11. Burston, *op. cit.*, 6.

Chapter 10

Issue Management: Dissolving the Archaic Division between Line and Staff

Public policy and profit are equal in importance.
Neither is secondary to the other.

W. Howard Chase and
Teresa Yancey Crane

The environmental movement of the '90s is similar in many ways to environmentalism of the '70s. Both are based on the concept of stewardship of the earth and its natural resources. But something else happened during those interim years that makes today's movement much more pervasive in its second wave. Trend analysts would say the difference results from the increased awareness of how the environment affects our health and fitness, the continued pluralism of our society, and the advances made in technological communications.

Issue management of the '90s also differs from the original system named and outlined in 1976 by Howard Chase, and developed into a more detailed model by the authors and Barry Jones in 1977. Between then and now, business has been exposed to methods such as management by objective, total quality management, process re-engineering, and green marketing.

Meanwhile, companies find that issues have not "gone away." Indeed, their impact on the corporation penetrates deeper, across more constituencies, and in more measurable ways than ever before.

What you have seen during the early '90s, therefore, has been a "revisiting" of the issue management process. In its second wave, issue management—like environmental management—is much more pervasive, more sophisticated, more tightly linked with business performance.

This chapter will provide an introduction to the issue management process; discuss changes that have occurred twenty years after its development; offer a list of steps to take in developing the reader's own in-house issue management initiative; and suggest a new corporate structure that will support our thesis that the line once distinctly drawn in the sand between line and staff responsibilities, exists no more.

What is an Issue?

Let's begin by examining basic terminology. What is an issue? *An issue exists when there is a gap between corporate action and stakeholder expectation.*

One of the first people to apply "gap analysis" to the identification and management of issues was David Grier, then at the Royal Bank of Canada. As illustrated in Andrew B. Gollner's book, *Social Change and Corporate Strategy,*[1] Grier's model appears (on the following page). It encompasses the following specific steps:

1. Set reputation objectives—"desired perception" goals
2. Identify relevant target groups—"publics"
3. Research public perceptions
4. Assess how the reality of corporate performance differs from "desired perception" goals. Conduct "gap analysis" to determine:
   a) performance gap, and
   b) perception gap
5. Devise and implement business actions to narrow performance gap
6. Devise and implement communications actions to narrow perception gap
7. Evaluate and report on a regular basis
8. If necessary, revise strategic business goals

Reputation Goal: To achieve a situation where Canadians believe that:
"Corporation XYZ is a leader in environmental protections and concern."

Target Groups: Governments, Media, Environmental groups, Community groups

Current Situation Point Scale:

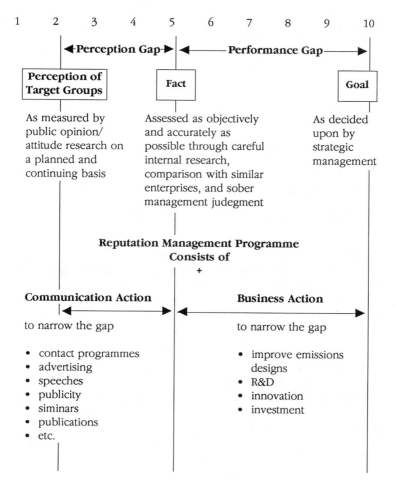

1   2   3   4   5   6   7   8   9   10

◀Perception Gap▶ ◀————— Performance Gap —————▶

| Perception of Target Groups | Fact | Goal |

As measured by public opinion/ attitude research on a planned and continuing basis

Assessed as objectively and accurately as possible through careful internal research, comparison with similar enterprises, and sober management judegment

As decided upon by strategic management

**Reputation Management Programme
Consists of**
+

Communication Action   **Business Action**

to narrow the gap   to narrow the gap

• contact programmes
• advertising
• speeches
• publicity
• siminars
• publications
• etc.

• improve emissions designs
• R&D
• innovation
• investment

Source: David Grier, The Royal Bank of Canada, as shown in *Social Change and Corporate Strategy*, page 153 by Andrew B. Gollner, (Issue Action Publications, 1983)

By observing that a "gap" necessitates change in either perception (communications) or performance (operations), Grier shows that issue management is both a staff and line concern.

The Issue Management Process

If an issue can be described as a "gap" between corporate action and stakeholder expectation, consider this:

Issue management is the process used to close that gap.

The Issue Management Process Model developed by the authors in 1977 included five primary steps:

- Issue identification
- Issue analysis
- Priority setting
- Issue action
- Evaluation of results

Further development of these steps resulted in a detailed Program Evaluation and Reveiw Technique (PERT) chart that included 88 distinct "steps." These actions were depicted in a series of concentric circles, as explained in Chase's book *Issue Management: Origins of the Future:*[2]

> To understand the dynamics of the issue management process, imagine the Model as a pond, and public policy issues as stones. When a stone drops into a pond, ripples move outward and form concentric circles. When an issue is dropped in the public policy process, at the heart of the Model, the resulting ripples disturb the smooth functioning of (traditional) business practices. How great these disruptions will be depend on their size, number, and how they interact with each other to affect public policy decisions.

A Broader Application

There is more than one way to implement issue management. The gap caused by an issue may be closed by adjusting to meet expectations—creating a new product, or modifying operations. The gap

may be closed by adopting a new policy—a different way of looking at natural resources may result in a revised policy that drives
operations and philosophy in many areas. Or, the gap may be closed
by changing constituent expectations—public education initiatives
on a complex issue, or community dialogue on safety procedures.

The first example, modifying operations, is led by line managers. In the second case, the Board of Directors sets the new policy
and senior management ensures its implementation. In the last example, communications expertise leads the action.

Thus, issue management involves many parts of the organization.
This is why it is unique from traditional strategic planning (finance
and operations-bound), or corporate governance (entailing top officers), or public relations (relationships with the corporation's publics).

Issue management provides the mechanism for all of these functions to work in a team on one specific objective—closing the gap,
or—managing the issue.

The Second Generation

While the preceding paragraphs seem so simple and obvious, it
has taken nearly twenty years for the once revolutionary concepts
of issue management to become "common sense." In the heady,
expansionary years of the 1980s, issue management became a working function in most of the largest U.S. firms. Hundreds of "issue
managers" were hired, mostly working in a research capacity, although some 300 companies did go so far as to create senior level
or Board of Directors Committees on public issues.

What were the vulnerabilities of issue management, as corporations headed into the down-sizing decade on either side of 1990?

- The issue management "department" worked in isolation
  from the core activities of the firm. This predicament has
  been eliminated, as companies increasingly base their
  strategic planning process on issues due to the resulting
  competitive advantage, cost savings, and increased revenues.

- The impact of issues often was measured in qualitative,
  rather than quantitative terms. While there are many "subjective" components of dealing with values (a key raw material

in issue management), business measurement and validation
of resources depends on quantified results. This problem is
being mitigated by advancements in issue management, buf-
fered by developments in the accounting, legal, investment
management, and computer sciences professions, where the
impacts of issues are increasingly considered.

- There was no "accountability" figure for key issues, with
  compensation linked to performance. As a result, issues that
  were identified were sometimes improperly or inadequately
  addressed. Today, companies assign an "issue owner," usually
  head of the department most directly affected by the matter,
  to spearhead actions taken on an issue. The fact that the
  "issue owner" often works in an operations capacity further
  illustrates the obsolescence of erecting barriers between line
  and staff.

- The impact of issues was not well communicated to senior
  management. Companies were fascinated by these phenomena
  called "issues." How many were there, and which ones had
  anything to do with our company? Well, there were almost
  limitless numbers of issues, and the earnest issue managers
  worked tirelessly to identify hundreds of them. Among the
  34 tenets in his book *Maxims for the Issue Manager,*[3] Randall Scheel warns, "Don't drive a dump truck when you go
  to senior management. Decision-makers want intelligence, not
  massive amounts of data and information. . . . Most senior
  managers do not have the time nor desire to wallow in the
  minutiae of analytical detail," Scheel continues. "They usually require only two things: an understanding of how you
  arrived at your recommendation and confidence in your ability to reach a sound conclusion."

- Speaking of confidence, that too was often a missing ingred-
  ient. As James Lukaszewski observes in his book, *Influencing
  Public Attitudes*, "Failure has a variety of well-known, but
  far too common ingredients." Among them: "timidity, hesita-
  tion, and lack of foresight." Courage, salesmanship, credibility, and character are personal traits that should not be
  underestimated in championing a new way of doing business.

- Issue management was not well understood by its own practitioners. Too many well meaning novices gave lip service to the process, without really understanding its disciplines. Indications of issue management ignorance include statements like, "Issues can't be managed." When put into a position of proving their contribution to profitability, persons of these persuasions often proved expendable.

With the pitfalls of issue management identified, let's turn to a step-by-step list of actions to take in introducing and implementing issue management. These originally appeared in the 15 August 1994 edition of *Corporate Public Issues and Their Management.*[4]

Issue Management
from the Ground Up

What are the first steps in establishing an issue management initiative? It's not an overnight achievement: in fact, the suggested activities which appear below require four years for implementation. The suggested time frame assumes the manager will be able to focus "full time" attention on these initiatives.

Goals for the First
24-month Period

1. Study (Company) business structure, product/service lines, methods of operation, etc.
2. Review existing issue management capabilities at peer organizations through personal visits, consultative assistance, referencing organizations such as the Issue Management Council, or searching literature.
3. Determine issue management structure and process that is suitable for (Company).
4. Brief senior management and Board regarding findings to date, and recommend appropriate involvement for top executives. Secure their approval and support.
5. Work with human resources and others to structure issue action as part of the performance and review evaluation process.

6. Identify appropriate individuals and assemble Issue Management Committee.
7. Conduct stakeholder assessment surveys among primary stakeholders (customers, employees, shareholders), as an initial internal benchmark, and for "hard data" in building credibility and support for issue initiatives.
8. Identify top ten issues.
9. Determine "mile posts" and goals for change in issue development.
10. Assess progress to date, report, add resources or "sunset" as appropriate.

Goals for the Second 24-month Period

1. Assess impact of key issues, set priorities on top three to five issues.
2. Working through the Issue Management Committee and the Corporate Management Committee, determine position on key issues.
3. Assist in the creation of issue action plans.
4. Prepare Issue Briefs for key issues.
5. Help staff departments to communicate issues throughout the organization, for unified position, broader involvement, and employee "empowerment." Offer in-house issue management orientation and training sessions.
6. Establish on-line issues database for access to limited audience, and eventually broader use. Over time, make the system "interactive" with internal managers.
7. Consider assigning "full time" managers for (Company's) most important issues.
8. Conduct follow-up assessment to measure results with primary stakeholders.
9. Work with appropriate departments to expand stakeholder focus to secondary stakeholders, including communities, suppliers, special interest groups, media, financial analysts, opinion leaders, etc.
10. Assess progress to date, report, adjust as necessary and appropriate.

Down the Line:
4 Years and Beyond

- Seek opportunity aggressively by using issue management to help identify new markets, enhance image, secure leadership position in industry and private sector.
- Create non-voting stakeholder advisory panels on priority issues for truly interactive management.
- Broaden on-line services to include more detailed information about issues, stakeholders, issue action, etc., keeping privacy concerns in mind.
- Produce Annual Emerging Issues Survey
- And so on . . .

Once issue management is producing sound results, and action teams are working in cross-functional, interdisciplinary teams, it will become necessary to modernize the century-old corporate organization chart, to accommodate this new breed of management, and to provide corporations with the flexibility and agility to move into the 21st century. "The Corporate Imperative: Management of Profit and Policy," with its proposed model for corporate reorganization, appears as Chapter 13 in *Issue Management: Origins of the Future.*[5]

The Inevitable Corporate
Reorganization

An antiquated or traditional corporate organization chart, with inadequate or no provisions for managing societal change factors, as well as profit, can destroy morale, create executive and staff disillusion, frustrate announced corporate policies, and make even a profitable company a sitting duck for its adversaries.

Most corporate organization charts today are obsolete. They are designed to achieve performance in one single monolithic function—the manufacture of profit. All the traditional boxes connected by solid and dotted lines, representing profit center management, and the service staffs presumably on board to help the line managers, are keyed to the myth that profit is the first, foremost, and literally the *only* reason for being of capitalist institutions.

This is a costly myth, and it is time to dispel it. There is a second prime function of management—effective participation in the formulation of public policy, rather than mere reaction to policies made by others. Public policy and profit are equal in importance. Neither is secondary to the other.

"Business strategic planning" is a buzz-phrase and a misleading prop that helps perpetuate the myth that the sole objective of management is profit. In reality, strategic planning is two separate and discrete, but interdependent functions, with each deserving the most senior executive attention and top management skills.

The first of these twin functions is strategic profit planning. The second, equally important, is strategic policy planning.

Each must be coordinated with the other. Each demands executive commitment, talent, and budget. Each can be organizationally designed, charted and its results measured. Each is part and parcel of the control function of management. Management demeans its own profession by failure to manage policy with the same skills it applies to profit.

To demonstrate this thesis, we propose a real world corporate organization chart (see below). It challenges the myth that profit— now—is the most important of all management objectives, and suggests operational processes to achieve an even more basic corporate objective—survival itself. Profit is an end-product of meeting perceived needs through production and marketing. Survival, however, is based on corporate capacity to meet deeper needs arising from technological, social, economic, and political tidal waves.

This is a chart of *functions*—not of people. Smaller companies may well have one person occupying several of the boxes. Note the two principal functions of the "new management," as they appear in the ovals at the top left and right. The purpose of public policy management is positive—not reactive—participation in the formulation of public policy in order to assure corporate survival. The purpose of the operational units is, in one word, profit.

The **Board of Directors'** function is traditional: to determine over-all corporate policy, to evaluate results produced by management, and, when necessary, to change management.

The function of the **Chief Executive Office** is to execute policies laid down by the Board, earn a profit, justify investors' confidence, maintain productivity and an adequate share of the market, reward its employees, AND to manage public policy with as much skill as it exercises in managing the profit centers.

Note the composition of the **Executive Offices**, sometimes called

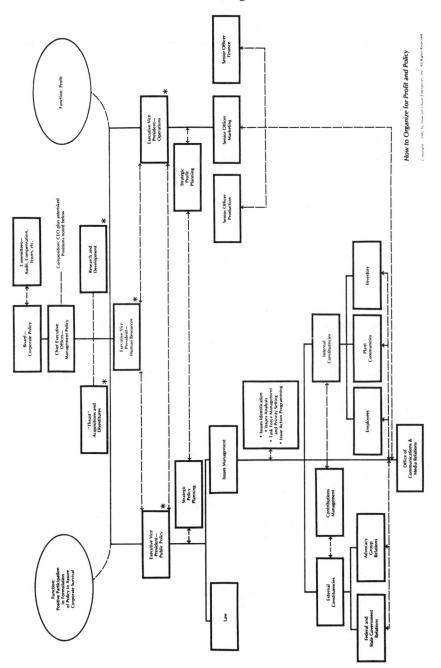

Source: Howard Chase, *Issue Management: Origins of the Future*, p. 141.

the Executive Management Committee. The chart calls for six members, officers in charge of: Corporate Thrust (direction of acquisitions and divestitures, etc.); Research and Development; the Executive Officer in charge of Operations; the Senior Officer for Human Resources; and the new Senior Officer in charge of Public Policy.

It is important to recognize that this organizational road map represents a 180-degree deviation from the traditional line and staff concepts. Historically, staff has been regarded as providing the services to the profit makers, either at their direct request or—often—because the CEO thinks the services *ought* to be useful. A too-frequent result of this division is that the profit center managers regard themselves as being taxed too heavily for services they have never requested and say they do not want.

In this real world organizational model, there is no line versus staff. There are, instead, two inter-related and integrated functions of equal importance—Public Policy and Profit. Note the uninterrupted dotted line representing continuous and full interchange of information between the Executive Vice President-Public Policy and the Executive Vice President-Operations.

We have conspicuously and consciously omitted detailed charting of hundreds of corporate functions relating to profit, and for purposes of this discussion and audience, focus more closely on the left side of the chart, public policy.

Public Policy Functions

Heading the left side of the chart is the **Executive Vice President-Public Policy**. Note specifically the two major subdivisions of this function: **Law and Issue Management**. There will be enraged reactions from the corporate general counsels who are accustomed by tradition to report directly to the CEO. Yet law professionally is recognized as the summation of "the customs and mores of the people." These are precisely the causative factors of economic, political, and social change with which the Public Policy executive must be concerned.

The appearance of communications at the bottom of the chart does not diminish its importance. As the ultimate stage of issue action programming, communications has as much opportunity to contribute to public policy as any of the other issue management specialists. In addition, the communications manager will be expected to listen to the distant drums of public sentiment, and to command and use the entire range of communications skills on behalf of the corporate public policy to which he or she has contributed.

The **Manager of Communications and Media Relations** has overwhelming responsibilities as charted. That office is the coordinated and articulated voice, as shown by the dotted lines, of all phases of both Policy and Profit management. Its responsibility not only for story placement and creative writing, but also for media research, content analysis, and above all for the "listening process" is vital to the issue identification and analysis stages of the issue management system.

To conclude: The functions of Profit and Public Policy are coordinate and equal in importance. It is the new responsibility of management to act accordingly. The more traditional organization charts ignore or underestimate the manageability of public policy. This can no longer be taken lightly. The authors hope that this chapter helps to chart a route to a more desired future.

Notes

1. Gollner, Andrew B. *Social Change and Corporate Strategy: The Expanding Role of Public Affairs.* Leesburg, VA: Issue Action Publications, Inc., 1983.

2. Chase, W. Howard. *Issue Management: Origins of the Future.* Leesburg, VA: Issue Action Publications, Inc., 1984.

3. Scheel, L. Randall. *Maxims for the Issue Manager.* Leesburg, VA: Issue Action Publications, Inc., 1991.

4. Crane, Teresa Yancey. "Issue Management from the Ground Up," *Corporate Public Issues and Their Management*, 15 August 1995.

5. Chase, W. Howard, *op. cit.*, pp. 135-150.

Chapter 11

Redesigning Corporate Philanthropy

John F. Coy

There is little question that the role of corporate philanthropy has changed dramatically in the last ten years. Many people in the field, including grant recipients and community organizations, would say that the term "corporate philanthropy" rapidly is becoming an oxymoron as more companies seek to strategically align their contributions with business interests. This does not imply that companies are self-serving, but more are expecting investments in contributions to at least address issues that are of interest to the business.

The trend toward such "enlightened self interest" is so strong in corporate giving that the use of the term philanthropy is seldom used by contributions managers. What used to be called philanthropy more often is a part of the corporate enterprise referred to as corporate citizenship, corporate support and contributions. Although these terms have slightly different meanings in different settings, the generally accepted definitions would include:

Corporate Citizenship is defined as those activities that the company voluntarily undertakes to have a positive impact on society and the environments in which it conducts business.

Corporate Support is defined as resources—cash and non-cash, grants or expenses—that the company uses to meet its citizenship goals.

Contributions are specifically the cash grants and measurable non-cash resources donated by the company to achieve corporate citizenship/community relations goals. Contributions may be made directly from the company, a foundation or a trust vehicle.

The greatest challenge, and perhaps the most difficult transition for corporate support in the modern corporation, will be casting aside the general perception that corporate giving is isolated, marginally relevant, and controlled by a very limited group of managers. The intended state for this function should be one of a thoughtful, strategic, and valued investment that reflects the vision, goals and interests of the company, that achieves results and makes a difference in the life of the company.

Striking a Balance

Most corporate officers and managers of contributions activities agree that corporations are not in the business of giving away money. Nor should companies expect these dollars to directly market or sell products, or only benefit the company. Most would agree that there is a middle ground between being altruistic and being self-serving.

There are three major targets or markets that benefit from contributions:

1. the community;
2. key stakeholders (employees, stockholders, public policy makers, etc.);
3. the company (values, goals, strategies, issues, etc.).

Graphically, these three targets or markets for contributions can be viewed as separate or converging as depicted in Figures 1 and 2.[1]

Few companies invest all of their contributions in serving only their own interests or, for that matter, any single target audience. Driven by changing corporate culture, community needs and corporate goals, most contributions programs find a balance between the target markets. There are certain programs and activities that companies will support regardless of the nature of their business. If a company employs people, has made significant investments in assets, and depends on the goodwill of a community to function effectively, that company will support those activities that serve the

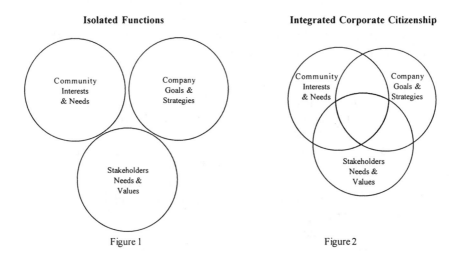

Isolated Functions   Integrated Corporate Citizenship

Community Interests & Needs

Company Goals & Strategies

Stakeholders Needs & Values

Community Interests & Needs

Company Goals & Strategies

Stakeholders Needs & Values

Figure 1   Figure 2

best interests of the community. The company receives indirect benefits by being a part of the community it supports. Generally, programs addressing the arts, culture, youth, health and human services, and education are the types of programs all companies will support in the belief that what is good for the community is good for the company.

Companies also make contributions related to the nature of their business or their core expertise and competencies. Telecommunications companies have an interest in communications technology; health-related companies support health intervention and prevention programs; and food companies are interested in nutrition.

Contributions also are made to organizations that represent the business of a company-customer connection, policy issues, research, and business relationships. Examples would include a cosmetic company supporting women's issues, a financial institution supporting economic development, a pharmaceutical company supporting a disease-related consumer or research group, or a retailer supporting consumer-related interests.

As more companies assess the value and relevancy of their investment in contributions, the more the three primary targets will converge. The shaded areas of figure 2 reflect those programs where community, key stakeholders, and company interests intersect. Support programs that address issues common to two or more markets add greater value to the function and often reflect a contributions program that is integrated with the goals of the company. In addition to balancing support for target markets, there are a number of other factors that need to be considered in developing a contributions program. The most common factors that need to be balanced include:

1. Local, regional, national, and international priorities;
2. Dollars available for reacting to requests versus dollars allocated to proactive strategies;
3. The level of support to be directed by employees through matching or other employee involvement activities;
4. The amount to be budgeted for corporate activities versus the level of contributions directed by operating units and department functions;
5. The level of support going to community versus business interests.

Trends Shaping the Contributions Function

CEO and Executive Leadership

The contributions function has been and will remain a highly placed function within most companies due, in large part, to the sensitivity and involvement of senior management. However, today's corporate leaders have a very different agenda than their colleagues did ten and fifteen years ago. Reengineering, right-sizing, globalization, and increased scrutiny from investors and board members are but a few of the issues competing for CEO and executive officer attention.

Although CEOs and senior management will remain closely involved in contributions activities, trends indicate they will delegate the strategy development, execution, and accountability to their management teams. Recently, a CEO of a *Fortune* top 50 company gave an excellent summary that reflects the thinking of most of his colleagues when he expressed his expectations for contributions:

The company's investment in these (contributions) activities should (1) be strategic enough for our employees and outside friends to understand what it is we hope to achieve; (2) make sense given the nature and location of our business and the issues we need to address; (3) reflect and involve the interests of our employees; (4) add value to our relationships with communities, organizations, and people with whom we share common interests and concerns; and (5) produce results and change that make a difference.

The New Corporation, Organization and Workplace

As with any corporate staff function, contributions managers and their departments are a part of the reshaping of the modern corporation. Their future will be driven by organizational concepts like horizontal, matrix, and process-driven organizations, and management styles that emphasize teamwork, cross-functional operations, customer focus, technology, and value-added outputs.[2]

Contributions programs will have to move from being seen as a highly placed, yet somewhat isolated activity to being strategically networked and integrated with company goals and a broad range of departments, field activities, and external stakeholders.

The four greatest challenges facing contributions managers as they position their role within the new corporation include:

1. Designing the function to be relevant within the company;
2. Adding value to the company;
3. Developing ownership, buy-in, and leadership within management;
4. Measuring outcomes and results.

As contributions managers find themselves competing for capital and management attention, they will have to utilize the same techniques and tools used by others within the company. If not, contributions will be relegated to an adjunct department and provided less than deserved attention and resources.

Changing Definition of Community

Given the dynamics of modern communications, the impact of technology, and the growth of highly visible special interest groups, society is redefining the meaning of community. Geographic boundaries alone no longer define a community.

In a broader sense, community can refer to very dispersed groups of people and organizations, yet united by a common, professional or emotional cause. Contributions and community relations managers, once tied to the more traditional definition of community, need to rethink what this new sense of community means and how these new communities can affect matters that are of interest to the corporation. These newly defined communities can be important to public policy, marketing, and relationship building much like traditional communities. However, working and communicating with these new communities will require new technologies, processes, strategies, and partnerships.

Valuing Employee Involvement

Employee involvement is one of the fastest growing components of corporate social responsibility in the 1990s. This is due, in large part, to the changing nature of work and the evolving relationship between employers and employees. It also reflects the realization that people are a natural extension of corporate citizenship and provide tremendous leverage to company investments. Today, nearly all corporate vision/mission statements address the value of employees and/or state the commitment to encourage and reward employee growth and empowerment.

As a result, more companies see their talented and motivated employees as important resources and as natural extensions of contributions and community relations activities. The added benefit of involving employees is that it links employee and company interests, enhancing morale and employee commitment.

Even in a time of "right-sizing" the work force, many of the nation's leading companies are placing a high priority on engaging employees in community and corporate citizenship activities. Employee involvement is a "win-win" proposition for the company, its communities and its employees. For companies that are sensitive to image and recognition, employee involvement is much more likely to receive media attention than other contributions or community relations activities.

Linking Contributions to the Marketplace

There is a growing body of research that indicates that the public is becoming more aware of a company's responsive citizenship.

One theory, supported by Frank Walker, Chairman of the Walker Group,[3] is that the life cycles of service and quality have matured as ways to differentiate products. More educated and sophisticated consumers now seek products associated with companies they can trust and know are responsible citizens.

Although this research topic is more than can be included in this chapter, it is important because it positions contributions as a potential element in establishing brand awareness and in linking image to customer and buyer activity. Recent consumer research shows that social responsibility and corporate citizenship increasingly influence consumer purchasing decisions:

1. Walker Research, 1994 - 47% of survey respondents are much more likely to buy from a socially responsible company;
2. Cone/Roper, 1993 - 78% of consumers are more likely to buy a product/service associated with a cause they care about; and
3. Wirthlin Group, 1993 - 33% of the public polled said that citizenship had a major influence on purchasing decisions.

More definitive research needs to be conducted to determine the linkage between contributions and its relationship to public and consumer perception regarding social responsibility and corporate citizenship. However, the increased evidence that consumer buying habits can be influenced by corporate citizenship holds promise that contributions and community relations are relevant and can be more closely linked to the success of a company.

The Competitive Nature of Contributions

The very nature of corporate contributions makes it less competitive than other corporate functions. As in the human resources, quality management, planning, stockholder relations, and even public affairs functions, information is shared freely within the contributions community with the goal of strengthening the field and society rather than gaining any particularly competitive advantage. This may change.

The opportunity to tie contributions to the customer represents good news internally, but could expand the competitive nature of contributions externally if contributions are linked to image, brand and product differentiation. Already many companies are responding to a more competitive environment. For highly regulated industries, like telecommunications and energy, contributions historically have been an extension of their right to do business within a protected franchise or regulated area. Contributions activities were simply a part of the company's obligation to the community and were structured accordingly.

Deregulation of the energy and telecommunications industries, greater competition from overseas companies, the growing use of corporate advertising to promote citizenship, and brand and corporate imaging campaigns all are making contributions activities more competitive. The more aggressive use of cause-related marketing and paid advertising to highlight good deeds is an indication that competition will be a greater factor in future contributions strategies.

The increased nature of competition will draw contributions closer to those corporate activities that are deemed to be industry competitive—marketing, recruiting, research, public policy, brand awareness, employee morale, customer relations, and market value. How any one company uses its contributions resources will be determined by what the company deems its greatest priorities and how it can best leverage its resources. The circles in Figure 1 will increasingly overlap as companies seek to support those activities that are mutually beneficial to the community and are consistent with business interests.

National Trends in Contributions

Research conducted on more than 150 U.S. companies[4] surfaced a number of key trends that are influencing the direction of corporate contributions.

1. Companies are developing comprehensive strategies that are aligned with company vision, mission and goals to leverage resources and to influence key stakeholders.

2. Corporate citizenship (contributions, community relations, corporate support) includes a range of company cash, non-cash, and human resources—a portfolio approach to investing company core resources and competencies.

3. Contributions and related community affairs activities are integrated with other key corporate functions such as communications, human resources, marketing, research, and government and customer relations.

4. Companies are becoming more issue-driven and proactive rather than reacting to requests for support. Most are making larger, long-term investments in priority areas. Nonprofit organizations are more often the channel and partner for implementing a solution to an issue.

5. Long-term partnerships with nonprofit organizations are becoming more important than annual or sporadic support.

6. Companies, more conscious about achieving results and having an impact on an issue, are measuring the results of larger grants.

7. With the changing nature of the workplace, employee involvement is becoming a high priority activity for contributions and community relations.

8. Communications, recognition, image, and branding are having an increased influence on contributions strategies and expectations.

9. Companies are expanding the use of outside services for data processing, special program management, administrative functions, and program assessment.

Future Management

The modern corporation and workplace of the future pose a number of challenges to contributions managers. Yet, in many ways, the future is a natural fit for how contributions should be managed.[5] *Effective* contributions management is not solely the responsibility of a department *within* the company. Rather, it is a function *of* the company—one that is networked, is highly integrated, has strong management leadership, has employee ownership, and is contributing to the long-term success of the company. Contributions managers need to understand that their function is one of corporate stewardship, not departmental ownership. They will need to know how to manage a program that should have the vested interest and involvement of a wide range of managers. Although contributions and community relations activities are a departmental responsibility, it is a company-wide responsibility to implement an effective program.

> We must wake up to the fact that authority is no longer vested in a place on the organization chart, but in the ability to do a job better for the customer.
> — James Champy, *Reengineering Management*

Given the pressure of costs and staff size, contributions managers benefit by doing all of the things expected in the modern organization—establishing teams, decentralizing process, and empowering business units and employees. Increasingly, the contributions manager's job will be to identify and interpret issues and opportunities of mutual benefit to the company and its external constituencies. This will mean that the successful manager will need to have both a firm grasp of the direction of the enterprise and a thorough understanding of the needs and opportunities in the outside environment. The challenge of being an effective and successful contributions manager includes the ability to understand and match the interests and needs of both the internal and external worlds and to become a valued advisor to senior and operations managers.

Designing the Future Program

To assume that contributions and community relations will look and act the same after a company has been reengineered, right-sized, or has established a new vision and culture is a mistake. It may take time for the processes and culture to finally find their way to the contributions function, but eventually contributions comes under assessment. Smart managers don't wait for the process to trickle down. The redesign or reengineering of the contributions function should be undertaken just as aggressively as any other function in the modern corporation.

Redesigning or reengineering the contributions function should be guided by a number of key questions.

1. What role and value should contributions provide the company?
2. What are the major success factors and how will these be measured?
3. What are the critical actions needed to fulfill the success factors?
4. What are the best or required processes to support the critical actions?
5. What actions, information, data, or inputs drive each process?
6. Who are the major providers of inputs into each process?
7. How should the function be structured to achieve success?

Self-Evaluation

In any field, it is helpful to conduct a self-evaluation. The following checklist of characteristics has been developed from years of assessment and benchmark work. It represents the standards demonstrated by the country's leading corporate contributions and community relations programs.

Senior Management Commitment

_____ A three-to-five year commitment to invest a certain level of income in the grantmaking process.

_____ A program based on long-term outcomes, not driven by annual profits and grantmaking budgets, yet responsive to shifts in profit.

_____ A well-informed, involved and committed chairman and senior management team.

Strategic Direction

_____ A clearly defined mission statement and set of objectives that establish company expectations for contributions and related activities.

_____ A strategic plan or program focus that defines the direction and interest of contributions and all related activities, and reflects the company's community, social, and business interests.

_____ A company-wide strategy that integrates and leverages contributions, community relations, and related employee and non-cash giving activities into a broader corporate support function.

_____ A program that involves employees.

Program Management

_____ Senior management approval of a concise set of corporate policies, procedures and guidelines for developing and implementing the program.

_____ The involvement of key corporate departments, operating units or management and employee advisory groups to help guide and implement corporate support activities.

_____ A program/department that utilizes management tools like strategic planning, quality management, program assessment, and evaluation.

_____ A program that focuses more on issues than on organizations and categories of giving as the justification for department and grant budgets.

_____ A budgeting and management accountability process tied to a strategic plan or program focus, to include formal reporting procedures.

_____ A management team that makes effective use of outside resources and peer associations to explore new management, funding, and program opportunities.

_____ A program that invests in internal and external communications to build support and value for its activities.

_____ A process for managing exceptions to policy as a part of doing business, yet structured to fit within existing program guidelines.

Program Staffing

____ A program directed by a manager who reports to a vice-president or higher management level, and has access to the senior management team.

____ A results-driven, creative, and responsive program manager and staff.

____ A manager and staff who are as knowledgeable about nonprofit management as they are about corporate management practices and issues, and who have the stature to broker the mutual interest of both within the company.

____ An appropriate investment in staff, training and professional development, technology, and related resources in line with program objectives, grant budget, and program focus.

If the program includes 14 or more of these characteristics, it is among the nation's best contributions and community relations programs.

A score of 10 to 13 characteristics indicates opportunity for improvement.

Less than 10 suggests the company is not leveraging its contributions and community relations resources effectively.

Notes

1. David Ford, Vice President & Director of Philanthropy, Chase Manhattan Bank, is credited for introducing the author to the converging circles concept of contributions.
2. In the past two years, *Fortune, Business Week*, and other business journals have covered numerous topics related to reengineering, the organization

and processes of modern corporations, leadership, and the future work place.

3. Walker Group is the 13th largest marketing research firm in the country. Its 1994 *National Survey Measuring the Impact of Corporate Social Responsibility* produced major findings about the relationship between corporate character and public and consumer behavior.

4. The Consulting Network has conducted more than 50 benchmark studies, in addition to authoring *Managing Corporate Support: Responses to Challenging Times*, a study of 100 companies published by the Indiana University Center on Philanthropy in 1992.

5. There are three texts recommended for contributions and community relations managers interested in reengineering and the future workplace. They are: Michael Hammer and James Champy, *Reengineering the Corporation* (New York: HarperCollins Publishers, Inc., 1993). James Champy, *Reengineering Management* (New York: HarperCollins Publishers, Inc., 1995). Joseph H. Boyett and Henry P. Conn, *Workplace 2000* (New York: Penguin Group, 1992).

Chapter 12

Public Affairs and
Risk Communications

William J. Koch and
Patrick A. McGee

The scenario is one that unfolds day in and day out across the country. Citizens, concerned over perceived risks to their personal health and safety, demand action by government. Public officials, elected by those citizens and ever cognizant of responding to constituent needs, pass legislation to eliminate the risks. Along the way, the voice of reason is often silenced by the fury of emotions.

Asbestos. Alar. Three Mile Island. Exxon *Valdez*. Savings and loans. Landfills. Seat belts. Passive smoke. Tylenol. Ivan Boesky. AIDS. Nuclear waste. Breast implants. Saccharine. E-coli bacteria. Tainted blood supply. Dalkon shield. Firestone 500. Mothers Against Drunk Driving. Love Canal. Nestle baby formula. Agent Orange. Air bags. Oklahoma City. And the list goes on and on.

The primary problem faced when dealing with questions of risk is that science often loses to sentiment and facts are replaced by fears.

Peter Sandman, Ph.D., is a faculty member at Rutgers University and founder of the Environmental Communication Research Program at that institution. He is a noted risk communication researcher, speaker and consultant and he is well known for promoting this formula for risk communication:

Risk = Hazard + Outrage

If you make a list of environmental health risks in order of how many people they kill each year, then list them again in order of how alarming they are to the general public, the two lists will be very different. Risk managers often deduce from this that people's perception of risk is ignorant or irrational. But a better way to conceptualize the problem is that people define 'risk' more broadly than the risk assessment profession. It helps to stipulate new definitions. Call the death rate 'hazard'; call everything else that the public considers part of risk, collectively, 'outrage'. Risk, properly conceived, includes both hazard and outrage.[1]

In his equation, Sandman indicates that the *hazard* might be death rate statistics, or in other words, the facts of the matter. *Outrage*, on the other hand says Sandman, can be driven by a number of factors identified by risk perception researchers. They include: voluntariness, personal control, fairness, process, morality, familiarity, memorability, dread, diffusion in time and space. These factors tend to be gut and heart originating. In other words, the visceral and emotional.

The significance of the use of the word "risk" to describe that which is of concern to the public points out one of the fundamental problems inherent in "risk communications."

In defining the word "risk," Webster's uses comments such as the "possibility of loss or injury," "peril," "a dangerous element," and a "specified hazard." No matter how you slice it, dice it or package it—those all add up to trouble.

Consequently, any discussion about risk or any attempt at risk communication automatically starts from a negative context before the first explanations are even given. Therein lies the greatest challenge for public affairs practitioners. It also explains the cause and effect relationship that makes public affairs so much a part of the risk communications environment.

While Sandman's equation has served us well over the years, we believe it's time to revise the equation slightly to put the topic into clearer perspective. We suggest replacing Risk with Threat, creating the following formula:

Threat = Hazard + Outrage

It appears that the business world and academia both have a fondness for the word risk. There are risk managers and risk assessments. Indeed it is a word evocative of reasoning and it can be spelled out in black and white and shown on a balance sheet as to its impact on the bottom line.

Unfortunately, agreement on what constitutes "reason" is usually never to be found in public discussions of risks. To the contrary, those discussions almost always become emotional and defensive. And in some cases, they deteriorate so far as to appear irrational and unreasonable. (Company representatives try not to show their emotionalism in public, although it often comes out. But they usually refuse to equate it with the emotion of the community.)

People facing risks—perceived or real—feel threatened.

In his lectures, Sandman sometimes uses an analogy where a first-time skier voluntarily "risks" life and limb to ski down a steep slope. On the other hand, Sandman describes the "outrage" of a second person bound head to foot and dragged against his will to the edge of the same slope. He uses this analogy to try and show us the difference between voluntary and involuntary participation in risk assessment.

We can use this same analogy to make our point. The voluntary skier is taking a risk, a chance. It's like a roll of the dice in Las Vegas. He might make it down the hill in one piece, and he might not. But in no way do thoughts of peril or threat enter his mind— the rush and excitement of skiing down the slope are paramount. The second person, however, has no thoughts of excitement. Instead, he feels threatened by the thought of rocketing down the hill.

To engage in a risk assessment discussion with these two people would result in entirely different intellectual and emotional responses. But we doubt that anyone would have difficulty understanding the reaction from the involuntary skier, faced with a threat through no real fault of his own. He appears to be an innocent victim. Most of us, would think it a criminal act to subject this person to such a threat. We know he can't get away and we're not much interested in arguments about the risk of sliding down this particular hill.

Extending this analogy takes us neatly into the public affairs arena. Once again, most of us would be hoping that the authorities would step in and save our victim from his precarious fate. In other words, seen in the light of *risk = threat* and *public = victim*, we would expect intervention. A legislative, regulatory or judicial intervention would not surprise us. In fact, it would be welcome. But in business or in the day-to-day operations of most organizations, that intervention would be a very unwelcome intrusion. Therein lies the essential challenge of risk communications.

Just Whose Words Are We Using?

The problem with using "risk" to describe the field of risk communications is that it is almost always the proponent's word, seldom the opponent's word.

Proponents usually say: "What is this wild emotional response we get from these people, they won't even listen to reason. They just refuse to discuss it." Most times, the "it" they are referring to is the risk. The public, on the other hand, sees "it" as the threat. Their conversation goes like this: "I can't believe that they think they can just come in here and threaten our health like that and we're supposed to just sit here and listen to their scientific explanations of how this can't hurt us." Of course, the rest of that dialogue is usually unprintable in a family newspaper.

While legislators and public servants with enforcement responsibility may be counseled by experts on risk, they are often persuaded quite readily by those who feel they are being threatened. They may understand the intellectual argument of risk assessment and risk management, however, the emotion—the "outrage" as Sandman would put it—is a potent force to be faced, particularly by elected representatives who face the "assessment" of their constituents on a regular basis.

"A common side effect of a public perception crisis is an unwanted increase in attention from the public sector. Regulatory, health and safety agencies often get into the act, and with them come the special interest groups. Few things are as disruptive to a chief executive's operating style as having to testify at congressional hearings and submit to endless investigations by regulatory agencies," says Gerald Meyers, former Chairman of American Motors.[2]

Meyers also reflects Sandman's comment about risk managers' views of the public when they don't understand or agree with the company's risk assessment.

There is a strong tendency for an executive caught in situations like these (crisis) to argue about the difference between 'perception'— the way the world sees what's going on—and 'reality'—the way he sees it. In fact, there is no gap between appearance and reality. Reality is what the public perceives to be true, and if the public grasps reality in a certain way, that is what it becomes. Reality is what your customers, suppliers, bankers, regulators, and other constituencies believe. But what about scientific truth, the facts that can be proven? They don't apply. Most commercial crises are not subject to repeatability or laboratory tests under controlled conditions to establish 'truth'.[3]

It would appear from these comments that risk communicators should have an understanding of how the public thinks and what makes them act. Behavior driven by outrage and the perception of threats should not be chalked up to mere ignorance, nor is it irrational or illogical. It is often perfectly logical behavior from the opponent's perspective.

One theory of behavior explains why perception is such a strong trigger for public outrage.

Perceptual Control Theory (PCT) is about the inborn nature of human beings as independent organisms who control themselves, who are inherently in charge of what happens to themselves.

PCT says that what drives us to do what we do is our comparing what we want to how we see things and if there is a difference between them, we act to correct that difference, either by changing what we want or by acting to change what doesn't conform to what we want.

The details of how we perform the actions are of little importance to us. Getting the environment to conform to what we want is our major concern. We act in whatever ways are necessary to perceive what we want to perceive and we attempt to get around any disturbances we encounter.[4]

If our want is the good health of ourselves, our families and our friends, but we perceive that a proposed facility to be sited near our home is a threat to that want, we will act to change the environment to make our perception—that we are safe—conform to our want. (PCT does allow for our want to be changed or modified, rather than or in conjunction with, a change in the environment.)

In a good health example, some of the actions we are likely to take are to tell the authorities who have permitting responsibilities that we don't want that facility near our home because it is a threat. As long as we are not prepared to change our want, then we are very likely to continue to take whatever actions we can to change the situation to match our perception of what it will take to ensure our good health.

Perhaps one of the most comprehensive sources of information on the subject of risk communication is the Student Manual for the Chemical Manufacturers Association (CMA) Risk Communication Workshop.[5] In it is a list, compiled by risk researchers, of the eight categories of community concerns:

Community Concerns

1. Health
2. Safety
3. Environmental
4. Aesthetic Issues
5. Equity Issues
6. Cultural/Symbolic Issues
7. Legal/Statutory Issues
8. Public Policy Issues

While the CMA labels these concerns, they also speak to the basic values of the community. Values are a key to really understanding the members of the community—they are the essence of their wants. How do we educate and inform the public about the true nature of any given "risk"? How can a proponent change a threat perception into an acceptable risk perception?

One must first understand the values of those one is addressing. This is because outrage is driven by the wants and needs of the individuals and communities; they are central to the logic of the opponent in dealing with and trying to gain control of situations perceived not to be in sync with their wants and needs.

Values research has been around for some time. It identifies values held by an individual and the factors that affect those values negatively and positively. There is most often a hierarchy of what triggers behavior based on values. A technique called "mapping" allows researchers and practitioners to lay out the data in order to establish a route and sequence of communication to positively connect with the most deeply held values of the subject.

Bridge the Credibility Gap

While understanding the values of those impacted by risk is a major element in risk communication, another is trust and credibility. Most risk communications advocates today talk about these essentials. Yet "their words don't inform their intentions," to borrow a phrase from Shakespeare. We still use the word "risk"—the proponent's word—while the authorities hear the word "threat"—the opponent's word. There is a credibility gap apparent immediately.

Trust and credibility—the building blocks to relationships—take time to build and to grow. There is no such thing as a "drive-by relationship," as many executives and senior managers would prefer. Relationship-building is an evolutionary process, not a revolutionary process and one that is often carried out by endangered species. Corporate downsizings, rightsizings and reengineering often eliminate relationship-builders on one hand while voter discontent or revolt takes its toll on relationship partners on the other. To show how changing faces can affect relationships, we'll use education reform as an example.

In 1989, then-President Bush convened an Education Summit— attended by governors from 50 states—to focus attention on reform. Today, more than 40 of those 50 governors, as well as Mr. Bush, are no longer in office. Not much is heard about the Education Summit today and education reform remains largely stalled.

Relationships are between people, not institutions. And only through effective relationships, built over time, will trust and credibility be earned.

An essential element in risk communications is the trust in the communicator by the receiver. That level of credibility determines the impact of the information or messages communicated.

Therefore, if the communicator is trying to provide information to an audience to allow that audience to better judge the risk or threat of a situation, the success of that communication is dependent less on the weight of the facts than on the strength of the trust that the receiver has in the communicator.

Vincent Covello, Ph.D., a respected authority on risk communications and Director of the Center for Risk Communication at the University of California at Berkeley, says the first goal in risk communication is establishing trust and credibility. He says that research indicates that four key factors influence trust and credibility:[6]

- Perceived caring and empathy   50%
  (assessed in the first 30 seconds)
- Competence and expertise   15-20%
- Honesty and openness   15-20%
- Dedication and commitment   15-20%

If the proponents do not have trust and credibility, or are an un-
known quantity, it is extremely precarious to have their foothold
anchored only in statistics and actuarial models of probability. This
is especially so while people who control their fate are responding
from fear and outrage. Our experience is that in these situations,
the opponents are quite ready to chip or hammer away to dislodge
a proponent if they believe that it will eliminate the perceived threat.

In these scenarios, the proponents can forget about treating the
situation as a community relations problem. They'd better start thinking about it as a public affairs problem because that's where it tends
to go when the opponents don't believe what the proponent's spokesperson has to say. The solution for the opponents is a choice of
legislation, regulation or litigation.

Don't Throw Statistics at Perceptions
and Emotions

Why did the Exxon *Valdez* incident drive new rules and regulations? The perception was that the company did not care about the
threat to the environment, to the local economy or to the health of
the citizens of Alaska. As far from the truth as this might be, the
perception remained and the legislators acted. Perhaps they just
didn't ever feel that Exxon understood how people felt being under
the threat of another spill. It appears to be two separate worlds when
discussing risk on the one hand while someone passionately wants
to talk about the threat on the other hand.

Leading edge communications thinker and PRSA Fellow Patrick
Jackson lists risk communications as one of the 15 key trends that
he sees in public relations. Jackson believes that all communications challenges should involve the principles of risk communication.[7]

He likes to say that people apply only about 10 percent logic
(brain) to communication and 90 percent intuition (gut) and emotion (heart).[8] It is amazing that so many organizations rely totally
on the propositional argument in communicating to important, and
often hostile, audiences. They become frustrated when their communication is met with a visceral response. Given Jackson's ratio,
it should be no surprise.

Clearly, risk communication is far more complex than just communicating statistical data reflecting risk assessment. Effective risk

communication must draw on the social and behavioral sciences for communication theories and research. That, combined with specific communication skills and techniques, will enable the communicator to effectively reach an audience not particularly open to science, statistics or risk assessment.

It would appear that, as Marshall McLuhan once postulated, "the medium is the message." This may explain why an audience feels the communication rather than listens to it. Relational communications are infused with feelings rather than facts. Transactions are what Sgt. Friday of the old *Dragnet* series was into: "The facts. Just the facts."

The CMA manual provides a set of rules to guide practitioners in risk communication:[9]

Seven Cardinal Rules of Risk Communication

- Accept and involve the public as a legitimate partner
- Plan carefully and evaluate your efforts
- Listen to your audience
- Be honest, frank and open
- Coordinate and collaborate with other credible sources
- Meet the needs of the media
- Speak clearly and with compassion

Is there anything different that must happen in communicating risk in a public affairs context? We don't believe there is anything fundamentally different in the approach. However, as John Paluszek, Fellow PRSA and President of Ketchum Public Affairs, says, "public affairs is a special kind of public relations because there's almost always a lot more at stake in a public affairs program."[10]

Legislators may find risks acceptable and refuse to indulge those who complain about a problem. However, if the public frames the issue not as a risk, but as a threat, it will be difficult for most elected officials to ignore their pleas. Most likely they will respond to the concerns of one's constituents.

How often have we seen that emotive energy drive legislators, even when close advisors or experts say there is no risk? From their perspective, what better service can a legislator provide than to ease, reduce or eliminate a threat to one's constituents?

While public opinion may be the engine that drives public policy, there is little doubt that public reaction to real or perceived risks throws that engine into overdrive.

As noted above, risk communications is an evolving field. The

---

An Historical Perspective

Baruch Fischoff, professor of Social and Decision Sciences, Carnegie Mellon University, created an historical perspective of 20 years of risk communication. *pr reporter* condensed it for us in July, 1994:

1. All we have to do is to get the numbers right;
2. All we have to do is tell them the numbers;
3. All we have to do is explain what we mean by the numbers;
4. All we have to do is show them that they've accepted similar risks in the past;
5. All we have to do is to show them that it's a good deal for them;
6. All we have to do is treat them nice;
7. All we have to do is make them partners.

---

behaviorists continue to study how people make decisions, relate to each other and their environment. Risk communications specialists work on translating the academic theories and research into practical techniques. Organizations and individuals apply all of this—for better or worse—to their relationships with their publics.

Public affairs practitioners are, as well, deeply involved in the development of the field. At the nexus of these endeavors lies an ongoing challenge to improve our knowledge and application of these fields of communication.

A Contemporary Public Affairs
Case of "Risk As Threat"

The concept of genetic engineering or recombinant DNA technology has been around for a long time, but when scientists started making great progress with plants and animals, Hollywood raised the "threat" of this new technology in the hit movie *Jurassic Park*. Not only was the movie a special effects masterpiece, but it carried the additional credibility of superstar filmmaker Steven Spielberg. And where does the public sit on the issue of biotechnology, the field of science responsible for genetic engineering?

A consumer study for the Canadian government found that consumers in that country were "unfamiliar with the subject of biotechnology; have not reconciled how biotech developments fit into their value system; are optimistic regarding potential benefits, yet may not accept all biotech products due to wariness of previous mishaps of technology; believe that governments should regulate biotech with a view to public safety; and support the idea of labeling biotech products."[11]

Douglas Powell, doctoral cinadiate at the University of Guelph in Ontario, Canada says that, "genetic engineering has now replaced nuclear energy as the science out of control." Powell's prescription for communicating with a "shopping public (to whom) trust is more important than science" is to use carefully constructed risk messages.[12]

In 1995 Canadians were able to buy *Jurassic Park* on videocassette but not biotech milk. Although it is on the shelf in the U.S., the Canadian government is not prepared to allow its sale without further study.

Contributing to this decision is a stream of media reports and letters to the editor against biotech milk, claiming too much health risk. Curiously, there is no consumer outrage. Politicians have a *perception* of significant opposition suggested by polls showing a strong suspicion of biotech products.

The major proponents, Monsanto and *some* of the dairy farmers, have relied on propositional arguments to support their case.

Notes

1. *Risk Communication: Facing Public Outrage*, Peter Sandman, *EPA Journal*, Pages 21-22, November 1987, Environmental Protection Agency, Washington, D.C.

2. *When It Hits the Fan*, Gerald C. Myers, John Holusha, Page 58, Houghton Mifflin Company, Boston 1986.

3. Op. cit. p. 64.

4. Perceptual Control Theory (PCT), is a model of how the brain works, based on the research and writings of William T. Powers, a physicist and

research scientist. Edward E. Ford, a Phoenix social workers, author and lecturer on the application of PCT to discipline in schools, describes PCT on page 12, *Discipline for Home and School*, Brandt Publishing, Scottsdale 1994.

5. *Risk Communication, The CMA Workshop Student Manual*, prepared for The Chemical Manufacturers Association by Rowan & Blewitt Incorporated and The Center for Risk Communication at Columbia University, edited and produced by Bob Amyot, Vincent Covello, Erin Donovan, Sarah Peasley and John Slavick. © Chemical Manufacturers Association 1989.

6. *Improving the Odds*, page 1, *Rapport*, Vol. 9, No. 3, Summer 1994, National Institute of Nutrition, Ottawa, Canada.

7. Patrick Jackson, APR, Fellow PRSA, Senior Counsel, Jackson, Jackson & Wagner, Exeter, N.H., speaking at a Canadian Public Relations Society workshop, February 8, 1995 in Toronto, Canada.

8. Ibid.

9. *Risk Communication, The CMA Workshop Student Manual*, © Chemical Manufacturers Association 1989.

10. Brochure, Ketchum Public Affairs Division, Ketchum Public Relations, New York, New York.

11. *The Agbiotech Bulletin*, April 1995, page 10, Ag-West Biotech Inc., Saskatoon, Canada.

12. *Talking About Food Biotechnology*, Douglas Powell, AG Care UPDATE, Spring/Summer 1994, Agricultural Groups Concerned About Resources and the Environment, Toronto, Canada.

Chapter 13

Public Affairs in the Public Sector

Gary D. Avery, Janet M. Bedrosian,
Sylvia J. Brucchi, Lloyd B. Dennis,
James F. Keane, Gary Koch

Let the public service be a proud and noble trust.
—John F. Kennedy

Paraphrasing F. Scott Fitzgerald, the practice of public relations in the public sector really is different from the craft practiced elsewhere. To begin with, unlike the private sector, one looking expressly for an "Office of Public Relations" in government will almost never find it. In fact, if the search is in the Federal government one will positively never find it for there is an abhorrence of the term public relations in the Federal Government as old, at least, as 1913: "Appropriated funds may not be used to pay publicity experts. . . ."[1] This ban was reiterated verbatim in 1966 (P. L. 89-554), in the Great Society Congress. Moreover bringing this odd stream of vilification of an entire profession—public relations—virtually up to the moment, one could find in the FY 1996 federal budget language requiring one Federal department to reduce the size of its public affairs staff: "This committee believes these positions should not be preserved at the expense of staffing for direct mission-related programs."[2]

Notwithstanding this long-standing and unwarranted denigration of a legitimate profession, the fact is that public relations exists in government at all levels and serves the interest of both the governed and governors well. This Chapter will explicate this fact and move beyond it to explore other important considerations involving the practice of public relations in governmental settings.

At the end of the Chapter, two "hands on" documents are added to aid the reader in moving past theory to real-world applicability and implementation. These include: (A) Public Sector Public Affairs Goals; and (B) Developing an Action Plan for Working with Communities.

Nature and Scope

In 1981, one observer of the Washington scene commented that "President Reagan is supported by a 'cast of thousands'—agency public affairs specialists who not only dispense information but also promote their agencies."[3] Just how accurate was that assessment of the scope of Federal government public affairs activity then and now?

The starting point for this analysis must surely be with an appreciation of a single fact: That *the practice of public relations called public affairs* can be discerned in public sector offices at virtually every level whether federal, state, county or municipal. While numbers cannot begin to explain the nature or extent of public affairs practice in governmental settings, they can add understanding to a discussion of this activity. The National Association of Government Communicators estimates that, across all standard levels of government, some 40,000 public affairs practitioners are at work.[4] This is an intriguing number because, if one examines the latest available Federal Government civilian workforce statistics, public affairs practitioners government-wide total just 4,438.[5] But however modest this number appears, it would at least appear to be consistent with a prior count of "public information" professionals—some "2,323"—which appeared in the same civilian workforce statistics in 1967. Relying on these data solely, one could easily conclude that, against a backdrop of some 2.5 million civilian federal employees, the number of public affairs practitioners is small, if not minute.

As is often true with statistics, and perhaps especially true of statistics generated in the public sector, a closer look may yield new or different information. For example, in 1993 the Hon. David Pry-

or, chairman of the United States Senate Subcommittee on Federal Services, Post Office and Civil Service, requested the United States Government Accounting Office to study this specific question and provide Congress with "information on the number of personnel engaged in public and Congressional affairs activities in 31 selected agencies."[6] This request sought, in effect, an update of a similar GAO report provided in 1986. Covered by the 1993 Report were civil service employees as well as political appointees in these categories for the years 1991 and 1992. The findings of the 1993 GAO Report are stated forthrightly:

> Based on agency-provided data, excluding the Department of Defense, the estimated full-time equivalent (FTE) count of personnel engaged in public and congressional affairs during fiscal years 1991 and 1992 appears to have increased since fiscal year 1985. For example, agencies reported that the estimated combined public and congressional affairs FTEs during fiscal years 1991 and 1992 was 6,382 and 6,673 respectively compared with 6,293 in fiscal year 1985."[7]

Given the broad sweep of this GAO study, its reliability would appear to be quite high. The GAO surveyed the same 31 agencies each time, including 14 cabinet departments and 17 independent agencies.

Mission and Function

This data establishes beyond refutation the fact that public relations is, indeed, present and practiced at all levels of American government despite an ironic propensity on the part of government policy makers to (a) deny it and (b) give it the name 'public affairs.' It does provide helpful guidance to those seeking public relations 'shops' in governmental settings although it does nothing to bring clarity to the long-standing confusion in the minds of many about the practical, definitional differences between public relations and public affairs.

Motivation

A key starting point in attempting to understand the mission and functions of public affairs in government can be discerned in *motivation*. Public affairs practitioners in government settings derive satisfaction not from watching their corporate employer grow and prosper, perhaps even sharing in that prosperity personally in terms of compensation or upward mobility, but from a sense of mission. Specifically, they derive a sense of identity and satisfaction from serving fellow citizens. Public affairs practitioners in government "know their jobs exist because various publics need to know about the goods and services offered by government agencies."[8]

Moreover, while public affairs officers in corporate settings may or may not find their energies focused on a truly mass audience, by definition the audience for public sector communications activities is large with a capital "L". After all, "citizens need to know how to file their taxes, obtain social security benefits, get their trash removed, summon the police or fire departments, and obtain many other government services. Government public affairs specialists provide this information, and more. Frequently the biggest challenge of government public affairs is overcoming public apathy to give people the information they need to make informed choices."[9] Equally important, of course, is the need to obtain from the public informed consent to governmental policies and practices.

Social Purpose

Finally, while public affairs officers almost always utilize the same tools and tactics as are used in private sector settings, the public sector practitioners have the satisfaction of knowing that their work not infrequently benefits larger *social purpose*, not merely to increased earnings or market share. Indeed, the source of much gratification for public sector practitioners originates in "the mission-oriented nature of government [which] means agencies often devote more resources to products with a purely social value than can be justified in the private sector."[10] Some government public relations practitioners are called *public information officers* which seems to indicate the expectation for simple one-way information out communications. Most federal level practitioners are called *public affairs officers* or *specialists* which implies broader, more complex duties. The public information model may be appropriate for some government organizations and institutions (perhaps such as the Supreme Court and the Office of Management and Budget) but the two-way asymmetric model is probably most appropriate for government agencies at most levels.

As to the chief functions of public affairs in government, *major goals* typically are:

- increasing public awareness
  — of the results of government research
  — of the availability of government services
  — of rights under new laws or regulations
- changing inimical personal behavior;
- keeping legislators informed;
- providing a 'window-out' function for agency managers, soliciting, obtaining and analyzing public input/opinion;[11] and
- facilitating the two-way communication between agencies and citizens that often results in modification of agency action as well as citizen behavior.

Above all else, communicators in government "practice public affairs when they develop plans to build and maintain relationships with various constituencies, such as industry associations, consumer groups, professional associations, and groups of officials at other levels of government. . . ."[12] In fact, a more complete listing of these relationship-building functions might include activists, "consumer affairs, legislative affairs, media relations, publishing, audiovisual production, liaison with various specialized organizations, internal communications, and responding to requests for information under the Freedom of Information Act or other government programs."[13]

As is readily apparent, these typical functions performed by public affairs practitioners in government, with the single exception of FOIA, parallel those to be found in similar settings outside government.

Professionalism in the Government Practice: Agency Advocate or Public Servant?

Most nongovernmental public relations practitioners quite clearly understand their role as client advocates. The same may be true for public sector practitioners but the problem of defining the client is not always an easy one for public affairs specialists in government. Is it the current Administration of elected officials who naturally possess a political agenda which bears on their own re-election and survival? Or, again, is it the amorphous "public" that all civil servants are sworn to serve? The answer is clearly both. Among the entire universe of public affairs officers, this split personality is unique to *government* public affairs specialists at all levels.

This is typified by the two primary categories of public affairs specialists, *career* versus *political* appointees. Political appointees, generally at higher levels, serve at the pleasure of the Administration currently in power. While their primary role is to serve those who appointed them and they deal with political strategy, they are also paid by the taxpaying public and are engaged in what could be called "honest advocacy." Career public affairs specialists are hired through competition, are protected by civil service rules, and while they obviously serve the current Administration, and the public that elected it, they generally survive through several or many Administrations. They must, and typically do, balance current political directives with their long-term credibility as public servants and their role as objective disseminators of responsible and reliable government information.

Finally, government versus private sector public relations specialists do have in common one vital core responsibility. Their most important role is to serve as *management counselors*. In this role, it falls to the government public affairs officer to maintain excellent working relationships with the agency's constituents and serve as advocates of the public interest in guiding government decisions and policies. While they must satisfy their current masters, they also are duty bound to always keep the public interest, however defined, as their overriding obligation and concern. In the final analysis, allegiance to the national or public interest is the full measure of their performance and professionalism.

A Contemporary Challenge: Rebuilding Confidence in Government

Readers of other chapters in this book know that the 1960s are often cited as a watershed decade in American history, one with profound implications for the current practice of professional public relations and public affairs. So it is with the virtual free-fall in public confidence in government's credibility and effectiveness in recent years.

While much of this attention has been directed at the Federal government, substantial evidence also exists that the general relationship between those who govern and those who are governed is perhaps the worst it has been since creation of the Republic.

This growing distrust of government at all levels presents a serious problem for public affairs practitioners who serve in government; it also presents enormous opportunities for salutary service.

If one uses the Public Relations Society of America's definition of public relations, i.e., "Public relations helps an organization and its publics adapt mutually to each other,"[14] the unfortunate current relationship between government and the citizenry makes the role of the government public affairs officer extremely important. It is the practitioner's job to serve as a facilitator in bridging the gap of credibility that is ominously eroding the public's belief in the government as fair and effective and, simultaneously and sadly, increasing some government workers' fear of the citizens they serve. In fact, it could be said that the most important role of the government public affairs practitioner is being a connecting link between the public and the bureaucracy.

History holds some of the reasons why this key relationship in American democracy is so strained today. In *The Government/Press Connection* (1984) Stephen Hess traced the origin of the government public affairs officer to President Woodrow Wilson's creation of the Committee on Public Information during World War I. Hess likens the Committee to a "ministry of propaganda" which issued an average of more than 10 releases a day. Unfortunately, the "propaganda" label stuck and several generations have embraced it as their image of government public affairs practitioners. Of course, in reality most practitioners in government, while continuing to issue news releases, find that activity to be a very small part of their job today.

The need to bridge the confidence gap between citizenry and bureaucracy remains. It is also arguably the greatest challenge confronting government public affairs officers today and for the foreseeable future. Since the Vietnam War and Watergate, there has been a precipitous drop in the public's confidence in government. This is particularly true of the 30 to 55 year old group, often called the Vietnam generation. While older Americans generally have more confidence in government, American youth are growing up to be at least as cynical if not more so than their parents. A bevy of key opinion polling findings in the mid-'90s underscored both government's diminished credibility and pervasiveness of that sentiment across all age groups.

It is ironic that the very group of people who are in the late '90s the foremost advocates of public participation, building relationships with affected publics, developing two-way communication, i.e., government public affairs specialists and officers, is the group targeted for criticism, elimination and downsizing by those wishing to reform government by shrinking it. Government public affairs people are seen as publicity agents instead of their true role in helping government agencies become more responsive to citizens, even facilitating active collaboration with the public in solving problems and improving the quality of life for those affected by public agencies. A major challenge for public affairs officers at all levels and in particular at the federal level is to provide leadership in turning around the anti-government attitude that is currently so pervasive. Non-public affairs management must be persuaded that publicity alone is not the answer, but that a comprehensive program of two-way communication within a strategic framework is the foundation for improving public perception of government's value. Building and maintaining mutually beneficial relationships with those publics on whom success or failure depend is just as true in the public sector as in the private sector. Targeting specific publics is absolutely necessary. No public agency can afford to communicate with the "general public."

Clearly, helping governmental administrators understand this challenge, meet it and master it, once again restoring the relationship between the governed and the government to a more normal and acceptable range, is the most difficult and challenging one confronting public affairs practitioners in the public sector. Facing the challenge points up perhaps better than any other example can, the essential difference between practicing the craft in the private sector, on the one hand, and in the public sector, on the other.

Notes

*   Contributors to this chapter are all current or past public affairs/public relations/public information officers in government service at the municipal, regional and federal levels.

1.   5 U. S. Code, 54, Chapter 32, Section 1 (last paragraph under "Interstate Commerce Commission").

2. House of Representatives Report #H104-173, Committee on Appropriations, June 30, 1995, p. 6.

3. Dom Bonafede, "The Selling of the Executive Branch—Public Information or Promotion," *National Journal*, (13) June 27, 1981, p. 1153.

4. Richard A. Lindeborg, "Government Careers In Public Relations," *Public Relations Career Directory*, Chapter 18, 1993, p. 105.

5. K. Doddridge, Congressional Reference Division, Congressional Research Service, Library of Congress, Memorandum to Hon. James Moran, August 9, 1995. Authors gratefully acknowledge the aid of Congressman Moran and his aide, Anstice Brand, in facilitating this chapter.

6. *Public Affairs Personnel Engaged in Public and Congressional Affairs in Federal Agencies*, U. S. Government Accounting Office, March 1993, p. 1.

7. Ibid.

8. Lindeborg, op. cit., p. 103.

9. Ibid.

10. Op. Cit., p. 104.

11. Ibid.

12. Ibid.

13. Op. Cit., p. 103.

14. "Public Relations: An Overview," *Monograph Series*, Public Relations Society of America, November, 1991.

Practical Documents
for

Defining Public Sector
Public Affairs Goals

Developing an Action Plan for
Working with Communities

PUBLIC SECTOR
PUBLIC AFFAIRS GOALS

Standards For Measuring Success

♦ The (name of agency) is referenced as a government agency that adds value to society.

♦ Top executives and other officers are respected and, though not always in agreement, are on good terms with Members of Congress, influential activists, opinion leaders, and people in other agencies.

♦ (Name of agency) has reputation of producing top quality products, conducting top quality activities, providing top quality services.

♦ The agency has reputation for treating employees well.

♦ Top management, etc., are well known personally to members of key constituency groups.

♦ News media include agency points of view in articles and often have feature stories of agency activities.

♦ The "10% swing vote" most often "swings" toward agency positions in controversial matters.

♦ There is minimum distortion of facts in articles and in public perceptions about the agency.

♦ People who are interested in an agency's jurisdiction generally (1) know what the agency is about and (2) agree that its mission and policies are in the public interest.

♦ People in local communities generally agree that the agency is a good neighbor.

♦ People believe that the agency tries to bring different views together in a socially- and scientifically-acceptable solution.

♦ The agency has reputation of planning for the future and looking at long-term public interest.

♦ Employees of the agency have reputation for being political-ly astute and neutral.

♦ The agency is seen as concerned about the consequences 'on the ground' of policies made in Washington.

♦ The agency is seen as accommodating the needs of an aging population.

♦ The agency is seen as being sensitive to women's and minorities' issues.

♦ The agency is seen as employing a diverse workforce.

Principles To Which Public Affairs Will Adhere

♦ We will focus on the future and avoid being defensive about the past.

♦ All our relationships will be based on respect for other people and acknowledgment that there are different values and opinions about public policy issues.

♦ Our public affairs and communications efforts will reflect integrity, professionalism, and understanding of the First Amendment.

♦ Reputation, not image, is important. What we say is based on what we do.

♦ We will inform our employees first.

Operations Standards For Public Affairs

♦ Public affairs efforts are focused, coordinated and behavior-driven.

♦ Public affairs strategies are developed with involvement of management and public affairs practitioners.

♦ Public affairs priorities are determined by line and top management.

♦ All public affairs campaigns will be evaluated as they are conducted and after completion to assess effectiveness.

Long-Term Public Affairs Strategies

♦ Enlist others in re-thinking goals and methods of agency management as changes occur in society and resources.

♦ Diversify the public support of the agency.

♦ Build support for new directions.

♦ Build and tend relationships with a broad array of publics who can help influence agency-related public policy.

DEVELOPING AN ACTION PLAN
FOR WORKING WITH COMMUNITIES

This document is intended to provide some ideas useful in developing an action plan for a field office of a government agency to address its community relations in a focused, analytical manner.

Evaluating your situation

Taking a realistic and hard look at the multiple factors that contribute to the existing state of relations between the field office and its local communities is a first step and can be the most critical and cost effective one in the long term.

How is the agency perceived?

What is the reputation of the agency in your communities? Is the agency considered a participant in the local community? What questions or complaints do the employees of your agency get from their friends and neighbors? What do the employees of your field office say to their friends and neighbors about their jobs and the agency? Who in the field office are influential in the community for other than job-related reasons? Does the agency benefit from their influence? What problems has the agency caused the local community in the past or currently? How have these problems been addressed?

How well do you know the people in your local communities?

Who are the influential persons in the community? Do these people take a position on agency issues? How many of these people have you or someone else in the field office talked to in the last six months? Who influences the influential persons in the community? Who are the persons that may not be community opinion leaders but who are considered experts on one or more agency issues? Who do they influence that has clout in regard to issues that affect the agency? How do the 'values' or 'interests' of the influential persons differ from the 'values' or 'interests' held by the managers of your local agency management?

How well do you communicate with the people in your local communities?

Other than the news media, where do people in your local community get their information about the agency? Other than agency officials, whose opinion do people listen to when they are forming their position on agency issues? How does your field office learn about the needs of the interest groups in the local community? Other than through the mail or news media, how do these groups receive information? How do you communicate with them? Does your field office management consider the local media biased? "Fair"? Does the agency public affairs officer agree? Does the local community agree? What keeps getting in the way when the agency tries to communicate internally and externally? Do your agency employees have an accurate, brief, concise answer to the controversial issues that concern the agency?

How well do you involve the people in your local communities in project analysis and project implementation?

Is your initial notification of a proposed project reaching all the potentially affected interests with clear, easily understood language? Do you provide enough information and ways for all the interests to interact with you—and each other—on each project? Do you maintain communication throughout the lifetime of the project analysis and implementation?

Determining needed actions

The following are some examples of action plan elements and questions that may help determine priority activities.

What are the short-term and long-term objectives that we need to establish?

Is the agency perceived as the legitimate agency to provide the services or commodities (solve the problem, take the action, perform the service, etc.)? Is the agency mission accepted by the local communities? Are the local communities working with us to find solutions to local problems? Do we have multiple ways for two-way communication with people in the area?

What do we need to do to identify all the people with whom we should be communicating? What actions will we take to establish communications?

Who has an economic stake in our actions? Who has an 'interest' or 'value' that we affect? Who has regulatory or legislative authority over us—or perceived authority? Who will take specific action for us or against us?

How can we best describe the decision space in which we are operating with the people in our communities?

Why is it important and in the public interest that we successfully do what we are trying to do in a given situation? What are the decision criteria, variables, constraints and who has the decision-making responsibility?

What are the activities which we will conduct to improve our relationships with our local communities?

What methods, approaches, techniques will best work in your field office zone of influence? What is working already? How might something that has not worked well in the past be successful with some changes? What specific actions will the field office undertake? When? Who will do it? What resources need to be allocated? What needs to be done to ensure that these activities are in compliance with the Federal Advisory Committee Act (or other applicable federal, state or local laws regarding public access to government decision making?).

How will we measure our success in improving our community relationships?

What checkpoints do we need to schedule to check our progress? How do we get feedback from the communities that goes deeper than newspaper headlines? What actions will we take to adjust our plan as needed?

What are the training needs for the field office to implement the action plan to improve relationships with your communities?

Do employees such as the project planners and interdisciplinary team members who must develop informed consent have the needed training? Does the local field office leadership have the training needed to implement the action plan successfully? What does the field office need from the headquarters office in terms of assistance or training?

Chapter 14

Public Affairs and the Community: Corporate Social Responsibility Now

John L. Paluszek

Community relations? In this day and age? In a period of downsizing, when you're closing plants and laying people off? When job
'security' and 'loyalty' are obsolete concepts? When companies are
abandoning their established communities for the lure of new 'low-
cost business environments'? You're going to make 'nicey-nice' with
the neighbors? Are you crazy?

It's a sentiment heard often these days. And the answer is, as
the saying goes, "crazy like a fox."

Context For Contemporary
Community Relations

To answer the cynics' basic question, "why community relations
now?", we first have to return to ground zero, to the basics of why
public relations in the 1990s and beyond. And that begins with a
serviceable description of contemporary public relations:

Public relations is the management function that helps an organization to build and maintain quality relationships with the groups of
people who can influence the organization's future.*

That means the groups of people, the publics, who can help you do what you want to do, or prevent you from doing what you want to do. Pretty basic stuff, yet elegant in its simplicity and quite relevant to any discussion of community relations. Because there should be no doubt that a community can prevent a company, or virtually any institution, from doing what it wants to do.

WalMart will attest to that quite readily. The company, one of the most successful in American business history, has run into a number of roadblocks to its expansion plans because of community resistance. Other macro retailers—Home Depot and several national shopping mall developers among them—have likewise had to shelve or cancel expansion plans because of such local resistance. Often such cancellations or revisions of plans have come at great cost.

Cost? Consider the mighty Walt Disney Company, colossus of the American entertainment industry and, to many Americans, beloved icon of family values. In 1994, Disney gagged on a bit of hubris when its multi-million-dollar plan for a Civil War recreation park near Manassas, Virginia, met heavy resistance—locally and, eventually, nationally—and had to be abandoned.

But it doesn't have to end that way. In a roller-coaster case with a happier ending, in Westbury, Long Island, a multi-million-dollar waste incineration plant was built, torn down and built again in a cycle of very bad and then very good community relations. Local citizens and community leaders, fearful of toxic emissions, had the first plant dismantled. But after an extended, sophisticated, empowering community relations program by a new operator, American Ref-Fuel, the community granted permission for construction and operation of the new plant. As I drove by the plant, (I'm one of the "local citizens"), I marvelled at how American Ref-Fuel was staging—and benefitting from—a community relations "staple", an open-house reception, at the site where secrecy and fear once prevailed.

American Ref-Fuel has been innovative in many aspects of community relations at Westbury. In addition to hosting some 2,000 visitors a year, it has sponsored soccer tournaments and a recycling contest and has even distributed children's booklets on waste management.

Of course, community challenges don't always relate to plans for the future. They sometimes relate to "rollbacks" of a long-granted approval to operate a facility in a given location. In a classic example, Mobil Oil Company was recently confronted with a community "uprising" at the site of its Torrance, California refinery. In a local political campaign, a candidate raised the issue of whether a "highly toxic chemical" should be allowed to be stored and processed at the refinery. The issue became a question on a local referendum and Mobil spent the better part of a year developing and implementing a sophisticated community relations effort.

The effort was successful and it saved Mobil millions of dollars.

In all of these cases—and, of course, in many others—there resides an over-arching universal. It is that effective community relations programs now exist at the intersection of good business practice and personal, humane values.

In this regard, good community relations becomes one of many elements in what has come to be known as "social responsibility." This concept recognizes that today—and, likely, far into the future—an organization has three concurrent obligations: In addition to fulfilling its "natural" mission (for a company, that would be products or services, jobs, profits and taxes) it also has an obligation to limit or eliminate any consequent social harm and, on an initiative basis, do "a little extra" for society.

The concept is by no means new. Various articulations—and manifestations—go back at least twenty years.[1] In fact, today there seems to be a blurring of the imaginary line between "natural mission" and social sensitivity. Nowhere is this more apparent than in the wave of "cause-related marketing" that has swept over American industry in the 1990s. In my judgement, it may even be time to inter the term "corporate social responsibility" in the belief that smart managements at successful organizations are *incorporating* social sensitivity into their strategic thinking and business plans. All of this feeds into an organization's reputation. The very word "reputation"—as opposed to the more hollow term "image"—has the ring of substance to it:

> A reputation is the sum of what you do and what you say, plus what others think and say about you. (Some contend that at heart, public relations is really "reputation management.")

Why Community Relations Now?

There are several basic reasons for building and maintaining a sound and effective community relations program.

The first is that your organization's reputation is increasingly important to your key publics. Take customers, for example. By customers, I mean those people who will buy what you're marketing, whether your organization is a corporation, a hospital, a university, a philanthropic organization, a government agency or—well, you fill in the blank.

In 1994, a Walker Group research study concluded that about 75% of consumers will not buy, no matter the discount, from a company they perceive not to be "socially responsible." I believe that you have to take such numbers with a large grain of salt. But even if the number is 50%—or 25%, or 10%—it is significant in an era when many brand managers and product managers will virtually "kill" for an increase of a couple points in market share. It's no wonder we've been experiencing a cause-related marketing frenzy.

And if you don't think that marketing belongs in the chapter on community relations—that there is often overlap across public relations audiences—reflect on how negative events (demonstrations, boycotts, environmental incidents etc.) taking place in a "home community" can be magnified across the country—and even around the world—when macro media choose to report on them.

In the spring of 1995, Royal Dutch Shell became the unwilling shuttlecock between the environmental organization Greenpeace and the British government. Shell thought it was doing the right thing— and the economical thing—by planning to scuttle one of its obsolete North Sea drilling platforms. "Oh no!," said Greenpeace, which, in its inimitable penchant for generating macro-media coverage, launched a worldwide blitz attacking Shell as perpetrating something akin to a 1990s version of the Exxon *Valdez* environmental disaster.

A key issue for Shell: Greenpeace's ability to generate consumer boycotts of Shell stations in communities in many parts of the world. Shell reconsidered, much to the chagrin of John Major's British government, which had approved the company's original disposal plan for the rig.

If reputation is more important in marketing and other operations these days, the next logical question is what makes for a good reputation—what favorably impresses—important publics.

New "values research" (beyond the Walker study)—attitudinal research on what various publics hold to be important in attributing "success" or granting "respect" to a subject organization—is confirming this hypothesis and developing a data base to support it.

More specifically, in the case of the corporation, researchers are finding a shift in the criteria on which a company is judged to warrant "respect"—not only by customers but also by investors, government officials, media, employees and, yes, neighbors too.

Picture, if you will, a matrix with horizontal and vertical axes, the horizontal axis labelled "commercial-financial" and the vertical axis labelled "corporate citizen."

Not long ago, a "successful, respected company" would have appeared far to the right on the horizontal axis, meaning that it was good at, essentially, making and selling something and making a solid profit at it. The vertical axis, if it existed at all in such deliberations, would not have been an important factor. Today, this "corporate citizen" axis is rapidly increasing in importance. As a result, the path of the company that is highly-respected among influentials is a diagonal, integrating high placement on both axes.

There are also corollary answers to Why community relations now? They, too, support the position that whatever the humane or altruistic content of such efforts, the predominant element is that today, sound community relations equals smart organizational management.

Again, from a corporate point of view: No community is an island. How a company treats the communities in which it operates is bound to have an effect on the degree of welcome it receives when planning new or expanded facilities in other communities.

Cynics may say, "Today, communities are glad to get almost any kind of jobs-and tax-generating enterprise." Tell that to WalMart and Disney.

Although jobs and a sound economy are critically important to communities, other important values, especially environmental, may well prevail.

An underlying corollary is that in the last few decades society as a whole has evolved in a more democratic direction. Cliches such as "empowerment" not withstanding, it is a fact that power is being diffused with increasing velocity.

The prevailing American governmental debate of the mid-1990s is how much federal authority will be dispersed to state and local governments—and just how this is to be accomplished with minimum social dislocation and pain. (In the twelve months prior to July, 1995, fifteen states passed resolutions re-affirming the U.S. Constitution's Tenth Amendment: "The powers not delegated to the United States by the Constitution, nor prohibited by it to the states, are reserved to the states respectively, *or to the people*." [Emphasis added.])

The plain truth is that neither the federal government, nor General Motors, nor say, Harvard University have even a semblance of the raw power they had in the 1950s or 1960s. Like it or not, each of our institutions must now partner with various constituencies to address mutual interests.

Nowhere is this more true than in the communities in which institutions operate. For this reason—and even more fundamentally, because you *live* in the communities in which you operate—it's important to become aware of the more seminal developments in contemporary community relations.

Communities: Where the Action Is

Community relations is now one of the more vibrant public relations practices. It's evolving so rapidly that only the bold would venture to click the shutter in the hope of capturing its essence. Nevertheless, try to capture it we must, incurring the risk that today's pioneers and heroes may stumble tomorrow; and that the current "cutting edge" may be blunted before the next edition.

To try to impose some degree of order on so unfocused a subject, I've arranged the evidence for community relations' "vibrancy" in three categories: Seminal trends, specific cases by business categories, and "outside-the-box" techniques.

Seminal Trends

1. The "Centralization" of Community Relations

The key findings of a 1994 national study conducted by the Center for Corporate Community Relations at Boston College, as reported by *Public Relations Reporter*[2] include:

- A greater community-relations role in employee motivation. Employee volunteerism is an important driver for selection of community causes winning corporate support.

- More linkage to business goals and measurable results. "Projects, in addition to being justified in the monetary sense, must also have a measurable impact on the community and the company."

• Environmental projects are increasingly valuable. They demonstrate, in real-life terms, social responsibility that is valued by both fence-line neighbors and the community as a whole.

2. Professionalism/Standards of Excellence

In another contribution to the advancement of community relations, the Center For Corporate Community Relations coordinated the development of what *Public Relations News* has headlined as "New Community Relations Excellence Standards [That] Provide Road Map To Align Function With Corporate, Community Priorities."[3]

These standards, developed under the auspices of the Center by a group of community relations and public affairs executives from leading companies, "put community relations on the map as being

---

**Community Relations
Excellence Standards**

1. Formal commitment to a social vision.
   - documented and widely communicated
   - senior management communicates vision, leads by example
2. Designated responsibility for managing the function.
   - managers have CR expertise and sufficient resources; operate on business plan
   - CR managers counsel top management; drive implementation of social vision; build community links, information/intelligence systems
3. Function, programs shaped by internal dialogue.
   - centralized facilitation of planning; decentralized planning, implementation of CR programs
   - internal communication of policies, training for internal staff
4. Programs reflect both corporate and community priorities.
   - programming springs from strategic plans, based on research, strategic planning
   - ongoing quantitative, qualitative evaluation
   - collaboration and communication with other companies, institutions

Source: Center for Corporate Community Relations, Boston College

---

one of the strategic functions within the corporation," according to Earl Plummer, manager of public affairs programs at Southern California Gas Company, and a participant in the standards committee.

3. Embracing the Community's Agenda

Effective community relations, like all effective public relations, requires a long-term commitment. And it requires, as Professor James E. Grunig of the University of Maryland has so well expressed it, "two-way symmetrical public relations"—substantive (policy and action) response to target audiences' needs and desires throughout the relationship.

This kind of commitment injects "juice" into what might otherwise be rhetoric. It breathes life into the concept of partnering. Often, it's accomplished by establishing a community advisory board with a company representative as one of several members.

The Dow Chemical Company has been a pioneer in developing and promoting the community advisory board concept. Its first CAB was formed in Canada in 1989 and by 1995 the company had 20 such groups in communities across the country.

Dow has even extended the basic concept to form a national advisory board on environmental issues. Members reflect a broad spectrum of expertise and viewpoints on the environment and the board's views weigh heavily in Dow's policy development.

The concept of public participation, persuasion and consensus-building in the community has been institutionalized in many ways but none, perhaps, as effectively as in the establishment and activity of the International Association of Public Participation Practitioners (IAP3). This Portland, Oregon-based professional society of about six hundred professionals in corporations, government agencies and consulting organizations, was founded in 1990 to share experiences in designing and conducting public involvement programs.

Some of IAP3's recent programs—available on audiotape cassettes—include "Community Visioning: Partnership in Planning", "Partnering with Stakeholders and Community," "Public Policy Consensus Building: Sustained Infrastructure to Connect Leaders and Citizens" and "Reengaging Citizens in Democracy."

At root in much of this community relations activity is a long-term commitment to the community's welfare. This often means involvement in the things that matter to the community even if your organization is not directly involved or responsible. In other words, it not just how your company will handle disposal of its waste, it's also at least awareness of—and, perhaps, monetary or "manpower" contribution to—matters of vital interest to the community such as economic development, education, crime and welfare.

Just where to draw the line between your organization's interests and the broad community interest is more art than science. Involvement in institutions such as community advisory boards will help you to make that decision on a case by case basis. However, a few recent corporate decisions made at this interface may be instructive.

Hallmark Cards, long a devotee of reputation management as being central to its strong brand, in 1991 faced the agonizing decision of having to transfer some production facilities out of Robersonville, N.C. and Osage City, Kansas, communities where the company had a presence for many years. As part of a plan to temper the impact of the withdrawals, Hallmark voluntarily contributed about $40,000 to charitable organizations in each community; the contributions were made even after the withdrawals. And in Robersonville, Hallmark was instrumental in finding a company to move in and take its place in the community.

On another important front—urban renewal—"a growing number of businesses [are making] their inner-city debut on the arm of a local church or other group," according to John Naisbitt's *Trend Letter.*[4] "An ambitious example is the Atlanta Project, launched by Jimmy Carter in 1992. Funded with $32 million from Atlanta businesses, the project's goal is to help 20 regional 'clusters' solve their own housing, health and other problems."

4. Trouble in Paradise: "Environmental Justice"

One of the more explosive issues facing community relations professionals is the alleged disproportionate level of environmental risk facing the nation's poor and minority communities.

The issue became much more virulent in 1993 when local groups filed complaints under Title 6 of the Civil Rights Act of 1964 which bars discrimination on the basis of race, color, national origin or sex in programs receiving federal assistance (state permitting programs are funded directly or indirectly by federal funds). According to experts, under Title 6, advocates must only prove there is a discriminatory effect—not necessarily intent—when new facilities are sited in a given community.

Even with the attempts at reduced regulation that came with the Republicans' "Contract With America," it's clear that the controversy over alleged "environmental justice" will not go away during the balance of the 1990s. Although it isn't likely to be a hot Congressional issue while the Republicans control the House and Senate, the Clinton administration appears to be committed to pursuing it. A 1994 Executive Order required federal agencies to develop plans for dealing with it at their own facilities. The agencies delivered such plans in mid-1995. Whether, and how, these plans eventually impact the private sector is worthy of high-priority monitoring.

By any name, "environmental justice" is, of course, a very sensitive issue with a high emotional quotient that threatens to rend the fabric of harmony being built in many communities. As summarized in a recent PRSA Environment Section newsletter, "the movement provides additional incentive for industrial facilities to invest in the communities that surround them by implementing aggressive community relations plans."[5]

5. Intellectual Ferment: "Communitarianism"

Perhaps the most encouraging "seminal" development in community relations in the mid-1990s is that its development is far from finished. Some impressive intellects are at work in conceiving and describing where it may be heading in the next century.

One such intellect is Amitai Etzioni, professor of sociology at George Washington University, Washington D.C. The founder of the Communitarian Network and a recognized authority on the subject, Etzioni penned the communitarian manifesto in 1993 under the title, *The Spirit of Community*. The book is visionary, idealistic, naive or prescient depending on where you're coming from.

Fundamentally, Etzioni challenges each of us as individuals and as managers to accept our responsibility as citizens to assure the survival, indeed the advancement, of the "community." One of the basic communitarian principles, as reported in *Public Relations News*[6] is that "communities happen in *public spaces*" (emphasis added). And the public spaces that are so vital to communities in this concept depend on strong institutions (schools, hospitals, places of worship, etc.) as well as protection of outdoor public spaces—streets and parks.

Communitarians also extend the idea of community inward: *the organization* as a community; and, more controversially, outward:

toward the formation of an ultimate *"community of communities"*. The "organizational community" concept is expressed in some of the new trends in design of corporate offices, in which common areas for team interaction are liberally dispersed. The more ambitious "community of communities" will require a successful macro balancing act: encouraging diversity while helping to sustain core values—those beliefs and predispositions that shape attitudes and behavior.

Specific Cases—Business Categories

"Trends" are important in the long term, but the real work, and progress in community relations, takes place day-in and day-out "in the trenches" in individual communities. It's not unlike the difference between climate and weather: climate is what you expect, while weather is what you get. And although meetings and dialogue will always be important in community relations, it is performance based on, and feeding, such communications that really matters.

There are literally hundreds of successful community relations programs in place across America. (The Public Relations Society of America annually bestows several "Silver Anvil" Awards for excellence in this category of public relations.) So to choose a just few for inclusion in this volume is less a matter of determining excellence—although excellence there may well be—than to illustrate the sweep and scope of effective community relations programs in the latter half of the 1990s.

1. Chemicals: The "Responsible Care Program"

No industry reputation has absorbed more slings and arrows in the past twenty-five years than that of the chemical industry.

(Arguably, the oil industry has had a comparable experience, but it is largely related to dramatic incidents played out on the world's media stage. The chemical industry's reputation problem, beginning with Rachel Carson's *Silent Spring* in the mid-1960s, has been unabating and generic—although Bhopal certainly exacerbated the problem.)

In 1988, American chemical industry leaders, assembled at their Washington D.C., trade association, The Chemical Manufacturers Association, determined to do something to change public perception of the industry. Adapting a national commitment made earlier

by their Canadian counterparts, they vowed to "continuously improve health, safety and environmental performance and . . . to do
this in parallel with open and honest dialogue with the public,"
according to *Public Relations News*.[7]

This "Responsible Care" Program (later adopted by chemical industries in dozens of nations around the world) is rooted in the
principle that the "public has a right to know about the risks and
hazards to which it is exposed, and what is being done to reduce
them. People should be told what type of chemicals are made or
stored in their community, as well as what is transported through
it. Stakeholders are also to be given a voice in shaping chemical
company operations that affect them."

What is particularly impressive about "Responsible Care" is that
although it is voluntary—ahead of some proposed legislation, as it
were (although the federal SARA Title III legislation was a factor)—it is also enforceable by the industry. A company cannot be a
CMA member if it doesn't adhere to the "Responsible Care" codes.
Although there is no public "drumming out of the corps" with, in
effect, epaulets being stripped from tunics of a lapsing company,
the moral suasion of an industry almost universally committed to
the codes is usually enough to prevent backsliding. Some CMA mem-
ber-companies will not even do business, as a supplier or a customer, with a chemical company that does not adhere to
"Responsible Care" codes.

A few highlights of "Responsible Care" progress: Chemical companies now participate in more than 250 community advisory panels across the country; an emergency response capability, known
as Community Awareness, Emergency Response, is now in place
in communities across the country; community leaders now know
what to do in the event of an emergency because local police,
fire fighters and hospitals have been educated in special emergency
procedures.

2. Tosco Education Partnership Program

In a completely different vein, Tosco Refining Company, Concord, California, is helping to answer one of the more troublesome
questions in community relations: What's our fair share of the solution to a pressing community problem?

Tosco's answer: Let our employees tell us.

Having determined that involvement in improving the educational experience in Concord could be in its own interest, Tosco asked for employee volunteers for this mission. It was surprised and delighted to find that almost 30% of its 900 employees stepped forward. So Tosco gave the employees time off from work to judge contests and science fairs, work with school clubs, participate as classroom assistants, mentors and tutors, and give plant tours or conduct environmental, first aid, fire safety and cultural workshops.

Tosco sees the program as a win-win-win: community improvement, better employee morale and self promotion. Tosco director of public affairs, Jim Simmons, summarizes the benefit to the company this way: "This program is a direct effort to ensure that we can continue to operate with the permission of the community. It's all about staying alive and staying viable."[8]

3. Banks

At another end of the industrial sector, banks and related financial institutions with a presence in various communities face a two-edged community relations challenge.

On the one hand, there is the potential payback for practicing advanced, progressive community relations that banks share with all manner of businesses. If this is the "carrot", it is all but overshadowed by the "stick"—the Federal Community Re-Investment Act (CRA), which requires banks to meet the credit needs of communities they serve and allows regulators to block mergers of banks that don't comply. Is there a better business reason for effective community relations programs?

Even with evolutionary changes by Congress, CRA remains a formidable stimulant for banks' meaningful commitments to the communities they serve.

The recent Chase Manhattan case is illustrative. In 1994, Chase sought to merge its bank in Connecticut into its lead bank in New York City. The application was attacked by a Bronx-based activist group, "Inner City Press/Community on the Move" which alleged that the merger should be denied because "Chase does not lend enough in minority and low-income areas of the Bronx and upper Manhattan"—an allegation that Chase vigorously denied.[9]

(In the most recent federal examination of the bank's community reinvestment activities, Chase received a "satisfactory" grade, the second highest of four ratings.) Several months later, federal regulators sided with Chase—but only after costly delay and expenditure of a considerable amount of Chase resources.

New York media, of course, loved the fight. *Newsday* headlined, "Robin Hoods of the '90s" and "The South Bronx' David Beats Banking Goliaths," referring to Inner City Press' earlier victories of 1994 in which "it negotiated settlements worth \$85 million."[10]

And Inner City Press represents just the tip of the iceberg of activist groups pressing for more investment by banks in lower-income communities. Broadly-based activist organizations such as the National Community Reinvestment Coalition in Washington D.C. and ACORN have been attacking banks' community reinvestment performance across the country since at least the late-1980s. In 1989, ACORN and the United Mine Workers of America used community reinvestment accusations to delay a Manufacturers Hanover Trust acquisition of 11 Goldome branches by six months.

One substantive answer to more funds for community lending—although not necessarily to low-income applicants—is Federal Home Loan Bank funds. According to Eugene J. Sherman, director of research at a leading investment bank, M.A. Schapiro Co: "Every dollar of FHLB affordable housing program funds is leveraged 14 times. As a result, the limited amount of subsidy funds contributes importantly to a large amount of affordable housing."[11]

Clearly, however, banks must create and implement far more comprehensive community relations programs to accomplish the outreach that will deflect many criticisms from activists, community leaders and individuals alike. As banks expand their mortgage lending and retail banking in lower-income communities—under prodding, but also because it has become apparent that banking in such areas can be profitable—they may well benefit from the experience of Massachusetts-based BayBanks, Inc.

In 1994, BayBanks launched a sweeping community relations program to involve community organizations in Boston-area lower-income neighborhoods in building awareness that the bank was committed to servicing those communities. The program was an educational exercise reaching many audiences whose primary language was not English. So the bank worked with Casa Nueva Vida, a homeless shelter active in the Hispanic community and the Vietnamese American Civic Association, among many others.

The main elements of the program included training materials—brochures, videos, and seminars—developed in English, Spanish, Portuguese, Vietnamese, Haitian Creole and Khmer; on-site showings of the videos; and the introduction of basic finance education programs for neighborhood schools. Although the program is long-term, an early evaluation showed that after about a year, some of the BayBanks branches in "diverse" neighborhoods became profitable faster than some suburban branches because the bank dramatically expanded its business in the targeted neighborhoods.[12]

4. Retail

Retail organizations (including, of course, bank branches) are perhaps the best laboratories for community relations programs. They touch their audiences—and are, in turn, touched by those audiences—constantly. So it might be expected that some of today's most creative and effective longterm community relations programs are being developed by retail establishments.

That is certainly the case with McDonald's.

As noted in *Inside PR*, "over the years, few companies have given as much back to the communities in which they operate than McDonald's. The company's Ronald McDonald House program is among the most powerful and highly regarded cause-related public relations programs in the country, and senior management credits its outreach efforts with boosting sales, forging links with consumers and even protecting franchises during the Los Angeles riots."[13]

McDonald's overall unwavering commitment—in corporate programs and in franchisees' programs as well—is to make a positive difference in the community by unilateral or partnering activity. And that activity is tailored to the needs of the community as determined by sensitive, on-site study.

In Detroit, for example, the company partnered with Detroit Edison to educate children to "Play It Safe With Electricity," a program to strengthen ties with schools and, through the schools, with the community. The program was one of unabashed cause-related marketing. Bill stuffers to Detroit Edison's 1.9 million residential customers presented a McDonald's coupon offer to all adults pledging to advise family and friends to stay away from fallen electrical wires; the utility estimates that 65% of its customers expressed awareness of the program—and awareness of the electrical safety issue doubled. A parallel program with schools generated some 40,000 coupon redemptions and "a lot of positive feedback from superintendents, principals, teachers and parents."

In Wisconsin, McDonald's Restaurants of Southern Wisconsin developed the "Magic School Bus Reading Program," tied to the company's national television sponsorship of Public Broadcasting

System's *Magic School Bus* show. In addition to promoting reading among children and adults—studies indicated that in Wisconsin, about 500,000 people are below functional literacy and 85% of juvenile delinquents are functionally illiterate—McDonald's also wanted to establish a relationship with community libraries. Library system directors advised that educational and entertaining programming during the summer would be most helpful in attracting young readers. So McDonald's, in partnership with Scholastic, Inc. arranged for an actress portraying the main character in the Magic Book, to visit 80 local libraries, reaching more than 8,000 children and their parents. Librarian response was overwhelmingly positive.

Finally, in Richmond, Virginia, McDonald's representatives decided that they could make a difference in crime prevention. So they partnered with five regional law enforcement agencies to introduce The Know Crime Institute, a year-long series of free classes designed to educate citizens about the root causes of crime, how to improve citizen safety, and how to help police fight crime in their communities. The program involved outreach to churches, schools, housing projects and "neighborhood watch" groups.

Other McDonald's operators are considering similar programs.

5. Foreign-owned Companies

Another "cut" at the dynamic of contemporary corporate community relations was provided by the 1994 Conference Board report, "Community Involvement of Foreign-Owned Companies."[14]

Perhaps the only surprise in this study of 108 large and small foreign-owned companies operating in the United States is that there is no great difference between these companies and their domestic counterparts in the commitment to community relations. Highlights of the study included these findings:

- 81% of the companies had a community involvement policy and 71% responded that community expectations were a "very important" or "moderately important" part of their business plan;

- Giving levels were comparable to domestic companies (about 1% of pretax profits) and patterns of giving also followed those of domestic companies;

- Although 55% of the foreign-owned companies were satisfied with their community relations programs, 39% felt that their companies should be more involved in the community.

That final finding led to this Conference Board analysis:

Leveraging international knowledge . . . foreign-owned companies have [many opportunities] to draw on their international connections and understanding to enrich the life of U.S. communities. The ability to introduce a truly global perspective into a community's activities in the spheres of education, the arts and serious social and environmental problems makes the foreign-owned company a unique cultural resource for U.S. communities. Much can be done in this realm.

To take advantage of this opportunity, The Conference Board urges communities (1) to encourage foreign-owned companies to be more "adventurous" in their social involvement; and, (2) conversely, become more "systematic" about quickly introducing foreign investors to the norms of community involvement around the country. It also recommends that communities should recognize companies (presumably domestic as well as foreign-owned) "that provide leadership toward meeting increasingly numerous and complex community needs."

"Outside the Box" Community Relations

As noted at the outset of this section, the many outstanding community relations programs extant, combined with the velocity of change in this field, make it extremely difficult to identify only a few as "cutting edge". Nevertheless, in addition to the programs cited above as identifiable with a type of business, there have been other pioneering efforts which deserve reflection.

1. Former Employee-Entrepreneur Rescues "Condemned" Plant

Disaster loomed for 340 semi-skilled workers in Cartersville and Milledgeville, Georgia. In the summer of 1994, Spring City Knitting, a subsidiary of Sara Lee Corporation, announced that it was getting out of private label apparel manufacture (sweatshirts, active wear) and would be closing the Cartersville mill and a small factory at Milledgeville, leaving sewing machine operators and other employees, mostly women, not only out of a job but also without prospect of employment.[15]

Enter Jerry Kemp, a former Sara Lee vice president at Cartersville who a year earlier had turned entrepreneur and, with three
partners, had purchased the Sara Lee plant at Wrightville, Georgia,
where 350 workers made men's underwear. After talks with Sara
Lee, the state, local banks and business leaders, employees and some
friends who would invest their savings, Kemp agreed to try to make
a "go" of all three plants—no small risk in the light of international competition in the apparel industry.

Although number-crunching eventually supported the decision, it
was the "people factor" and the sense of community that drove it,
not only for Kemp but also for the local bank, Trust Company Bank
of Northwest Georgia. Kemp: "We decided to gamble . . . because
of the management, the people and because we ourselves are here."
David Johnson, the bank's senior loan officer: (After due diligence),
"our interest is in Cartersville. It is a viable employer. It has great
potential and is important to the community there."

At the end of the day, Jeff Kemp's entrepreneurial gamble with
the former Sara Lee plants, like so many corporate decisions in this
era of accelerating socio-economic change, was an amalgam of good
business strategy and progressive community relations policy. It's
been written that Kemp and his partners, "like mice scampering
between the legs of elephants," are trying to find niches in the apparel market and compete aggressively. But Kemp himself articulates his mission with a somewhat different apologia: "They're good
people here, and a lot of these jobs are in towns where there's not
a lot of opportunity. Just writing this off is just not right."

2. Community Relations During/After A Crisis

A crisis is inherently "outside the box." You work hard for years,
maybe decades, to establish and maintain good relations with the
community in which you operate—after all, you do *live* there—and
suddenly an apocalypse threatens all you've accomplished.

Crisis management is, of course, a large and growing public
relations professional practice and it's dealt with in other chapters
of this book. So the intent here is not to examine at length the
many important facets of crisis management but, rather, to remind
readers that in addition to communicating through the media, successful crisis management also often requires important *direct* communications with the community. And, of course, effective communications in a crisis, as always, begins with sound policy
decisions.

For a case in point, we return to the textile-producing area of Georgia. At 2 p.m. on January 31, 1995, the Milliken & Co. carpet plant in LaGrange, Georgia, burst into flames, an inferno that would engulf the entire plant and wipe it out in a matter of hours. According to *Business Week*, Milliken's response to the disaster "demonstrates the payoff from effective disaster planning and strong customer ties. It's also a powerful, if anachronistic, image of small town Southern paternalism—a company taking care of its company town."[16]

Well, the description of Milliken's "company town" is a far cry from the pejorative of the 1930s. Because Milliken, which accounts for one in five LaGrange jobs, turned the disaster into what the company called a "tremendous opportunity"—to show how good a supplier Milliken-LaGrange could be. By 3 A.M. the next day, the company had organized 30 teams of employees to address every local concern from personnel to reconstruction. The next afternoon 720 employees met in the LaGrange College gym and heard not what they expected—that the plant would not be re-built—but that Milliken would provide jobs for as many as possible and immediate unemployment benefits for the rest. Within two weeks, 600 of the employees were back at work, some as far away as in Britain and Japan.

"Everything went like clockwork," said Jean Rainey, a mid-level Milliken employee at LaGrange. "But I don't know anybody who doubted for a minute that it wouldn't be that way."

3. Wisconsin: The State as a Community

The states have been called our laboratories for improving government. Few states have outpaced Wisconsin in this regard. From the populist thrusts of the LaFollette Progressives to the bold initiatives of the 1990s under Governor Tommy Thompson, Wisconsin ideas on government have earned national attention (although not always adoption).

Now comes "Wisconsin: The 21st Century", a sweeping plan to create a framework to "establish an atmosphere of continuous renewal; balance public and private initiatives; leverage learning and technology; and value good government and government service." Governor Thompson calls the plan "a vision of noticeably better citizens, noticeably better communities, noticeably better government and noticeably better quality of life compared to any other state."[17]

This blueprint for the state as a seamless, successful community was the result of input and support from all parts of the Wisconsin public and private sectors. Among its goals is "Cooperating Communities—Partnerships to Enhance Community Capacity." To achieve this goal, the plan calls for "tools such as conflict resolution, negotiation, mediation, cooperative pacts and certificates of cooperation for public advantage."

Visionary? Perhaps. But that's what the doubters said about some of the Progressive Party's suggestions that eventually became national policies.

Community Relations, Public Relations and the Bottom Line

The very idea of "community" is protean. In a physical sense, it means location, the streets and avenues, bricks and mortar circumscribing a "place." On a human level, it means, of course, a group of people with common interest—neighbors, employees, colleagues. And, as conceived by intellectuals such as Amitai Etzioni, it connotes something more universal—the core values of a society.

Wherever "community" occurs, there is a process relying, not surprisingly, on communications. And it's here that public relations and public affairs professionals should feel especially comfortable.

Eric Miller, of the Foundation for Community Encouragement, has presented a series of thoughts that, it is hoped, will feed yet challenge that comfort. In a brief article in *Public Relations Reporter*, "Community Building = Communications. Is Public Relations Ready For the Challenge?"[18] he quotes M. Scott Peck:

> Community requires communication—and not the mere exchange of words, but high-quality communication. . . . A genuine community is a group whose members have made a commitment to communicate with one another on an ever more deep and authentic level.

Finally, CEOs themselves have addressed the Doubting Thomases on the appropriateness of for-profit institutions' investments in community relations. In "Justifying Community Relations to Bottom Line Business Needs," an article in *The Community Relations Report*[19] James E. Burke, now chairman of the board emeritus of Johnson & Johnson, makes the case as a CEO.

Burke, of Tylenol fame, presented the findings of a J&J Business Roundtable study of fifteen companies that had a longstanding commitment to a written, codified set of principles stating the philosophy that serving the public ("corporate social responsibility") was central to their being. The study concluded that these companies achieved a 10.7% growth in profits compounded over three decades (GNP grew at 7.6% during the same period); and shareholder value exceeded many norms.

Burke offered this summation:

> I would like to turn your attention toward the intangible asset of any corporation that goes well beyond the 'goodwill' listed on the balance sheet—and that's its reputation with the public, *all* the publics that it serves. For I believe that public service is not a thing apart . . . it is, in truth, our very reason for being. It is implicit in the character of every American corporation . . . that's what makes our enterprise system so special.

Dr. James J. Reiner, CEO of Honeywell, Inc. has provided an equally pragmatic summation for progressive corporate policy:

> There are hardhearted business reasons for working to better the lot of our people, to improve education and to garner the benefits of successful communities.

Reduced to the very bare essentials, my own advice to companies and other institutions re-evaluating their community relations and overall corporate social responsibility policies is rather stark: To be successful tomorrow, do three things: Do well what you're supposed to do (your mission). Do no social harm. And, anticipating future expectations and demands, do a little "extra."

Notes

* This sweeping description presumes many "vertical" professional practice areas within public relations including customer relations, employee relations, investor relations and—to our point here—public affairs and community relations.

1. *Will The Corporation Survive?* John L. Paluszek, Prentice Hall, 1976.
2. *PR Reporter*, October 10, 1994.
3. *PR News*, November 7, 1994.
4. John Naisbitt, *Trend Letter*, December 8, 1994.

5. PRSA Environment Section Newsletter, "On the Horizon," Spring, 1994.

6. *PR News*, January 23, 1995.

7. *PR News*, December 19, 1994.

8. *PR News*, January 23, 1995.

9. *New York Times*, November 5, 1994.

10. *Newsday*, February 19, 1995.

11. *Community Investment Reporter*, December 5, 1994.

12. *PR News*, November 21, 1994.

13. *Inside PR*, March 27, 1995.

14. "Community Involvement of Foreign-Owned Companies," The Conference Board, Report Number 1089-94-RR.

15. *New York Times*, November 5, 1994.

16. *Business Week*, February 27, 1995.

17. "Wisconsin: The 21st Century," The State of Wisconsin, January 10, 1995.

18. *PR Reporter*, March 20, 1995.

19. *The Community Relations Report*, June, 1987.

Chapter 15

Citizen Groups, Public Policy, and Corporate Responses

John M. Holcomb

Citizen interest groups have had a profound impact on corporate America since the 1960s. During the New Deal and through the 1950s, labor unions were the most common adversary for business in public policy battles. Since that time, though, citizen groups have emerged to bring about the greatest wave of social regulation in American history, during the 1960s and 1970s. During the late 1970s and 1980s, while liberal citizen groups attempted to defend the gains they had made for the previous two decades, conservative interest groups emerged to bring about a partial rollback in the regulation of the previous era. In the late 1980s and 1990s, citizen groups have pursued more direct action against corporations and relied less on government as an intermediary. Simultaneously, new social movements have emerged that complicate still further the political environment of business.

With this brief history as background, this chapter will explore the citizen group terrain along the following dimensions: (1) origins, (2) old truisms, (3) political tactics, (4) political ideologies, (5) recent developments, and (6) new social movements. The chapter will then explore the implications that citizen group activities have for business. Specifically, the chapter will address: (7) implications for corporate public affairs, and (8) modes of response and response mechanisms.

Origins

There are a number of special factors that gave rise to the growth and proliferation of citizen groups during the turbulence of the 1960s and 1970s. First and foremost was the tension and division of that era, caused mainly by civil rights conflicts and the Vietnam war. Those events served as catalysts for the two major social movements of that era, the civil rights and anti-war movements. They, in turn, served as models for the development of later social movements, including the ecology and feminist movements, as well as newer movements of the 1980s and 1990s.

The emergence of a generation of talented protest leaders and social policy entrepreneurs was another important causal factor in the rise of citizen groups. Martin Luther King as leader of the civil rights movement, Ralph Nader as leader of the consumer movement, and Gloria Steinem as a leader of the feminist movement are just a few of the more prominent examples.

Rising educational levels among the American public provided fertile ground for the growth of a greater issue consciousness by citizens. Investigative reporting, which gained ascendance during Watergate and Vietnam, along with media exposés of corporate misconduct, fed the public's growing cynicism as well. With the decline of the political parties as articulators of major issues and aggregators of many conflicting interests, citizen groups emerged to channel the public's growing anxiety and issue awareness. Hence, rising educational levels, the role of the media, and the declining roles of the political parties all interacted to propel citizen groups to the forefront.

Among other causal factors for the rise of citizen groups are the financial support of leading liberal and conservative foundations and patrons, as well as government subsidies and contracts that sometimes flowed to certain interest group sectors, such as women's groups and anti-hunger groups. Finally, laws and government regulations played roles as both cause and effect in the rise of interest groups. While lobbying by environmental and consumer groups often led to the passage of certain laws and regulations, the laws themselves often generated the formation of groups that organized to benefit from certain government programs and campaign for larger appropriations.

Old Truisms

There are some truisms about citizen interest groups that are still true and will remain so into the foreseeable future.

Rapid Proliferation of Groups and Constant Turnover of Group Population

The number of groups continues on an upward spiral, and the tendency of people to join groups continues unabated. The Times/Mirror Center for People and the Press has found that 27% of Americans belong to a cause organization. Further, the landmark studies of political scientist Jack Walker found that 50 percent of all the groups in existence in the 1980s had formed since 1960. To be informed about the upward spiral of all varieties of groups, it is clearly not sufficient to know only about mainstream groups like Common Cause, the Sierra Club, and the NAACP. The configuration of groups, along with their agendas and tactics, becomes more complex with the passage of time.

Staff Domination Among Groups

In focusing on groups at the national level, it is clear that members have little voice in the direction of those groups. One of the earliest studies of public interest groups (Berry, 1977) found the decision-making structures to be oligarchic. National citizen groups are largely undemocratic by nature. One prominent cause for this phenomenon is the reliance that most national groups place on foundation funding, which incidentally also discourages militant protest among such groups. Membership surveys and analyses of groups such as Common Cause and the National Organization for Women demonstrate that the vast majority of those belonging to such groups are merely checkbook members, who send in their dues but do not participate in organizational decisions.

At the grassroots level, community organizations behave differently. Their members are more actively engaged in organizational decision-making and tend to use more aggressive and militant tactics (Paget, 1992). This difference in operating styles between national and grassroots citizen groups must be appreciated by corporations and other targets of their influence, in order to make sensible and meaningful responses.

Counter-Cyclical Group
Formation and Activism

It is an ironic truism of politics that groups prosper more when they are in the opposition or when their programs are threatened. In an electoral context, conservative groups thrive more during Democratic administrations, while liberal groups thrive more during Republican administrations. For example, the rise of conservative activist groups and think tanks peaked during the Carter Administration. Environmental, women's, and civil liberties groups grew rapidly during the Reagan era of the 1980s. Since Clinton's election in 1992, memberships among the so-called "big five" environmental organizations have nosedived, while subscriptions to conservative publications such as *National Review* and the *American Spectator* have climbed dramatically. When any interest group sector finds "its person" in power, it tends to grow complacent and lose members, but when it is out of power, its supporters feel threatened and become galvanized. Hence, the counter-cyclical aspect of interest group organizing reinforces the swing of the pendulum in American politics.

Gridlock and Paralysis in
Policy-making

The ever-growing spiral of interest groups complicates public policy-making to the point where change is either frequently incremental or halted altogether. Each group or coalition of groups has a greater ability to veto or prevent change than to advance it. Early studies of the impact of economic interest groups confirm this finding (Olson, 1982). More recent studies, focused on the impact of all varieties of groups and on the growth of so-called hyper-pluralism, come to the same conclusion (Rauch, 1994).

Political Tactics

The political tactics utilized by citizen groups range from the conventional to the more creative. Concerns that emerge as social movements, applying militant tactics such as political demonstrations, gradually evolve into interest groups that apply more conventional tactics, such as lobbying, litigation, and research. All the social movements of the 1970s, such as civil rights, women's rights, the environment, and consumerism, now have a major presence in Washington and many state capitals. The public interest law movement, launched in the 1970s with critical support from the Ford Foundation and other smaller foundations, now boasts a large population of both liberal and conservative legal foundations. The universe of think tanks, once dominated by the Brookings Institution and the American Enterprise Institute, now includes a network of localized conservative think tanks in each region of the country, as well as many specialized think tanks, focused on a specific issue agenda (Ricci, 1993; J. Smith, 1991). The Economic Policy Institute generates liberal policy ideas on economic issues, and the Progressive Policy Institute is the research arm of the centrist Democratic Leadership Council. Research centers based at academic institutions, such as the Tobacco Liability Project at Northeastern University Law School, are also central players in the development of public policy.

Beyond the range of conventional tactics, many citizen groups also apply a host of different creative tactics.

Grassroots Activism

National organizations from the National Rifle Association to the Sierra Club are infamous for generating grassroots pressure from their members on national legislators. Parallel to the rise of activism in state legislatures, and at the local level, many groups have also developed state chapters to advance public policy at those levels. Networks of grassroots community groups include ACORN, which operates in 27 states, and Citizen Action, a federation of 20 statewide organizations. Such networks bring together labor, consumer, and environmental representatives to focus on grassroots issues. At the national level, groups such as the Citizens Clearinghouse on Hazardous Waste offer support and technical assistance to grassroots anti-toxic groups.

Increasingly, grassroots organizations have become involved in local electoral activity as well. State affiliates of Citizen Action get involved in both congressional and local elections, while the Christian Coalition, with its 1.5 million members, has allegedly taken control of several state Republican Party organizations.

Ballot Measures

Ever since the wave of tax limitation measures placed on the
ballot in the late 1970s, groups on both the left and the right have
increasingly brought volatile issues directly to the public for a vote.
In the 1990s, conservative populist groups made use of ballot measures to advance term limits and limits on gay rights and abortion.
Liberal groups have attempted to advance issues like campaign finance reform through ballot measures.

Boycotts

Groups of all different stripes have used the boycott tactic to
pressure the business community generally and specific companies.
The Boycott Colorado campaign was organized to protest the passage of a ballot measure that limited gay rights. PUSH, led by Jesse
Jackson, has threatened to boycott several corporations, including
Nike, as part of a campaign to pressure those companies to sign
covenants with PUSH to elevate their relationships with the black
business community. Conservative religious groups have boycotted
companies that advertise on television programs that offend family
values. Since 1985, 330 boycotts have been sponsored in the U.S.,
with 260 of those originating after 1990. The boycott industry has
even spawned a quarterly *Boycott News*, published by the Institute
for Consumer Responsibility.

Shareholder Activism

Two different varieties of shareholder activism have emerged to
advance the cause of corporate social responsibility. Social investment funds and services have been formed to serve the needs of
socially conscious investors. Such funds even have their own association, called the Social Investment Forum. Activist groups, meanwhile, introduce over a hundred shareholder resolutions annually to
protest such issues as investment in repressive nations, environmental
abuses, and corporate political activities. The shareholder resolution
tactic, developed by radical organizer Saul Alinsky in the 1950s,
now finds its chief sponsors in church organizations that are members of the Interfaith Center on Corporate Responsibility. Pension
funds have also joined the fray, sponsoring resolutions on mainstream corporate governance issues.

Cross-Sector Coalitions

While political interest groups have always built coalitions to fight lobbying battles, citizen groups are increasingly joining hands across sectors or communities of interest to fortify their strength. Environmental groups do not just work together within their own community of interest. They reach out to work with religious groups, consumer groups, and farmworker groups, as they have on the pesticides issue. They have also built bridges to work with religious groups and civil rights groups on the issue of environmental racism. The Citizen Trade Campaign, a coalition organized to lobby against NAFTA, included labor unions, environmental groups, consumer groups, farm groups, religious organizations, and the Rainbow Coalition. Coalitions built across ideologies even exist. Free-market libertarian groups have joined with environmental groups to oppose corporate welfare and government support for risky technologies.

Direct Action

Whether through use of protests, boycotts, or shareholder resolutions, citizen groups are more frequently pursuing direct action against corporations today, rather than relying solely on indirect impact through lobbying and public policy campaigns. A tuna boycott launched by Greenpeace, for example, prompted H. J. Heinz and other tuna companies to announce they would no longer accept tuna caught with methods that endangered dolphins.

Often the direct action campaigns are going in a more cooperative direction. The National Toxics Campaign, for instance, has initiated "Good Neighbor" campaigns, asking industries to open their gates to citizen inspections and to discuss environmental decisions. The campaign also negotiated an agreement with five supermarket chains to achieve pesticide reduction goals. The supermarket chains agreed to ask food suppliers to disclose all pesticides used to grow produce sold to the chains and to phase out certain dangerous pesticides by 1995. The Alyeska Pipeline Service signed a formal contract to establish a Regional Citizens Advisory Committee, chaired by the Alaska Director of the National Wildlife Federation, to review Alyeska's oil spill response plan. Negotiations and direct action campaigns are increasingly direct. They may be combative or they may be collaborative, but they are often settled outside the arena of government.

Political Ideologies

Since most citizen groups are cause oriented, they have distinct political ideologies and orientations. Since the social movements of the sixties called for government or regulatory solutions to most problems, groups tied to those movements would fall into the liberal category. That would include the environmental, consumer, civil rights, and feminist groups that originated during that era. The think tanks and organizations that promoted economic rationality, regulation, and regulatory reform during the 1970s would fall into the neo-conservative category. Groups that promote social conservatism and have a moralistic view urge a strong government role to regulate abortion, control crime, protect school prayer, and promote family values. Such groups would fall into the new right category, which would include religious right organizations, right-to-life groups, and even think tanks like the Heritage Foundation. Libertarian groups advocate a limited role for government in both the economy and in social issues. They go beyond the call of neo-conservatives for deregulation and regulatory reform to urge that government drastically scale back its role in our lives and in the economy, and attack corporate welfare and other government subsidies. The Cato Institute is the leading libertarian think tank. Other libertarian organizations include tax limitation groups and various regional think tanks.

Populist organizations distrust the elites and believe power should be exercised at the grassroots level and returned to the hands of the people. Left-wing populist groups want to confront corporate behavior directly and include aggressive community organizations, militant environmental groups, and some union locals and consumer groups. Right-wing populist groups seek to limit the power of the national government and return power to the people through tax limits and term limits. Populist groups often make use of the initiative mechanism and communicate with their followers through talk radio. The most extreme populist elements in the mid-1990s are right-wing paramilitary and pro-gun organizations.

Recent Developments

Beyond the old truisms already discussed, more recent developments have occurred among citizen groups as they have evolved and matured. A rising level of professionalism marks the operations of many citizen groups. As social movements become transformed into interest groups, it is natural for them to adopt more traditional political tactics. As they have matured still further into the 1980s and 1990s, what is even more impressive is the diversity of their total package of tactics. Two-thirds of citizen groups are now full service public interest organizations and have the capacity to engage in research, public education, lobbying, litigation, and other functions under one organizational roof. In 1977, that was true of only fourth of the existing citizen groups. Citizen groups are also making greater use of high technology in their education and organizing campaigns, as well as applying scientific and economics expertise in their public policy analyses. The Environmental Defense Fund (EDF) has been in the forefront of the drive for market-based environmentalism and has departed from a doctrinaire liberal approach to pursue one based on market incentives. Based on their scientific expertise, the EDF and the Natural Resources Defense Council also produced reports critical of the degradability claims for certain products. The advocacy of certain citizen groups is now much more moderate and sophisticated and commands respect even among scientists and scholars.

Along with the rising professionalism and moderation of many groups, and partially caused by it, has been a growing fragmentation within several citizen group sectors. The environmental community is perhaps the foremost example. Splits have occurred between older mainstream groups, largely at the national level, and newer more militant groups, largely found at the local level. Lois Gibbs, leader of the Love Canal homeowners' protest, and now a grassroots organizer, refers to mainstream environmental groups as "elitist, highly paid, detached from the people, indifferent to the working class, and a firm ally of big government." The fight over NAFTA is symbolic of the fragmentation within the environmental sector. The following table (see over) compares those groups that supported NAFTA to those opposed to the agreement.

Women's and feminist organizations are also more divided than ever, along both ideological and economic lines. Major disagreements have emerged between so-called "difference feminists" and "equality feminists." Difference feminists, led by legal scholar Catherine MacKinnon, believe women have different psychological and behavioral predispositions than men and that those differences must be accommodated by public policy. Equality feminists believe wom-

Table 1: Environmental Groups and NAFTA.

Pro-NAFTA	Anti-NAFTA
National Wildlife Federation	Sierra Club
World Wildlife Fund	National Toxics Campaign
National Audubon Society	Greenpeace USA
Natural Resources Defense Council	Friends of the Earth
Environmental Defense Fund	Public Citizen
Defenders of Wildlife	
The Nature Conservancy	

en only need be provided with equal opportunity to succeed as well as men. Differences among feminist leaders and groups have therefore emerged on such issues as hate speech and pornography.

Within the civil rights community, cleavages have developed between various ethnic groups and even within the African American community, on such issues as affirmative action. As the power of the religious right expands, differences over strategy are even emerging among those groups. Some want to emphasize only social and moral issues, while others want to stake out positions on mainstream economic concerns like the budget deficit.

To the extent fragmentation occurs, it produces a more complex political environment for business, but it also poses new opportunities for business. Business is now more likely to find some elements within a citizen group sector more approachable than others, leading to the possibility of more creative political coalitions or, at least, constructive dialogues.

A final and disturbing development among some citizen groups, as well as within society at large, is a trend to incivility and violent breakdowns. Right-to-life groups have escalated their violence to include murder of doctors practicing abortion, while the right-wing militia movement has targeted federal agents and law enforcement officials for intimidation and violence.

New Social Movements

The 1990s has seen the emergence or strengthening of at least three new social movements. The property rights or wise use movement poses the greatest threat to environmental laws and regulations. It believes that the government should compensate landowners when the impact of a regulation diminishes the value of the owner's property. Legislation ordering such compensation has already been proposed, and environmental groups fear that such legislation will deter further necessary regulation. The western faction of the wise use movement further wants to open access to federal lands for logging, ranching, and mining. The property rights movement combines elements of populist and libertarian thinking, as it both distrusts federal authority and seeks to protect property ownership from government interference. It allegedly includes over 700 grassroots property rights groups throughout the country, and the coverage it has received in major environmental publications attempts to portray the movement as funded and controlled by major natural resource companies.

The family values or cultural values movement is another major social movement of the 1990s. Its foundation lies in the religious right, and it includes many national and regional organizations, such as the Christian Coalition, the Family Research Council, Focus on the Family, the Traditional Values Coalition, and Colorado for Family Values. Forty of the major evangelical and family values organizations are now headquartered in Colorado Springs. Gay rights has clearly been the wedge issue for the family values movement into the mid-1990s, and it has vigorously promoted several ballot measures at both the local and state levels to restrict gay rights. Other issues on the family or cultural values agenda include abortion, school choice, religious freedom, creationism, and anti-multiculturalism. The growing strength of the family values movement and religious right agenda has been a concern among civil liberties organizations and has generated a counter-reaction from the ACLU, People for the American Way, and Americans United for Separation of Church and State.

The communitarian movement is the third social movement that has gained ascendance during the 1990s. It has its base in academia and policy think tanks and, similar to neo-conservatism, is an elite movement. Its critique of traditional liberal ideology includes a criticism of the heavy hand of government, and of the proliferation of rights in our political culture. Communitarians seek to balance the scales, by promoting regulation based on market incentives and by building a sense of responsibility for both individual and institu-

tions to counter-balance the explosion of rights. Leading communitarian organizations include the Communitarian Network, found by
Amitai Etzioni and William Galston, and the Progressive Policy
Institute, the research arm of the Democratic Leadership Council.
Communitarian thinking has had a heavy influence on both Democratic and Republican moderates. Specific items on its policy agenda include initiatives to reinvent government, education reform,
community service, family support programs, protection of religious
freedom, and campaign finance reform. In a less extreme fashion,
it shares some of the cultural views of the family values movement.

It is interesting that none of the major social movements emerging in the 1990s find their base on the left. This may be further
evidence that traditional liberalism is not doing a good job at defending itself or redefining itself.

Implications for
Corporate Public Affairs

It is readily apparent that citizen groups are central to the functions of all key public affairs components and have a pervasive
impact on the operations of each.

Government Relations

Government relations officers, caught in the swirl of various issue networks, must be keenly aware of the importance of competing interest groups, including citizen groups. Lobbyists realize that
groups are involved in every stage of the public policy cycle, and
must adapt to their presence. Demonstrations by social action groups
or studies by policy think tanks can put issues on the public policy
agenda, just as Nader put auto safety on the agenda and the American Enterprise Institute put deregulation and regulatory reform on
the agenda (Derthick & Quirk, 1985).

Regarding the policy formulation stage, witnesses who testify in
legislative committee chambers commonly represent citizen group
interests. At the policy implementation stage, when regulators take
center stage, business increasingly confronts citizen groups becoming more and more adept at regulatory liaison, whether the issue
be food additives, nuclear power, or energy pricing. Finally, at the

policy evaluation and review stage, when judges scrutinize regulations on various legal or constitutional grounds, once again citizen groups can be key actors. They may act as plaintiffs, represent plaintiffs if they are public interest law firms, or file *amicus curiae* (friend of the court) briefs (Caldeira & Wright, 1988; L. Epstein, 1985).

While lobbyists at the national level recognize that citizen groups are involved at every stage of the public policy cycle, corporate lobbyists at the state level recognize their growing impact as well, especially since groups have shifted their focus in the wake of government retrenchment at the national level. Activist legislators and activist judges, friendly to the legal concerns of citizen groups, are more likely to be found at the state level in the 1990s than the federal level.

Media Relations

Media relations staff also realize that the barrage of criticism they must handle is often generated by citizen groups responding to events, or generated by reporters who turn to groups for information and criticism of the firm or industry. For every new product development or product failure, for every corporate acquisition or restructuring, and for every corporate position taken on a public policy initiative, media relations staff realize that citizen groups will be in the front line of corporate criticism. They are publicity maximizers, to insure their own survival and visibility.

Corporate Philanthropy

Corporate philanthropy is also preoccupied with interest groups. In the broadest sense, all recipients of corporate contributions are interest groups, whether they be arts organizations, health and welfare groups, or public policy think tanks. In a political context, citizen group concerns have generated three types of strategic philanthropy by business. First, in response to liberal activism and to advance pro-business issues on the agenda, many corporations have given substantial support to conservative think tanks or legal foundations (Himmelstein, 1990; Blumenthal, 1986; Edsall, 1984). Second, corporations will often respond to a social problem or criticism of its practices by launching a new contributions effort, to both alleviate the problem and blunt the criticism. Third, corporations will often fund their critics, as a way of building bridges and facilitating ongoing relationships, as many firms have done with environmental groups (Smith, 1994).

Community Relations

Corporate community relations officers are also highly focused on citizen groups, especially civil rights groups like the National Urban League, the NAACP, and many localized groups. Community relations concerns have focused as well on local anti-toxics groups and on activist low-income groups like ACORN and National People's Action. Community relations staff also promote public-private partnerships to address urban problems, involving government, business, labor, and community groups (Gittell, 1992).

Consumer Affairs

Consumer affairs professionals focus on a range of citizen groups as well, especially consumer organizations like the Consumer Federation of America, the National Consumers League, and Public Voice for Food and Health. However, their attention also often goes to women's groups, senior citizen groups, civil rights groups, and even religious groups, when those organizations focus on consumer issues.

Modes of Response and Response Mechanisms

The response by the business community to activist pressure has ranged along five dimensions—confrontation, imitation, cooperation, participation, and negotiation.

Confrontation

Sometimes, corporations will attack the motives of a citizen group or the legitimacy of the organization. These are obviously hardball responses, not designed to facilitate bargaining or compromise. There have been instances where companies have also attempted to undermine the funding base of an organization, by complaining about taxpayer support or foundation grants going to the recipient group. Some companies have also initiated libel litigation against critics, in order to silence them or even deplete their resources. Such litigation has gained the label SLAPP suits—strategic lawsuits against public participation—and has been criticized by legal scholars. Companies that take any of these confrontation approaches are engaged in a reactive mode of response to criticism and public pressures.

Imitation

Other companies, perhaps learning from their earlier defeats, have copied the successful tactics of their adversaries. Business support for conservative think tanks and litigation centers is a leading example of successful adaptation of tactics developed by citizen groups. Further, corporations were not the first organizations to create political action committees or grassroots lobbying capabilities. Here again, they adapted successful models often used by their critics.

Cooperation

Many firms have learned that it is prudent to form coalitions with erstwhile critics when their interests converge, just as they would with any mainstream economic interest groups. Allstate Insurance Company cooperated with Ralph Nader in the campaign to make airbags mandatory in automobiles, even while they opposed each other on no-fault insurance. Monsanto has lobbied with environmental groups on behalf of increased funding for the EPA. Based on the bridges it has built through its contributions program, Philip Morris has built a coalition with civil rights groups to fight smoking regulations and advertising restrictions. Some would say that both imitation and cooperation are common-sense proactive strategies to defend one's interest in the public policy arena.

Participation

Firms that take one step further into an interactive response mode seek deeper levels of collaboration with citizen groups. Participation by citizen groups in corporate planning or decision-making is an advanced form of collaboration that has been attempted by some firms. They have formed citizen or consumer advisory panels, issue councils, or even product panels. Energy and telecommunications companies, supermarket chains, and health insurance companies have often experimented with such interactive mechanisms, and they have benefitted firms both economically and politically. Banks and insurance companies sometimes collaborate with activist community groups like ACORN to address redlining concerns.

Negotiation

Another interactive response is negotiation with citizen groups. One-on-one negotiations now are quite common, for example between firms and religious organizations that are sponsoring shareholder resolutions. Beyond those ad hoc relationships, more structured negotiations have evolved. The National Coal Policy Project, developed by energy and chemical companies, along with leading environmental groups, provided one of the original models. Participants were able to reach agreement on over 200 separate issues, though few of them were actually implemented as law (McFarland, 1993). Since that experiment in the late 1970s, independent convening organizations like the Conservation Foundation, the Institute for Resource Management, and the Keystone Center have sponsored dialogue groups and consensus-building forums involving a wide range of industry, government, and citizen participants (Amy, 1987).

A genuinely interactive strategy will involve the following elements: systematic monitoring of citizen group activities and concerns; initiation of communication with such groups across a broad range of concerns, not just ad hoc responses to narrow issues; maintaining a continuing dialogue with relevant citizen groups; and development and participation in structured dialogue and negotiation efforts.

Of the five response modes assumed by business, the confrontation mode is the most unfortunate and damaging. Imitation and cooperation are shrewd, sensible, and inevitable proactive responses. However, they do little to prevent needless conflict or advance positive change. The most desirable and functional modes of response for business are those of participation and negotiation. Through them, business may adjust corporate policy to the needs of multiple constituencies and contribute to sound public policy.

References

Amy, Douglas J. (1987) *The Politics of Environmental Mediation*. New York: Columbia University Press.

Berry, Jeffrey M. (1977) *Lobbying for the People*. Princeton, NJ: Princeton University Press.

Blumenthal, Sidney. (1988) *The Rise of the Counter-Establishment*. New York: Harper & Row.

Caldeira, G.A. & Wright, J.A. (1988) Organized interests and agenda setting in the U.S. Supreme Court. *American Political Science Review*, 82 (4), 1109-1127.

Cigler, Allan J. & Loomis, Burdette A., eds. (1991) *Interest Group Politics*. Washington, DC: CQ Press.

Derthick, Martha & Quirk, Paul J. (1988) *The Politics of Deregulation*. Washington, DC: The Brookings Institution.

Edsall, Thomas M. (1984) *The New Politics of Inequality*. New York: W.W. Norton & Company.

Epstein, Lee. (1985) *Conservatives in Court*. Knoxville, TN: University of Tennessee Press.

Gittell, Ross J. (1992) *Renewing Cities*. Princeton, NJ: Princeton University Press.

Himmelstein, Jerome L. (1990) *To the Right: The Transformation of American Conservatism*. Berkeley, CA: University of California Press.

McFarland, Andrew S. (1993) *Cooperative Pluralism: The National Coal Policy Experiment*. Lawrence, KS: University of Kansas Press.

Olson, Mancur. (1982) *The Rise and Decline of Nations: Economic Growth, Stagflation, and Social Rigidities*. New Haven: Yale University Press.

Paget, Karen. (1990) Citizen organizing: many movements, no majority. *The American Prospect*, Summer (2), 115-128.

Petracca, Mark P., ed. (1992) *The Politics of Interests: Interest Groups Transformed*. Boulder: Westview Press.

Rauch, Jonathan. (1994) *Demosclerosis: The Silent Killer of American Government*. New York: Random House.

Ricci, David M. (1993) *The Transformation of American Politics: The New Washington and the Rise of Think Tanks*. New Haven: Yale University Press.

Smith, Craig. (1994) The new corporate philanthropy. *Harvard Business Review*, 72 (3), 105-116.

Smith, James A. (1991) *The Idea Brokers: Think Tanks and the Rise of the New Policy Elite*. New York: The Free Press.

Walker, Jack L., Jr. (1991) *Mobilizing Interest Groups in America: Patrons, Professions, and Social Movements*. Ann Arbor, MI: University of Michigan Press.

ADMINISTERING THE PUBLIC AFFAIRS FUNCTION

Chapter 16

The CEO's Role in Nurturing
Public Affairs

Ronald E. Rhody

The CEO has more at stake than any one else in the organization that the corporation's case be made persuasively and that constituent buy-in be secured. Which is why the CEO should take a personal hand in setting the strategy and helping with its execution.

Toward that end, he or she should recognize that this is a game that demands professionals, not amateurs, and establish a solidly professional staff with budgets sufficient to allow them to do the job that needs to be done.

If You Don't Play, You Can't Win

This is intended for the CEO. If you are or intend to be one, read on. If you are not in that august category and don't aspire to be, (not every one wants to be a CEO—it's devilishly hard work) but expect to be working with CEOs on matters of importance, there may be something here that will make it easier. If you are in neither category, welcome—but your time will probably be better spent in other sections of this book.

To make sure there are no unfulfilled expectations here, this is going to be very fundamental stuff—no dancing around or fancy footwork, just basic blocking and tackling—a primer on what the function is, what it can do, how it can be used, and the role the CEO should play in it all.

A few CEOs, of course, know quite a lot about public relations. Unfortunately, even more think they know a lot—but don't. By far the largest number, though, don't know anything about the matter at all, don't think they need to know, and stumble along in blissful ignorance until a major opportunity is missed or a flaming crisis flares and they find themselves up to their ears in alligators when all might have been easily contained if the right steps had been taken in the first place.

To be fair, most executives who win the CEO's chair come to their new responsibilities not wholly prepared for the role they must play in presenting the organization to its publics and not realizing that they are the ones under the gun. The organization's reputation and success is theirs to manage and sustain. The spotlight is on them. They can't avoid this or delegate it and very few are ready.

For the most part they come from finance, or marketing, or production. They've had very little experience and practically no training in how to deal effectively with broader constituencies: like shareholders and employees en masse; or with the movers and shakers in the towns and states they operate in; or with critical shareholders and skeptical analysts; or ambitious federal legislators and regulators; or angry special interest groups and militant activists, or with a not always respectful media.

Having little experience or training in these matters, they sometimes fail to understand that not everyone sees the nobility of their cause as clearly as they do or appreciates the rightness of their actions. Consequently, they don't understand that the organization has to take steps to make sure that the people and groups whose actions and opinions can help or hurt do understand and do appreciate—the result of which is to secure the support the organization absolutely must have if it expects to be successful.

CEO's who are good at this game do understand this. They have a feel for it almost as a matter of instinct, or if not instinct, then the intellect and understanding to appreciate what the tool can do for them and to use it with premeditated skill. Lee Iacocca at Chrysler, Cornell Maier at Kaiser Aluminum, Sam Walton at Wal-Mart were naturals. Tom Clausen at Bank of America, Jack Welch of General Electric, Dick Mahoney at Monsanto, if not naturals, had the quality of mind and managerial savvy to put the tool to work with great effectiveness.

CEOs have little choice but to be adept at positioning their institution acceptably with its key constituents. They face the pressures and demands of a business environment in which the pace and dimensions of change are hazardous coupled with the pressures and demands of a socio-political environment in which it is necessary to be seen as responsible, responsive, constructive, and principled. Boards of directors are not very tolerant of CEO's who stumble in the public arena, who fumble the corporate reputation and set the company up for criticism and complaint; shareholders become restive, employees unhappy, customers critical, governments and regulatory bodies punitive, and the public in general indifferent or hostile.

CEOs, of course, are as different as the companies they head, but regardless of their differences, they share a fundamental reality—their success depends on their ability to create and sustain buy-in. Never mind the financial brilliance or marketing wizardry or technical sophistication they may posses and irrespective of their ambition and their drive, in the final analysis they can't succeed unless and until they can get people to buy in to what they are trying to achieve.

Creating buy-in is what public relations is all about. Which is why the tool is so important.

What Is It?

Unfortunately, the label this function carries confuses users as to its purpose.

It isn't about relating with the public or communicating corporately. It is about getting the organization from where it is to where it wants to be with maximum support and minimum interference. It is about getting people to do something, not do something, or letting you do something. It is about affecting behavior.

In pursuit of this objective and driven by the nature of the function, all public relations operations, regardless of the organization they represent, have certain qualities in common. They include an expertise in mass communications and interpersonal communications, a knowledgeable and skillful media relations capacity, a corps of creative people constantly looking for new and more effective ways to phrase, package, project and deliver ideas, a number of standard and shared techniques in the social sciences and in political affairs, problem solvers in crisis management and damage control, experts in press relations and governmental affairs, in financial communications and employee communications and community relations.

But even with the similarities, the differences from company to company are considerable and they derive principally from the culture of the organization and the personality of the CEO.

The principal objective, however, remains the same: to motivate people to do something, not do something, or let you do something because they understand what the organization is up to and can be shown how their interests are served.

You want them to buy your products and support your stock price, understand your side of the story. You want them to be good employees and supportive neighbors. You want them on your side, or at the very least, you want them to give you the benefit of the doubt.

The "them" in this case isn't everyone. You can't afford to reach everyone. But you absolutely must reach and convince the individuals and groups whose opinions and actions can make a real difference in what you're trying to achieve. As for those who are against you and to whom no amount of reasonable argument will make a difference, you listen politely to their arguments, accept the sincerity of their position, and do what you can to neutralize them.

All these things can be done, not easily and not in every case but most of the time if the CEO wishes them done, sets the necessary priorities, and is a player.

Public relations or public affairs or corporate communications or whatever label the function carries in your organization is, then, a serious management tool which can do what no other single tool can do when properly used. It can create buy-in.

How It Works

The tool works best when it works against a plan. Oddly, for a discipline whose stock in trade is the management of ambiguity, the function is highly planable. It lends itself to clear thinking, goal setting, and managed execution. It is a tool for action, not reaction. If the function is reactive, if it spends most of its time fire fighting, then the organization is wasting its money and the CEO is being ill served.

The way to be proactive is to set goals and go after them. That means a plan. With a plan, the focus is on what needs to be achieved, not on what circumstances throw your way. The right kind of plan, properly executed, puts down fires before they flare.

This is the way the planning process works.

First, objectives are set.

Then the constituencies most important to your success and the critics most likely to impede your way are identified, by individual name if possible but if not, then by groups. Very careful attention should be paid to this step. If this analysis is not correct, the desired results cannot be achieved.

For most profit making organizations, the key constituencies are their shareholders; the professional financial community; customers; employees; retirees; local, state, and national (and sometimes international) governmental and regulatory influences; community leaders in the areas in which they operate; special interest and consumer activities groups; and the media in all its forms—print and electronic, local and national, trade, business, and general interest. Not for profits can substitute donors and clients for shareholders and customers, and the list would be about the same.

As for the critics, each organization is on its own for this one, but the research and analysis ought to be every bit as rigorous as it is for constituents.

Having determined who your true constituents are, you then determine what actions you need to take and what points you need make in order to help them buy in:

- Figure out how to most effectively articulate, package, and deliver your key points to the key constituents so that they take note and are persuaded;

- Decide how and when the points are to be delivered so as to be mutually reinforcing and to deliver sustained impact over the full schedule of the effort;

- Cost it all;

- Do it, checking at regular intervals to gauge if the points are registering and are persuasive and if not, making corrections as you go.

Not a very complicated process as processes go, but very demanding in each step. Overlook a key constituent group, misphrase a message, deliver it in a haphazard way, and the effort fails.

What It Can Do

There are at least seven basic ways in which the tool can be used to help the organization reach its goals:

1. By presenting and explaining the organization's actions and objectives to employees in such a way that they associate their self interest with the success of the organization. (Internal Communications).

2. By creating a climate of understanding and acceptance for the organization's actions and goals which generates cooperation and support from individuals and groups whose opinions and actions can make a difference in the achievement of those goals. (Public Information and Education)

3. By creating (and sustaining) interest in, and understanding of, the strengths and prospects of the organization which supports the stock price and overall financing efforts. (Financial Communications)

4. By creating an atmosphere of public understanding around issues or actions important to the organization which allows law makers and regulators to be supportive of initiatives the organization favors and which mitigates restrictive or unfavorable legislation or regulation, and by fashioning and managing the persuasive presentation of the organization's case to law makers and regulators. (Governmental Relations)

5. By drawing attention to, and creating interest in, the organization's products and services in direct support of marketing efforts. (Product Publicity)

6. By identifying potential problems before they arise and either defusing them or laying strategies to minimize their impact. (Crisis Management)

7. If a crisis is up and running, by taking control of the information flow, assessing the organization's options, marshaling the best arguments, and taking the actions necessary to put the problem down. (Damage Control)

This isn't meant to be an exhaustive list of the function's scope. Responsibilities such as corporate contributions, corporate advertising, research, etc., are often part of the function. But these are the core disciplines.

Organization and Budgeting

The determination of how the organization presents itself, and with what voice, and to whom is too important a matter to be outside the CEO's personal concern. So ideally the function reports directly to the CEO with no intermediary stops or second guessing.

Sometimes the function reports to legal, or to human resources, or to the head of a grouping of various staff services. This isn't the best of arrangements. Each of these functions has its special mindset, its particular values, its own agendas. However enlightened the executive in charge of these groups may be, there is pressure, consciously or unconsciously, to bend the public relations function to their way of doing things, to judge actions by the practices of their disciplines, to measure value by the value scale of their specialty. The result often can be that the CEO doesn't get the hard, unvarnished view of key issues which public relations professionals are trained to provide, doesn't get the candid advice he or she needs on a critical issue or a sensitive situation. Putting people between the senior public relations officer and the CEO who are often more concerned with what the CEO wants to hear rather than what the CEO should hear or apprehensive about what the CEO might not like rather than what ought to be done, isn't smart. It may be organizationally more convenient (the complaint heard is that the CEO has too many people reporting to him, etc.) but gate-keepers at this gate don't serve the CEO's, or the organization's, best interests.

In some cases, however, that's the way it is and that's the way it is going to stay. If so, then the CEO should be sure that the chief public relations officer has unfettered access and a seat at the table as key decisions are being considered.

Of all the organization's officers, only one beside the CEO needs to consider the organization in its entirety; only one other is charged with seeing all its strengths and understanding all its weakness; with keeping the organization's overall goals in sight while working on the minutia of the moment; with being advocate and defender, cheer leader and constructive critic—that is the chief public relations officer. All others can have tunnel vision, indeed are expected to have tunnel vision as they focus on achieving the individual goals of their particular unit or division. This puts a big responsibility on the public relations head to be knowledgeable about all the company's businesses, to work for them all, and to advance their interests and the interests of the corporation together.

As the matter of creating buy-in is too important to be outside the CEO's personal control, it is also too important to be left to amateurs.

Turning the public relations function over to a non professional is a bit like turning open heart surgery over to the hospital administrator. Professional managers can indeed manage the function, and if they are blessed with professional staffs of sufficient quality and dedication, they can get good results. But rarely will the professional manager be able to give the effort the spark, or drive, or leadership necessary to achieve truly outstanding results, the sort of results the CEO needs to create solid buy-in.

What is needed are "managing professionals," people who have the management credentials to run a complex function in addition to the personal creative and professional credentials necessary to motivate and lead an effective professional team.

However the reporting relationship is resolved, to get the most mileage out of the effort, to get the sort of efficiency and synergy and impact the function ought to deliver, the functional portfolio should include:

- employee communications
- media relations
- financial communications
- public information and education
- governmental relations
- community relations
- contributions
- product publicity
- corporate advertising
- issue management
- crisis management and damage control

Many companies do group these connected functions in this manner. In cases where they are housed in various parts of the organization, this is more a matter of practice and tradition than a practical analysis of organizational effectiveness. All these functions are discrete parts of a larger whole. They share disciplines, skills, and mind-sets. Put them together and a remarkably effective tool results.

As for budgets, the dollars needed to run a good operation are quite low in comparison to other expenses. On average, a budget level representing one-tenth to one-quarter of one percent of sales is not unusual among Fortune 500 companies. As the attorneys would say, *de minimus.*

The Role of the CEO

Conventional wisdom notwithstanding, performance almost never speaks for itself. At least it does not speak loudly enough to a wide enough audience in a complex society to make much competitive or persuasive difference rapidly enough.

The short of which is to say that if the organization's story is to be told convincingly, it must do the telling itself.

You have to help people see and appreciate the organization's performance. They cannot be counted on to discover it. Their attention has to be drawn to those things they need to know and appreciate. They have to be helped to understand why they should care, shown how their interests and the organization's interests intertwine.

None of this happens unless the CEO wants it to happen and is serious enough about the matter to be personally involved. This can be uncomfortable. It can mean that the CEO must take a more public role, must be in the media spotlight, must carry the organization's story personally to legislators and community leaders and even critics.

It means as well that the CEO must be personally involved with setting the organization's public relations and communications strategies and with reinforcing existing ones when necessary.

The CEO is the organization's de facto chief public relations officer. He or she may delegate the day to day management of the function to another, but the principal responsibility lies with the CEO. It is the CEO who personifies the organization's values, the CEO who articulates the vision, the CEO who sets the objectives, and as noted earlier, it is the CEO who increasingly takes the rap when things don't work out as well as constituents might have hoped.

Given these facts, it is the CEO who ought be most concerned about how his or her organization is presented to its key constituents. He or she ought to care very much about how its reputation is maintained, how its progress is described, how its problems are explained and its potential projected.

The reporting line for the function should be directly to the CEO, but if organizational gridlock makes this undesirable, the chief public relations officer should have direct access to the CEO under all circumstances, should be included as a member of the deliberative team on issues of consequence and sensitivity, and should have the authority to act on matters within his or her sphere of responsibility.

If the CEO has the right chief public communications officer the team can be formidable. They'll understand each other, have confidence in each other, trust each other and the result of their joint efforts will be the achievement of the goals they have set out to secure.

Working relationships like this are not uncommon, but they are not built easily. They are the result of the opportunity to work together on issues that matter in situations of considerable pressure with each able to gauge the others' performance under fire and have confidence in the outcome.

However such working relationships are arrived at, if they are arrived at, the organization, in the end, is the beneficiary.

No organization's public relations programs can succeed, of course, if its policies and practices are flawed.

To guard against that possibility, the CEO should insist that the organization be open and candid and fair in its dealings with all its constituencies and that it be both responsive and responsible in meeting its obligations to them. The CEO should verify the importance of these values through personal action. And most importantly, the CEO should be a player in this most demanding of games.

Those who don't play can't win.

Chapter 17

Anticipatory Management: Linking Public Affairs and Strategic Planning

William C. Ashley

Given that change has become the essence of today's business climate, the real strategic consideration for leaders is whether that change will befall the organization as a series of crises. Or, will the organization use foresight and anticipation to deal such with change in a calm, informed and systematic manner? Setting one's own future agenda can only be done with knowledge. Knowledge comes from balancing—and in some cases challenging—inside knowledge with outside knowledge. To compete for the future, companies will have to perfect their outside-in thinking skills. Many Japanese companies believe that new and strategic knowledge cannot be created without an intensive interaction between inside and outside information. One of the ways that an organization can capitalize on strategic outside knowledge is by establishing a closer and more systematic relationship between public affairs and strategic planning.

Public affairs adds value to the strategic planning process by incorporating strategic stakeholders (legislators, regulators, media, customers, educators, special interest groups, etc.) information and strategic trend intelligence (external trends, events and driving forces) on a regular basis. This information can be transmitted regularly to assure emerging issues are considered when setting the strategic agenda.

239

An emerging strategic issue is an internal or external development that: (1) could impact the organization's performance; (2) the organization must respond to an orderly and timely fashion; and (3) over which the organization may reasonably expect to exert some influence. Wilson (1982) articulates the life cycle of an issue in four phases. He stated in an unpublished monograph, "[w]ithout a proper business response, the societal expectations of today become the political issues of tomorrow, legislated requirements of the next day and the litigated penalties the day after."

The complexity of today's issues make it necessary for managers to think beyond neat organizational boxes (in some cases foxholes). Emerging issues possess complex qualities incompatible with hierarchical organizational charts. The new perspective requires circumventing the organizational chart. It requires establishing decision models that link with accountability models, so that in periods of unprecedented change the organization will recognize strategic issues, know what to do about them, who will do it, how and when it will be done and what the outcomes might be.

To increase public affairs value to the company, in terms of the strategic process, new models and new methods of interaction must be used. If public affairs expects to participate, it must adopt a systematic approach to anticipate issues early in their life cycle and bring them to the attention of senior planners in a way that assures only emerging issues of strategic significance are considered, if not acted upon.

The Anticipatory Management Decision Process Model

The anticipatory management decision process model diagrammed above suggests an outside-in information processing schematic that has been employed in corporate settings with great success.

1. Identifying Issues

Scanning, monitoring, and forecasting provide raw information for anticipatory issues management. Although there are many approaches to identifying issues, the primary consideration is that

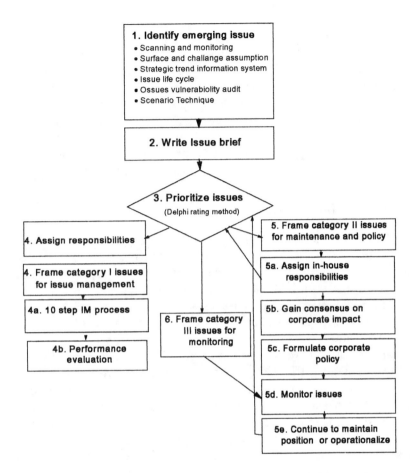

Anticipatory management decision process model

trends and events are monitored by public affairs to ascertain dura-
tion, direction, acceleration, and amplitude. *Trends* are descriptions
of *social, technological, economic, environmental,* or *political*
(STEEP) movements over time. They define the context within
which the organization will function in the future (e.g., the increase
or decrease in households with incomes over $50,000). *Events* are
developments that change the future when they occur (e.g., an international free trade agreement). Trends and events converge to
form *issues* like population growth, pollution, and poverty.

2. Writing Issue Briefs

Analysis of the trends yields a rich quantity of information about possible issues that could influence the way the organization does business. An *issue brief* summarizes the issue for management consideration in a concise document. In general, issue briefs should be no longer than two single-spaced pages. They should contain (a) a statement of the focus of the issue; (b) a discussion of its background; (c) a description of the trends, driving forces, and stakeholders influencing it; (d) a forecast describing its future prospects; and (e) a listing of potential implications for the organization.

3. Prioritizing Issues

Sorting issues involves answering several critical questions: What is the probability that the issue will go critical? What is the probability that it will affect the organization? Can the organization influence the issue? Should the organization try?

Prioritization categorizes issues into three types: high priority, those requiring action (Category I); those that do not require immediate action due to their maturity, their inability to be managed, or their relative unimportance (Category II); and those requiring no action (Category III). Category I, high priority, issues will be discussed according to the 10-step Issues Management (IM) process. Category II issues are too mature in the issue life cycle to manage effectively but may require organizational policy statements or actions on the part of certain sectors of the organization. Category III issues require no action but due to their potential impact on the organization need to be monitored and periodically revisited.

4. Framing Category I (high priority) Issues for Issues Management

To manage those issues requiring an action plan a 10-step IM process provides an effective step by step approach to managing an issue.

4a. 10-step Issues Management Process

1. Issue owner.
2. Issue action team.
3. Situational assessment.

4. *Impact analysis.*
5. *Stakeholder assessment.*
6. *Organizational position.*
7. *Stakeholder objectives.*
8. *Technical or operating objectives.*
9. *Action plan implementation.*
10. *Measurement and fine tuning.*

4b. Performance Evaluation

Performance evaluation is the review of the action plan implementation. It assesses how well objectives are attained and how stakeholders respond to the plan. Since the action teams disband once the plan is set in place, performance evaluation is the responsibility of the issues management function.

5. Framing Category II Issues for Maintenance and Policy

For Category II issues, the emphasis is not on external management and influence but internal containment and compliance. The organization cannot influence the issue under present circumstances. However, the issue may require an internal structural or policy readjustment to align the organization with the direction the issue appears headed in. The 1992 Disability Act was not something that could be managed in 1992. Internal policies regarding hiring and architectural adjustments needed to be established.

Such adjustments generally require the involvement of several departments or divisions. Questions must be asked early on about which departments will be affected most. Who in the organization has the most information about the issue?

5a. Assignment of In-house Responsibilities

Establishing policy on a mature issue whose full impact is unclear requires the best strategic thinking the organization can muster. This work should not be left entirely to the issues management function but include those departments most affected.

5b. Consensus on Corporate Impact

At this point in the process, senior management knows that the issue will affect the organization. Reaching consensus on what, where, and how it will do so requires linking "hard" and "soft" information to strategic thinking.

5c. Formulation of Corporate Policy

Using strategic thinking, the issues management staff and members of affected departments examine the dynamics of the issue from both the outside in (finding trends and driving forces) and from the inside out (linking those trends to the operations of the organization). In so doing, the group will identify information needs (e.g., positions within the industry and similarly affected industries).

It is important to remember throughout the issues management process that whereas an issue may be in its emergent stage for one's own organization, it may have progressed much further for another. Someone else may have worked on the issue for a much longer period of time and have valuable information on which to draw. When United Airlines confronted the video display terminal (VDT) issue, a check with companies outside the airline industry revealed information that made policy formation much easier.

5d. Issue Monitoring

Once the group has done its work, the course to be followed should fall into place. It is important to identify further information needs and charge the issues management staff with monitoring the issue.

5e. Decision to Maintain or to
Operationalize Strategic Response

Because the future is unpredictable and issues do not always behave as expected, one must be able to move an issue into management mode easily. Shifts in the environment (social patterns change; economic variables emerge that were not present when a policy was formulated; a new technology surfaces that makes the position less tenable) could lead to a decision that the issue is now Category I. The shift may also be within the organization: a new strategic direction or new product introduction makes the existing policy less valid. The Anticipatory Management (AM) decision/process model provides for such contingencies.

The AM model emphasizes early identification and analysis of an emerging issue, making use of an issue brief and prioritization rating form. The rating process is essentially an algorithmic deci-

sion method. When used, the issue is prepared for strategy, maintenance, and/or policy making. The organization either builds a plan
to manage the issue or establishes a position for use throughout the
organization and with the various stakeholders.

When an emerging issue needs to be managed, the 10 step IM
process provides a series of steps that allow the organization to
maximize the fit between the issue's direction and the organization's
goals.

6. Framing Category III Issues for Monitoring

While category III issues may require no action they continue to
be monitored for shifts that could affect the organization's future.
If such shifts occur, the issues are re-evaluated and may be dropped
or assigned a category I, high priority status.

The Anticipatory Management
Accountability Model

Understanding the movement of information through an organization goes beyond delineating the decision phases of the issues
process. To make anticipatory management part of the organizational
mind set, one must make it part of the management structure. The
components of the accountability model describe what is done, who
does what to whom, when and how.

The accountability model diagrammed below shows the movement
of strategic information from outside the organization in through
various accountability gates. Without such a road map, many companies find themselves befuddled by an issue for which ample
information already exists somewhere in the organization. Also,
many in-house programs fail because the information languishes in
a file in a division or department with no system to monitor its status or to bring it to the attention of the strategic planners.

Anticipatory management relies heavily on processes and responsibilities. Marrying the flow of strategic information through an
organization to the accountability for that information is critical to
the successful operation of the anticipatory management process.
While emerging issues may be complicated and difficult to understand, the process by which issues are dealt with should not be. The
use of the AM decision/process described above and the account-

ability schematics shown below help managers follow the flow of strategic information and the accountability for that information in the process of managing an issue.

The accountability and decision/process model share a key component, the 10 step IM process. When an issue is classified or prioritized by a senior steering committee as a high priority or category I issue it is dealt with through the use of a standard set of procedures and check points. Referred to as the 10-step IM process, it assures that each class I or high priority issue receives the same or similar investigative methodology. The use of this process also allows management to become familiar with dealing with issues that are still in the emerging stage.

Understanding the flow of information through an organization is central to the successful implementation of an in-house anticipatory management program. The structure should be kept simple. Management's time is at a premium. Although the overall anticipatory management process can have significant bottom-line potential, it need not be complicated, cumbersome, or intrusive on day-to-day operations.

1. The Public Affairs Issues Management Function

The issues manager oversees the issues management function. The manager must:

- Maintain the strategic trend intelligence system;
- Identifying issues from numerous sources;
- Analyze trend information into issue briefs for consideration by the steering committee.

2. Steering Committee

The Steering Committee is selected by the CEO to screen and prioritize emerging issues presented by the issues management staff. Individuals selected for this committee generally report directly to the CEO. They possess not only an in-depth knowledge of the organization but also a broad perspective on the external forces with influence on it. They must:

- Review issue briefs prepared by the issues management staff;
- Determine implications and degree of organizational opportunity or vulnerability;

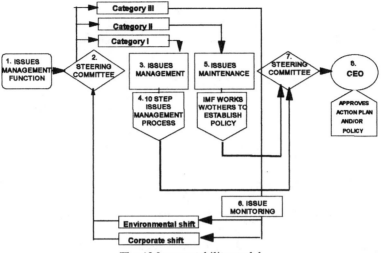

The AM accountability model

- Use specific criteria to rate issues on probability of occurrence, impact, and degree to which the organization can and should influence them;
- Determine the degree of organizational involvement, based on consensus opinion, i.e., sort issues into categories.

3. Issues Management Process

If an issue has been rated Category I, it will likely continue in the direction it is headed and its impact on the organization will be high. The organization should attempt to influence either its direction or its effects on the organization.

Responsibility for resolving the issue must rest at the senior management level. To relegate responsibility to a lower level is to belie the rating scheme and the organizational commitment.

Once the steering committee determines an issue to be Category I, it assigns issue ownership by determining the department that could most benefit from or be hurt by the issue. The officer responsible for that area is designated the owner.

Ownership does not imply that work on the issue should be carried out exclusively within the owner's department. Establishing ownership is merely the first step in preparing Category I issues for management. While a senior manager may own the issue and be responsible to the CEO for its successful resolution, the manag-

er may appoint someone else as chair of the action team. The issues manager works with the chair to select the action team, set
the agenda, and facilitate team meetings as necessary.

4. 10-step Issues Management Process

The organization analyzes the issue using the 10-Step methodology.

5. Issues Maintenance

Should the steering committee classify the issue as Category II—
that is, an issue that does not require management by an action
team—the committee returns the issue to the issues management
function for policy formulation. Other departments may need to be
involved so that the internal position is consistent with the issue's
status.

6. Issues Monitoring

The monitoring activity for issues in categories II and III concentrates on *environmental* shifts (changes in the direction of events,
trends, and driving forces) and *corporate* shifts (changes in organizational policies, products, services, marketing strategies, or operating procedures) that could turn them into high priority, category I
issues needing analysis and management. Monitoring systematically collects and analyzes information related to the issue: changes
in public attitudes, fiscal policy, regulations, legislation, or academic
theory.

Understanding corporate and environmental shifts is the essence
of anticipation. A major obstacle to anticipatory management is the
evaluation of managers on efficient performance under relatively
short-term targets, criteria being based on strict administration of
resources. Whenever a new opportunity or threat is revealed, recognition will be resisted by managers whose performance will be
affected by *any* shift in ongoing activities. (*If it ain't broke, don't
fix it.*)

Issues monitoring is a responsibility of a separate issues management staff for that reason. If the issues manager determines that
an issue needs to be reconsidered as Category I, the manager re-

submits the issue to the steering committee in the form of an updated issue brief.

7. Steering Committee

At this stage, the steering committee reviews the action plan, including details of what is to be done, why it is to be done, who is to do it, when it is to be done, how much it will cost, and where the money will come from. Because many action plans involve cross-disciplinary work teams, it is crucial that all parties agree to it.

The steering committee then forwards the plan to the CEO.

8. CEO

The CEO is responsible for reviewing the action plan. The CEO will usually ask the issue owner and action team to present the plan at a steering committee meeting. Because the issue may not have crystallized fully, stakeholder positions along with technical and operating objectives should be presented to ensure everyone's involvement and commitment to the principals.

Summary

Public affairs must adopt a systematic approach to anticipate issues early in their life cycle and to bring them to the attention of senior planners in a way that assures only emerging issues of strategic significance are considered, if not acted upon. Thereby providing valuable lead time, better allocation of resources, increased and informed and timely participation in dealing with strategic issues.

Understanding outside-in thinking, and the increasing role of stakeholders, public affairs and public relations will gain very important and well earned seats at the strategic planning table. It is fiscal folly for organizations to wait until an issue goes critical then expect their public affairs folks to contain it and their public relations folks to explain it. Through the use of the tools and techniques discussed in this chapter public affairs comes to the table with a well thought out methodology for bringing the outside in, in a systematic, easily comprehensible manner, that takes a minimum of senior manager's time. In becoming involved in the strategic planning process, public affairs professionals must understand that operations managers develop a paradigm or mind-set that is heavily influenced by experience and training and thus places heavy emphasis on an inside out perspective. Metaphors and analogies abound in discussing this somewhat one-sided perspective; *keep your head down and charge, keep your nose to the grindstone, if it ain't broke don't fix it, stay out of other peoples sandboxes (or more correctly, in our present business environment, foxholes)* are just a few. The ideas and systems discussed above suggest that while change and uncertainty is inevitable, it need not be terminal. Organizations cannot count on a policy fix or a natural evolution to a more predictable world. Success and in some cases survival will require a sophisticated intelligence system plus new, ongoing relationships between public affairs and strategic planning and a shift in managerial mindset. Shifting from the organization as a profit maximizing, economic entity, to an awareness of the strategic significance of stakeholders and seeing the organization as a major player in social, technological, environmental and political arenas will be required.

Chapter 18

Public Affairs: Profit Center?

Nick L. Laird

Is it enough for a corporate public affairs department to promote a positive corporate image in the media, good relations with public officials, and goodwill in the community? Or should public affairs be required to operate as a "profit center" contributing to the corporation's profitability? Do operating departments expect public affairs to add to the company's profits? More specifically, can a public affairs department operate as a profit center? Is it possible to quantify with credibility the profit contribution generated by public affairs?

The answer to these questions is easily answered "yes" in today's environment of reengineered corporate staffs. In companies that have implemented the shared services approach, public affairs departments know well the implications of adding (or failing to add) to operating units' profits. Unfortunately, many of our colleagues who were capable at implementing the public affairs strategies no longer have jobs because of their failure to focus on identifying internal issues specific to their company's operating and staff units.

I. Source of Issues

Despite nearly a decade of emphasis on quantifying contributions to the company's bottom-line profits, corporate public affairs departments still too often develop issues as reactive *ad hoc* responses to external events.

External Issues

In companies where public affairs contributions are viewed as "soft," public affairs issues are most likely identified by analyzing the external environment and advising the operating and staff units of the issues identified. Too frequently, the issues identified externally are not relevant directly to operating and staff plans, especially as they relate to new lines of business or new revenue-generating opportunities. As a result, operating and staff managers often question the "value added" by the public affairs efforts.

Crisis Issues

Another source of issues comes from operating and staff units who ask for urgent help on crisis issues. The matter of urgent help is often news to the public affairs staffs. Generally, public affairs staffs are asked to perform miracles on a crisis issue that is far along in the process. Many times, the effort to salvage the crisis is less than satisfactory.

Internal Identification

Public affairs departments operating as profit centers focus on identifying issues having bottom-line earnings impacts. They focus on working closely with operating and staff units. By doing so, public affairs staffs increase their opportunities to add value to the company's operations. More importantly, chances of being successful on each issue improve by identifying the issues *early* in the planning process. Successful resolution of those issues contribute *quantifiable* results—results that would not have been realized but for the initiative taken by the public affairs staffs.

II. Issues Identification

In a recent benchmarking study of public affairs "best practices" across industries, Dr. Rita K. Roosevelt documented public affairs staffs that operate successfully as profit centers. In each case, the staff relied on an issues management process that interacted with business groups, business units, and shared services staffs to identify issues and projects with clear strategic and operating bottom-line profit impacts.

In the *"Quantifying Impacts" (QI) Handbook*, prepared by the writer and Dr. Roosevelt, presents a detailed issues management process for identifying strategic and operating public affairs issues. Much of the discussion on issues management that follows is based on the *QI Handbook* methodology. *QI* shifts the *focus* from primarily *externally* generated issues to *internally* identified issues that will uniquely benefit the company's profits, operations, and competitive positions. *QI* also shifts the public affairs agenda to a challenging *proactive* agenda. Figure 1 illustrates the *QI* shift in focus.

The "Quantifying Impacts" *(QI)* methodology focuses on operating and staff personnel identifying issues and projects that would improve their operations if specific changes in the external environment were accomplished by the company's public affairs staffs. More importantly, operating and staff personnel identify issues and projects where changes could *increase* earnings for their units.

Figure 1

"QUANTIFYING IMPACTS" *(QI)*
ISSUES IDENTIFICATION

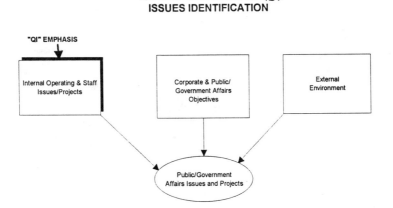

Operating Expertise

Success of the issue identification process depends heavily on the public affairs staff's initial interview and ongoing discussions with operating and staff personnel. The goal of these discussions (as reflected in Figure 2) is *to identify profit-generating or cost-reducing issues and potential projects that would not be identified by operating and staff managers in the normal course of business.*

Typically, operating and staff personnel develop operating and strategic plans based on limitations, regulations, and restrictions known to them at the time of developing their plans. Understandably, they cannot fully appreciate or assess the potential for changing the external limitations. Therefore, their planning documents and contingency plans and projects are developed "inside the box" of known limitations. Their "inside the box" plans and projects reflect operating within a known external environment. They are not based on changing the external environment.

Figure 2

QI INTERVIEW GOAL

GOAL: To identify profit-generating or cost-reducing issues and potential projects that would not be identified by operating and staff managers in the normal course of business.

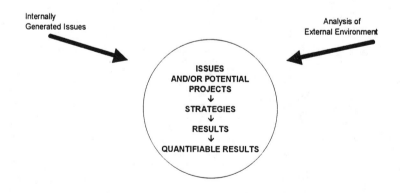

The public affairs staff's interviews should seek to generate creative "outside the box" thinking by operating and staff personnel. To stimulate such creative brainstorming, the public affairs staff interviewer may ask, *"Assuming that you could change anything in your external operating environment, what would you then do differently to increase your unit's profitability?"* The interviewer may ask the follow-up question, *"What size of potential earnings increases, cost savings, avoided costs or competitive advantages would your unit be able to realize under the changed environment?"*

The interviewer's objective is to identify new operating and staff issues and/or projects that potentially would be undertaken if some change in the company's external environment could be achieved.

Public Affairs Expertise

Just as operating and staff personnel cannot be experts on the extent of potential changes that could be made in the external environment, public affairs staffs cannot know the spectrum of operating and staff initiatives or projects that potentially could be undertaken if changes were made in the external environment. For that reason, the public affairs staff interviewer should create a dialogue where the operating and staff personnel are convinced of the following: *Public affairs staffs are dedicated to helping the operating and staff units to generate profits.* In other words, the public affairs staffs are "customer focused" and targeted on issues relevant to the customer's profitability.

As Figure 3 illustrates, the public affairs staff interviewer's objective is to develop from each interview a "brainstorming" list of new projects or initiatives that the operating and staff units would like to undertake if the public affairs staffs could change some aspect of the current external environment.

The public affairs interviewer should obtain gross earnings impacts (earnings increases, cost savings, or avoided costs)—even if only a "guesstimate"—for each of the most likely issues or projects.

III. Issue Evaluation

The brainstorming "wish" lists of potential issues and projects developed from discussions with operating and staff personnel must

Figure 3

QI INTERVIEW OBJECTIVE

ASSUMPTION #1: Operating and staff departments develop operating and capital plans with limited appreciation of what changes the company's public and government affairs staffs could potentially accomplish.

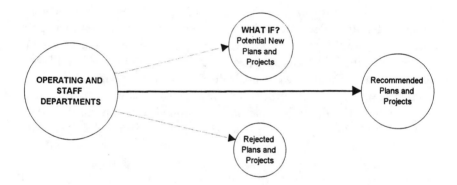

ASSUMPTION #2: Operating and staff departments could identify potentially <u>new</u> projects or plans to increase earnings or to reduce costs if all external restraints were removed (thinking "outside the box").

Figure 3 (continued)

ASSUMPTION #3: Public and government affairs staffs can change some aspects of the company's external environment.

ASSUMPTION #4: Some potential new plans and projects are dependent on changes in the company's external environment.

Operating and Staff Departments' Potential New Projects and Plans

TARGET ISSUES

Company's External Environment Potentially Changeable by Company's Efforts

be evaluated in order to reduce them to a manageable number of key issues.

Potential public affairs issues and projects can be evaluated by any number of factors. Most public affairs departments operating as profit centers apply two measures to the "wish" lists of potential issues and projects: (1) significant bottom-line earnings impacts (earnings increases, cost savings, or avoided costs) and (2) probability assessments of being successful in achieving proposed changes in the external environment.

Earnings Impacts

During interview discussions with operating and staff personnel, the public affairs interviewer should obtain gross earnings impacts for each of the issues and projects for which changes in the company's external environment *may* be achievable by the public affairs staff. Even if the estimated earnings impacts are a guesstimate, they are useful in assessing the issue. At this stage in evaluating potential issues, the estimated earnings impacts do not have to be precise. However, operating and staff personnel should agree that the guesstimates are reasonable financial estimates.

Relying on operating and staff units to quantify the estimated dollar impacts of potential issues or projects enhances the credibility of the public affairs staffs' evaluations. The greater the **earnings impacts** the more likely that an issue or project will be included in the final agenda of public affairs issues.

Probability Assessments

Evaluating a potential issue or project requires making **probability assessments** of the likelihood of achieving the objective or the required changes in the external environment. Public affairs staffs make the assessments based on their knowledge, research, judgment, experience, contacts, and available resources. Their insights and the factors they weigh are unique to each issue or project.

The **probability assessments** put the public affairs staffs into an equal partnership with operating and staff units in (1) evaluating potential issues or projects and in (2) determining priorities and resources to be assigned to each issue or project.

Evaluation Matrix

Determining the "preliminary" list of public affairs issues and projects involves weighing carefully the **balance** between *earnings impacts* and *probability assessments* for each potential issue or project.

The Evaluation Matrix in Table 1 can be used to plot the estimated earnings impacts in dollars and the percentage likelihood of achieving specific changes in the external environment. Issues and projects falling in the upper right quadrant of the Evaluation Ma-

Table 1

EVALUATION MATRIX
OF
QI POTENTIAL ISSUES

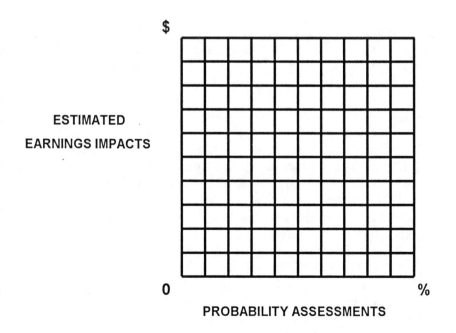

(Estimated Earnings Impacts = Earnings Increases or Costs Savings)

(Probability Assessments = Percentage Likelihood of Achieving Specific Changes in External Environment)

trix have the highest probabilities of success and the greatest potential earnings impacts. Consequently, those issues and projects should be included in a **preliminary agenda** of public affairs issues. In addition, the Matrix can be used to assign *priority* rankings to each of the issues on the preliminary agenda.

IV. Issue Analysis

Issue Analysis is used to evaluate more thoroughly the issues and projects included in the preliminary issues agenda. Issue Analysis provides the documented basis for determining the company's **final** public affairs issues agenda.

Issue Papers

In addition to *earnings impacts* and *probability assessments*, Issue Analysis assures that other aspects (especially external) of each issue or project are included in assessing its potential impacts and viability.

In Issue Analysis, each identified issue or project is viewed as a unique problem or situation requiring some form of action. To determine ultimate viability, an "Issue Paper" generally is prepared for each issue or project that responds to a structured set of interrogatories.

- **WHAT** is the issue or project? Does it have universal impact or is it technical in nature and specific to the company? What is known about the issue or project from external scanning?
- **WHO** is affected? A large or small number of people? A broad cross-section of the population or some particular segment?
- **WHEN** are the effects likely to be felt? Currently or in the future? Are the effects inevitable or only as a consequence of some other development?
- **HOW** can the issue or projects be resolved? What options are potential responses? Who will be involved?
- **HOW MUCH** will each of the options cost? How much will earnings increase? How much cost savings or avoided costs will be realized? How are these figures derived?

The answers to these questions provide a measure of the impact of each issue or project on the company and will serve as the basis for setting the final **public affairs issues agenda**.

Prioritized Rankings

Issue Analysis may eliminate some of the issues or projects on the preliminary issues agenda. Likewise, the analyses may produce new issues or projects to be evaluated.

As the final step in determining the final agenda of key public affairs issues, the Evaluation Matrix (Table 1) can be used to plot each issue's **earnings impacts** and **probability assessments** and to assign *priority* rankings to each of the issues or projects included in the final agenda.

The company's final public affairs issues agenda may also include issues or projects that meet other corporate or operating goals. Such issues or projects will have justifications based on other factors.

Issues Agenda

After obtaining appropriate corporate approval of the final agenda's issues and projects, the company's **public affairs issues agenda** is established.

Management and operating personnel will have a clear understanding of what the public affairs staffs are trying to accomplish and how their efforts fit into the company's operating and strategic plans.

The **public affairs issues agenda** will provide a tangible standard of performance review. While not the only measure of performance, it is likely to be the most important measure. Management's annual review and approval of the public affairs issues agenda will set a clear standard in advance.

Successful results on the issues agenda will provide justification for public affairs staff's budgets, staffing, and salary levels, and help to justify expenditures on other public affairs activities that are difficult, if not impossible, to quantify results.

Management's prior approval and rank ordering of key issues will provide operating and staff personnel with an appreciation of where their issues fall within the public affairs staff's priorities. Public affairs successes on operating and staff issues will cause those managers to advocate increased resources for the public affairs staffs (so that additional issues can be resolved to increase operating and staff units' earnings).

The **public affairs issues agenda** will establish clear lines of responsibility for managing the issues within the company. It also will help senior executives to assess management potential and determine salary increases, bonuses, and other compensation incentives and rewards.

Within the public affairs staffs, the issues agenda will facilitate clear delegation of assignments, individual performance reviews, and justification of performance critiques, promotions, and salary adjustments, as well as evaluation of performance of outside consultants.

After the public affairs issues agenda is established, public affairs must develop and implement the external strategies needed to bring about the desired results specified for each issue or project.

Strategies and action plans must be uniquely formulated for each issue or project, as well as for the targeted audiences. After public affairs staffs resolve each issue, operating and staff units can take "new or changed actions" (as identified during the issues identification interviews) that will produce earnings increases, costs savings, or avoided costs.

V. Performance Measures

The public affairs issues agenda represents *opportunities* for public affairs staffs to create "value added." To do so, public affairs staffs must change the company's external environments as specified in the issue analysis paper developed for each issue or project. The changed environments will permit operating and staff units to generate quantifiable **earnings impacts** from new or changed actions.

Public affairs operations can be evaluated by "Performance Measures" applied on a staff unit and/or project basis.

Applying Performance Measures on Department Basis

Applying performance measures on a department basis is relatively simple and credible. As each public affairs issue or project is resolved, operating and staff units provide reliable estimates of the earnings impacts resulting from the changes achieved by the public affairs staffs.

Public affairs staffs maintain a running compilation of the earnings estimates for resolved issues and projects. At the end of the fiscal year, the earnings estimates are added to determine the total of the documented earnings impacts. Recognition of those earnings impacts are justified because the specific earnings impacts would not have been generated but for the issues identification and changes achieved by the public affairs staffs.

Applying Performance Measures on a Project Basis

Figure 4 illustrates application of the performance measure to evaluating a staff unit's activities on a project basis. Projects are analyzed on both a *quantitative* (earnings) and a *qualitative* (secondary, goodwill) basis.

Project analyses should emphasize the following *"Types of Impacts"*:

Earnings Impacts—quantifiable earnings increases, costs savings, or avoided costs;

Secondary Impacts—actions, such as media coverage, that are independent or indirect from company's own initiatives;

Goodwill Impacts—improved external relationships and company images.

Public affairs departments with projects primarily in the "Goodwill Impacts" category have difficulties in documenting quantified value added from their activities. In contrast, Dr. Roosevelt's benchmarking study found that public affairs units operating successfully as profit centers identified issues and projects primarily in the "Earnings" and "Secondary" impacts categories.

Measuring Performance of Public Affairs Activities

Most corporate managers use a financial measure to calculate return on investment (earnings ÷ investments = percentage ROI). This financial performance measure is easily utilized to measure public affairs performance. A public affairs unit's total documented

Figure 4

APPLYING *QI* ON A PROJECT BASIS

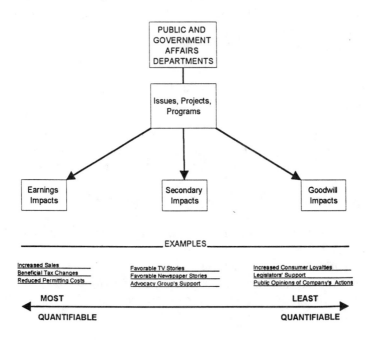

earnings impacts for the year can be compared to the unit's **annual budget** (or total annual expenditures) to determine whether the staff unit added value or earned a profit.

As Figure 5 illustrates, the measure of performance requires dividing a public affairs unit's annual budget (or total annual expenditures) into the total of the documented earnings impacts (earnings increases, costs savings, or avoided costs) applicable to that year. A resulting quotient of more than one (1) indicates that the unit returned earnings greater than its costs.

VI. Conclusion

Should public affairs departments operate as a "profit center"? As noted at the beginning of this chapter, the answer is "yes"! As

Figure 5

CALCULATING PERFORMANCE MEASURE

$		$		
EARNINGS IMPACTS	÷	TOTAL DEPARTMENT BUDGET	=	MEASURE OF PERFORMANCE

Dr. Roosevelt's "best practices" benchmarking study demonstrated, the most successful public affairs units emphasize the systematic identification of quantifiable operating and staff departments' issues or projects on which public affairs staffs can potentially make positive changes in the company's external environment. The **earnings impacts** growing out of the positive changes achieved by the public affairs staffs provide documented value added to the company's profits—*thereby establishing public affairs as a credible "profit center."*

Chapter 19

Benchmarking: Evaluating the Public Affairs Operation/Function

Craig S. Fleisher and
Sara Burton

If there is one constant that public affairs (PA) professionals face in their organizational lives, it is continuously fighting battles to keep their heads above water. One crisis is almost always followed by another. Yet in the midst of trying to survive the crises, PA professionals need to demonstrate the unit's ongoing value to top executives and line managers in their organizations. Similar to the contemporary forces which have affected professionals in other staff functions, PA professionals have had to fight an increasing number of more vigorous battles while at the same time weathering resource cutbacks.

However, unlike some of their other staff colleagues, PA professionals regularly struggle with supporting an answer to questions such as "What have you done for me, lately?" or "What has the PA unit contributed to the bottom-line this last quarter?" Many PA professionals encounter difficulty communicating their role or value to top management and others in the organization. For a closer look at PA as a profit center see Chapter 19).

It is our objective to illuminate the role of benchmarking in helping PA functions and practitioners achieve, sustain, and keep management's confidence. This chapter provides several pertinent reasons as to how PA adds value to the organization, suggests why PA has encountered difficulties in gaining management's confidence, defines the process of benchmarking, and identifies how benchmarking can benefit the PA function and the entire organization.

The Value of Public Affairs

Most experienced PA professionals inherently believe that the PA unit adds great value and makes important contributions to the organization. However, many professionals are unsure as to the quantity and the quality of value in both an absolute and relative sense, they have contributed to the organization. The challenge is to find a means by which PA professionals can improve their ability to demonstrate and communicate their value and importance while improving what they do and how they do it.

A premise underlying this article is that PA can add significant bottom-line value to an organization even though PA is indirectly linked to an organization's ultimate product or service market customer. This bottom line contribution is enhanced when PA professionals perform effectively. For example, PA professionals and their units can be the key to sustaining an organization's reputation and integrity during a crisis situation. Few observers of the business world are unaware of the contribution made by PA professionals and units during Johnson & Johnson's Tylenol or Pepsi's product tampering crises.

Through its management of actions and inactions during crises, PA adds to or at least preserves both tangible and intangible forms of organizational value in the eyes of product/service market customers and other stakeholders. This value can take years of sustained effort to generate; however, it can be lost in a matter of hours. Although senior organizational executives recognize the value of PA during these crisis situations, PA's value is often forgotten after the crisis subsides or goes unrecognized because of its indirect nature to the end customer.

The successful management of public affairs is like walking the edge of a two-sided sword: PA professionals and/or units gain management's confidence when they effectively respond to crises; but if they proactively avert, minimize or prevent these crises, as most managers are taught to do and are rewarded for, their value goes un- or under-recognized or un- or under-rewarded. How can PA professionals manage this difficult balancing act and capably walk on the edge of the sword?

Improved PA management begins with the recognition that PA professionals add the most of their value on a day-to-day basis through leveraging the efforts of other departments and units. Outcomes to PA's customers are enhanced when the PA unit improves its inputs, processes and outputs. When these outcomes are depended upon by other line and staff members, these functions will operate at higher performance levels. By helping other functions perform at their highest levels, PA increases the value of these functions and the entire organization which can better satisfy the ultimate product/service market customers. Figure 1 depicts this relationship between PA and the ultimate customer.

Difficulties PA Faces in Gaining Management's Confidence

If PA truly creates value, why does it have such difficulty in achieving, sustaining, and keeping management's confidence? There are a number of reasons which can create a lack of managerial confidence in PA. The following section discusses three critical issues which may lead to lessened executive confidence in PA.

Role Differences Between PA and Other Organizational Areas

There is a fundamental difference between the role of PA and the role of many other organizational functions. As was previously discussed, PA tends to have indirect relationships with the organization's ultimate customer. PA's internal customers could be completely satisfied with the outputs of PA, however those outputs may not have an observable effect on the bottom-line. This can create a problem for PA when management requests "proof" of PA's value vis-a-vis the bottom-line.

PA members are also known as boundary spanners in that they operate both within the organization and in the external environment.[1] To external stakeholders, PA professionals are viewed as organizational agents. To internal stakeholders, PA professionals are viewed as those individuals who are out there interfacing with ex-

Figure 1

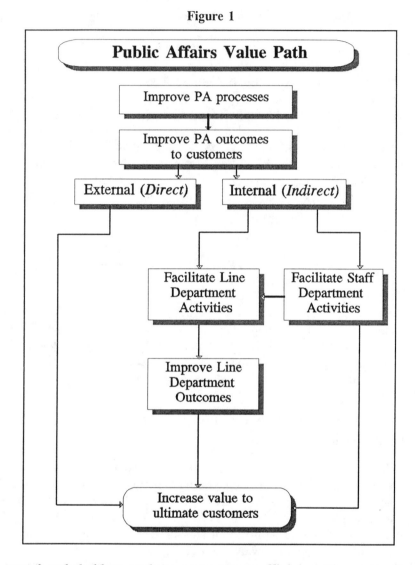

Public Affairs Value Path

Improve PA processes

Improve PA outcomes
to customers

External (*Direct*)   Internal (*Indirect*)

Facilitate Line   Facilitate Staff
Department   Department
Activities   Activities

Improve Line
Department
Outcomes

Increase value to
ultimate customers

ternal stakeholders such as government officials and community representatives. To many line managers, PA professionals are corporate staff types who are to be avoided like other corporate staff types. In other words, PA professionals are frequently viewed with suspicion by internal and external stakeholders. No wonder it has been so difficult to clarify the PA role in a way that can build confidence.

In addition, PA has generally been slow to adopt management improvement efforts that are attempted by other parts of the organization.[2] This has created two key problems: First, PA is not improving as rapidly as others in the organization who attempt to implement such efforts; second, PA professionals do not know how to communicate the unit's efforts and achievements using the language of "Quality." Because of their tardiness in adopting quality improvement efforts, PA units run into the problem that they are "always among the last to know, and among the first to go" when the organization's budget reduction axe swings. Questions will remain about the function's value to the extent that PA cannot prove its worth in actions and terms used by the rest of the organization.

Lack of Strategic Orientation and Integration

PA professionals who constantly fight fires do not have time to take preventive measures. These measures may be avoided by PA decision makers in the first place since they get minimal or sometimes even "negative credit" for them. A comment sometimes offered by PA executives at professional meetings suggests that there is "nothing like a crisis" for getting executives to recognize PA's value; conversely, many executives do not acknowledge or vaguely understand and recognize PA's efforts at heading off or preventing problems. This situation means that the PA function is not always used as a strategic tool within the organization. PA can in fact be a very powerful tool in gaining and sustaining competitive advantage; however, the tool has to be effectively used.[3]

PA units can be instrumental in affecting the public policy risk faced by business units. PA programs which enhance a community's understanding of a plant's expansion plans, leading the community to view these plans as opportunities and not threats, can reduce the likelihood of community groups formally organizing to defeat the expansion proposals. PA can also act in ways that directly increase business opportunities (e.g., opening up new markets for competition through proposing and supporting relevant legislation such as that promoted by telecommunications firms in opening up the telephone market), decrease business expenses, and/or increase business revenues. These strategic PA efforts can have direct, long-term, measurable impacts on the bottom line.

PAOs Underemphasize Strategic
Measurement and/or Evaluation

More than ever, senior executives depend on quantitative financial indicators when making strategic decisions; PA executives
frequently have not exhibited a similar reliance on "the numbers."
Admittedly, the nature of PA does not easily lend itself to being
measured. In addition, numbers cannot always communicate how
well or poorly the PA unit in particular is performing; nevertheless,
an underemphasis or lack of effort in trying to show the bottom-
line impact of PA activity has been problematic to most PA units.[4]
Why does this situation exist?

Public policy cycle times and processes are more difficult to
measure because they are affected by sociopolitical factors.[5] Complex sociopolitical issues are highly variable, fraught with
uncertainty and can often take many years, even decades, to resolve.
The challenge for PA professionals is to communicate this unique
problem to managers who are used to measuring performance in
fairly understandable quarterly cycles.

Unmeasured functions are likely to be under-resourced functions.[6]
Though measuring PA is not a simple matter, it must be done.
Managing a function without measuring it is akin to a sailboat without its rudder—the boat is capable only of responding to the
prevailing winds of the moment and must rely upon the goodness
of mother nature for locomotion.

In light of these difficulties and problems PA faces in achieving,
sustaining, and keeping management's confidence, we will examine
an improvement technique called benchmarking. PA benchmarking
has the potential to help PA professionals and units to effectively
address these challenges.

Benchmarking as an
Improvement Technique

What is PA benchmarking? Dictionary definitions describe benchmarking as a surveyor's term, generally associated with a point of
reference from which measurements may be made or something that
serves as a standard by which others may be measured.[7] From this
perspective, it is easy to understand the general concept underlying
benchmarking activities. We offer the following definition of PA

benchmarking. This definition includes several important elements that build on the dictionary definition and reflect the best components of definitions in practice.

Public Affairs Benchmarking **is defined as an ongoing systematic approach by which a PA unit measures and compares itself with higher performing and world-class units in order to generate knowledge and action about PA roles, practices, processes, products/services, or strategic issues which will lead to performance improvement.** The following discussion will examine each element in detail.

1. **Ongoing.** In general, there are few management performance improvement activities that PA units perform on an *ongoing* or continuous basis. By seeking to apply and sustain a methodology like benchmarking on an ongoing basis, PA professionals will be able to baseline their competencies and performance, and learn ways for improving them over time. The issues that arise and confront the unit may differ; however, through benchmarking, PA professionals will be familiar with effective processes for dealing with those issues. Therefore, introducing a sustainable technique to be performing on an ongoing basis is a critical step toward helping the PA unit overcome the problems associated with the communication and performance of the PA role.

The value of benchmarking increases geometrically when it is an *ongoing* technique as opposed to a one-time endeavour. A critical aspect of benchmarking is to work toward specific goals and then to move ahead those goals or benchmarks after a certain level of success is reached. This *ongoing* recalibration keeps the unit improving and moving toward higher performance. It also serves to remind the unit that world-class PA leaders are also improving, making the benchmark of best practices a moving target. PA will gain valuable, empirically researched information to communicate to management the extent to which it is performing the best practices and achieving success compared to other organizations on a regular basis.

2. **Systematic.** As with any other improvement technique, if there is no plan or logical set of steps to follow, it is very difficult to accomplish anything. A systematic plan gives a sense of direction and keeps pointing to the next step in the process, thereby ensuring that important elements are not overlooked. It also results in a greater feeling of accomplishment.

Systematic approaches can also be documented. This has two main benefits. First, if processes are documented, they can be communicated to others in the organization more easily. Second, a documented systematic approach helps the PA unit cope with unexpected events such as if a key individual decided to leave the organization for another employment opportunity. This is especially critical to the PA unit because it is not uncommon for one individual to be responsible or to "own" a particular issue.

PA benchmarking is systematic. There is a logical order of steps that should be followed to arrive at a desired result. Unfortunately, the benchmarking process does not have a standard number of steps. Often, it seems there are as many models as there are different initiatives.[8] It is not critical whether an organization chooses to use a 4, 6, 8 or 10-step benchmarking process. The important thing is that there is a logical flow of activities that is planned from the onset of the initiative.

The method we employ is a four-phase process: planning, data collection, analysis, and implementation. Each of these four phases contains several sub-steps. It is not our goal here to describe each of these in detail.[9] Figure 2 presents a graphical portrayal of the four-phase process.

3. **Approach.** PA has historically been slow to utilize managerial improvement approaches. An approach is a formal or systematic method used to accomplish a task. PA professionals need to use approaches and tools to systematically solve problems or discover

Figure 2: The Four Benchmarking Phases

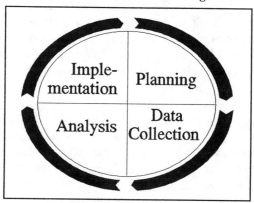

opportunities that will in turn help improve the quality of outputs. Other organizational functions have gained management's confidence by being familiar with and using the language of benchmarking and other improvement techniques. When PA starts to use this language, it will be better able to communicate managerial performance information with other organizational members.

Benchmarking is only one improvement approach or tool. Like any tool in your garage or kitchen, one tool is not useful for every job that needs to be done. It helps to keep in mind the old adage that says, "If all you've got is a hammer, everything starts to look like a nail." Benchmarking will NOT be the panacea for all PA management performance problems; however, it has been demonstrated that it is a useful tool PA professionals and operations can use to improve and communicate improved PA performance.[10]

4. **Measures.** PA officers do themselves a disservice when they underemphasize strategic measurement and evaluation. The TQM gurus have argued that you cannot manage what you cannot measure.[11] Measurement is key to understanding where you have been and the value you have created from your actions. It acts as a "baseline" for performance in order to see improvement over time. Measuring effectiveness, efficiency, or adaptability will give evidence as to whether the unit is achieving success in a particular area. Communicating positive changes in measures of key PA processes over time can show senior executives that PA managers are performance-oriented.

PA benchmarking requires dedicated measurement. In fact, though PA professionals have not routinely measured their own activities, they do have an innate advantage in learning and applying benchmarking quickly because of their basis of experience in research techniques emphasizing measurement such as opinion polling, focus group utilization, and reputational surveying, etc. Professionals just have to apply their knowledge of these research techniques to measure their own performance.

5. **Compares.** Benchmarking adds value through a comparison of a PA unit with higher performing units. Comparison has two main benefits. First, the unit has a relative ranking as to how it is performing compared to another unit. It is virtually impossible to achieve a realistic or valid picture of the unit's level of performance without using an external referent. For example, a comparison may

show that one operation is the expert in certain areas. The same comparison may also show that there are many areas for improvement that had not been previously considered. Second, the unit can gain knowledge of how to improve. A benchmarking unit will gather and analyze data illustrating how world-class leaders perform the process (i.e., through an examination of flowcharts, descriptions, numbers, etc.). The benchmarking unit can take this information and make substantial progress by adapting high performance practices using the information gleaned from successful organizations. Practice adaptation, instead of a wholesale adoption of practices, will not only allow the unit to address any important differences that exist between the units, but also will let the unit creatively build upon the concepts and procedures the world-class unit employs.

The PA unit can use this measurement and comparison information to become more strategic and effective in its efforts. In addition, the PA unit will have performance-related information to report to senior executives that is in a form and context that they can relate to and understand.

6. **Higher-performing and world-class units.** It is important to benchmark an organization that is better at the study topic than the benchmarking unit. PA management should know what the "best" PA units are doing. It is advantageous to comprehend a unit's performance levels and progress in comparison to higher performers. It is equally as important to understand the reasons for the gap. Making a conscious effort to compare the unit to units which are reputed, reported or known to be the best will also increase the efficiency of the benchmarking initiative.

It is unlikely to find a PA unit that is an across the board world-class performer. This situation presents an excellent opportunity for sharing information on a *quid pro quo* basis which suggests a give and take of information. A PA unit can share information about processes in which it is the expert to gain information about processes in which it needs improvement. It is also important to note that it is not always necessary to study the best of the best. For example, if a unit is only beginning the journey toward quality it is generally inadvisable for that unit to benchmark a unit that is light years ahead of it. It is possible to have an extant performance gap that is too large and too difficult to make valuable comparisons. Professionals in the lower performing unit could end up more confused than when they started as there would be too many things that need improvement.

7. **Knowledge and Action.** So many times, PA could integrate itself into the strategic management of the organization if it were only known where it could best make a difference. Knowledge is the main output of the benchmarking process. Benchmarking should result in a clear understanding of how the PA unit performs its processes and how it realistically compares to other world-class performers. Information is extremely valuable in and of itself; however, knowledge and action need to flow from the information. Knowledge beneficially contributes to the development of actions via new strategies and improvement tactics. Setting these strategies, tactics, and policies can be done proactively with confidence because the actions were based on empirical evidence. PA professionals will be better able to do their job and understand how they can better integrate into the organization and organizational strategy. Benchmarking can spur preventive activities that are normally managed in a reactive fashion. Also, the number and value of breakthroughs will increase to the extent that benchmarking helps PA professionals to begin thinking "out-of-the-box."[12]

8. **PA roles, practices, processes, products/services, or strategic issues.** It is possible to benchmark each of these items. Separating PA activities into these five areas allows PA to be viewed in terms of identifiable targets to measure. It is unusual that everything is wrong with a PA unit. An analysis can be made to determine which areas will gain the most from benchmarking. Depending on the nature of the organization, some benchmarking efforts will be more critical than others in achieving, sustaining, and keeping management's confidence. In this next section each of these items will be defined and examples will be given for each.

A *PA role* is an organized set of behaviors which illustrate the relationship between a PA professional, group, or process and another individual, group, or process. Every PA professional's job consists of some combination of interrelated roles which can vary over time and context in terms of organizational importance. It is essential that the cluster of tasks which makes up a PA professional's role is clearly identified and understood in order to meet stakeholder expectations. Benchmarking PA roles attempts to help

Table 1

Examples of PA benchmarking initiatives that study roles:
• The role of the PAO vis-a-vis his/her relationship with other top executives
• The role of PA vis-a-vis its relationship to another organizational function (e.g., Human Resources)
• The role of PA strategic planning and how it relates to organizational strategic planning
• The role of the senior PA executive in PA planning

PA professionals decrease role ambiguity and conflict. This often requires PA professionals to systematically address performance expectations held by key PA customers.

Table 2

Examples of PA benchmarking initiatives that study practices:
• The practice of choosing whether to use internal or externally contracted resources for publications
• The practice of using the industry association versus "going it alone" in responding to issues
• The practice of choosing a grassroots versus a grasstops approach in responding to an issue
• The practice of deciding whether to promote employee voluntarism versus using a philanthropic approach to contribution

A *PA practice* is a component of a process that usually has an "either/or" decision. Knowledge about practices can facilitate improved planning and decision making.

A *PA process* is a series of repeatable, definable, and predictable work activities consisting of people, equipment, procedures, and material organized to produce a specific result. PA processes explain how essential PA tasks are carried out. The benchmarking

Table 3

Examples of PA benchmarking initiatives that study processes:
•   The process used to develop a PA strategy •   The process used to analyze stakeholder interests •   The process of evaluating communications performance •   The process of developing PA training sessions

initiative that studies processes tends to be most popular because organizational professionals have had more experience applying measures to processes due to its association with TQM initiatives.

Products/services are the outputs of a PA process. Outputs are delivered to PA customers. Initiatives studying products/services can

Table 4

Examples of benchmarking initiatives that study products/services:
•   Benchmark annual reports as to effective versus non-effective features •   Benchmark the content of speeches written for effectiveness •   Benchmark the content of issues briefs •   Benchmark the content, structure, and effectiveness of PA training sessions

examine and compare aspects of the products/services that promote effectiveness.

Strategic issues. Strategic issues are those public policy environment conflicts which can significantly impact the organization's ability to achieve its mission. There are many strategic issues that regularly challenge PA professionals. These can be benchmarked in order to better understand how others manage organizational responses to similar issues.

Table 5

Examples of benchmarking initiatives that study strategic issues:
•   Benchmark the nature of internal management challenges faced by PA operations and how other managers face these challenges •   Benchmark ways that technology is utilized in performing critical PA activities •   Benchmark the management challenges faced by PA professionals when the organization enters new geographic locations, closes a business, or enters an alliance •   Benchmark PA and/or organizational goals established for managing in down-sized or under-resourced conditions

9. Performance improvement. The ultimate goal of benchmarking is to improve performance. Specifically, the purpose is to improve the unit's quality of outputs, productivity, and/or adaptability. A PA unit that constantly improves benefits the entire organization. In an era of downsizing and resource restrictions, benchmarking will help the unit to survive and thrive through improving its performance of, and communication of, value-adding activities.

How Benchmarking Helps Achieve, Sustain, and Keep Management's Confidence

Management's confidence has to be gained through both words and action. If a PA unit lacks in either area, management will not give PA the confidence that it desires. The underlying quality goal for the PA unit should be to, "Do and communicate the right things right the first time every time."

Obviously being able to do the right things right and communicate those results in a manner that is "right" leads to the best result (i.e., the most confidence from management). Benchmarking helps the PA unit discover what the "right things" are from the vantage point of those operations which excel at doing these things. From that point, it becomes a question of communication. In this next section, we will discuss what some of these "right things" are and show how benchmarking can lead us to these right things.

Benchmarking spurs an organization to improve its performance. Performance improvement takes the form of the unit and/or its professionals becoming more effective, efficient, and/or more adaptable. These are the "right things" to improve upon in a strategic management sense. Through a systematic and focused examination of the best practices of other organizations and operations, benchmarking points out where small improvements can be made or where involved restructuring of the process is needed. Benchmarking gives targets for comparison both in the present and beyond. Through this examination the PA unit will begin to develop a healthy view of what is truly superior work and what is mediocre. The PA unit can then focus on accomplishing higher performance efforts. Once the unit begins to understand that improvements can be made as well as knowing how they can be accomplished, that unit is on a journey to doing the "right things."

The second part of the goal is to communicate in the right way. Benchmarking can act as a key input to the communication process. There are a number of different kinds of messages which can result from benchmarking. These messages will be discussed in the following paragraphs.

Messages

The first information that is useful to communicate is qualitative and quantitative benchmarking data that ranks the unit with respect to the other players in the environment. Upon the conclusion of an analysis of benchmarking data, the unit may find it has the best practices; however, it is more likely that it will not. In any case, progress in its performance over time is tangible information which is quickly recognized by senior managers. In fact, it is not much different than positioning a product in the marketplace. The only difference is that the product being measured is something that is very different from what is usually monitored. Worthwhile PA performance products include cycle time reduction (e.g., the amount of time needed to respond to an inquiry from a government agency), increased levels of customer satisfaction, decreased costs in producing PA products and services, increased exploitation of opportunities, and/or decreased risks.

For example, the PA unit could demonstrate:

> We have established measures that show we have improved by _____.
> Our return on investment in this communications effort is ____%.
> We are rated _____ among world-class performers in _____ area.
> We have reduced our time to respond to inquiries by _____ hours.
> We have reduced our cost of producing this PA product by _____.

Benchmarking forces the PA unit to examine who its high priority customers are and how PA can best satisfy them. Satisfying PA customers usually comes through helping them better understand and respond to critical public policy stakeholders and issues. Improved response will allow organizational stakeholders to compete more effectively over time.

Similarly, benchmarking information can be used to better communicate how long PA processes take through the use of flowcharts or other descriptive methods. As every PA professional knows, cycle times and processes are affected by sociopolitical factors. Though PA tends to have its hands tied with respect to the length and variability of the cycle, PA can report to management the steps involved in the process, how far along they are in the process, and can show them approximately when specific results can reasonably be expected to occur.

Benchmarking also creates knowledge for the PA unit about which processes are successful. If PA knows what it can do well and how that affects the success of the organization, it can communicate and persuade management to use PA strategically. Linking the PA function to the organizational strategy integrates PA into the rest of the organization. PA will then have the opportunity to tangibly show how it is contributing to the success of the organization. This will not only help PA in the present but also in the future to define the direction of the unit.

Examples

It is helpful at this point to specifically show some examples of benchmarking initiatives that are related to improving the ability of other organizational departments to compete. The next chart shows how PA adds value to the organization within different departments or areas (See pages 288 and 289). We have then given some examples of benchmarking studies that could be done to improve those particular processes or activities.

Harnessing the power of the public affairs function produces improved results for the entire organization. PA professionals can use benchmarking to understand where their particular strengths lie or do not lie and learn how to gain improvements in the PA function. Benchmarking information can also be used to communicate the value of PA to management. When management truly understands how PA creates value for the organization and when management begins to strategically use PA resources, PA will surely be on its way to achieving, maintaining, and keeping management's confidence.

Notes

1. Some of the earliest management-oriented works labeled the work of PA professionals to be boundary spanning. This label, used heavily in the 1970s through early 1980s and associated with much of the systems resource theorizing of the day, has generally been absent from the literature since that time. Among the best works stressing PA as a boundary spanning function are:

Boston University Public Affairs Research Group. 1981. **Public Affairs Offices and Their Functions: Summary of Survey Responses**. Boston, MA: School of Management, Boston University.

Gollner, A.B. 1983. **Social Change and Corporate Strategy: The Expanding Role of Public Affairs**. Stamford, CT: Issue Action Publications.

Murray, E.A. 1982. The public affairs function: Report on a large-scale research project, in Preston, L.E. [ed.], **Research in Corporate Social Performance and Policy**, 4, 129-155, Greenwich, CT: JAI Press.

2. Much of the research being conducted at the North American Public Affairs Research Group (NAPARG) at Wilfrid Laurier University, Waterloo, Ontario, has been of the management of the PA function in light of changing organizational paradigms. Some of this research is summarized in the following publications:

Fleisher, C.S. and Nickel, J.R. 1994. Analyzing the TQM adoption experiences within a corporate staff unit: A progressive learning model, **Total Quality Management**, 5(3), 77-91.

Fleisher, C.S. 1993. Quality management for corporate staff functions: the public affairs example, **Total Quality Management**, 4(2), 159-164.

Fleisher, C.S. and Nickel, J.R. 1993. New kids on the block: A status report on quality in public affairs, **Continuous Journey**, 1(3), 26-33.

3. Although the literature continues to demonstrate a dearth of research which addresses the competitive value of PA, among the most effective empirical research which looks at the association between PA and strategic organizational performance includes:

Bhambri, A. and Sonnenfeld, J. 1988. Organization structure and corporate social performance: A field study in two contrasting industries. **Academy of Management Journal**, 31(3), 642-662.

McMillan, C.J. and Murray, V.V. 1983. Strategically managing public affairs: Lessons from the analysis of business-government relations. **Business Quarterly**, summer, 94-100.

Miles, R.H. 1987. **Managing the Corporate Social Environment: A Grounded Theory**. Englewood Cliffs, NJ: Prentice Hall.

Miles, R.H. 1982. **Coffin Nails and Corporate Strategies**. Englewood Cliffs, NJ: Prentice Hall.

4. Several writers have addressed the difficulties of showing the bottom line impact of PA, notably:

Andrews, P.N. 1987. **Public Affairs Offices and Their Evaluation**. Unpublished doctoral dissertation, School of Management, Boston University.

Bissland, J.H. 1990. Accountability gap: Evaluation practices show improvement. **Public Relations Review, 16(2), 25-35.**

Fleisher, C.S. 1993. Public affairs management performance: An empirical analysis of evaluation and measurement, in Post, J., [ed.], **Research in Corporate Social Performance and Policy**, 14, 139-163, Greenwich, CT: JAI Press.

Laird, N. and Roosevelt, R. 1994. **Quantifying Impacts: A Comprehensive Guide to Identifying the Bottom-line Impact of Public and Government Relations Activity**. Washington, DC: Laird and Associates.

Nowlan, D. and Shayon, D. 1984. **Leveraging the Impact of Public Affairs: A Guidebook Based on Practical Experience for Corporate Public Affairs Executives**. Philadelphia, PA: HRN.

Smith IV, G.L. 1991. Building a public affairs operation that works in the '90s, remarks of a speech given to the 1991 Corporate Affairs Conference, Washington, DC, May 15.

5. Attempting to address the rarity of models for managing sociopolitical management issues, the following authors have promoted the use of life cycle concepts for PA managers:

Bartha, P. 1982. Managing corporate external issues: An analytical framework. **Business Quarterly**, fall, 81-90.

Buchholz, R.A. 1990. **Essentials of Public Policy for Management**. 2nd ed., Englewood Cliffs, NJ: Prentice Hall.

Kingdon, R.A. 1984. **Agendas, Alternatives and Public Policies**. Glenview, IL: Scott, Foresman and Company.

6. This is the view frequently offered by PA professionals who have moved toward TQM and related, management-measurement related paradigms, described in:

Lacopo, J. 1993. Demonstrating value: PA as a strategic function. **ImPACt**, July/August, 1-2, Washington, DC: Public Affairs Council.

Shafer, P. 1992. An informal poll of PAOs yields "Quality" insights. **ImPACt**, September, 1-4, Washington, DC: Public Affairs Council.

Whitney, B. and Pedersen, W. 1993. Is public affairs being reinvented? **ImPACt**, May, 1-3, Washington, DC: Public Affairs Council.

7. Several authors have noted the number of definitions in use. One author, Spendolini, studied numerous definitions in use and noted elements that most definitions had in common.

Spendolini, M.J. 1992. **The Benchmarking Book**. New York: AMACOM.

Websters New Collegiate Dictionary. 1976. Springfield, MA: G&C Merriam Company, 103.

8. International Benchmarking Clearinghouse. 1992. **Common Steps in Benchmarking Models**. Houston, TX: International Benchmarking Clearinghouse.

9. Readers interested in exploring the benchmarking process in detail can consider consulting:

Camp, Robert C. 1989. **Benchmarking: The Search for Industry Best Prac-**

tices That Lead to Superior Performance. Milwaukee, WI: ASQC Quality Press.

McNair, C.J. and Liebfried, K.H.J. 1992. Benchmarking: A Tool for Continuous Improvement. New York: Harper Collins.

Spendolini, M.J. 1992. The Benchmarking Book. New York: AMACOM.

Watson, G.H. 1993. Strategic Benchmarking. New York: John Wiley and Sons.

10. Successful benchmarking experiences within PA are addressed in a series of management handbooks published by the PA Council:

Fleisher, C.S. 1995. Public Affairs Benchmarking: A Comprehensive Guide. Washington, DC: Public Affairs Council.

Shafer, P.S. 1994. Adding Value to the Public Affairs Function: Using Quality to Improve Performance. Washington, DC: Public Affairs Council.

11. Total Quality Management (TQM) experts (or gurus) have been arguing for the improved measurement of organizational activity as being necessary for the improved management of organizations, including:

Harrington, H.J. 1987. The Improvement Process. New York: McGraw Hill.

Juran, J.M. 1992. Juran on Quality by Design: The New Steps for Planning Quality into Goods and Services. New York: The Free Press.

12. Several authors have recently been pushing professionals to "break out of the box" of traditional management improvement paradigms and to re-engineer their organizations. This view can be found in:

Akao, Y. 1991. Hoshin Kanri: Policy Deployment for Successful TQM. Cambridge, MA: Productivity Press.

Hammer, M. 1990. Re-engineering work: Don't automate, obliterate. Harvard Business Review, July/August, 104-112.

How Public Affairs
Adds Value
to the Organization
Within
Different Departments
or Areas

Table 6

Depart- ment	How PA Adds Value to the Organization	Benchmarking Studies For Improving Value Added
Marketing	• Lobby government agencies to improve labelling requirements on certain products • Maintain or improve corporate reputation or image	• Benchmark the process that the most effective companies use to influence these government regulations • Benchmark the processes used for managing and evaluating corporate reputation
Human Resources	• Help recruiting by promoting an image of the company that shows the company is ethical, cares for employees, is involved in the community • Develop employee communications that boost morale, lowers absenteeism, and/or increases productivity	• Benchmark the products and services produced by other organizations which are used to communicate such an image
Accounting	• Lower the volume of paper filing requirements on applications for government grants	• Benchmark the strategic issue of the use of on-line filing requirements and improved database and digital technologies

Finance	• Increase the available capital from foreign banking institutions at decreased rates	• Benchmark the issue of how organizations influenced the requirements in other nations where these changes were made
Production	• Reduce restrictions on importing certain sources of raw materials	• Benchmark the practices used by other companies which were successful in reducing these restrictions
Senior Management	• Improve the strategy of the organization through improved contributions from PA	• Benchmark the role of the senior PA officer in corporate strategic planning • Benchmark the processes used to link PA strategic planning to corporate planning.

Chapter 20

Interfacing with Peers, Trade Associations and Professional Societies

Robert A. Neuman and
Kenneth P. Arnold

Washington, D.C., arguably the information industry capital of the world, is a city of trends and timelines. No other industrial center feels the immediate pulse of business and public policy change like Washington. So, when American business engages in deliberate and painful downsizing to meet the financial demands of stockholders and budget-cutting CFOs, the impact on Washington representatives is the same—in some cases, reduced personnel and an increase in reliance on specialists and consultants, neither of which are in short supply in the Nation's Capital.

Not all companies downsized their Washington representation, however. Some, mostly those in the sensitive areas of finance, energy resources, and health care, feeling that the Clinton presidency would launch a new era of activism, actually bolstered staffs for the expected flurry of regulatory and legislative activity.

According to the authoritative publication, *Political Finance and Lobby Reporter,* some 700 U.S. and foreign companies have offices in Washington. Added to the company offices are more than 9,000 associations and special interest groups and an estimated 12,000 lobbyists, some 6,500 of whom have actually registered with the Congress.

What, you may ask, do all these people do? Good question. And since 1993, when the Congress eliminated the tax deduction for lobbying, many top executives have asked this question at budget time.

This new scrutiny was not lost upon the Washington hordes. The 40th Anniversary celebration edition of the newspaper *Roll Call* (1955-1995) carried a full-page advertisement paid for by the American Society of Association Executives. Under the headline "How Associations **Help** Congress" (emphasis theirs) were listed the following:

- Education — Associations educate their members about legislative issues and processes allowing for increased participation;

- Outreach — Associations inform their members of pending legislation and related compliance issues;

- Access — Associations act as a communication link between Congress and key constituents, groups, and local decision makers;

- Research — Associations provide Congress with research and study results for more informed decision making and better policies;

- Feedback — Associations inform Congress of the impact pending legislation may have on an industry, profession, or segment of society.

The association executives could have included another bullet point—"Financial—Save your company some hefty fees and utilize your association memberships."

Associations, be they representing an industry or a social cause, have a highly visible and indelible place in the making of public policy.

Who are these people? Are they lobbyists, public affairs specialists or public relations practitioners?

In the words of a character in a children's book, "When I use a word, it means just what I choose it to mean—neither more or less."

And so it goes with public relations and public affairs. Morris K. Udall, the long-time Member of the House Representatives from Arizona once told the story of the law school professor who asked a student to explain the difference between fornication and adultery. "Well, sir, to tell you the truth, I've tried them both and I can't tell you the difference."

Looking in the abstract, public relations has audiences and public affairs has constituencies. Further, one person's constituencies are another's special interest group. And we all know the difference between a constituency—that politically viable and nobly motivated group of like-minded individuals or organizations— and a special interest—a mean-spirited, wantonly greedy outfit that is trying to extort policy or funds from the same place as my constituency.

At its simplest, a lobbyist works to influence legislation. The public affairs/public relations practitioner works to influence the attitudes of legislators by mobilizing their own election constituencies rather than directly soliciting their votes.

Policy making, after all, is reactive. That is, people feel they don't get policy made until there's some indication that there is a public clamor for it.

And that is where we find the emergence of the new resources, peers, trade associations, and, to a lesser extent, professional societies.

The downsizing of corporate offices in Washington and the resultant growth of single-issue organizations and associations in Washington, D.C., combined with the reality of how political campaigns are being funded, has essentially changed how information is being provided to those who make much of our public policy.

Indeed, some have suggested forcefully that the explosion of new constituencies and their power to exert influence through campaign contributions and skillful use of communications and grass-roots campaigning has done much to create the policy gridlock between Congress and the Administration.

Special Interests and New Constituencies

When did this trend begin? We contend that the era of special interests first really surfaced at the time when President Lyndon Johnson discovered that he just could not pay for all the elements of the Great Society and conduct a costly war in Vietnam. The Federal pie began to shrink at the same time the national appetite for government money grew. Those competing for the Federal dollars, the cities, the farmers, universities, researchers, the poor, the handicapped, etc., saw the need to organize their efforts, take their case directly to those making the budget decisions. There was a direct correlation between the drying up of resources and the startup of organizational and political activities. And, as more and more social issues failed to get new funding, constituency groups rallied for those causes as well.

The presidency of Richard M. Nixon saw more and more growth of new constituencies. Environmentalism, for example, became a newly legitimate, well-funded cluster of policy advocacy organizations. The "peace movement" became a training ground for a new kind of political activism that did not disband as the Vietnam war ended. It generated a whole host of causes, committees, and individuals well-versed in grassroots activism, with an eye and ear for media exposure and expert in the use of fund-raising techniques ranging from direct mail appeals to foundation grants.

From Presidents Ford, Carter, Reagan, and Bush the trend of new constituencies and interest organizations has blossomed and bloomed to where those constituencies have a permanent place at the policy-making table.

Who are these new constituencies and how do they relate to public policy?

In but one page of the 300-plus pages of organizations in the publication *Washington Representatives* the following groups or causes are listed:

National Frozen Food Association
National Frozen Pizza Institute
National Gay and Lesbian Task Force
National Geographic Society
National Glass Association
National Governor's Association
National Hay and Feed Association
National Grape Growers
National Grocers Association
National Hand Tool Corporation
National Head Injury Foundation
National Head Start Association

National Health Council
National Health Lawyers Association
National Hemophilia Foundation
National Hockey League

All are bona fide organizations with fully functioning staffs, offices, telephones, fax machines and in all probability, on-line service addresses.

At an average of 30 such listings a page, that's some 9,000 or so special interests or constituencies. And that's a lot of message development meetings and power lunches.

The proliferation of new constituency building and alliance formation is not confined to the private sector. While the 104th Congress did adopt rules that limited the use of public funds to special caucuses, there still exist such organizations as the Congressional Automotive Caucus, the Congressional Coal Caucus, the Congressional Bearing Caucus, the Congressional Sportsman's Caucus and the Congressional Truck Caucus. All these caucuses had liaison with counterparts in the private sector. Services ranging from the recruitment of new members to the funding of expenses for publications, research, and event meals and drinks, come from private sources.

The purpose of these special interests or constituencies is simple: to influence policy by getting the government to fund or continue to fund a program; easing a regulation; extending or searching for a special exemption in the tax code. These objectives are not necessarily bad. When combined with the singular objectives of some 7,000 to 10,000 other policy advocates, however, all seeking a share of a shrinking financial pie in a possibly slowing economy, there is a distinct possibility of policy gridlock.

Recognizing the New Resources

The old ways of lobbying and the old ways of getting messages and new policy initiatives heard and acted upon are as long gone as cash contributions and carbon paper.

We are in a new era, a time when the ways of representing constituencies, old and new, have dramatically and irreversibly changed. For not only are we in an era of new and emerging constituencies, we are in an equally fascinating period of new strategies.

First and most important in this new strategizing is the full recognition and utilization of all possible resources key to the successful
resolution of objectives in a communications strategy or public relations action program.

Those of us who practice in Washington, D.C. have an abundant
source of out-of-office resources available for the type of public
affairs/communication strategy that goes with those in extra-govern-
mental campaigns designed to influence public policy by rallying
public opinion for revising old policies, elimination of others, and
formation of new policies. In-house resource and research capabilities have been totally revolutionized by the power of on-line services such as Lexis and Nexis, CompuServe, America On Line, the
Internet and others. Gathering of information and source materials
can be accomplished in minutes, not hours. Facts can be checked,
legislation tracked, and statistics gathered in a fraction of the time
it took only a few years ago.

Using Resources Provided by Peers

One of the myths of Washington, D.C., is that it is mainly pop-
ulated by lawyers. In fact, Washington has nearly as many public
relations and public affairs practitioners as lawyers. An article in
The Washington Post noted that there are more than 10,000 federal
employees whose primary duties are in public relations. "Watching
the government's $2 billion PR industry intermarry with Washing-
ton's immeasurable (but huge) PR industry, a cynic might be tempted
to conclude that virtually everything that happens in Official Washington is part of a PR campaign. But that would be exaggerating.
Slightly." (*Washington Post*, Feb. 11, 1990).

There are, in fact, some 400 political consulting, advertising, and
public relations firms in Washington with billings in the hundreds
of millions of dollars. Throw in the law firms doing advocacy and
lobbying work, and you can see that this is a major segment of
Washington's gross product.

Washington firms are especially valuable in resourcing policy
initiatives and advocacy campaigns because of the richness of governmental and congressional experience and political involvement.
Since the election of the 104th Congress in November of 1994,
Washington firms have seen a new openness to former Administration and Congressional personnel of the Republican persuasion.

How best to utilize this resource? Among the strategic and tactical opportunities available to the practitioner from his peers are the following:

- **Alliance building**—On major public policy issues in which there are multiple organizations or companies affected, the opportunity exists for organized task force operations in which the personnel and resources of individuals and their firms are mobilized for the common objectives. While there is normal reluctance to share proprietary information and long range planning, it is not uncommon for Washington, D.C., public relations firms to engage in cooperative efforts to attain goals and objectives.

- **Information gathering** — Clearly one of the most useful resources, Washington public relations firms employ hundreds of key campaign operatives of both parties who maintain strong ties to colleagues and former employers both on Capitol Hill and in the various Administration Branch departments.

- **List building** — Painful as it may be, some individual firms will share lists of contacts and allies if the common good is at stake. It has been our experience that such generosity rarely comes from altruism, rather the opportunity to update one's own list motivates firms in the sharing of lists.

- **Media contacts** — Meetings of allied public relations firms working on common objectives often include sessions where names of prominent reporters, columnists, producers, and bookers are offered up for the taking. Individuals from some firms like to show the enormity of their own influence by actively bidding for the most influential targets. Peers can be helpful in this area, or disingenuous, if so inclined. Our experience is to guard against giving too much authority to a single partner in the campaign. The most effective contact campaigns will reserve a follow-up authority for the lead agency or client group.

The massive and successful utilization of peers was dramatically proven effective in the putative effort by the Clinton Administration and a Democratic majority in the Congress to enact meaning-ful health care reforms in 1993 and 1994. Armed with a "mandate" in the form of his election victory in 1992, President Clinton cited public polls and the overwhelming concern of special groups of citizens, the elderly, the poor, the underinsured, as reason enough for the Congress to rally behind his reform package and enact a comprehensive, if complicated, health care reform legislation.

The specter of reform energized health care providers, insurance companies, and other institutions affected by such legislation into a nearly unparalleled and united front that galvanized public attitudes and opinion in the form of a tremendous barrage of letters, tele-phone calls, fax messages and political organizing in opposition to the Clinton plan. Much of this effort was the result of combined resources utilizing the public relations and lobbying consultants and firms hired by individual companies and associations. Efforts by such organizations as the Pharmaceutical Manufactures Association (PMA) were funded by special assessments to member companies.

Other pharmaceutical companies, worried about the negative im-age of the PMA, organized their own campaign under the rubric RX and hired a public affairs firm to conduct an effort independent of PMA. (Interestingly, PMA itself shed its name and, in the inter-est of reforming the message of progress and research, renamed itself the Pharmaceutical Research and Manufacturers of America, or PhRMA.)

The most famous of the media campaigns arrayed against the President and the First Lady was the "Harry and Louise" advertise-ments produced by the specially formed task force of the Health Insurance Alliance of America. The television ads flooded the air-waves as the Congress began deliberations on the massive legisla-tion. Many political observers and journalists credit the messages carried by these ads, clear messages that hit the reform as denying Americans of their right to choose their own doctors and the type of coverage, as crucial elements of the demise of the Clinton pro-gram.

It seemed as if no combination of Administration or Congressional advocates and their many private sector allies could cut into the negatives raised by the HIAA campaign.

The success of the Harry and Louise campaign has spawned a new segment of the advocacy business, those independent consult-ing firms that specialize in political-style campaigning, including paid advertising, for non-political issue campaigns.

Using Resources of Trade Associations

Though it may be hard to dispute the fact that one of the most difficult clients to please—quickly—is a trade association or any other multi-faceted, multi-issued, and multi-constituency organization, it is also true that a trade organization is an invaluable resource in the formulation of an effective and successful campaign.

Case in point: an international body that represents importers of wine, beer, and spirits into the U.S. is not only weakened by the highly competitive nature of the industry, brand against brand, country against country, and type against type, but by competing interests in the arcane and very important set of statutes and regulations arrayed before this industry.

Thus when the association is ordered by a powerful member to utilize its resources to minimize an action by the EPA against a certain type of spirit, the market in which is dominated by a single manufacturer, a host of competing interests can be arrayed against the effort by the association's public affairs counsel.

Cases such as this provide an opportunity for the public affairs counsel to skillfully and carefully meld the resources and positive aspects of an apparently disjointed entity, unifying it to win common goals.

The glue that sticks trade associations together is fear. Fear of failure, fear of the tag "obstructionist," fear of being isolated and fear of having the in-house laundry exposed for all to see can be powerful motivators.

One of the most essential parts of any campaign involving trade organizations is defining the issues, the objectives and the message. It should be clear from the start that division within the ranks will most certainly undermine the campaign. Opponents will recognize and exploit any divisions.

Is a trade association a democracy? Should every member have common goals before the association is formed? Can a public relations or advocacy campaign be developed and made effective even with a client that is splintered and divided?

Well, in fact, yes.

But it takes intelligence and grace, elements that are not always present.

The titanic battle between the long distance telephone companies, AT&T, MCI, Sprint, etc. and the regional Bell companies (RBOCs) is a classic case of fierce competitors burying their own differences and unifying in a struggle to dominate the huge telecommunications industry.

Unable to reach accord for years, the long distance companies combined resources and energies in the mid 1990's, under the leadership of a coalition led by former Senator Howard Baker, to take the fight to the Congress. They were joined by consumer organizations who have long fought the local companies which have enjoyed near monopolies in providing local telephone service. The RBOCs, or "Baby Bells" have themselves united in an unprecedented grassroots campaign utilizing such resources as customers, employees, vendors, and their own consumer organizations.

Utilizing the Resources of the Professional Society

The resources provided members of the Public Relations Society of America (PRSA) for fellow practitioners is only good if it is used. It is our experience that the PRSA workshops and publications are excellent resources, but are not utilized nearly as much as they should be.

As the public relations/public affairs profession has become more specialized, the professional societies that service the industry also have become more specialized in order to meet the growing needs of their constituencies. The Public Relations Society of America, which represents more than 16,000 professionals throughout the United States, has been developing new sections and program areas to address the ever-expanding public affairs field.

Currently, PRSA has a "public affairs" membership section, along with several other sections with a strong public affairs focus, including the recently-formed "environment" section. In addition, PRSA's vast array of programs and resources, ranging from workshops to on-line services, all are designed to give the professional readily-available tools.

In fact, the PRSA Information Center, alone, is a treasure trove of information for the typical over-stretched public affairs practitioner. This extensive data bank has access to more than 1,000 public relations subject files, including case studies.

PRSA workshops and professional development seminars are other worthwhile forums for expanding the public affairs resources base. Not only does the practitioner learn from the instructor, but these workshops and seminars provide an important opportunity for peers to interact—learning through the exchange of experiences.

Utilizing the Resources of the Professional Society: A Case Study

Environmental issues are often the most contentious and emotional of public policy debates. Environmental advocates and industry representatives often offer widely different opinions regarding the state of the environment, what the key issues are and, most important, what public policy actions should be taken to protect the environment.

On a number of occasions the chemical industry has been pitted against environmental advocates in public policy debates surrounding issues such as the Clean Water and Clean Air Acts. The issue is not whether or not you are for or against clear air and water—everyone is in favor of those—but, rather, what is the best way to ensure that we have clean air and water. Certainly many benefits of modern society have been built in large part on commercial chemistry—pharmaceuticals, air bags for automobiles, computer hardware and software, for example. At the same time, scientific questions have been raised over the years about possible negative near and long-term health effects from exposure to these commercially produced chemicals. And in the middle of this discussion is the realization that the scientific community, while an important contributor to the process, never will have all of the answers or the last word on environmental issues.

So it is within this context that government officials, both legislative and regulatory, must make public policy decisions. The process is a blending of scientific fact and politics based on public opinion. This is where the public affairs professional enters. His/her job is to help frame the debate, develop key messages and implement proactive and reactive communications strategies to drive public opinion as the process moves forward.

In Washington, D.C., the local PRSA environment section decided to explore one such public policy issue for a workshop. Specifically, the section looked at the public debate surrounding certain chlorinated chemical compounds. The timing was right, as the Clinton Administration had put forward a legislative proposal that could, if enacted, begin the phase-out of a number of chemicals. The proposal was hailed by environmental advocates and criticized by industry. The public policy battleground had been identified.

During this public policy debate, a PRSA workshop was held in Washington, D.C., and brought together representatives from the chemical industry, environmental community, and the media. For public affairs professionals—from both sides—involved in the public policy debate, the forum was yet another opportunity to position the issue and test key messages. For peers who attended the workshop, the "live" case study offered insights and experience that would be useful for their professional activities.

In Conclusion:
The Move to Common Sense

The world of Washington, D.C., has been changed markedly by the dynamics of Congressional implementation of the "Contract With America," a key part of the historic Republican surge in 1994 resulting in the GOP takeover of the U.S. Senate and House of Representatives. Though all political situations are necessarily in flux, nonetheless, the way Washington's public affairs and public relations practitioners are doing business has seen changes ranging from removal of certain privileges of access for registered lobbyists to realignment of firm and corporate human resources to bolster the number of identifiable Republicans on staff.

The new Committee and Subcommittee chairs of Senate and House Committees have shown increased acceptance to information and suggestions as to reforming and in some cases abolishing regulatory impediments to corporate objectives. This, of course, makes staff members with access to such key decison makers very valuable indeed.

The new strength of corporate resources has put public interest and environmental interest organizations in an unfamiliar position outside the influence loop. To counter that situation, these groups have intensified efforts to raise funds through direct mail soliticitations and foundation grants.

The new demands on public affairs professionals means more utilization of resources outside the comfortable confines of their own offices. There will be more peer arrangements. There will be new associations and special interest consortia to take advantage of specific talent and expertise. And, there very well may be more change ahead.

One author, Philip K. Howard, seems to have captured the moment of change in how government will react and public policy will be made during this significant philosophical and polticial transition. Howard contends that the Administration's "reinvention of government" and the Gingrich-inspired "downsizing of government" are not mutually exclusive.

"Reinventing Government preaches the credo of flexibility without emphasizing the cold truth that flexibility only comes from abandoning the procedural orthodoxy on which modern government is now built," Howard writes. "An unworkable contradiction lies at the heart of the modern state. Process is a defensive device; the more procedures, the less government can do. We demand an activist government while also demanding elaborate procedure protections against government." [*The Death of Common Sense*, (Random House, 1995), p. 105.]

Howard's thesis provides public affairs and public relations practitioners with a fertile environment to participate in what may well be a revolution in how government works and how policy is made.

How they utilize the resources at hand will be a key both to their influence and their effectiveness.

Chapter 21

A Change in Direction: New Careers in Public Affairs

Barbara E. Whitney

If you are in the public affairs field and your corporate job has been reengineered out from under you, take heart! There is a new job market developing out there.

Some of the companies that reorganized their operations and eliminated whole departments are discovering that they may have cut too deeply. In external affairs, particularly, problems arise unexpectedly and escalate quickly with increased media interest. Confronted with the possibility of a crisis, these companies look inside for someone with experience in troubleshooting only to find that they no longer have anyone to call on. They may then ask their general counsel or some other operations officer to step into the breach. This often only exacerbates the situation. Predictably, a decision is made to go outside to find someone who can "fix things."

It is very difficult for companies to go against the principles they committed to in reengineering, one of which is to retrain and promote from within whenever possible. The way they are able to justify an outside hire is by asking for extra qualifications that no one inside who is promotable is likely to have or could learn in a reasonable amount of time.

Expectations of Outside Candidates

Organizations that are hiring will expect an outside public affairs candidate to. . . .

1. . . . *be multifunctional*—capable of pulling together a lot of loose ends in internal and external communications, community affairs, grassroots and PAC administration areas. He/she will also be able to provide valuable input to business units in market development and strategic planning.

2. . . . *exhibit a "marketing mindset" in his/her approach to finding solutions.* The focus of all company managers today has to be "customer satisfaction." This usually requires taking a leadership role in representing the business units and planning your strategies in the same entrepreneurial way a sales force would operate.

3. . . . *demonstrate the ability to motivate others to achieve the highest levels of productivity by "unleashing their brainpower."*[1] This may be the toughest expectation to satisfy. When their company is downsizing all around them, employees begin to be concerned about their own jobs and morale deteriorates. How do you go about making them feel "empowered," eager to commit themselves to the high level of productivity necessary to achieve corporate goals?[2]

   Don't plan to use James Champy's new book *Reengineering Management* (1995), to solve the problem. Champy offers plenty of well-intentioned suggestions but none of the hard answers you'll need to motivate a staff that has been through one or more corporate reorganizations. Creating a "culture of willingness," where employees genuinely support the reengineering mission statements companies are adopting, takes far more than clever rhetoric.[3] Whatever positive statements Champy may make about the spirit of ongoing change and how it enables organizations to implement more and more successful programs, many staffers only see the reality of: Today you are a valued member of our team; tomorrow we may be more cost-effective without you.

   Look around. There actually are organizations that have devised credible plans for reaching out to their employees— fair and straightforward approaches that work! *Why* do they work? Because they have been conceived by decent and ethical individuals who have earned the respect and trust of those who work for them. They are the managers who are the leaders and role models. You'll see evidence of the successes they have achieved just by observing the level of enthusiasm and the work ethic of those who report to them.

4. . . . *be technologically on the cutting edge of change, plugged into newest and most time-saving breakthroughs on the "information superhighway" that could benefit the functions for which he/she would be responsible.*

Right now, this requirement seems to be more important for public relations positions than for those in other areas of public affairs. Recently, in two searches involving senior-level public relations jobs, the finalists who were hired were no more proficient in other critical skill areas than their competitors, but they were capable of introducing a new technology that could improve workplace productivity. This intrigued the corporate officers with whom they met and clinched the hiring decision.

There is still time if you need to update your technical skills. New jobs are just beginning to surface. Ask those you know who have a grasp of the technological possibilities in your field to refer you to the best resources for getting the training you need. Then test your newly updated skills in one or two consulting assignments. You want to exhibit a certain comfort level in this area when you go to interview for the next big corporate opportunity.

Other Options

At this point, you may decide that "reinventing" yourself to get back into a company with the possibility of being restructured out a second time just may not be worth it. Let's look at your other options.

Trade Associations

The first step away from the corporation is, of course, the trade association. In some industries today, where companies have severely trimmed their employee numbers to get closer to their "custom-

ers," the primary trade association will be asked to take greater
responsibility for the functions members themselves can no longer
handle effectively. The mandate these associations are given usually translates into a well-paid position and a generous budget com-
mensurate with the broad, senior-level responsibilities involved.

You may even be fortunate enough to uncover an opening with
an association that is geographically desirable—i.e., you could com-
mute to work from where you live now and not have to uproot your
family or cope with the problem of finding another career opportunity for your spouse.

"Outsourcing"

Another area of employment opportunity that has developed as a
result of the reorganization going on in corporate America is the
"outsourcing" of *entire "non-core" operations.*[4]

Companies that privately admit that their reengineering has failed
may continue to apply the process again and again, believing that
the fault somehow lies with them and not with the formula itself.[5]
While they are reviewing the processes they have in place, these
firms are able to conduct their business activities as efficiently as
ever by hiring independent contractors to operate like a small company within their larger organization. These contractors will carry
staff salaries and benefits on their own books so the company gets
the expertise it needs and the arrangement is very bottom-line
friendly.

Have you ever thought of starting your own business in this way?
It *is* a big leap from working as a salaried employee, getting a paycheck every two weeks and getting a lot of "perks" and good benefits as well. The reality of the here and now, however, is that there
will be more and more of these "outsourcing" situations developing in the corporate world just as fewer and fewer senior-level traditional jobs are being created. *This may be the best transitional
career you could choose.* (I say "transitional" because I believe there
will eventually be other ideas for change embraced by the business
community with the same enthusiasm they have shown for reengineering. When that happens, then all the rules will change—
again.)

You may be nervous about assuming the role of entrepreneur, not
having ready answers to the questions of how large a staff you

would need, what you should pay them, what, if anything, you should subcontract, and, most important, what is a competitive but also profitable amount to charge a client.

One solution might be to spend a few years working for one of the consulting firms already well-established in the "outsourcing" business. You may even decide once you're there that you may want to stay. After all, you'll be getting a regular paycheck and the cost of your benefits will be covered—two advantages you wouldn't find if you choose to run your own business.

And Remember—

Whatever you decide to do, taking an alternative career direction will force you to stay on the "cutting edge" of change in the field you have chosen. Whatever corporations may do with their internal operations in the years ahead, you will always find a way to survive. You have today's difficult and unpredictable business environment as your training ground!

Notes

1. *Industry Week*, February 26, 1995, "Lessons From the Best," by John H. Sheridan, pp. 13-14.

2. *The Washington Post*, April 9, 1995, "The Case for Corporate Downsizing Goes Global," by Frank Swoboda, p. H5; *Business Week*, October 17, 1994, "The New World of Work," pp. 76-87.

3. *Reengineering Management (The Mandate for Leadership)*. James Champy, *Harper Business*, New York, Copyright 1995, Chapter 6, "What Kind Of Culture Do We Want," pp. 75-95.

4. *The Wall Street Journal*, March 25, 1995, "The Network Society," by Peter Drucker, editorial page.

5. *Across the Board*, March 1995, "Reengineering: A Light That Failed?" (interview with James Champy), pp. 27-31.

General Source

Reengineering the Corporation (A Manifesto for Business Revolution), Michael Hammer and James Champy, *Harper Business*, New York, Copyright 1993.

Chapter 22

New Communications Resources for Global Public Affairs

Hernando González

When the end finally came, the swiftness of socialism's downfall in Eastern Europe and the Soviet Union came mainly as a surprise to outsiders. It was the "domino theory" played in reverse, with one regime after another being swept away by revolution (Goldfarb, 1992; Remnick, 1993). By the time Russia parted ways with communism, it was not simply the end of the Cold War, but the end of history, as Fukuyama (1992) described it. He emphasized, however, that this does not mean the end of change, which has accelerated socially, politically and economically across the globe with the opening of more democratic space.

The end of the Cold War has provided U.S. corporations with new markets in Eastern Europe, Russia and Vietnam, which are all hungry for U.S. products and services, from Mars bars to fast food to computer technology (Bennis and Moushabeck, 1993; Goldfarb, 1992; Islam and Mandelbaum, 1992). The thaw in economic relations is apparent even in North Korea, which has expressed interest in U.S. nuclear power plants, and in Cuba, where telecommunication deals were concluded to the satisfaction of both sides. In an effort to end the U.S. embargo, Cuba has expressed its willingness to provide compensation for U.S. property seized after the 1959 revolution, even as it actively solicits foreign investment. Following hard bargaining and the threat of sanctions, China has agreed to protect U.S. software and other intellectual property and has established a court to settle such claims. Other markets have also been transformed. Western Europe is moving toward closer economic integration, ASEAN countries have become a powerful economic bloc, and Latin America is selling off state-owned enterprises (United Nations, 1995). These developments underscore the triumph of market economy over competing systems worldwide.

In this new business environment, practitioners in international public affairs require more accurate, up-to-date and focused information. Time and again, reliance on traditional information channels, including the mainstream media, appears to be insufficient for issues management. U.S. business was caught unaware by the "rebellion" in Chiapas, and the subsequent collapse of the Mexican peso. Ironically, this economic shock wave immediately followed NAFTA and the 1994 Summit of the Americas in Miami, which was briefly touted as the beginning of a new era of prosperity in the region. If the mainstream media could not provide early warning for an ailing economy next door, how well can they serve public affairs managers with interests in Senegal or Singapore?

The inability of the mainstream media to anticipate structural change, particularly in other countries, does not appear to be confined to isolated cases. The stream of "surprises" seems to represent a worrisome pattern, which blindsides U.S. corporations operating abroad. The mainstream media failed to predict the rapid collapse of communism in Europe. Much earlier, their flawed reporting on Iran failed to gauge the depth of opposition toward the Shah and popular support for the mullahs. They misread Saddam Hussein's hostile intentions toward Kuwait, and initially portrayed democratic opposition to the Nationalist party in Taiwan as being subversive and extremist (Chirot, 1994; Darwish and Alexander, 1991; Fathi, 1979).

Part of the problem appears to be the mainstream media's dependence on official sources in government and industry, which do not necessarily represent the only interpretation of what is going on socially, politically and economically in those countries. Mexico, for example, has long been described as a democracy, notwithstanding its anomalous one-party rule, long record of fraudulent elections and systematic exploitation of indigenous peoples (Kandell, 1988; Rius, 1993; Ruiz, 1992). The Chiapas "rebellion" appears to be more of a desperate plea for help, rather than a serious armed attempt to overthrow the social order (Collier with

Quaratiello, 1994; Marcos, 1994; Ross, 1995). With such weaknesses in mainstream media coverage, decision-makers with business interests abroad clearly need other information channels.

A Contingency Framework

As the global market economy increases in both complexity and interdependence, U.S. corporations will require more perceptive sources of information and analysis for strategic planning. Clearly, the U.S. mainstream media will not be sufficient, even those that purportedly "cover" the globe. As some communication researchers have noted, the mainstream media tend to favor the status quo and often ignore social and political movements outside of the mainstream, even in the U.S. For years, the growth of armed militia groups across the country received scant attention in the mainstream media, until the terrorist bombing of the federal building in Oklahoma City (Aho, 1990; Gibson, 1994; Macdonald, 1980).

The gathering and sifting of information by public affairs managers may be guided by the following communication contingency principles (González, 1991).

1. Since no single information source can provide corporations with all the information they need for international public affairs, then multiple sources of information are necessary. The inability of the mainstream media to provide sufficient information for decision-making on key issues is not an argument to stop trying to identify other information channels, or to stop using the mainstream media altogether.

2. Some information sources are better than others. Their relative advantage depends on the subject matter, participants involved, timing, place, and circumstance. This contingency principle also implies that some media are worse than others. Even after the revolution that swept away communist regimes in Eastern Europe and the former Soviet republics, the press in those countries remain under varying levels of social control and dependence on government subsidy (Goldfarb, 1992; Remnick, 1993). As a result, there are limits to how much they can report or comment on certain institutions and participants (Hiebert et al., 1994a, 1994b).

Social control of the mass media is not confined to poverty-stricken countries, such as Burma or Somalia, but include economic successes such as Singapore, South Korea and Taiwan. Economic democracy does not necessarily lead to political democracy. China and the other remaining communist regimes may be pursuing the "Asian dragon" model, where high economic growth is accompanied by minimal political expression. Even prior to re-assimilation in 1997, China has curbed critical commentary in the Hong Kong press (Barnathan, 1995). In Mexico and other hierarchical countries in Latin America, media reportage and commentary often exclude topics which are taboo to the dominant coalition (Heuvel and Dennis, 1995; López, 1991; Virtue et al., 1995). As a result, any "real news" on those topics can only be found outside of the mainstream media.

3. Information on social, political and economic developments in any country will always be limited or incomplete in some way. Corporate decisions are often made with "bounded knowledge," as explained in the writings of Nobel laureate Herbert Simon (1982; 1992). Partial knowledge of what is going on may be due to the way that the real power network is organized within a country. In China, formal organizational charts do not necessarily correspond with how influence is wielded within the state and the party (Lieberthal, 1995). With the passing of Deng Xiaoping from the scene, "outsiders" could regain influence, in the same way that Deng returned to power after losing to Mao Zedong (Salisbury, 1992). Political succession is also problematic in regimes built around charismatic leaders, such as Cuba and Indonesia (Chirot, 1994; Fogel and Rosenthal, 1994; Orozco, 1993).

Alternative Communication

Given this contingency framework, public affairs managers can minimize gaps in "bounded knowledge" about countries where they do business by using the following alternative sources of information.

Foreign Mainstream Media

Depending on their relative freedom of expression, the mainstream media in countries of interest to U.S. companies can provide information and analysis on social, political and economic developments which are not found in U.S.-based media. Inordinate government and industry influence on the media do not appear to be a problem in Western Europe and Japan, but caution has to be taken in many emerging markets, which have real constraints on press freedom, as regularly noted by organizations such as Amnesty International (1994) and the International Press Institute (1994).

By providing a non-U.S. perspective, public affairs managers can compare and contrast the insights and emphasis of these media with U.S. mainstream media. These media include the *Economist* in London and *Far Eastern Economic Review* in Hong Kong. Both newsweeklies also publish regional and country reports. Several prestige newspapers, such as *Asahi* and *Mainichi* in Japan, *Le Monde* in France and *Frankfurter Allgemeine Zeitung* in Germany, provide in-depth analysis and commentary on their own countries and the world. Many Latin American countries are now publishing their own business newspapers and magazines, although many problems remain, particularly those related to political corruption and editorial independence. Unlike the U.S., many journalists also work concurrently in public relations in several Latin American countries. The *World Press Review* is a useful introduction to foreign mainstream media. U.S.-owned media based abroad, such as the *Asian Wall Street Journal*, also provide coverage on the scene.

Alternative Media in the United States and Other Countries

Almost as a rule, public affairs practitioners tend to ignore the alternative media, particularly abroad. To be certain, not all alternative media are equally important. Some are more influential than others, especially if they represent the views of an emerging social, political or economic coalition. In the past, U.S.-based mainstream media tended to dismiss alternative communication channels, such as the widely-circulated audiocassettes of the Ayatollah Khomeini's teachings prior to the Iranian revolution (Fathi, 1979; Shawcross, 1988). As a result, most of the U.S. public knew little, if any, of the depth of the opposition to the Shah's rule prior to his ouster.

Similarly, U.S. corporations in Central America could have learned about the intentions of various insurgent groups, such as the Sandinistas and the Farabundo Martí National Liberation Front, even before they gathered enough strength to challenge their respective governments by paying attention to their newspapers and radio stations (LaFeber, 1993). *Barricada*, which started as an underground publication, eventually became a mainstream newspaper and remains popular even after the Sandinistas have lost power in Nicaragua (Inter-American Press Association, 1995). As radical Islamic groups try to gain political power in Algeria, Egypt, Indonesia, Malaysia and Morocco, U.S. corporations doing business in those countries need to pay attention to media and other channels supporting these causes (Bennis and Moushabeck, 1993; Daniel, 1993; Viorst, 1994).

In the U.S., alternative media, such as *Mother Jones, Progressive, Utne Reader,* and *Village Voice,* report on foreign affairs from time to time and offer analysis which often differs from the mainstream. Instead of ignoring these sources of information, public affairs practitioners can compare them with their own analysis of what is happening in key sectors of the countries where they operate.

Ethnic Media in the United States

Various print and broadcast media by different immigrant groups also comprise a sub-set of alternative media available in the U.S. Most of these media also report and comment on important developments in their countries of origin.

Haitian newspapers and radio stations in Miami and New York, for example, provided insider points of view on the ouster and eventual return of President Jean-Bertrand Aristide. Using reliable sources in their countries of origin, some ethnic media have scooped the U.S. mainstream media on important issues. Years before the Pulitzer prize-winning report in the *San Jose Mercury* on President Ferdinand Marcos' fake war medals, the *Philippine Times* in Chicago made a documented exposé on the same topic (Simons, 1987). To be certain, not all ethnic media in the U.S. require attention, and public affairs practitioners need to winnow out the grain from the chaff, probably with the help of local staff in countries where they do business. Of particular interest within the next few years will be ethnic media among immigrants from Eastern Europe, the Middle East, East Asia, and Africa.

Worldwide Television

CNN's vision of worldwide media by satellite is being challenged by other players, including BBC World Service Television and Star TV, the first pan-Asian satellite television network. The competition could benefit U.S. companies, which are interested in non-U.S.-centric perspectives. As direct broadcast satellite technology becomes cheaper across the globe, access to this new category of "world media" is expected to climb. In India, pirates stealing from Star TV's signal and reselling them to others over cable may have only succeeded in broadening Star TV's potential reach. Instead of hurting the company's bottom line, these pirates have enabled Star TV management to raise their advertising rates (Dwyer and Edmonson, 1995; Gross, Coy and Port, 1995).

Planet Internet

What started as an attempt to create a communication network capable of surviving nuclear warfare has become the single most important global-spanning medium in the 1990s. Online services in both the U.S. and Western Europe are joining the Internet, even as users multiply by the millions worldwide every few months (Edmonson, 1995). Dominance in the field by a few online services will eventually be decided by their coalitions of institutional and individual content providers, telecommunication carriers, cable TV operators, computer companies, local resellers and bulletin boards, among other players. U.S.-based online services need content from Europe and elsewhere in order to attract subscribers worldwide, while European-based services need U.S. content and information from other countries to remain competitive. Even as governments and interest groups try to control the flow of information, U.S. companies need to figure out what type of content would be most useful in making them more attractive in countries where they operate. As technology improves, the information tide will continue to swell.

The World Wide Web was one of the very first attempts to impose order over the mass of free-form information on the Internet by organizing it into easily understood pages. It probably will not be the last. But the idea is fundamental to taming the information tide. Without order, available information becomes very difficult to access and use. As the amount of information approaches the carrying and processing capacity of organizations, information surplus becomes information deficit. Beyond a certain point, available information could overwhelm a corporation's ability to make sense of the data. Furthermore, the Internet could be oversold by bogus claims and hidden costs. Boosters claim that the Internet can solve everything from educating children to restoring participatory democracy. It is expected to cut down medical costs, turn corporations into super efficient businesses, and finally overcome boundaries of poverty, race, and inadequate education (Stoll, 1995).

These promises have a familiar ring. The same technological "solutions" were offered when radio, television, and satellite technology were introduced at various times since the 1920s. Like the "cargo cults" of the South Pacific, these promises were never quite fulfilled anywhere close to their overheated claims (González, 1991). Some practical questions remain, including encryption and security of online transactions and better indexing systems to keep people from drowning as they surf through a sea of information to find exactly what they want. More information and faster access to databases are not necessarily better, even for public affairs practitioners. Information Highway pioneer Clifford Stoll (1995, pp. 45-46) said, "Simply by turning to a computer when confronted with a problem, you limit your ability to recognize other solutions. . . . Computers punish the imaginative and the innovative by constraining them to prescribed channels of thought and communication." He added that "Information is not knowledge" (Stoll, 1995, p. 193).

Making Sense of the Data

To anticipate and respond to possible changes in the social, political and economic landscape in various markets abroad, public affairs managers need to expand their analytical abilities. The following suggestions can help in making sense of the information obtained from alternative communication sources.

Tapping Local and Regional Expertise

Corporations can add depth to their capability to scan the environment by calling on local and regional expertise to provide regular analysis of social, political, and economic events. For example, they can help sponsor seminars with local chambers of commerce where recognized government, business and academic representatives analyze present and future prospects of specific topics of interest.

In many countries, business schools and universities also publish their own analysis of current events and future trends. Out-of-pocket cost is as little as purchasing these reports. Whether these analyses conform with those made by the public affairs staff is not as important as comparing their differences and understanding why. From time to time, corporations can ask academics to serve as consultants on specific projects. Many universities and research institutions in the U.S. also produce annual analyses of various countries and regions. These reports may be used as additional input in strategic planning by corporations. As in any type of research, these reports vary in quality, coverage and authority.

Understanding the Local Culture

Patience and persistence are necessary in trying to understand other cultures, beginning with learning the local language as a key. These values do not seem to come easily to many U.S. corporations, given their tendency toward isolationism and impatience for "getting on with the business." Although there is no love lost between China and Japan based on recent history, Japan continues to lead the world in trade and investment in China, by making an effort to understand how the Chinese want to do business. U.S. companies often find themselves at sea with cultures radically different from their own, as dramatically shown in their perplexity in Japan, Korea and elsewhere. While Japanese companies require their senior overseas staff to learn the local language and culture, comparable efforts by U.S. companies appear to fall short of the mark (Gelsanliter, 1990; Katzenstein, 1989; Stross, 1990).

The Pacific Rim is widely considered the market of tomorrow. At present, it is the fastest-growing region in the world (Elegant, 1990). Hiring local bilingual managers is not a substitute for U.S. executives posted overseas, since local staff are rarely represented at senior levels of management. Again, academics from local colleges and universities can help the public affairs staff with their in-house analysis of the environment. Aside from quantitative methods, practitioners can employ social science meta-analysis, anthropology, and various non-obtrusive methods. These skills can be used to examine enduring beliefs, values and practices, and to help identify institutions aside from the government that could become major players in structural change. Knowing the culture can also help U.S. companies anticipate reforms or understand the maintenance of certain policies and legislation.

Building Relationships

Coming to terms with another culture from the insider's point of view also enables public affairs practitioners to build relationships. The new markets in former socialist countries provide a case in point. As they struggle toward political and economic democracy, former state bureaucrats try to transform themselves into managers and technocrats. They are unaccustomed to U.S. ways of doing business, as many U.S. corporations are unaccustomed to theirs (Bennis and Moushabeck, 1993; Goldfarb, 1992; Islam and Mandelbaum, 1993). Over the next few years, these emerging economies will rewrite their rules for trade and investment.

Although U.S. companies tend to emphasize short-term profitability and immediate results, they could benefit greatly by building for the long-term. U.S. business can only lose these markets by default, by failing to plan several more years into the future. This may mean initially establishing a presence, even if returns appear to be minimal for the first few years, foregoing larger profits for market share, assigning U.S. staff overseas for a longer term, arranging living arrangements for these staff closer to the local people, and building personal bonds instead of simply relying on legal paperwork (Copetas, 1991; Katzenstein, 1989; Stross, 1990). These efforts will not come easily because U.S. companies do not appear to be instinctively internationalist.

A recurring criticism of U.S. businesspeople abroad is their lack of empathy and insensitivity for other cultures (Goldfarb, 1992; Gelsanliter, 1990; Katzenstein, 1989; Stross, 1990). The emphasis on short-term returns puts long-term success at risk, because time-consuming relationship-building is ignored. Public affairs practitioners have the responsibility of educating their management and staff in building relations with their consumers, local partners and other public and private agencies that they interact with.

Lending a Hand

Pervasive social problems, particularly in emerging economies, could affect the conduct of business. They include population pressure, racial hatred, insurgency, drugs, AIDS and other diseases, homelessness, crime, environmental damage, corruption at various levels of government, as well as state-sponsored human rights violations. To be certain, even helping solve some of these concerns are beyond the ability of many companies doing business abroad.

The opportunities to make a difference would vary in each case, and the channels for such assistance would depend on whether social welfare agencies and similar institutions are not only available, but trustworthy. Russia in transition is experiencing inequity and discontent as the private sector slowly takes over the remnants of the old economy. In Haiti, the transition to democracy means more than a ballot box, but the opening of new opportunities to make a better life possible for the impoverished majority. In the past, national development models usually ignored pervasive government corruption in many Third World countries, as if the private sector alone could make a difference. But recognizing an unaccountable and unresponsive government as part of the problem does not make the solution any easier. Part of the resistance to privatizing state-owned enterprises in some Third World countries is the perceived loss of social safety nets.

Almost by definition, capitalism creates economic inequality and unequal recognition. How to convert this weakness into strength will be a challenge for those corporations doing business in emerging markets. Non-participation in trying to find solutions to these social problems, however, does not appear to be a viable option, especially if those corporations intend to do business in those countries for any period of time. By not lending a hand, they could be perceived by the local population, perhaps wrongly, as being in business for profit alone. This perception could impact on the corporation's long-term success.

Openness

Competing in new world markets requires flexibility and openness to other, even opposing, points of view, particularly against those held by management. While openness is more of an attitude than a strategy, it impacts on what kind of information is gathered, processed, and eventually used for decision-making.

Symmetrical models of communication, as envisioned by James E. Grunig and his colleagues (Grunig, 1992; Grunig and Hunt, 1984), can only occur in relatively open corporate environments. Otherwise, lower-level managers and staff, including those in public affairs, will rely mainly on sources of information which management considers acceptable (González, 1989). The main strength of using alternative communication is that these sources are commonly dismissed as being less reliable or authoritative by those who rely only on mainstream sources. Unfortunately, so-called "safe" sources of information very often echo the establishment point of view. As previously discussed, U.S. corporations who simply joined the chorus admiring the emperor's new clothes found themselves blindsided on imminent structural change, such as the revolution in Iran, the invasion of Kuwait and the peso meltdown in Mexico (Darwish and Alexander, 1991; Marcos, 1994; Ross, 1995; Viorst, 1994).

Alternative futures

The purpose of opening the corporation to new flows of information other than those from mainstream sources is to enable management, through the public affairs staff, to consider alternative futures. Based on information gathered on social, political and economic developments, public affairs practitioners can apply this working knowledge to construct at least three scenarios or "futures" based on their probability of happening, namely: (1) The most likely scenario, (2) the likely scenario, and (3) the least likely scenario vis-a-vis certain corporate activities. Since some events are considered more likely than others, corporate strategies and action plans can be prioritized accordingly. The corporation can prepare for more than one contingency, based on the estimates prepared by the public affairs staff.

Short-term scenarios can be constructed annually, with a review of assumptions and actual events every six months. Longer-term scenarios may also be prepared, between three to 10 years, and updated periodically. As Herbert Simon (1982, 1992) observed, even this type of information gathering and processing will represent "bounded knowledge." However, the likelihood of being "surprised" or passively overtaken by major events appear to be reduced by considering all major participants in social change, paying attention to their own media and other channels, and critically analyzing their content for intentions and possible courses of action. Even the Central Intelligence Agency recognized that economic information will become more competitive among nations as the Cold War receded from view (Waller, 1995). Current country reports prepared by the CIA are openly available in hard copy or online to anyone interested in this type of analysis (Central Intelligence Agency, 1995).

The idea of alternative futures may appear threatening to some people in management. Part of the reason is that conventional economics focuses mainly on buying and selling transactions in the marketplace, and virtually ignores the possibility of social, political, and economic change. But the winners of the 1994 Nobel Prize for economics—John Nash of Princeton University, John Harsanyi of the University of California at Berkeley, and Reinhard Selten of the University of Bonn in Germany—have turned conventional wisdom on its head. Using game theory, they analyzed not only why existing social and economic arrangements are stable, but what the alternatives might be, based on the interactions of economic "actors" such as individuals, corporations and governments (Harsanyi, 1982, 1986; Harsanyi and Selten, 1988). The possibility of many stable outcomes or "multiple equilibria" is being used more and more to explain a wide range of activities, such as the behavior of central banks to the spending patterns of corporations. Michael Mandel (1994), *Business Week* economics editor, said that "Almost every economic and social game turns out not to have just one stable outcome, but many." In other words, the status quo is not inevitable. In trading new markets for old, public affairs practitioners have a brave new world full of possibilities.

References

Aho, James A. *The Politics of Righteousness: Idaho Christian Patriotism.* Seattle: University of Washington Press, 1990.

Amnesty International. *The 1994 Report on Human Rights Around the World.* Alameda, CA: Hunter House, 1994.

Barnathan, Joyce. "Hongkong: Beijing is Already Muffling the Media." *Business Week*, June 12, 1995, p. 60.

Bennis, Phyllis and Michel Moushabeck, eds. *Altered States.* Brooklyn, NY: Olive Branch Press, 1993.

Central Intelligence Agency. *The World Factbook.* Washington, D.C.: Central Intelligence Agency, 1995.

Chirot, Daniel. *Modern Tyrants: The Power and Prevalence of Evil in Our Age.* New York: Free Press, 1994.

Collier, George A. with Elizabeth Quaratiello *¡Basta! Land and the Zapatista Rebellion in Chiapas.* Oakland, CA: Institute for Food and Development Policy, 1994.

Copetas, A. Craig. *Bear Hunting with the Politburo.* New York: Simon and Schuster, 1991.

Daniel, Norman. *Islam and the West.* Oxford: Oneworld, 1993.

Darwish, Adel and Gregory Alexander. *Unholy Babylon: The Secret History of Saddam's War.* New York: St. Martin's Press, 1991.

Dwyer, Paula and Gail Edmonson. "CNN Copycats get set for a Catfight," *Business Week*, March 6, 1995, p. 50.

Edmonson, Gail. "Europe enters the Cyberspace Race." *Business Week*, February 13, 1995, pp. 91-92.

Elegant, Robert. *Pacific Destiny: Inside Asia Today.* New York: Avon Books, 1990.

Fathi, Ashgar. "The Role of the Islamic Pulpit." *Journal of Communication* 29 (3), Spring 1979, pp. 102-106.

Fogel, Jean-Francois and Bertrand Rosenthal. *Fin de Siglo en la Habana.* Santafé de Bogotá, Colombia: Tercer Mundo Editores, 1994.

Fukuyama, Francis. *The End of History and the Last Man.* New York: Free Press, 1992.

Gelsanliter, David. *Jump Start: Japan Comes to the Heartland.* New York: Farrar Straus Giroux, 1990.

Gibson, James William. *Warrior Dreams: Violence and Manhood in Post-Vietnam America.* New York: Hill and Wang, 1994.

Goldfarb, Jeffrey C. *After the Fall: The Pursuit of Democracy in Central Europe.* New York: Basic Books, 1992.

González, Hernando. "Mass Media and the Spiral of Silence." *Journal of Communication* 38 (4), Summer 1988, pp. 33-49.

González, Hernando. "Interactivity and Feedback in Third World Development Campaigns." *Critical Studies in Mass Communication* 6 (3), September 1989, pp. 295-314.

González, Hernando. *Some Myths of Communication and Development.* New York: International Institute of Rural Reconstruction, 1991.

Gross, Neil, Peter Coy and Otis Port. "The Technology Paradox," *Business Week*, March 6, 1995, pp. 76-84.

Grunig, James E. "Communication, Public Relations, and Effective Organizations: An Overview of the Book." *Excellence in Public Relations and Communication Management*, edited by James E. Grunig. Hillsdale, NJ: Lawrence Erlbaum, 1992, pp. 18-19.

Grunig, James and Todd Hunt. *Managing Public Relations.* New York: Holt, Rinehart and Winston, 1984.

Harsanyi, John C. *Game Theory.* Norwell, MA: Kluwer Academic Press, 1982.

Harsanyi, John C. *Rational Behavior and Bargaining Equilibrium in Games and Social Situations.* New York: Cambridge University Press, 1986.

Harsanyi, John C. and Richard Selten. *A General Theory of Equilibrium Selection in Games.* Cambridge, MA: MIT Press, 1988.

Heuvel, Jon Vanden and Everette E. Dennis. *Changing Patterns: Latin America's Vital Media.* New York: Freedom Forum, 1995.

Hiebert, Ray, Peter Gross, Dean Mills, Timothy Kenny and Maurice Fliess. *Highlights of a Summit of Journalism Educators from Central and Eastern Europe and the United States.* Arlington, VA: Freedom Forum, 1994a.

Hiebert, Ray, Peter Gross, Dean Mills, Timothy Kenny and Maurice Fliess. *Looking to the Future: A Survey of Journalism Education in Central and Eastern Europe and the former Soviet Union.* Arlington, VA: Freedom Forum, 1994b.

Inter-American Press Association. *Press Freedom in the Americas: 1995 Annual Report.* Miami: Inter-American Press Association, 1995.

International Press Institute. *IPI Report,* December 1994.

Islam, Shafiqul and Michael Mandelbaum. *Making Markets: Economic Transformation in Eastern Europe and the Post-Soviet States.* New York: Council on Foreign Relations Press, 1993.

Kandell, Jonathan. *La Capital: The Biography of Mexico City.* New York: Henry Holt, 1988.

Katzenstein, Gary. *Funny Business: An Outsider's Year in Japan.* New York: Prentice Hall, 1989.

LaFeber, Walter. *Inevitable Revolutions: The United States in Central America* (2nd ed.). New York: W. W. Norton and Co., 1993.

Lieberthal, Kenneth. *Governing China: From Revolution to Reform.* New York: W. W. Norton, 1995.

López Vigil, José Ignacio. *Rebel Radio: The Story of El Salvador's Radio Venceremos.* Willimantic, CT: Curbstone Press, 1991.

Macdonald, Andrew [William L. Pierce]. *The Turner Diaries.* Hillsboro, WV: National Vanguard Books, 1980.

Mandell, Michael J. "How Game Theory Rewrote All the Rules," *Business Week,* October 24, 1994, p. 44.

Marcos, Subcomandante. *EZLN: Documentos y Comunicados.* México: Ediciones Era, 1994.

Orozco, Román. *Cuba Roja: Cómo viven los cubanos con Fidel Castro.* Santafé de Bogota, Colombia: Javier Vergara, 1993.

Remnick, David. *Lenin's Tomb: The Last Days of the Soviet Empire.* New York: Random House, 1993.

Rius [Del Rio, Eduardo]. *Su Majestad el Partido Revolucionario Institucional* (Novena edición). México: Grijalbo, 1993.

Ross, John. *Rebellion from the Roots: Indian Uprising in Chiapas.* Monroe, ME: Common Courage Press, 1995.

Ruiz, Ramón Eduardo. *Triumphs and Tragedy: A History of the Mexican People.* New York: W. W. Norton and Co., 1992.

Salisbury, Harrison E. *The New Emperors: China in the Era of Mao and Deng.* Boston: Little, Brown and Co., 1992.

Shawcross, William. *The Shah's Last Ride: The Fate of an Ally.* New York: Simon and Schuster, 1988.

Simon, Herbert A. *Models of Bounded Rationality* Vol. 2. Cambridge, MA: The MIT Press, 1982.

Simon, Herbert A. *Models of My Life.* Basic Books, 1992.

Simons, Lewis M. *Worth Dying For.* New York: William Morrow and Co., 1987.

Stoll, Clifford. *Silicon Snake Oil: Second Thoughts on the Information Highway.* New York: Doubleday, 1995.

Stross, Randall. *Bulls in the China Shop and Other Sino-American Business Encounters.* New York: Pantheon Books, 1990.

United Nations. *World Economic and Social Survey.* New York: United Nations Publications, 1995.

Virtue, John, Agatha Ogazón, Ana Cecilia With, Roy E. Carter, Mario Diament and Sandra Navarro. *Journalists in the Andes.* Miami: Florida International University, 1995.

Viorst, Milton. *Sandcastles: The Arabs in Search of the Modern World.* New York: Alfred A. Knopf, 1994.

Waller, Douglas. "Spies in Cyberspace." *Time,* March 20, 1995, pp. 63-64.

ISSUES IN PUBLIC AFFAIRS MANAGEMENT

Chapter 23

Information Preparedness:
Harnessing Technology

Stuart Z. Goldstein

There is an exercise I often use when speaking to young communications professionals at local universities. I'd like to share it with you to introduce and emphasize an important point in this chapter. First, I ask them to describe on a piece of paper the current functions, responsibilities and structure of a communications department in a major company. After 5-10 minutes, I then ask them to take what they've just defined and tell me what that communications role will look like in 15 or 20 years.

There really is no right or wrong answer. The point of the exercise is to underscore the need—for all of us, as communicators—to develop a conceptual framework that stretches our thinking and considers: how the different component pieces of what we do within the disciplines of corporate communications/public relations interrelate; an understanding of the trends affecting the communications industry in general; and how innovations in technology are changing this framework looking toward the future.

It's amazing, but in the last 20 years the basic strategies and structure of what we do in communications has not changed significantly. Is the world the same as it was 15 or 20 years ago?

Historically, the role of communications has been seen as adjunct to the business. Communicators were tacticians, called in to write a press release, speech, annual report, marketing brochure, etc. This snapshot of the profession may be a generalization, but it serves as a sharp contrast to the real demands today on communicators in a fast-paced, highly demanding and competitive business environment.

Over the past several years, the profession has been forced into a transformation as companies have downsized and demanded more accountability from their communications departments. While there will always be a need for people with skill levels to implement the tactical elements of communication, dynamic forces reshaping business demand that communicators have a better understanding of how to get to that strategic level. Companies are looking for communicators who can integrate their activities with the firm's business strategy and see themselves as catalysts for change. These seasoned communicators will have experience across the communications disciplines and will know how to leverage the pieces to influence outcomes and affect results.

Communications is no longer just "a nice thing to do." In the information age, it is a business imperative. The public no longer distinguishes between product performance and corporate action. The visual impact of media has created a sort of corporate persona, where every decision or product is seen as a sign of corporate judgement, ethics and responsibility.

Technology a Key Factor in Driving Change

Technology is dramatically transforming our world—and the way we communicate. However, describing a laundry list of software or hardware trends and their impact on our profession hardly seems relevant, since they will change by the time this chapter is published. More importantly, we should focus on how we think about using technology in the context of creating more effective strategies.

Technology has already redefined the role of corporate communications as a knowledge-based profession—some of us just don't realize it. Innovations in technology and telecommunications have expanded the:

- Quantity, quality and speed of communications worldwide;

- Impact of audio and visual media on public opinion; and

- Competition for reaching and influencing key constituencies.

But communications professionals today are so absorbed in dealing with the "here and now," they are not developing the infrastructure tools that will allow them to operate on a more strategic level. The end result is that more often than not they are reacting to today's realities rather than influencing them.

Let me give you an example. It involves the tainted meat scandal that occurred in Seattle, Washington. In that scenario, reports of tainted meat hit the news wires within minutes of the first reported illness. The television cameras arrived at the CEO's door 20 minutes later. The wire stories carried the news to New York, where the financial markets reacted and the company's stock started to plunge. In the midst of all this, the head of corporate communications is likely to have turned to his staff and said, "Tomorrow morning, we've got to organize a crisis communication task force meeting."

That's the real world that we're operating in today. It's often the tail wagging the dog. Our profession has already been radically changed, because information flows more rapidly than ever before. And that affects how we approach the job of communications.

The rationale for a crisis task force, as it *used to* be conceived, and even as we manage it today is, "Let's get the group together; let's talk about it." Well, the message is already out. Companies no longer have the luxury of time for lengthy discussions to formulate strategy.

Information Preparedness
the Key to Success

Information preparedness will determine communication success in the future. And various technology capabilities will provide the wherewithal to better manage and influence events—not after they occur, but before they occur by anticipating and planning the "if P then Q" scenarios in advance. . . . or as they are occurring.

Here is another example to illustrate how you can use technology to influence outcomes. During my tenure at American Express, I introduced into our department a method of tracking news wire stories through the local PC by subject.

The tools were in place when in the middle of the Gulf War crisis, I saw a Dow Jones news story scroll across the wires on the PC: "Bomb discovered at American Express headquarters in NY." You can imagine how disconcerting this was, since we were on the 48th floor and we had no idea that there was a bomb reported in our building below us. We quickly called downstairs and discovered that in a mail room near Shearson Lehman's fifth floor trading area, a package had arrived from overseas. It was unidentified and unexpected. As part of normal security procedures, the floor was temporarily cleared until they could verify what it was.

Bottom line, it was not a bomb. And within approximately 45 seconds, we were on the phone to Dow Jones. As we provided the real story, we could see the correction being reported on the news wire.

Now, a company can afford to have its trading floors cleared only so often before that disruption starts to hit the bottom line. And if that bomb story had been carried on the news wires and reported in the newspapers the next day, there is a high probability that further bomb threats would have been received. In effect, we had preempted a negative news story.

One of the current theories is that given the way information flows, you cannot allow a story to go out over the media channel without challenging it, or coming very close behind it, or else it will dominate the news. If your message is too far behind, you've lost.

It should come as no surprise that some of the top people in the communications field have political backgrounds. In the modern era of communications, political campaigns come closest to serving as laboratories for testing communication theories. For example, in the last presidential campaign, Jim Carville was credited for his success in managing the message by never letting something crowd the media channel, never letting a negative story get out in front of him.

Well, the same issue challenges us in corporations. The more we understand what capabilities are needed from a strategic point of view, the more effectively we can build the technology infrastructure that will support and leverage our effectiveness.

Defining "Strategic"

The word strategic has different meanings to different people. A number of my colleagues, for example, will talk about strategic communications from the standpoint of whether they have a plan which articulates their goals and objectives. Their idea of strategic is that they have an employee communications programs that reflects what they will do in 1995, or a media relations program that maps out what they're going to do in that area.

When I talk about strategic, I mean influencing outcomes and affecting results by:

- *Quantifying perceptions of various audiences through research;*

- *Using these perceptions in developing targeted messages to distinct groups;*

- *Creating the capacity to reach large, diverse constituencies with precision and speed;*

- *Managing communication messages through preemptive activities to influence news and views on various corporate issues;*

- *Verifying results based on action taken or by quantifying shifts in public opinion.*

In the future, a corporate communications department will function like a war room in a political campaign headquarters. As in a campaign, sophisticated research on perceptions of various publics will become standard practice. And technology will be used to reach those constituencies, once identified.

Routine tools in the political world such as overnight polling and focus groups will be used to provide the critical baseline of information for deciding strategy and for evaluating the effectiveness of that strategy once it is executed.

The shift toward research as a basis for communication planning is already under way. Union Carbide, for example, is already using overnight polling of employees as part of its internal communications program.

Experimentation by companies like Union Carbide and others underscores the growing competition for influencing various publics in the information age. And the period of time in which a company can respond to challenging situations from whatever public it deals with—that "window of opportunity"—is much smaller today.

Outside interest groups today are better organized and more sophisticated than ever before. They obtain marketing lists and carry out targeted mailings. They use 900 numbers to solicit funds as well as to identify supporters and mail literature. And they, too, have access to a growing arsenal of technology/ telecommunications tools to help them communicate and influence diverse audiences.

Building the Technology Infrastructure

So what technology is needed to help us achieve a more strategic approach to corporate communications? It is not one particular piece of software or hardware, but a foundation that you build to provide a more solid footing for strategy. This electronic infrastructure for corporate communications will include three major technology components:

- *An **integrated database** that allows you to proactively leverage internal information across all public affairs/corporate communications disciplines;*

- ***On-line** access to databases that allows you to receive and track information from external sources;*

- *A **diagnostic database** that tracks and helps analyze opinion data on a wide range of issues across key segments of your various constituencies.*

The Integrated Model

Today, public affairs professionals often see themselves across the different disciplines (e.g., media relations, government relations, employee communications, philanthropic activities) as clients to one another.

Each department within the corporate communications/public affairs umbrella has its own **administrative database** to help manage record-keeping for that particular program, and for that program

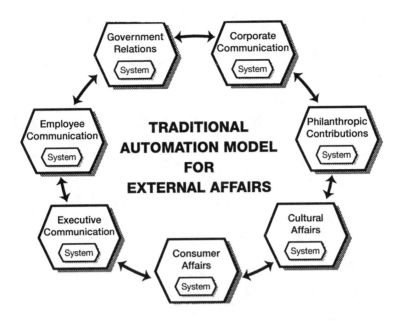

Government Relations System

Corporate Communication System

Employee Communication System

TRADITIONAL AUTOMATION MODEL FOR EXTERNAL AFFAIRS

Philanthropic Contributions System

Executive Communication System

Consumer Affairs System

Cultural Affairs System

alone. While these systems support each function, in almost all instances there is an inability to compare data across the departments.

Even when a strong team spirit exists within an organization, the design of the technology may limit its ability to respond. One department comes to the other and asks, "Can you give me this information?" The other department is likely to respond, "I can give you a list of names, but I can't give it to you the way you need it because of the system. And that request may take us 'til next week."

The **integrated model**, which some companies are already heading toward, will help position the organization for a higher state of readiness. This will be achieved by integrating databases that track and facilitate the cross-referencing of information from contacts with the media, elected officials, philanthropic group members, shareholders, employees active in their communities, etc.

In this scenario, the communications umbrella will consist of a string of departments that perceive themselves as integrated in terms of how they operate, integrated in terms of where data is kept, and integrated in their understanding of how to use data to "leverage the whole" of their public/external affairs effort.

Designing this relational database model requires that commu-

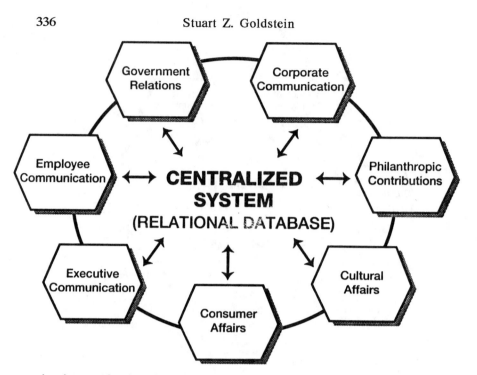

nication professionals see interconnections and leveraging opportunities. For example:

- *The ability to track reporters who have written positive articles about a particular issue or seem predisposed to your company, and identify them by Congressional district so media stories can be pitched to correspond where votes may be needed in Washington;*

- *The ability to track philanthropic grants and philanthropic group members by Congressional or state legislative districts, and communicate information to them on issues affecting the company;*

- *Comparing the biographical backgrounds of elected officials with the backgrounds of the employees who are involved in the local political contact program, which will help target areas of common interest that might assist your company in establishing stronger political ties;*

- *Providing our public relations people with direct, online access to information about our philanthropic activities to use in marketing stories to the press . . . or feed information to employees meeting elected officials that will help leverage these meetings to communicate other company concerns/ messages on key issues.*

This integrated database will also provide a large-scale institutional memory for easy, online access to news clippings, corporate statements, photo files, a video library of all production/operating facilities and linkages to external "information brokers" who can provide unlimited access to data when needed.

The Pepsi bottling scare is an excellent example of how information preparedness really saved the day. Within a week of news reports of a syringe allegedly being found in a bottle of Pepsi, the company was able to distribute a video on the safety of its bottling operations. Now imagine a company creating a video library that can distribute this footage over fiber optic networks or via satellite almost simultaneously with news wire reports. This represents a new dynamic in how messages will be managed.

Media Tracking

Many companies still do not track media contacts. But think about it: If you have 7,000 media calls coming in each year, what are they calling you about? What kinds of issues are they raising with you? What has your experience been with that reporter? Rather than viewing the calls operationally, think about them strategically. Tracking this information gives you the ability to analyze and proactively manage it.

If you're tracking reporters and their stories, you will know their areas of interest and you will have an ability to more proactively market stories. You know who the players are.

How you use this information can shift the whole focus of your media relations program. You will stop serving a **reactive** function and will become more **proactive**.

Equally important, automated media tracking preserves your institutional memory. This is particularly key because turnover in media relations is high. In two years, you may see a complete turnover in the media relations area of a corporate communications department. Whether it's one key staff member or several, it can be increasingly difficult to reconstruct what was said, when it was said, whom it was said to, how it was communicated, what the circumstances were and what insights on the reporter writing the story were captured. This information can be vitally important if the issue resurfaces—and most controversial issues do.

In a period when professionals are often at organizations only for brief stints, it is imperative that companies have effective safeguards to reconstruct how media situations were handled. That continuity, constancy and consistency of communication strategy will be key to the success of the organization.

On-line Access and Distribution

On-line access to external databases is another fundamental component of the communications infrastructure. Many companies already use external information databases. Some of these databases provide in-depth coverage of who's who in the media, legislative information, access to wire services . . . and there's a growing number of "information brokers" who specialize in an industry or type of data analysis.

Corporate communication professionals should not only broadly investigate avenues of information sources that will strengthen their efforts, but ensure the ability to capture and retain this information. While it is often cost effective to use outside data providers, there will be instances when capturing this information requires developing software to bridge with your internal technology infrastructure.

In addition to receiving information electronically, equal emphasis must be placed on innovative approaches to distributing your news and information to your various constituencies. While the technology curve still has some practical limitations (i.e., not everyone has PC-to-PC communications capabilities or access to the Internet), firms must develop an array of flexible and timely options for communicating directly with different audiences.

Diagnostic Database

A third building block for effective communication strategy is an internal database that will help track and analyze ongoing diagnostic research on the perceptions of your various publics, including:

- *Understanding how your company is generally perceived by various corporate constituencies;*

- *Gauging in advance how different if P then Q decisions will be perceived before action is taken;*

- *Measuring the effectiveness of messages as they are communicated and then using this information to modify the messages, if necessary.*

Smart companies today are beginning to ask themselves, "What is the basis for our communication strategy? What do we base our advertising on? Is it being driven by intuition or by research?" This issue poses a real dilemma for us as communicators.

Most of what we do in communications is intuitive, driven by our gut, usually drawn from past experience. A combination of things that we see, observe and feel. It is not very quantitatively based.

But we live in era when CEOs are demanding more accountability. If I were to ask: How would you demonstrate your effectiveness as a communicator? How would you prove that you've identified your audience properly, communicated to that audience the right message, you informed and influenced, and that you actually achieved your desired result? How would you do that?

In the information age, the margin for error in communicating the right message and influencing change is narrower than in the past. In this environment, communication strategy tied to intuition and experience should be tested for validity through periodic research.

Technology is allowing us to become more sophisticated in using measurement techniques. And through the diagnostic database, you will be able to track that information over an extended period of time. It will permit you to draw correlations that reinforce or correct intuitive judgements, and can be used to plot changes in strategy.

The Media Is Also Changing

Innovations in technology and telecommunications are also shaping trends in the media. Competition in network media and cable has not only impacted the style and content of news, it has also reduced the base of available advertising revenue. This loss of revenue is putting enormous strains on broadcast and print journalism.

Newspaper chains are rapidly consolidating the fourth estate. As a cost-cutting measure, local news reporting staffs are being reduced and greater reliance is being placed on syndicated coverage by the news chains. The result, sadly, is that there are fewer sources of independent news today. This trend applies to broadcast media as well, and it is going to continue.

Operating as a News Bureau

The opportunity side of this trend is that corporate communicators can get their story out by starting to operate as their own news organization. Drop the fluff, provide information that is newsworthy and you may find hotly competitive news organizations receptive to your material.

At the NASDAQ Stock Market, for example, when their communications staff traveled around the U.S., they had difficulty getting local TV coverage. Local stations couldn't spare the staff to cover the story. So NASDAQ now brings its own person to film events, and the tapes are then handed off to the local station. If this is done credibly, the video is run as news.

Credibility is essential to the success of this strategy, whether it's your own locally filmed news coverage, the distribution of video news releases or an audio news bureau that can be accessed online by external radio stations.

Creating Direct Channels
of Communication

As the control of media ownership (print and broadcast) becomes increasingly concentrated, however, companies will also need a technology infrastructure that helps them create more direct channels of communication: between the company and its stakeholders, and the company with segments of the general public.

While everyone is suggesting that the reality of 500 cable TV channels is just around the corner, I get nervous thinking about editorial decision-making once the shake-out is over. These cable companies may be owned by three or four huge media conglomerates.

Companies already have begun using technology offered by firms like ADP to speed the delivery of printed material directly to shareholders. Communicating directly with employees through dedicated cable TV channels is not far away. In this scenario, Social Security numbers are likely to be used to designate access for employee viewing rights in their home. Beyond the year 2000, this communication will be totally interactive which could expand the use of cable TV for annual shareholder meetings.

When General Motors is attempting to influence events in Washington or blunt negative or erroneous news coverage, they can call upon a database of over 5,000 shareholders who have been pre-identified as willing to write letters to legislators or to local media.

A few years back, a similar database of volunteers at Citicorp was used to generate 38,000 letters from employees to newspapers and Congress on banking law reform.

Regardless of where you stand on the issue of smoking, Philip Morris must be viewed as a leader in harnessing technology to support its communications activities. Confronted with an amendment on a bill pending in Congress, from a database of over 30 million names, Philip Morris can execute mailings overnight. The mailing can include a toll-free phone number that supporters can call to express their views. As the calls come in, computers can sort and redirect the call so the phone will ring in the Congressman's office. That's real. That's no longer imaginary. And whether it's Congress or letters to the editor, communicating directly with stakeholders can be a powerful method of managing perceptions and outcomes.

In the past, many of these approaches were used less effectively because they were so manually intensive or costly to implement. Technology, however, is removing these obstacles. It is also offering more dynamic approaches to segment audiences and target strategy.

In a media-dominated world, communicating directly with broad coalitions of stakeholders (as well as segments of the public at large) whom you can pre-identify as being predisposed to your views is absolutely critical. Corporate communication effectiveness increasingly will be differentiated by the degree to which communication strategy utilizes the infrastructure and tools that technology offers in reaching these groups.

The role that communications plays in a company's bottom line is greater today than it has ever been. And in a world where CNN comes into almost every home and news is reported with lightning speed, the absence of a strategic approach to communication can be devastating.

Using Research to Target Strategy

While survey research has long been used to gauge public perceptions on issues, we are entering an era where marketing segmentation analysis will be used to guide communication strategy. Instead of broad-brush strategies drawn from a large general sampling of opinion, technology supported research techniques will provide laser beam targeting capabilities.

At Citicorp in the late 1980s, we used outside research firms to measure public awareness about banking reform. The costs for this type of research were high, which restricted the number of questions you could ask. As a result, the information was very general and had limited use.

Let me contrast that with today's environment, where a company can take its own national survey on a range of critical issues and public perceptions. Ten years ago, you would have to reach 1,500 people in order to achieve a three or four percent error margin. Today, most national samplings can achieve this error margin with a 550-person sampling. Survey research, focus groups and other perception measurement techniques are becoming more economical and easier to execute.

Sophisticated geo-demographic targeting software combined with cognitive modeling (offered by social scientists) will allow you to identify by zip code large clusters of people with similar views across the country. This information can then be used to direct your corporate messages into highly specific media markets and to help prioritize how you allocate advertorial and advertising dollars in newspapers, broadcast TV, magazines and even direct mail—all with a degree of precision unimaginable just a few years ago.

Easy access to, and use of, direct database marketing techniques will significantly redirect how corporate PR professionals inform, influence and generate support among diverse stakeholder groups; e.g., employees, shareholders, customers and others.

Building on this example, let's take it one step higher on the ladder of sophisticated communication strategy. A consumer goods or consumer services company today, like Citicorp or GE, maintains large customer databases. You could take the analysis of the 10 key issues in your survey for supporters and break the group down by zip code. These zip codes could then be put back into the company's large customer data bases. The information technology will then permit you to selectively insert issue-oriented material into customer statements and to send separate direct mail.

If the company does not have its own customer database, it can contract out for these services to a telemarketing/database marketing company. Some of these companies already have more than 100 million names and addresses in a database, drawn from available public sources of information (usually catalogue sales).

None of the ideas I've raised should boggle anyone's mind. The capabilities are not five or ten years off; many exist today. In fact, various companies are experimenting with some of the strategies I've touched on.

There are further steps higher on the ladder, as we move toward interactive media. A few years ago during an ABC-TV Monday Night Football half-time show, callers could express their opinions on the best players in the game by dialing a 900 phone number. Computers were able to provide almost instant polling results, which were reported toward the end of the game.

What callers were unaware of is that the technology can now sort and identify the source of the caller. The interactive media, therefore, provides yet another method of survey research which can then sort and identify potential supporters, and closely follow the targeted communication strategy outlined above. And the cost of the survey is underwritten by the charge to call the 900 phone number.

Competing for Influence

In the information age, technology is also leveling the playing field for public interest groups. These groups are adopting the same techniques for communicating messages, mobilizing support and prompting action.

The Child Welfare Society, for example, published a full-page ad in *The New York Times* three years ago, dramatically calling attention to the problems of children and offering a package of information about the organization's efforts. The public was encouraged to call a 900 phone number for a fee, which more than covered the cost of the call and printed material. The Society not only used this approach to advertise its message and raise money; it also facilitated the creation of a database of supporters for future activities.

Does all this seem too futuristic? Whether or not you accept each of the scenarios I've described, the emphasis here is on the degree to which breakthroughs in technology and telecommunications are changing the way that messages are communicated and managed. These scenarios also underscore the influence of technology as the great equalizer in the competition for influence.

What Is the Downside of Technology?

It is important to underscore that technology is not an end in itself: it is a means to an end, a tool. People still have to analyze and interpret data. A technology platform will provide corporate communicators with a heightened state of readiness and more effective methods for researching, targeting and executing strategy. The best technology infrastructure in the world, however, will not substitute for good judgement.

In addition, there exists the potential for business to abuse technology and violate consumer privacy. Each of us in the profession must exercise judgement in carefully defining boundaries. When it comes to the issue of privacy, we should make certain that the information used is in the public domain and readily accessible. And if we err, it should be on the conservative side of the issue. The public will be unforgiving if a company encroaches on this fundamental right.

Finally, the most effective communication strategy in the world will not protect an organization that lacks a moral compass. It didn't take CEO Jim Burke at Johnson & Johnson a long time to decide what to do during the Tylenol scare. He immediately pulled the product from the shelves. There was pain involved (no pun intended), but some issues are crystal clear where public safety is involved.

The leadership of the CEO still plays a critical role in communication strategy. The best research and methods can be for naught, if the senior executive doesn't value communications as an integral part of the business. But that is changing, as more enlightened CEOs are bringing with them a better understanding and appreciation for the importance of an active communication program.

A New Era of Communication

The communications support required by business in the twenty-first century will be markedly different from what we know today.

Communications is becoming a knowledge-based profession, and the lines between corporate communication/ public affairs disciplines are converging. I believe the dynamic forces reshaping business will lead to communication departments that structure themselves as follows:

- *Research and technology to guide strategy development and to provide implementation tools;*

- *Senior-level communication strategists with experience across the disciplines.*

In this new era, media relations, issues management, advertising and the rest of the disciplines will be more closely integrated to ensure clear, consistent and constant emphasis on key messages. This integration, moreover, will offer the capacity to change advertising messages, sometimes overnight, to address the changing perceptions of various constituencies.

As we face a communications world that will be greatly influenced by technology, we must begin to look at developing new strategies, skills and tools for the world of the future. Our universities and professional trade organizations must be called upon to help us design new models and serve as laboratories.

I have described a number of issues and trends in this chapter, and proposed a technology infrastructure that I believe can move us toward a more strategic approach to communications. But I would like to end this discussion by returning to the exercise I use with college students. Looking out 10 to 15 years, what is your vision of the role of communications?

The exercise is intended to serve as a clarion call, a challenge to each of us in the profession to stretch beyond our current thinking. Once awakened to new possibilities, we can ensure our relevance as communicators and to continue serving as catalysts for change.

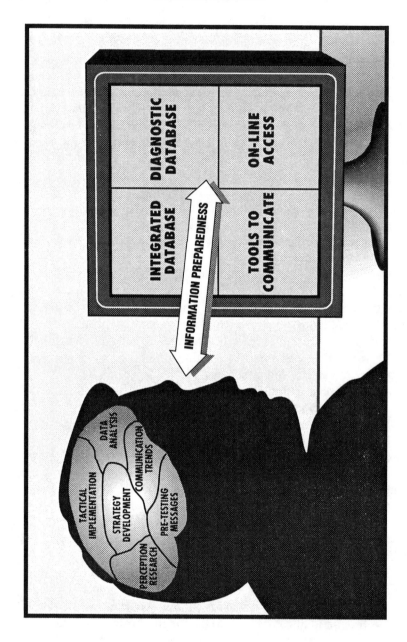

Chapter 24

The "Gipper's" Timeless Lessons on Communicating Effectively

Michael K. Deaver

To understand the secret of successfully integrating public relations programs with a public affairs agenda, it helps to remember the lessons of a man who carries the mantle as one of the great political communicators of our age.

When Ronald Reagan came to Washington, D.C. in 1981, it was at a pivotal moment in American politics. We had reached a point when the office of the Presidency had been dangerously devalued by a continuing loss of public trust. Far from a bully pulpit of prestige and power, the office had become an albatross for a series of recent inheritors. Lyndon Johnson had opted to retire rather than face the looming prospect of defeat during a time of war. Richard Nixon had resigned in disgrace, and Gerald Ford and Jimmy Carter had successively lost their respective re-election bids.

In this climate of shriveled public confidence, the possibility of anyone earning a second term seemed remarkably remote. And those chances seemed all the more unlikely as Reagan arrived with the highest negative public opinion ratings of any incoming President in the history of such polling. But Reagan had always been underestimated. And once again he defied the doubters and detractors by restoring belief in the possibilities of the Presidency with a successful first term, which was followed by a historic re-election mandate.

One of the keys to Reagan's success, of course, was his ability to communicate so effectively to the American people. And as I remind my clients, while there is only one Ronald Reagan, one of his lasting legacies is a communications blueprint that can be followed to this day by individuals, companies and organizations.

Sure, the communications industry has changed dramatically since then as the information revolution has surged forward with each new technology breakthrough. But we cannot forget that the core principles of successful message delivery remain the same regardless of the technology used to carry the message.

Whether the medium is the Internet, a fax or an old-fashioned press release, Reagan's rules for communicating are just as important today for companies facing public affairs challenges as they were during his confrontation with the incredibly shrinking Presidency.

Understand Who You Are

People felt comfortable with Reagan because he was comfortable with himself. In my early days as an aide to then-governor Reagan, I once suggested he strike a Kennedyesque pose for a photograph, with his suit jacket slung over his shoulder. "I can't do that, Mike," the Governor said. "That's not me and people will know it. The camera never lies."

For all of the credit given to others for creating the Reagan image, the truth is that Reagan knew who he was better than anyone else and never allowed himself to be in a situation that was contrary to his basic personality. The same holds true for any company.

Perhaps not surprisingly, this is why corporate communications programs so often fail to work. It does not mean that the communications professionals involved were not up to the task. To the contrary, I have worked with exceptionally talented people who were destined to fail. That's because they were representing an organization that had yet to adequately define a vision of itself. It's like the Cheshire Cat's wise words to Alice as she reached a fork in the road and wondered which one to take. "That," the clever cat advised, "depends on where you want to go."

Sometimes a company's self-definition actually can come into clearer focus after realizing how others view it. I once had the pleasure of working on an image campaign with America's three auto companies—Chrysler, Ford and General Motors. At the time, the companies had good reason to believe that public policymakers and policy influencers in Washington had a relatively low opinion of the U.S. auto industry. Over the years, they had heard plenty from people who had ideas about what was wrong with automakers. They also knew a lot more was right with the industry than people realized.

Innovative changes had occurred both in management structure and in the application of new technologies in the manufacturing process. The result was that cars were moving from the design stage to the driveway more quickly than ever before, enabling the industry to adapt to changing demands of consumers in half the time it used to take. Cars and trucks were being built more efficiently and effectively, and quality was higher at the same time. The problem was that while the U.S. consumer appreciated the difference and was buying more U.S.-made cars and trucks, the policymakers in Washington did not appreciate the extent of the industry's comeback.

As research was being conducted to better understand just how Washington viewed the U.S. auto industry, one fact became clear that had not been anticipated. It was not just that people had a negative view of the industry's performance; many people did not believe the industry was even going to be around for much longer. The automakers were off the charts when it came to identifying the types of businesses that would play an important role in the nation's economic future.

It was painfully clear that if Washington policy experts considered the country's automakers to be a "sunset" industry in unavoidable decline, there was less reason for them to listen to the industry's concerns of today. As the companies launched an aggressive image campaign targeted at the Washington audience, the future of the industry became a top priority and a central feature of how the industry defined itself. It took the viewpoint of others to realize just how important it was.

Know Your Strengths and Weaknesses

Once in 1972, during Reagan's second term as governor, he received a late night call from then-President Richard Nixon. Reagan was heading Nixon's re-election campaign in California, and Nixon was unhappy. He had been reviewing a report of every county chairman enlisted to support him and found the name of a man he disliked a great deal. As Nixon criticized the man and asked Reagan to replace him, Reagan cupped the telephone and asked us, "Who's this guy he's talking about?"

It was a classic example of the differences between the two men. There was Nixon, the President and master political tactician, with no detail too small to ignore, up late at night and reviewing lists of county chairmen from around the country. And there was Reagan, the consummate big picture thinker, not having a clue as to whom Nixon was talking about even though this chairman was from his own state.

Reagan's strength was in *communicating wholesale*—no one could do it better. He also knew he was not a detail person. He had plenty of other people working for him who could keep track of precinct committeemen.

When establishing a communications program, it is essential to first conduct a detailed, honest audit about your team's strengths and weaknesses. Make sure you have all of your bases covered—strategists, tacticians, researchers, writers and orators. You may find yourself short in a critical area and that's where you must focus when getting new personnel or when employing outside counsel. Too many people are caught up with the day's struggles without having an accurate assessment of what they are doing well and where they are falling short.

Speak Only When You Have Something to Say

Reporters still talk about how few press conferences Reagan held as President. But no one has any trouble recalling his central messages. Reagan knew the people wanted to hear from their leader when he had something important to say, and pretty much only then.

Recently, an energy company that is an important source of power for communities across the world was attacked by the environmental organization, Greenpeace. Greenpeace had broadly distributed a press release attacking the company for a history of environmental degradation, citing three examples of incidents that had occurred years earlier. The company responded as many others would. It wrote a long press release countering the accusations in minute detail and providing a much more complete and accurate explanation of the incidents in question. Now the company wanted to know what I thought of its release and my recommendations for distribution.

My response at first surprised them. I advised them to rewrite the release and provided a draft of a much shorter version. Rather than feel compelled to respond in detail to the accusations, I said the company should simply point out that the charges were a result of taking things out of context and in some cases just being plain wrong about the facts. At the same time, I told the company it had a positive environmental story to tell and should use this opportunity to highlight that commitment, including the ongoing participation of the company's founder in a number of national environmental programs and organizations. Finally, I told the company to use the statement as a means of communicating with the press only when asked. There was no reason to distribute it to anyone at this point. I warned against creating a story when there was no evidence the media was doing anything with the Greenpeace salvo anyway.

As things turned out, no newspaper ever did do a story based on the critical press release. The company's response, which was ready for distribution to the media if needed, was used to communicate with employees and other friends of the company, including those serving with the company chief on environmental boards.

It's popular these days to respond to any attack whenever one is made. And there are a number of examples of companies who erred by not responding sufficiently or in a timely manner to a situation that obviously required a thorough public response. But there are also times when it is inappropriate to give credence to an unfounded criticism. Organizations should also be selective in their proactive communications. Some companies still seem to measure their media relations programs by the sheer volume of press releases issued. And this brings us to our next point.

Keep Your Goals Limited

Reagan had a specific agenda when he came to office and stayed focused on it. To a large extent, his ability to focus was why he was so successful in implementing much of his stated agenda during his first term. Plenty of people had lots of different ideas for the President, but he knew that if he took on every cause he would provide insufficient time and energy to the issues that mattered most.

The same strategy marks a successful communications campaign. If you are trying to do too much, you will succeed at too little. I always advise clients to be a *well*, not a *fountain*. And don't be afraid to repeat your messages until you are sure they are getting through. Just look at Reagan. He gave essentially the same stump speech over and over again to audiences across the country for years and years. It took a while, but eventually his messages began to resonate—so much so that he was carried into the White House.

Message repetition works. It takes patience and perseverance. But I am convinced that this type of discipline is needed today more than ever. People are barraged as never before by competing messages from myriad delivery systems. And it seems that our collective attention span is growing shorter than ever as we surf through television channels and the Internet. It is rare that any one message is so powerful and memorable that it can be delivered on a limited basis and succeed in getting the job done.

I am reminded of a case involving a huge international company that had been accused by a competitor of engaging in unfair trade practices. The company responded with a thick document that countered every complaint in detail. It was a masterful report, and contained at least a dozen relevant messages that made for a powerful rebuttal case. A press conference attracted a huge crowd and stories were published and broadcast that put the besieged company in a favorable light. The corner was turned. And then the company representatives asked, "Now what do we say?"

Months had been spent preparing this huge document that no one could possibly read in one sitting, and now the team was ready to move on to the next task. It was pointed out that there were several important messages in the original report that had never been picked up by the media. These messages were worth repeating again and again until the media began reporting on them. If you have a good story to tell, keep telling it. Do not feel compelled to change subjects every day or week or even month. It's your story and no one will tell it unless you do.

Keep Laughing

Nothing endears communicators to people more than a sense of humor, especially when they can laugh at themselves. Once Reagan was being grilled by reporters for showing up at the Oval Office later in the morning than his predecessors and for leaving earlier. "Well, they say hard work never killed anyone," Reagan said. "But I figure, why take the chance?" People laughed and the issue was diffused.

Not everyone is funny, and not every situation is a cause for laughter. But having someone on your team who can find humor in a situation is a valuable asset, especially when times are tough. As you take stock of your communication team's strengths and weaknesses, make sure that you have someone who can make you laugh. Maybe the jokes will never be needed for prime time, but they certainly will make a difficult day in the office a whole lot easier to take.

Conclusion

In this chapter, I have provided a few timeless lessons from one of the great communicators of our time who is best remembered for his skills as a political orator. And the reason is simple: Everyone can count votes. The winners and losers are clear. In many cases, the bottom line of a communications campaign in the public policy arena is easier to isolate than in the business world. But these lessons are just as real for a CEO as they are for a Presidential candidate.

We must remember to look to the marketplace of public policy as the greatest testing ground for the practice of communication techniques. It is in this laboratory that successes and failures are so easy to find. Whether it is the successful tax plan or the failed health care proposal, lessons from these public policy battles can be applied to public affairs challenges of any company. They are the most visible examples of whether certain communications strategies, tactics and skills will work. Roosevelt, Reagan and Kennedy knew this. Carter, Nixon and Bush should have learned.

Chapter 25

Innovations in Public Affairs Programming: Collaborative Planning and Beyond

Kenneth D. Kearns and
Anna L. West

Collaborative Planning— Why is it Important?

Every modern definition of *public relations* includes, as an essential element, two-way communications between an organization and its publics.[1] An organization's decisions should be shaped by input from the people they affect. Collaborative planning goes one step further: it uses two-way communications, not just for input, but as an integral part of the decision process itself.[2]

Today, organizations are required to operate in a complex framework of policies, special interests, and market factors, making old decision processes ineffective. *Decide-announce-defend*, the practice of making a decision, announcing it, and then defending it, no longer produces sustainable results.

We live in a *participatory democracy* where people have a say in decisions that affect them. Whether public participation is institutionalized by law or achieved by other means (lobbying, the courts, information campaigns), today's decisions involve the

355

public. Stakeholders—groups and individuals—have capabilities and resources to either help or hurt an organization's decision.

Furthermore, when public participation involves communications through the media, the dominance of the *sound bite* and *instant analysis* inhibits a deeper understanding of stakeholders' interests and discourages a search for better solutions. The *information age* provides a profusion of data; it does not necessarily make us well-informed.

Too often the result is conflict. In their acclaimed dispute-resolution book *Getting to Yes: Negotiating Agreement Without Giving In*, Roger Fisher and William Ury suggest that society has allowed conflict to become a growth industry.[3] The proliferation of lawyers, personal lawsuits, courtroom backlogs and skyrocketing insurance costs are symptoms of this problem. And for an organization, conflict means delays, increased costs, and uncertainties.

People and organizations are frustrated with the adversarial nature of decision making. They are seeking better ways—ways that stress *we* instead of *us versus them* and processes that *build relationships* rather than create polarization, enemies and ill will. Collaborative planning is one of the ways.

Collaborative planning encourages, above all else, talking *with* each other instead of *at* each other, and building relationships. Fisher and Ury argue for *principled negotiation* among parties, focusing on the substantive issues at hand rather than personalities and positions which often only inflame conflict. By considering the underlying concerns of affected parties (with fair, but firm, rules of engagement), an organization enhances the quality of its decisions and anticipates problems that could derail final agreements.

What is Collaborative Planning?

Collaborative planning is a participatory process that helps parties, often with divergent views, solve problems, reach goals, resolve differences, satisfy needs, or complete tasks to the mutual benefit of the participants. It brings together all interested and affected parties, improving the quality of, and building support for, final decisions.

Collaborative planning is one of a number of processes grouped under the term *alternate dispute resolution*. The National Institute for Dispute Resolution (NIDR), an organization formed in 1982 to research and teach dispute-resolution methods, defines the ultimate goal of dispute resolution as "alleviating court congestion, enhancing access to justice, and strengthening the capacity of communities to resolve conflict."[4] NIDR has tracked significant gains in reducing conflict in courtrooms, in classrooms, and in state houses across the nation through the use of mediation techniques.

Arbitration and mediation are primarily used to resolve existing disputes. These methods are used in lieu of court proceedings, business-labor disputes and other conflicts. Collaborative planning could be termed *dispute avoidance* since it is most often used prior to a dispute's occurrence.

Collaborative planning does not ensure a "pure," or 100 percent, consensus. Frequently, participants develop a set of solutions palatable to almost all. Yet, there are often a few not willing to

Collaborative Planning	
Is	**Is Not**
Involving stakeholders in the decision process.	Relinquishing business decisions to external stakeholders.
Joint planning with stakeholders to pursue joint interests and minimize potential conflicts.	Another forum to argue the case.
Seeking mutually beneficial ways to expand *the pie*, as well as how best to distribute it.	Strategies for expanding just your *slice of the pie*.
Being clear about your business constraints.	Compromising your competitive advantages.
Involving all stakeholders, including those previously inactive.	Dealing only with vocal adversaries or only with allies.
Two-way dialogue—joint discussion through meetings, one-on-one conversations, and jointly developed documents.	One-way communications mailings, newsletters, the media—without dialogue.

agree. These minority views are often shared as part of the final outcome

Put simply, collaborative planning allows an organization and its stakeholders to achieve mutual gains while establishing an understanding of other interests, responsibilities and obligations. By combining the diverse backgrounds, skills, and learning of all participants, collaborative decisions can be comprehensive, innovative and, perhaps most importantly, secured in a conflict-reduced environment.

What Can Collaborative Planning Accomplish?

Collaborative planning is used to:

- develop *public policy recommendations*;
- make *siting* decisions;
- develop *facility operational plans*;
- develop *strategic plans*;
- develop *community action plans*; and
- lots more.

When is Collaborative Planning Appropriate?

Consider using collaborative planning when:

- establishing and sustaining *long-term stakeholder relationships is important*;
- your *decisions affect or impact the community*, external stakeholders or others;
- there is a *history of stakeholder challenges*;
- your *opponents have resources or capabilities* to oppose you;
- the *problems and solutions are complex*;
- there are *numerous possible outcomes* and a diversity of views about what they should be;
- *no clear choices* are available;
- it is *less costly* than traditional means;
- you need broad *accountability*;
- you need *broad support* to ensure the sustainability of the outcome;
- only *a few vocal opponents* are getting the attention; or

- you want to *demonstrate public involvement* to policy makers.

The Five Steps of Collaborative Planning

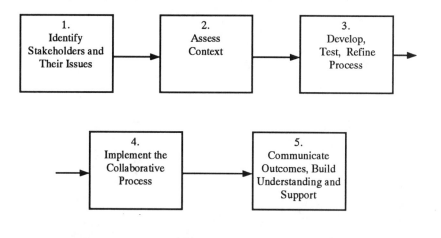

1. Identify Stakeholders and Their Interests

Steps for identifying and understanding stakeholders and their interests include the following.

- *Identify all parties who have an interest* in the decision-making process and the final outcome, including those who have a stake, but may not currently be active, and those who have the power and influence to undo the decision after the process is complete.
- *Seek balanced representation* of all parties with a stake in the process not just those who complain the loudest.
- *Conduct stakeholder research* to gain knowledge of their history, issues and concerns. Interviewing stakeholders helps determine key issues and concerns, and identify key players important for planning the collaborative process.

2. Assess Context

Determining the context of the situation is necessary to craft an appropriate design for the collaborative process. Following are questions to be answered.

- What are the *top issues* for the organization and stake-holders?
- What is the *history of the organization's relationships with stakeholders*? For example, is the organization seen as a community resource, as a polluter in the locale, or is it perceived (despite the reality) to have little or strong appreciation for the community at large?
- What are the *social, demographic and geographic* qualities of the community?
- What is the nature of the *news coverage* of related issues and concerns? Is it considered hostile or fair?

With this information an organization can anticipate the interests and dynamics of the process. This *intelligence* can assist in identifying potential sources of agreement and conflict. It may also provide an early signal of the need for research about issues or relationships that are poorly understood.

3. Develop, Test, and Refine the Collaborative Process

In the collaborative process there are really two efforts—the collaborative dialogue itself and the larger communications and research efforts. The dialogue involves stakeholders meeting with an organization or industry to explore options for mutual gain. However, much work must be completed between meetings: information must also be gathered in one-on-one and small group dialogues. These efforts further understanding, develop ideas to bring to the larger group, and test the dialogue design.

As a complement to the collaborative dialogue, communications and research—technical factfinding—are also a part of the program. Proactive communications and technical efforts are required up front, during and after the process. The extent of these complementary activities depends on the program objectives and the complexity and volatility of concerns being addressed.

Collaborative Dialogue

The following are areas to consider for the collaborative dialogue design.

- Conduct an *initial assessment of issues* based on advanced research.
- Determine *stakeholder participation.*
- Develop *dialogue structure.*
- Determine *ground rules* for the dialogue process (responsibilities for implementation, media ground rules).
- Develop each interest's *"must haves,"* established by the organization in the beginning.
- Determine *topics* to be addressed and the *framework* of the discussion that all participants will accept as fair.
- Determine the *period or length of the process* and participants' time commitments.
- *Test* the areas to address and the process design *with a cross-section of stakeholders.*

An important part of the process design is determining the organization's and stakeholders' "decision space." For example, does the organization want to have stakeholder input while retaining final decision-making power? Or is the organization willing to accept a shared decision with stakeholders? It is important to clarify the collaborative's role within the advise-only or fully-shared decision-making spectrum in advance.

It is also important that the organization determine and share its essential "must haves" as part of the ground rules at the outset. For example, an organization might require that any solution must be financially viable for the organization.

Communications and Research

The following are areas to consider when developing communications and research plans.

Communications

- Determine *target audiences* (who needs to be informed of, involved in, the process so they will support the outcomes?).
- Develop *key messages* on the collaborative story (why doing it, outcomes, implementation plans).
- Develop *activities to communicate* throughout the process using appropriate, reinforcing channels (newsletters, town meetings, focus groups, media, one-on-one visits, etc.).

Research

- Determine *issues* to explore based on the advance research.
- Scan, collect *existing information.*
- Determine *missing information, or areas of likely debate.*
- Prepare *options for addressing the technical information needs* for discussion with the collaborative group.
- Work through the dialogue process to determine *"must have" technical information,* and the best way to collect the information so that participants trust the findings.
- Conduct *additional research,* as needed.
- Provide *technical information* to support the collaborative process.

4. Implementing the Collaborative Process

With research completed, ground rules established, and the collaborative plan in place, implementation can begin.

Collaborative Dialogue

- *Invite participants* to the first meeting.
- Develop supporting *materials.*
- Conduct the *first session,* where ground rules, participation and the scope of the effort are reviewed and accepted.
- Conduct *off-line contacts* with stakeholders (one-on-one and small group discussions) between meetings to take the *temperature,* anticipate issues, set directions, and adjust the program.
- Use *documentation* in some form (updated white papers or notes from each meeting) to reflect the group's discussion and directions.
- Continue *meetings* to build understanding and explore solutions. Where possible, identify areas of agreement and disagreement.

Communications and Research

- Execute the *communications* plan, adjust as needed.
- Provide *technical information* support, as needed.

5. Communicate Outcomes, Build Understanding and Support for Decisions

Achieving success involves obtaining broader understanding and support than from those directly involved in the process.

Having developed a larger communications plan supporting the effort since inception, most external audiences should be informed and prepared. Sharing results and building interest in outcomes can be done through media briefings or announcements, white papers, newsletters, employee briefings, and other activities. The integrated communications effort sharing the decisions or outcomes are ideally supported by and involve the collaborative participants (e.g., bring a cross-section of stakeholders to an editorial board meeting to share the results and plans). The nature of the communications activities change depending on the type of collaboration and decisions reached (or not), and the audiences important for implementation or acceptance of the outcomes.

Collaborative Planning Cases

Aspen Institute Series on the Environment
National Policy
Innovation Through Collaboration

Situation

The current approaches for achieving U.S. environmental goals have been successful over the last two decades, but many have concluded that our environmental challenges require a different management system today that goes beyond or, as a complement to, our current system of command-and-control. To that end, the Aspen Institute convened a Series on the Environment in the 21st Century in the fall of 1993 to identify ways to achieve a cleaner environment at less cost by developing a better system of environmental management.

Process

Identifying stakeholders and seeking balanced representation
Environmental, industry, and local, state and federal government

leaders have participated, including leaders from the Sierra Club, Environmental Defense Fund, NAACP, Ciba Geigy, Amoco, 3M, Pacific Gas and Electric, U.S. EPA, the White House, U.S House and Senate, City of Los Angeles, State of New Jersey, and many others.

Collaborative dialogue and facilitation

The cross-section of stakeholders have explored issues through a series of facilitated conferences in an informal, non-partisan setting. Areas addressed include problems with our current system, the vision, mandate and principles for a new system, and models for implementation. Session outputs include an ever-expanding white paper capturing the ideas which emerge from the sessions. Off-line discussions between meetings with stakeholders help to shape future agendas, materials needed and continuously refine the program's goals and objectives.

Results

Participants gain directly through the opportunity to hear and truly understand different stakeholders' needs in a safe context. In addition, the ideas resulting from the sessions have directly contributed to a number of policy arenas, including President Clinton's plan for Reinventing Environmental Regulation, 1995 legislative initiatives in Congress, Department of Energy policy, and more.

Pacific Bell Education Initiative
Market Development and State Policy
Creating Options for Mutual Gain

Situation

Educators in California became concerned about the ability of educational institutions and libraries to link up to the *information superhighway*. Many policy initiatives were focused on ways in which the local telephone companies—Pacific Bell and others—could support, and *fund*, these initiatives by increasing telephone rates. Rather than being forced to absorb the costs of these enhanced services, Pacific Bell seized the opportunity proactively and convened a collaborative with concerned educational and community leaders to create a broad number of funding options.

Process

Stakeholder Enlistment and Decision Space

Pacific Bell convened approximately 15 diverse higher educational stakeholders representing community colleges, state universities, and universities. Also represented were state government and legislative participants, and library and community leaders. Each was invited to participate with clear commitments on the number of meetings and the time frame. It was established up front that the group served in an advisory capacity to Pacific Bell.

Collaborative Dialogue

The process included the following.

- *Determine and invite participants.*
- *Convene four meetings over three months* to define a shared vision, create funding options, and develop a set of recommendations.
- *Involve policy leaders and other experts* as speakers and observers in the process, building their ownership in the outcomes and enhancing the quality of the effort.
- *Build company leadership and support* by involving company executives in initiating the collaborative and a joint session to share results. Also, simultaneously the company developed an education sector business plan, elements of which were reviewed with the collaborative group.
- *Produce a white paper* of the final recommendations which included 26 funding recommendations, including the rate base option.

Results

The results include the recommendations being used directly in state legislative debate, former adversaries working together in various policy arenas, and Pacific Bell's simultaneously developing a business plan to provide enhanced telecommunications services to the educational community.

Duke Power Company Bad Creek Pumped Storage Station
Facility Siting
Developing Sustainable Decisions

Situation

Duke Power Company (DPC) built its 1065 MW Bad Creek
Pumped Storage Hydroelectric Project in the mountains of South
Carolina with approval from the Federal Energy Regulatory Commission. By the time construction was nearing completion in 1990,
it was apparent that public interest in the nearby Whitewater River,
which had been named number one among South Carolina rivers
for recreational fishing, natural features and wildlife habitat, had
grown tremendously. Therefore, the original recreational plans for
the Whitewater River no longer adequately supported public use
needs. DPC invited a coalition of 30 representatives from 13 resource agencies and environmental groups to participate in developing a plan to manage Whitewater River resources for maximum
benefit and minimum environmental impact.

Process

*Convening the Dialogue, Defining an Agenda with Shared Inter-
ests*

Called the Whitewater River Corridor Committee, the group
hired two consultants specializing in special area resource management. The Committee divided into sub-groups to address such specific issues as safety, special area access, endangered species
protection and watershed management. The Committee met regularly for more than a year.

Results

The result is a plan that accommodates public recreation use of
the Whitewater River in a manner compatible with its unique and
fragile resources. The plan called for a 50-car parking lot, trail
improvements, overnight camping areas, day-only use restrictions
in other areas, a steel bridge over the river and a viewing platform
for a spectacular waterfall. Further, the group decided that it would
be responsible for ongoing review and management of the area. It

continues to meet to review impacts of the nearly 5,000 yearly visitors to the area and make adjustments as needed. For its part, DPC received the "Conservationist of the Year Award" from the South Carolina Wildlife Federation and the Hydro Achievement Award for coalition-building from the National Hydropower Association.

Suggestions for Collaborative Planning Success

Exploring barriers to successful collaboration and the role of the facilitator can improve one's chances for success.

Barriers to Successful Collaborative Planning

Successful collaborative planners should understand barriers they will encounter and strategies for surmounting them. Six common barriers are described below.

- *Strategic Barriers*[5]—Dispute resolution, and specifically collaborative planning, addresses both the overall scope of the effort (*the size of the pie*) and distributive issues (how the pie is *sliced*). Traditional negotiations tend to focus on distributing benefits (who gets what slices) without much consideration to expanding the scope and, as a result, increasing the benefits.
- *Principled negotiation*[3] focuses on increasing benefits by understanding the underlying interests and needs of the participants and then generating options for mutual gain. However, revealing basic interests can often compromise one's ability to gain a larger share of the fixed pie and hence represents a strategic barrier to successful collaborative planning.
- *Principal/Agent Barrier*[5]—Sometimes the interests of the person at the table is not aligned with the principal (the organization or the person represented). For example, in traditional litigation, early and efficient resolution of an issue may be at odds with the lawyers' (agents') interests in billings based on hours.
- *Cognitive Barriers*[5]—Most of us are loss averse and will favor decisions to avoid losses over decisions to secure gains

even when the latter is rationally much better. This trait can inhibit searches for better solutions.

- *Reactive Devaluation Barriers*[5]—Options and solutions offered by other parties, particularly adversaries, are often discounted independent of the merit of the offer. This inhibits finding acceptable solutions.

- *Technical Information Barriers*—Parties in traditional negotiations generate technical information to support their own positions and distrust information used by other parties. In these cases, much of the dispute is on the technical data and inhibits getting to the participants' underlying interests and how they can be addressed.

- *Underlying Interests Barriers*—A participant's underlying interests may be so strategically in conflict with the organizations' needs that agreement is simply not possible. In one collaborative process, one stakeholder's principal interest was eliminating the organization leading the effort. This can be a collaboration *deal breaker*.

Third-party facilitators, or mediators, can help address these barriers. A neutral facilitator can encourage participants to reveal underlying interests, first to the facilitator, and then to the larger group. A facilitator can help assure that the principals are a part of the process or are being represented well. Solutions and compromises offered by the facilitator can avoid cognitive and reactive devaluation barriers. Joint fact-finding, implemented through jointly selected third-parties, can overcome the barriers related to technical information. And, to address difficulties with conflicting underlying interests, a facilitator can help focus the discussion away from *deal breakers*.

The Facilitator

One of the important factors in a collaborative planning effort is the role of the facilitator. This role most often is filled by an independent third party. However, in some cases, the hosting organization can serve in this capacity as well. Determining whether a third party is needed is based on the extent or nature of the controversy, the trust among the participants, and the likely credibility of the result.

The facilitator leads, focuses, and referees deliberations among stakeholders. The facilitator's role in the process is multifaceted. He or she:

- sets initial *ground rules* and enforces them;
- provides *structure and meaning* to the process;
- designs and *guides* the sessions;
- plays *"devil's advocate;"*
- *listens, explores and clarifies*;
- *records and displays* comments, takes notes, sorts and categorizes information;
- *sets and revises the agenda*;
- helps *identify areas of agreement and disagreement*;
- assures that *the process is equitable* to all participants;
- serves as the *process expert* with techniques for progress during and between meetings;
- implements the communications plan (for pre, during and post the collaborative process) along with the stakeholders.
- *ensures participation* by all stakeholders [goes somewhere]
- *builds trust* among participants and with the facilitator;
- *drives the group's schedule* to achieve meeting and program objectives;
- makes the *process transparent*—clearly conveying what the group will do and why, and what it will accomplish;
- *exposes hidden agendas* so the full group appreciates underlying needs and interests and much more; and
- *asks why*—at least five times to better understand underlying interests.

The facilitator should *never* openly endorse a position or form an opinion about issues under discussion, and must never make an arbitrary decision that will threaten the moderator's perceived neutrality in the collaborative planning process.

The key *characteristics* a facilitator should possess to effectively run the process and a session include:

- *knowledge about the issues* under examination, so that he or she can make meaningful contributions;
- *communication skills* both with individuals and groups;
- *willingness to be open and flexible* with new, perhaps uncharted ideas;

- *ability to take the heat* in tense situations; and
- ability to *elevate the session beyond one's own ego* or need for control.

Conclusion

Collaborative planning is a powerful approach for incorporating two-way discussions with stakeholders into the decision-making of an organization. It is effective in avoiding disputes and misunderstandings, and it can improve the quality of decisions made at all levels in our society. Collaborative planning deserves a prominent position in the public relations profession.

Notes

1. Cutlip, Center and Broom, *Effective Public Relations*, Sixth Edition, Prentice-Hall, Inc., Englewood Cliffs, NJ, p. 4.
2. Collaborative planning is discussed in this chapter as a public affairs tool for organizations.
3. Fisher, Roger, Ury and Patton, *Getting to Yes*, Second Edition, Penguin Books, NY, 1981.
4. "A Decade of Progress" *The National Institute for Dispute Resolution*, 1993 Annual Report. Pp. 4-5.
5. Mnookin, Robert, *Why Negotiations Fail: An Exploration of Barriers to the Resolution of Conflict*, NIDR Forum, Summer/Fall, 1993.

Chapter 26

The Newest Discipline: Managing Legally-Driven Issues

James E. Lukaszewski

The public affairs process is charmingly intuitive and delightfully broad ranging in its acceptance of plausible potential scenarios. The lawyer is far more focused, far less inclined to speculate, and often antagonistic to the idea of extensive public communication preparation.

Growing worldwide legal threats to business organizations require that management consultants—but especially public affairs and issues management managers—develop a substantial knowledge of the law, lawyers, the environment of legal risk, and how to apply this knowledge strategically and tactically.

Legal Affairs Are Growing in Importance

Primarily in the United States, but also in other Western democracies, large organizations are operating in more legalistic environments. This environment has a number of important attributes.

- *Rules and regulations*: The promulgation of rules and regulations has been refined to a maddening level of detail. While the recent decade-long gush of rule and regulation making in the U.S. may now be abating somewhat, government at every

level is still attempting to define behaviors, outcomes, and
even specific process steps at the most micro levels. These
governmental rules and regulations are backed up with very
stiff civil and, often, criminal penalties.

Outside the U.S., in the developed and emerging democracies, this gush of rule making is just beginning. The difference, however, is that even without the presence of relevant
rules and regulations, stiff civil and criminal penalties are
already in place. There is no more frightening prospect than
running afoul of the law in a country where bail bond procedures do not yet exist.

- *Aggressive government enforcement*: In every area where
industry and other large organizations are subject to regulation, it's clearly evident that the government is now more
inclined to investigate, take the initiative, and act on allegations with less evidence. The public overwhelmingly supports
these governmental approaches. In fact, survey research
indicates the public remains dissatisfied with enforcement
efforts and feels that government is not doing enough to
protect citizens. Therefore, aggressive government intervention and prosecution will expand.

- *Zero tolerance*: In a variety of areas—discharges, emissions,
medical practice, medical products, product safety, and the
like—the public no longer accepts even small accidents or
infractions. Instead the public applies a standard of zero
tolerance to environmental and health and safety issues. Most
publics, including employees, are expecting near-perfect
performance.

- *Public expectations*: American expectations of business have
always been high. Products are expected to work and not
cause injuries. Corporations are expected to act, at the very
least, in the public interest, and certainly not against it.
When negative events threaten or occur, fulminating public
and legal response can result.

- *Employee expectations*: One of the primary sources of information used in anti-corporate legal action and prosecution

comes from those within the organization—disappointed or disgruntled employees whose expectations of the company have not, are not, and probably will not be met. Surprisingly, a far larger number of these employee informers or "whistle-blowers" are credible, honorable people who have witnessed wrong, stupid, or unlawful behaviors and feel they have no other choice but to go to the authorities, around management.

- *Personal exposure and liability*: Increasingly statutes, rules, and regulations are written to pierce the corporate barrier, making individuals personally responsible for regulatory infractions, especially offenses involving health and safety laws, environmental laws, and hazardous waste or disposal laws. In cases where a corporate official or employee acts outside of his or her authority, silently allowing him or herself to be involved in a crime, fraud, or abuse, or where it isn't clear when an individual is acting in a representative capacity on behalf of the company, personal liability and additional liability for the organization are highly probable. One of the most frequently used areas of corporate criminal prosecution is conspiracy—defined as two or more people cooperating in an activity they know is illegal.

- *Legal concerns dominate*: A recent study of 35 representative crisis situations authored by Kathy R. Fitzpatrick and Maureen Shubow Rubin demonstrated that public relations advice and participation (and by extension, public affairs concerns) was non-existent or clearly secondary to legal advice and counsel.[1] The public affairs consultant is often left "outside the room" when issues have decidedly legal overtones. When this happens, the reputation and perceived ineffectiveness of public affairs and issues management are at fault, not the legal counsel brought in or the executives who trust attorneys and seek their assistance.

There is a continuing stream of additional indicators of the growing legal environment in which decisions, plans, and strategies are created, developed, and executed. One of the more fascinating is the push in the United States to deregulate certain industries. The unintended consequence of this governmental activity will be the imposition of regulation by legal precedent established through lawsuits and legal action, which will set standards and establish guide-lines.

A critical challenge for public affairs and issues managers is to remain on the key management advisory team. The public affairs practitioner of the future will need a higher level of sensitivity to legal issues, along with a concept of public affairs and issues man-agement that takes important legal considerations into account. The positive pay-off is that studying the law is a fascinating and useful intellectual endeavor that will draw public affairs and issues man-agers into the highest levels of organizational decision-making at the most critical times.

Knowing the Law

One of the most interesting aspects of this new environment of laws and litigation is learning just how useful, systematic, and com-monsensical the law really is. From the public affairs perspective, the legal issues of a business organization fall into four general categories: legal management, litigation, lobbying, and negotiation/conciliation (generally for the purpose of avoiding or shortening litigation).

Legal management, broadly defined, involves as many as 20 important categories—everything from personnel law, health and welfare law, unemployment law, workers' compensation law, and interstate commerce law (for those companies that ship product across state lines) to specific laws that focus on entire industries.

The job of inside Corporate Counsel is to understand the rela-tionship of the law to the corporation and to quickly provide the expertise necessary to handle any particular legal problem requir-ing expertise beyond the more general knowledge resident within the organization. In-house corporate lawyers generally know very little about specific legal issues. They hire specialist firms to man-age special problems. Even when there is substantial in-house ex-pertise, the practice is to hire outside legal expertise immediately. The larger the organization, the more likely it is that outside legal assistance is already in place. One public affairs challenge is to understand this matrix of outside legal consultants and be ready to work through it when something happens.

Litigation is, of course, the business of suing others or being sued. There are usually two types of lawyers involved in litigation—those who understand the issues and develop the legal framework the organization will use to take the offense or manage its defense, and litigators whose job it is to be out front either taking action, which is usually accomplished by filing a complaint and becoming the plaintiff, or responding to the legal actions of others and becoming a defendant.

Lobbying is included because so many lobbyists also happen to be attorneys. Lobbying is the process of influencing legislation and is described in great detail by other authors in this text.

Negotiation/conciliation, also called alternative dispute resolution (ADR), involves the use of lawyers in an environment where both parties agree not to sue or slow down the litigation process, and instead to negotiate, conciliate, bargain, and attempt to accommodate each other's concerns to the point where the problem can be resolved more or less amicably.

Public Affairs vs. the Law: Some Differences

There are important differences between public affairs/issues management expertise and the law. The five most readily identifiable differences are: (1) the legal process itself; (2) most aspects of the law are known; (3) the law automatically enjoys management's respect; (4) in the law many words have a very different meaning than they do in other usages; and (5) the legal thinking process is more logical, systematic, and strategic.

1. *Process.* Law is a process.

2. *Most aspects are known.* This is both a function of the process of the law and the fact that an entire branch of government has been structured to make certain that the legal process works from beginning to end—from initial filing of a complaint to appeals directed to the U.S. Supreme Court. Each aspect, each step, each variance, each procedure can be identified, defined, and positioned appropriately within the spectrum of legal activity.

3. *Automatic management respect.* Clearly, avoiding the specter of punishment, damages, humiliation, or other actions of a punitive or public nature cause management to respect the legal process and

its representatives. Management knows it must listen very carefully when lawyers speak—even when lawyers talk about things they know little about such as public affairs and issues management.

4. *Words in the law have very specific meanings.* One example is the word "evidence." In the legal sense evidence is that which is presented in court as a part of the legal process; or information to which litigants or parties to a legal action agree is evidence; or information which can be proven by one side or the other. In public affairs/issues management, evidence can be almost any document, newspaper clip, comment, or idea that seems relevant. Not so in the law.

The meanings of most words in the law are far more precise than in general usage. This tends to make the business of legal communication one of much more precision and care.

5. *The legal thinking process is more logical, systematic, and strategic.* Perhaps one of the most crucial differences is in the area of thinking and reasoning. The law is principally a process created to develop evidence. Evidence can be direct, which means observed first-hand by someone, or indirect, which means it can be validated by other means. The attorney's reaction to the intuitive nature of public affairs and issues management may be that both seem unintelligible and often of little value. The successful public affairs/issues management practitioner learns to propose ideas and concepts in more systematic, structured, well-reasoned ways.

Public Affairs vs. the Law: Some Similarities

There are also important similarities between public affairs/issues management expertise and the law. The four most readily identifiable are: (1) writing and speaking skills are essential; (2) novel approaches can win or convince; (3) people-focused action tends to predominate; and (4) the personality of individual practitioners and lawyers can dominate a proceeding, situation, or client relationship.

1. *Writing and speaking skills.* Law is very much a verbal process.

While it's true that many, many documents are produced and developed in the course of litigation or a legal situation, documents are not generally the persuading factor. They play only a supportive role, a factual role, and, to some extent, a bureaucratic role. It's the lawyer's arguing of a case, position, or perspective before a client, legislative body, or judge and jury that becomes the deciding factor—along with the evidence, which becomes part of any legal proceeding. Even during the appeals process—when lawyers receive only a very limited time to argue their cases and where appeals judges genuinely study and examine the records provided, it can be the lawyer's oral argument that focuses the court on the essential issues in the case.

2. *Novel approaches can win.* Despite all the process, the structure, the bureaucracy, and the enormous burden of paper generated, the lawyer who is sought after is the lawyer who can apply all of these pieces in client-friendly, strategically-effective ways. New law is made outside of the legislative process by how lawyers interpret and get courts and other legal jurisdictions to agree with their interpretations.

In law, just as in public affairs, the novel interpretation of a seemingly mundane set of facts can make a simple subject electrifying and exciting in the hands of the right individual and intellect.

3. *People-focus.* One truism seems to hold in the law just as it does in public affairs and corporate life: the individual who can focus on the needs and problems of the people, legitimately putting him or herself in the people's shoes, and work from the people's perspective, is the individual with the winning public affairs strategy. In law, there is nothing worse than what's called an "expert's case," where there is almost no testimony from a people perspective, but instead very technical testimony from academicians, economists, scientists, technologists, and subject matter experts. The lawyer with the people focus, especially when in front of a jury, can win. The same is clearly true for corporations who are striving to preserve their reputation and deal effectively with the issues that affect their important constituencies. Arguing an issue with a people focus helps overcome the daunting, often arrogant image of large organizations.

4. *Personality dominated.* Law is often a personality-dominated profession, especially among high-profile specialists such as defense and criminal attorneys and class action or public advocate plain-

tiff's lawyers. While there are virtually no nationally-famous public affairs and issues management practitioners, there are some very
big reputations and many individuals who are well known in the
corporate world. On an incident-by-incident basis, clients tend to
look for charismatic personalities who can motivate and aggressively
dominate the crucial public affairs issues they face.

Civil Litigation vs. Criminal Litigation

There are basically two kinds of litigation: civil and criminal.
In civil litigation, the individual or organization who sues is called
the plaintiff. The action is usually for money, but can also be for a
variety of other claims involving injury or damages such as libel,
loss of entitlements, loss of property, or to enforce a contract. The
individual or organization being sued is the defendant.
The result of civil litigation is generally the award of damages,
or property, or ownership, or custody, or additional rights, or other
remedies to repair or redress an "injured" plaintiff.
Anyone can be a plaintiff—individuals, companies, the government, or lawyers acting on their own. Virtually anyone can file a
civil suit.
In criminal litigation, the "plaintiff"—now called the "prosecution"—is always an agency of government. It could be a county
government, state government, the United States of America, or an
agency of government such as the Food and Drug Administration,
the Environmental Protection Agency, or the Occupational Safety
and Health Administration.
The defendant can be virtually anyone: another government agency, a foreign government, a corporation, an individual, or a private
organization.
Criminal law is established for the purpose of "preventing harm
to society." It declares what conduct is criminal and prescribes the
punishment to be imposed for such conduct. The principal difference between civil law and criminal litigation is this concept of
punishment in criminal law, which can mean incarceration and fines.
Keep in mind that the government can and often does file civil
lawsuits from which it is awarded and receives damages.
Practically speaking, in civil litigation, both the plaintiffs and
defendants have access to the same information, the same data, and
each other's witnesses and evidence. Civil litigation can be frus-

trating, irritating, maddening, and time consuming, but victory usually goes to the side that is best prepared in terms of evidence and case presentation.

Criminal litigation is an entirely different matter. Because criminal laws are designed to protect society and individuals from harm, the government has great latitude in how it conducts its investigations and when it informs the defendants of the information it has. Government also has the ability to search and seize information using a variety of lawful, but secret information collection processing methods. A corporation, organization, or individual cannot face a more frightening or seriously debilitating situation than criminal prosecution.

Some criminal statutes have been adapted for use in non-criminal circumstances, particularly what are called the RICO statutes (Racketeer Influenced and Corrupt Organizations Act). While this concept is a bit beyond the scope of this chapter, corporations and their public affairs/issues managers are well advised to study civil RICO statutes with respect to how they might apply to specific kinds of corporate activity.

In 1970, Congress enacted the RICO statutes to combat the influence of organized crime in interstate and foreign commerce. The statute makes it unlawful for any person to use a pattern of racketeering activity or the proceeds therefrom to control, conduct, or manage the affairs of a business operating interstate. This law imposes both civil and criminal penalties.

Due to increasing government prosecution of corporate executives, a solid knowledge of law, particularly criminal litigation, has become mandatory for consultants who advise senior management. This is because so many governments, at so many levels, are either beginning to focus on and emphasize criminal prosecution of statutes and laws, or are criminalizing laws, rules, and regulations that in the past only involved civil penalties. This trend of toughened enforcement continues and, despite much public policy rhetoric to the contrary, the public's increasing demand for punishment will strengthen the government's utilization and enhancement of punitive measures because they satisfy the public's expectations.

Knowing Lawyers

Today it seems fashionable to treat lawyers derisively. Yet, the reality for the public affairs/issues management practitioner is that often the first person the executive in trouble or the executive concerned about some future event looks to for counsel is a person with legal training. And, it is the legal counsel who decides whether or not public affairs/issues management or other staff counsel is necessary. This gatekeeping function should be no joking matter to the public affairs/issues manager.

What is it about lawyers that gives them such clout? Let's examine what causes organizational leadership to rely so heavily on legal advice and to perhaps undervalue or ignore public affairs/issues management advice.

First, let's look at what senior executives say when asked to compare public affairs practitioners to lawyers within their own organizations.

About public affairs:

- "They seem to be looking for appreciation of their knowledge of the issues rather than to contributing useful and helpful ideas."
- "They rarely put themselves in my shoes and are always advising from a 'distance'."
- "They often bring only one highly-focused option. When there are two or three questions they haven't thought of or can't answer, I don't invite them back."
- "They don't seem to understand the operating elements of the business enough to appreciate my problem."
- "They seem to be trying to teach me to be an issues manager when my goal is to solve the current problem and move on to the next."

About lawyers:

- "They seem to have a highly-focused, systematic approach to my problem."
- "They ask really good questions."
- "They are able to arrive at recommendations that address the problem at hand."
- "They show real expertise in the problem and its solution."
- "They help me select the correct option, but it's my decision after they've presented me with all the facts."

- "They seem to care more about my problem than the opinions of outside groups, the media, our employees, or government."

Having said all of this, what gives lawyers an edge over other corporate consultants? Lawyers are consultants just as are public affairs/issues managers. The value of any consultant is defined by the client. The client also controls the final course of action. There must be other fundamental reasons why lawyers have that edge:

- *Lawyer belief systems are different.* The motivation for the lawyer comes from a deep abiding respect for the process the law represents. The law provides a sense of civility, predictability, comfort, and confidence. And, the law is the law. You do what it says or face the consequences. The lawyer is very slow to buy into any belief or strategy that seems to have as its basis emotional, intuitive, or unprovable approaches (remember the concept of evidence).

- *Lawyers think systematically.* Public affairs/issues management is very much a creative/intuitive process. Cynically described, one could say that creative people jump to their conclusions while the lawyer tends to build a reasonable, rational, and logical series of provable steps to reach his or her conclusions and recommendations.

- *The lawyer is a problem identifier and solver.* This is reflected in the kinds of questions lawyers ask, which are often negative in nature: "Tell us how this won't work?" "What are the downsides?" "How many times has this been done successfully in the past?" "Where is the proof that this approach will work?" "What is the truth?" "What is the whole truth?"

These kinds of questions are not the hallmark of aggressive, creative, positive strategic thinking. However, most operating managers tend to live in this kind of environment themselves. They are subjected to, and subject themselves to very negative questioning, which tends to keep them sharp as managers. Public affairs people tend to ask few questions (having intuitively decided the answers). This inability to be "tough" diminishes the credibility of the public affairs/issues management function and sways the

executive listening to advice from both the lawyer and the
public affairs practitioner.

- *Constituency issues are probably the lawyers' last concern.*
  Lawyers are taught that less communication with outsiders is
  better. Law schools maintain that shorter answers allow
  attorneys to better control the information released and
  thereby better manage additional problems. Indeed, there may
  be very sound legal reasons why certain constituencies must
  be left in the dark.

  The public affairs manager has a dramatically different
  view, usually arguing for communication with particular
  constituencies. Lawyers need to be educated about constituencies, not the "spill your guts" school of communication.
  They need to understand the concept of scripting, careful
  statements, expanded but controlled speech, and the value of
  constituent feedback.

- *Lawyers are very suspicious of anyone who is not one of
  them.* Those involved in the law are a pretty exclusive group.
  They don't take kindly to those without legal training who
  attempt to interfere in the legal process.

  Since there are few courses to help the layperson understand the law, it's up to public affairs practitioners to develop useful ways to work within an increasingly legal environment. What the lawyer most needs to know is what
  experience the public affairs/issues management practitioner
  brings to the table from worlds beyond the law. The public
  affairs officer must be able to describe a similar real-life
  example that will better help the lawyer understand how the
  public affairs perspective will benefit the current legal
  situation.

  When the public affairs practitioner is called upon to assist
  with legal visibility management, the first step is to conduct
  a brief seminar for interested staff on civil and criminal law
  and litigation from the public affairs perspective. Lawyer
  suspicion of the non-lawyer will never be totally eliminated,
  but inviting corporate counsel and members of the legal
  department to interpret what is said in terms of specific real-

time corporate situations can be a helpful start to the necessary law/public affairs relationship.

- *Lawyers tend to have little curiosity.* Simply stated, once
  lawyers begin refining a problem, they stay focused on it
  and resist the urge to broaden the inquiry or scope of their
  interest unless something very concrete and provable moves
  them in that direction. This is probably one of the greatest
  areas of frustration between the public affairs/issues management practitioner and the lawyer. The lawyer is constantly
  focusing in on the issues, excluding extraneous data, and
  wondering why the public policy concept or the public
  affairs concept of the problem keeps expanding, keeps
  looking at options, keeps trying to forecast what's going to
  happen. From the legal point of view, all of these mental
  gymnastics are clearly unnecessary because whatever happens will happen and can be dealt with when it occurs, and
  probably in court.

  The toughest job public affairs faces is to demonstrate to
  senior management that in many circumstances, extensive
  preparation which results in nothing happening is the best of
  all possible outcomes. The worst of all possible outcomes is
  not being ready and not being able to manage problems as
  they occur.

- *Lawyers have a high degree of information possessiveness.*
  This is no surprise to those who have worked in the legal
  environment. Lawyers as a matter of habit tend to build
  walls, divide communication, hold information closely, and
  only reluctantly share information outside the legal circle.
  Ironically, public affairs/issues management practitioners, to
  the irritation of the lawyers, will quickly know most aspects
  of a legal situation when virtually no one else, including
  corporate counsel, does. It's simply the nature of the way
  practitioners think and process information. It does tend to
  make lawyers nervous when public affairs people have a
  broad brush understanding of what's going on. From the
  lawyers' perspective, preparing for the known is sufficient.
  By contrast, the public affairs/issues management practitioner

generally wants to prepare for a wide variety of scenarios because quick, competent response in the public arena may be the most effective technique available to reduce or eliminate reputational and other kinds of damage to the organization.

These lawyerly approaches resonate well with senior executives who are not interested in spreading the organization's potential bad news much beyond their own offices. The challenge to the public affairs/issues management practitioner is to build the level of confidence both in the lawyer and in the boss and to win the opportunity help increase the organization's readiness to respond to the potential threats legal visibility can cause.

Knowing the Legal Environment
(Legal Risk Analysis)

Legal risk assessment must be added to the practitioners' scope of issue investigation and problem prevention. Public affairs-related legal risks arise from several avoidable corporate behaviors.

- *Arrogance*. Example: A large multi-national petroleum company spills millions of gallons of oil in an environmentally-pristine area, appears to respond slowly and not really care what outsiders think, and uses its financial and economic muscle to keep neighbors, outsiders, activists, and the government from investigating the spill and taking action.

- *Coyness*. Example: A consumer product manufacturing company that sells a critical component used in millions of customer-owned machines discovers a defect, which has only the remotest possibility of causing user problems. This defect is disclosed to a select group of individuals who "understand" the situation and will not make a big issue out of it. No thought is given to what will happen when other owners discover the situation (which they inevitably will).

- *Expectation*. Example: A large national retailer, one of the finest companies in the U.S., provides a standard of service backed up by one of the most powerfully positive guarantees in American business. The company is discovered to be falsifying repair reports, not replacing parts correctly, and in many cases billing for but not making the indicated repairs. The company initially discounts published reports calling it an "isolated incident," but within weeks operations in 45 states are involved.

- *Ignorance.* Example: A medical products manufacturer, without notifying or receiving permission from the U.S. Food and Drug Administration, modifies crucial medical devices designed for use during life-saving surgical procedures. When, due to a patient death, the company is confronted with the alterations, it relies initially solely on its contacts with medical specialists, ignoring the concerns of hundreds of thousands of patients affected annually by their products and these surgical procedures.

- *Insensitivity.* Example: Following published reports of problems with implantable devices in women, the seven manufacturers band together to "get the facts" out. They focus on those facts rather than the emotional distress suffered by millions of women with these medical devices. The manufacturers persist in using this "factual" approach until public outrage reaches Congressional proportions.

- *Intolerance.* Example: A national restaurant chain, following one embarrassing situation after another related to discrimination on the basis of color and sexual orientation, announces a complete reorganization of its company, approach, and, to some extent, its management. However, instances of intolerance and discrimination continue.

- *Regulation.* Example: Allegations are made that the company used undue influence on the rule-making process through the use of highly paid lobbyists, experts, and research. Subsequent investigation, including information provided by a whistle-blower, reveals a pattern of kick-backs, bawdy parties in remote locations for the benefit of government officials, and collusion with other industries.

- *Reputation.* Example: A large regional restaurant chain experiences an incident where a number of customers, including several small children, become seriously ill. One child dies. The restaurant chain immediately announces that the food purveyor is at fault and attempts to shift public interest to that company.

- *Requirements*. Example: An internationally-known, up-scale boutique specialty store that sells both a high-profile food product and the equipment to process it, refuses to help a disgruntled customer with a product problem in an efficient and timely manner. The individual hires a lawyer and goes to the news media. The company, whose slogan is, "Your satisfaction at any cost," still refuses to help the customer. Stories about the problem continue to appear in major market newspapers.

- *Secrecy*. Example: The XYZ Corporation shuts down operations on a rather beautiful island location and announces that the plant will be torn down and the site turned into a park and donated to the city. As the opening of the park approaches, and after spending $7 million to develop the site, a black, smelly liquid is found oozing into the center of the main parking lot. The U.S. Environmental Protection Agency announces a criminal investigation of the company for non-disclosure of the existence of the contamination.

- *Stinginess*. Example: A national retail chain with more than 15 million credit card customers mistakenly over-bills 3,000 customers by amounts ranging from $2.50 to $65. After much discussion with the lawyers and in fear of many lawsuits, the company sends out a form letter, issuing each over-charged customer a precise credit for the amount accidentally billed. Two major class action lawsuits are instituted, mostly on behalf of those who were overcharged less than $10.

- *Stupidity*. Example: A large consumer food products chain, after having settled many cases related to burns caused by the spillage of hot beverages, decides that it will no longer settle these cases, but instead will pursue the next one to the bitter end.

- *Tardiness.* Example: A manufacturing plant suffers a major malfunction causing a noxious smelling gas to escape in large quantities. The emission forces the evacuation of hundreds of neighbors. Only after the public disclosure of the nature of the incident did residents learn that they had been exposed to very low levels of this same chemical for several years.

- *Testosterosis.* Example: The lending practices of a major bank are attacked publicly by a public interest research group. The bank labels the group as a "bunch of radical activists" and refuses to talk about the dispute or meet with the activists. The bank's public comment is, "We can't afford to set this kind of precedent."

Organizational Legal
Response Techniques

Corporate attorneys are generalists. One of the most important revelations in watching a corporate legal department operate is discovering how little specific knowledge corporate attorneys have. When problems with very serious legal overtones arise, the legal department reaches out to individual specialists and outside firms with the necessary expertise. The typical corporation of some size has six to twelve law firms or specialist lawyers either on retainer, or bound by some other arrangement, to quickly provide expertise in every major area of corporate activity—from patent law to employment law to termination law to takeover/rightsizing/downsizing law.

A similar approach should be considered by public affairs. Why should corporate public affairs/issues management operations have more resident knowledge than the law department? Yet, there seems to be a bias against using this approach to public affairs planning and the use of outside specialists—often until it's too late or the specialists are instead brought in by the legal department, another corporate division, or senior management.

A very credible approach for the public affairs/issues management group is to build its knowledge of the organization's legal environment and then to identify specific legal, paralegal, and non-legal resources that can be marshalled on a moment's notice for specific areas of potential threat. In other words, the law department model of operational behavior is an excellent model for the corporate or institutional public affairs operation to follow.

Applying Your Legal Affairs Knowledge to the Issues and Problems of Your Business or Organization

There is a model for applying legal knowledge and identifying areas of required preparation. It is based on proactive steps and approaches that build management confidence. It effectively contributes to resolving issues beyond simple legal questions. The model involves seven active areas.

1. *Pay attention.* Public affairs/issues management practitioners tend to live in the past, present, and future. To become more legally sensitive, the current issue monitoring, identification, and analysis process must be augmented with some additional tasks related to potential legal exposure.

Typically in the issue-identification process, any given issue is broken down into a predictable group of categories such as a description, the current status, company impact, the stakeholders, advocacy opportunities, current company position, unresolved questions, recommendations, related issues, and the potential unintended consequences of key actions.

From a litigation perspective, a new series of evaluative standards should be applied to the legal questions at issue and the victims/stakeholders affected. Specific areas for evaluation include:

- The nature of the effect on each;
- Settlement options;
- Inclination to settle;
- Likely opposing issues;
- Anticipatable repercussions beyond the litigation;
- Adverse consequences of settling; and the
- Adverse consequences of litigating.

2. *Have some specific approaches ready.* Fortunately, most approaches to public affairs issues have useful direct application to

Model for Introducing Public Affairs
Perspectives into the Mix

Step 1—Situation Analysis: Briefly describe the nature of the issue, problem, or situation.

Step 2—Situation Interpretation: Briefly describe what the situation means, what its implications are, and how it threatens the organization.

Step 3—Options Available: Develop at least three response options for the situation presented. You can suggest more, but three is an optimal number for management consideration.

Step 4—Most Recommended Option: Select the option you would choose if you were in the boss' shoes. Provide an explanation of why you selected it.

Step 5—Unintended Consequences Forecast: Explain those events or problems that could arise due to the options you suggested, or by doing nothing.

the litigation process. They do tend to go beyond where the lawyer might go in developing information. In practice, because litigation requires the review of so many documents and discussion with so many people, the public affairs manager needs to be more succinct, more direct, and more pragmatic than in most other circumstances.

On the following page is a model which is useful and effective for introducing public affairs perspectives into the mix of recommendations and decisions that need to be made.

This is a straight-forward problem-solving model. There are a variety of similar constructs using as few as four or as many as 11 steps. This five-step model seems to work well and can be accomplished on one side of one piece of paper. Victory in decision-making often goes to the individual who can be brief, pragmatic, and positive, both verbally and in writing.

3. *Use a "process" approach.* This means having a structured, step-by-step approach ready for the different kinds of decisions that will arise as a part of the litigation/public affairs process. There are two key elements of a good process approach.

First, work from a timeline. Trials, litigation, events happen over time. Develop a timeline or "calendar" approach beginning with today and working through the various milestone events and circumstances that can be forecast through the resolution of the problem.

In civil litigation, this means a calendar beginning today and moving out six or seven years. In criminal litigation, the timeline is often shorter—usually one year for the investigation, one year for grand jury deliberations, one year for development of evidence, and one year for trial conclusions and appeals,

For the most part, the legal process is predictable and scheduleable. Aside from developing a calendar of events through the start of the trial, the corporation may require specific messages and constituency management plans during the trial. Typical trial segments include:

- Pre-trial period;
- Jury selection;
- Opening arguments;
- Special witnesses;
- Initial rebuttal/arguments;
- Motions;
- Summations;
- Jury deliberation;
- The verdict;
- Post-verdict commentary; and
- Appeals.

Having an understanding of the flow of the process and major milestones helps the public affairs practitioner play a far more useful role in the overall communications litigation strategy approach.

The second key element of a good process approach involves simple, standard formats. A well-structured public affairs/litigation management plan might have four components: a contacts list; situation description; communication/issues management objectives; and a tactical approach. The tactical approach can be broken into six sections:

- Constituency issues;
- Scenarios—Actions/Statements/Q&A;
- Internal constituencies;
- External constituencies;
- Weekly assignments/action checklists;
- Follow-up scenarios/Actions/Statements/Q&A.

The message here is that an organized and focused public affairs plan will have more momentum. Using a process approach will also give your knowledge and opinion more weight.

4. *Anticipate carefully.* The public affairs process is charmingly intuitive and delightfully broad ranging in its acceptance of plausible potential scenarios. The lawyer is far more focused, far less inclined to speculate, and often antagonistic to the idea of extensive public communication preparation.

The public affairs/issues management practitioner might be asked why it's important to get ready for things that will never happen, or told that it really doesn't take any preparation to manage the problems suggested. Therefore, be very selective and pragmatic about the issues, concerns, problems, or constituency issues you choose to introduce into the legal preparation process.

In many ways, legal public affairs is the art of not communicating while maintaining constituency relationships. Once attorneys see a timelined, pragmatic approach, one which is not totally focused on external communications, they will participate in the process necessary to develop and maintain constituency relationship programs.

5. *Build relationships with the lawyers.* It's easy to know when a good relationship exists with attorneys. If they begin their comments by saying, "I don't know much about public affairs, but, . . ." there isn't much of a relationship. Building relationships means:

- Identifying today those law firms and specialists your organization has on standby or retainer to deal with various issues, and finding a way to introduce yourself and your function;

- Including key attorneys in your reporting and private issue-related communications network and preparing them for your approach and the differences in style that will occur when something happens;

- Asking advice ahead of time in areas where there may be legal consequences. (This can often be done with little or no charge to your organization, primarily because these individuals are probably already on retainer.)

6. *Prepare for rejection.* Attorneys have enormous clout when legal issues are at stake. Attorneys are used to working with consultants, but they're also used to having the last word. Providing

fewer options increases the likelihood that those you present will be rejected, questioned, or modified in some respect. Provide more options.

No scenario, litigation, or problem ever unfolds in a totally predictable fashion. Therefore, to expect your recommendations, no matter how well organized and presented to survive as a whole is unlikely.

If the focus is on the client's best interests and approaches taken make sense, even if they aren't totally public affairs dominated, move on to the next issue.

7. *Be unchallengeable.* Force the public affairs/issues management effort to face up to the important legal realities of the situation and communicate, advocate, cooperate, and execute in ways that build your credibility at every step, with every decision, with every action.

To be unchallengeable:

- Search for, find, and insist on the truth. Sooner or later, the organization will be forced to deal directly with whatever the truth is. The sooner, the better.

- Remember that there is more than one truth. The truth is defined by each individual constituency's point of reference. Victims will never see it your way. Angry neighbors will never see it your way. Government regulators will never see it your way. Opposing counsel will never see it your way.

- All litigation involves victims. In civil litigation, we create victims through the actions of our company or organization. In criminal litigation, the victim is society as a whole, certain groups within society, individual government agencies, or government as a whole. The function of the judge in the trial is to protect victims' rights. In the presumption of innocence environment, this means it's the defendant's rights which will be protected by the court. It's the plaintiff or the prosecution who must provide the proof.

   Think, plan, talk, and act with the victims' perspective in mind.

- Be a pragmatist. Settle what you can't win well. Settle quickly to avoid creating permanent enemies, even when you're right. A legal victory which creates permanent generational enemies is worse than losing a war.

- Understand your own belief system, your values, and explain and act on them constantly.

Apply the techniques in this chapter. Like most staff consultant activities, involving public affairs/issues management practitioners in legal issues and concerns will not be done automatically by management. The legal arena is one in which the non-lawyer needs to be proactive, making the assumption that for a limited but appropriate range of scenarios, public affairs and legal affairs will be teamed up in the interest of the corporation's reputation and constituent relationships.

Note

1. "Public Relations vs. Legal Strategies in Organizational Crisis Decisions," *Public Relations Review*, Vol. 21, Number 1, Spring 1995, pp. 21-33.

Chapter 27

Emerging Trends in Public Policy Issues

James F. Keane and
Gary Koch

Any attempt to predict the future of public affairs in such a rapidly changing world is fraught with peril. Who would have guessed ten years ago that such terms as fax, laptop, e-mail, virtual reality, homeshopping network or ATM machines would not only enter our vocabulary but transform our way of life? With the dramatic change affecting our profession, our nation and the world, gazing into the crystal ball can be quite an unsettling experience.

That said, some of the changes now occurring here and abroad allow us to detect certain patterns. Through review and analysis, some of these patterns will interconnect to form emerging trends. For those of us who help shape and monitor public policy, it is important to identify and understand these trends so we can be prepared for the future rather than left in its wake.

An examination of the Contract with America offered by the House Republicans after their stunning victory in the 1994 elections provides a unique opportunity to watch the emergence of new public policy directions or the repudiation of the new and reaffirmation of the old.

We have witnessed the ease with which House Republicans were able to initiate their agenda vis-a-vis the operation of government to make it more efficient; to reduce multi-million dollar settlements for personal injuries; and to espouse tax cuts.

Once these broad public policy issues had been voiced and it came time to relate them to specific programs, the going became tougher.

The policy issue of a balanced budget, while accepted conceptually, broke down when the policy represented by a secure Social Security system was raised in direct opposition. Other policy issues expressed in the "Contract" will undoubtedly come into similar conflicts with competing policy issues.

Many writers have talked about the second American Revolution that is now well underway. Examples of it are everywhere: the impact of a global economy on the United States; the rise of entrepreneurialism; the movement of business to the Far East; the rebirth of religion; the growth of the neighborhood movement; and the influx of new immigrants to our borders and shores.[1] These developments are creating a new America, one we are not familiar with and one vastly different from our childhood.

While it is impossible to categorize all of the current and budding trends, in this chapter we will examine the following trends that will greatly affect those of us in public affairs and public relations:

Major Trends

- Information Explosion
- New Federalism
- Greater Emphasis on Morality and Ethics
- Growth of Special Interests
- Changing Workforce
- Increased Professionalism
- Continuing Battle for Term Limits
- Campaign Reform

Information Explosion

An explosion in new ways to transfer information has forever changed the way many of us do business and go about our daily lives. Fax machines, e-mail, cellular phones and the like have made communication immediate and constant. In theory, you can now reach anyone, anytime, anywhere. While the advantages of instant access are obvious, there is also a down side.

For the old-school public affairs practitioners who believe in the personal touch of developing a one-on-one relationship with clients, the impersonalness of much of the new technology can be disturbing. For too many of us who dismissed personal computers and other electronic tools as "toys" and did not investigate their potential because we were too busy, the overnight mass acceptance of the new technology is disquieting.

As the banking community discovered early on with the advent of personal computers, wire transfers and direct deposit, there is no "float" time in the working world anymore. If you're a consultant with more than one client demanding their project be done right now, you always had the float time of a few days for mail delivery. Now clients can request and expect immediate response to their needs, thus causing more stress and longer work days for the consultant.

Anyone who has recently been the victim of corporate downsizing or layoffs knows first hand the changes new technology has made in the workplace. Computer experience and familiarity are now prerequisites for many jobs, from supermarket clerk to truck driver. Because of their ease of use and speed in disseminating information, computers and fax machines have tremendously increased the number of applicants for specific jobs. Some job openings are today only listed on computer bulletin boards.

Think CD-ROM is just the latest computer gimmick? Think again. While 4.9 million U.S. homes had computers equipped with CD-ROM drives in 1993, nearly 8 million drives were sold between October and December 1994.[2]

What all this means is that public affairs professionals must embrace the new technology. The future demands it. If you are to be competitive in the Information Age, you must be up to speed on technological advances. You must be able to use this technology to provide better service for your clients or employer. This means exploring the new databases created and using new avenues of communication to inform and educate. The important thing to remember is that it isn't necessary to know how these electronic marvels work to benefit from them.

Bottom line: become a player in the new technology or go the way of the dinosaur.

New Federalism

With the advent of the change of power in the new Congress and widely popular and respected books like *Reinventing Government* advocating massive change in how the federal government goes about its business, it is not surprising that a new federalism is on many people's minds.

Changes in the very structure of the federal government have been bandied about for years with little or no success. President Reagan, during his administration, promised a new federalism but actually did little more than reduce federal aid. Today the debate continues with the focus on dismantling several federal agencies, elimination of thousands of federal jobs and transferring responsibility for many matters to the states. Recently the Council of State Governments called for a "Conference of the States," billed as the first formal meeting of the states since the Constitutional Convention in 1787. The object of the conference is to restore balance in the federal system.

How all of this translates into real change is anyone's guess. However, certain points must be addressed. First, the voters in the November '94 election seemed to want "less government, better administered, more decentralized with less partisanship."[3] In other words, the electorate is going to demand smaller and more efficient government at all levels, more professional and better equipped to provide new and expanded service locally to a more sophisticated public.

Secondly, for years polls have shown that people favor their government at the local level. Local officials, they feel, are more accessible than their state and federal counterparts, more accountable and better equipped to provide workable solutions to particular problems. For these reasons, among others, it is likely that public policy will focus on shifting power and responsibility from the federal level to state and local government. Whether a complete shift ever happens remains to be seen.

Coupled with this transfer of power, major focus will be drawn to four particular issues.

Public Safety

Public safety may be the dominant issue for government officials for years to come. Health care, drugs, violent crime, gangs, youth crimes and school violence will occupy the minds of government officials and public affairs people for the foreseeable future as they seek solutions to improve the quality of life.

Education

It has been said many times that if you are not educated, you will not work in the future. It is estimated that by the year 2000, 65% of workers in America will need 13 years of education to get any job. Conversely, other studies show that the skills of new college graduates do not meet the needs of the workforce. Will this result in a new category of "non-workers?"

Unfunded Mandates

For years state and local governments have balked at being forced to accept the responsibility for the administration of programs and services without being given the financial resources to provide them. According to a recent survey by the National League of Cities, 75% of municipal elected officials indicated that the impact of unfunded mandates worsened in 1994.[4] Governments at the local level are going to continue to demand, in the words of Newark Mayor Sharpe James, "No check, no mandate."[5] An undecided question is if the federal government does in fact provide "block grants," what process and controls fashion the public policy issues?

Public Infrastructure

America's basic facilities are continuing to deteriorate at an alarming pace. Roads, bridges, water and wastewater treatment systems, public buildings and other structures all continue to age and break down. Cost estimates to replace or upgrade our national infrastructure are staggering. Failure to address the problem leads to an ever increasing backlog of maintenance, which will only grow more expensive in years to come.

Morality and Ethics

For over two decades now our national conscience has been pummelled by lapses in ethics. Beginning with the Vietnam War and

Watergate and continuing to present day, we have suffered through scandals at the highest levels of government, big business, churches, charities and other institutions. No repository of trust has been immune to legal and/or moral laxness. Negative campaigning, talk shows that appeal to the most primitive of instincts, and tabloid TV, where the dismantling of heroes is a spectator sport, all bring the ethical maelstrom into our living room. Our sense of right and wrong seems more and more limited to what a jury of 12 determines it to be. As commentator Jeff Greenfield has said, "As long as you can appear self-confident, aggressive and above all, unashamed of what you have been accused of, you are likely to prevail in the court of public opinion."[6]

However, this may be changing. The electorate of '92 and '94 seemed to indicate they want change, that the old ways of doing business are not acceptable anymore. As we enter a time when crucial and difficult decisions will have to be made, the public is going to demand honesty and integrity. The perception of impropriety in government, not-for-profit or business will not be accepted.

Big business has already seen the importance of ethics. As society comes to expect more of business, profit is no longer the only concern. Business leaders now must consider employees, customers and the community where they are located. Business schools across the country now include ethics courses in the curriculum. And while colleges cannot teach people to be ethical, they can at least impress upon students the need for honesty in the marketplace and the consequences of unethical behavior.

Ethics is important to public affairs practitioners for three reasons.

1. Public relations has a reputation for unethical behavior. In today's world we must be above reproach.

2. Often, public affairs professionals are responsible for ethical statements of an organization. Their credibility can depend on our own.

3. Our profession is based on trust. Many of the people we work for in public life are held to a higher standard and so are we. Many important decisions are made based on our

work. We have an inherent obligation to be ethical in our dealings with the public and those who employ us.

For the public affairs professional of the future, ethical behavior won't be a question. The public and the workplace will demand it. Public affairs people will be responsible for providing leadership in the question of what is ethically or morally right for the Age.

Growth of Special Interests

All kinds of special interest groups have proliferated and will continue to grow in power for the rest of this decade and beyond. Women, minorities, senior citizens, environmentalists, community groups, gay rights, consumer groups, pro-life and pro-choice, all will become more vocal and more active.

Special interest groups have become part of the fabric of our society. Each of us belongs to several of these groups, if not by specific membership, through definitions such as the catch-all "women's rights" groups who purport to speak for all women on "women's issues."

The power of special interest groups is obvious. The ability of senior citizens to make Social Security politically untouchable is a good example. Another example is the adeptness of those supporting AIDS research/treatment to far surpass, on a proportional basis, the efforts of similar and longer established groups suffering from disease or physical impairments.

Supposedly, the 1994 elections signaled the rise of the white male. This group is said to want to take revenge on affirmative action programs that mandate women and minority participation, often without regard to economic need, to the perceived detriment of white males.

The political reality of a shift in voting patterns of white males in the 1994 election may well change or significantly alter affirmative action public policy.

By their very nature special interest groups are designed to impact public policy. The seniors wish to maintain the benefits of Social Security. White males want to reverse the trends and programs enacted in the name of affirmative action. Pro-abortion and anti-abortion groups do battle for control of that public policy issue.

The impact of special interest groups and their effect on public policy is perhaps best exemplified by the initiative procedures available in California. Many of the major propositions that have been adopted there reflect not only the power of special interest groups on public policy issues, but also the process by which a few individuals can create and mobilize a special interest group around an idea.

To respond to the growing presence and expanding needs of special interest groups, public affairs professionals must:

- Become knowledgeable about these groups and their special needs;

- Focus attention of clients or employers on special interest groups that impact them;

- Seek out appropriate media to reach the targeted audience;

- Develop issues based on concerns of special interest groups; and

- Overall, develop a public policy consensus structure and guidelines that provide a basis for decision making.

Changing Workforce

One of the most shocking aspects of our future is the makeup of our workforce. As downsizing and industry consolidation continue unabated, the nation's workforce will continue to be lean and mean. Less people to perform more work. Efficiency, speed and competitiveness will be stressed.

But it is the people themselves who will make change so noticeable. Women continue to enter the workplace in ever increasing numbers. Between now and the year 2000, six out of every ten people hired will be female. By the year 2000, almost 50% of our workforce will be female.

When we enter the new millennium, the average age in this country will be 39. In India it will be 19. Today, 17% of persons entering the American workplace are either immigrants or minorities. In the year 2000, this figure will be 42%. Forty-one percent of all immigrants are Hispanic; 43% are Asian.

A Global View

The long lines to purchase gasoline during the Arab oil embargo of the mid 1970s are now a distant memory, but the events causing them are not. We learned then, as we continue to learn on a daily basis, that what happens thousands of miles away in a different corner of the world can have a direct impact on our life. Whether it's a drought in the coffee fields of Columbia, earthquakes in Japan or pipeline ruptures in Alaska, these events, to some degree, affect us all.

To be competitive in the future most businesses are going to have to take a global view. Executives will be forced to educate themselves on international issues and concerns.

As James Crupi explains,

> We have gone from having 50 percent of world market share after World War II to now having 15-16 percent. We are in a world where Mitsubishi is bigger than IBM, Bank of America, General Motors and Western Electric combined. We are in a world where the second largest trading center for the issuance of U.S. Treasury bills is Tokyo, Japan; where 13 of the top 20 banks in the world are Japanese; where you are witnessing around-the-clock 24-hour financial trading.[7]

As public affairs practitioners enter this brave new world, they will have to rethink their relationship with changing publics. They will have to regularly reexamine priorities and establish new communication methods. Cultural sensitivity will be a major concern as will developing databases that will provide information for easy access across national boundaries and international time zones.

While the international market offers immediate and long-term opportunities in public affairs, a word of caution. We currently are not well positioned in the international scene. In other words, public relations and public affairs in this country have been slow to develop a world view. For example, in 1980, New York was the public relations capital of the world and the U.S. had the top five agencies; today the U.S. has only one of the top five agencies and London is the new PR capital.[8]

It is evident that, as a profession, we must upgrade our skills and our perception to take our rightful place in the global marketplace. More than ever our people will be needed in a leadership role of bringing people together from different cultures, backgrounds and experiences. We need to shift from a national focus to an international one in order to serve our clientele.

Increased Professionalism

In his book *Powershift*, Alvin Toffler explained how old patterns of power are being restructured, transferred and transformed to new players at every level of society.[9] According to Toffler, the entire structure of power as we know it is disintegrating and a new, different type of power will be created. What does this mean for those of us in public affairs?

To begin with, individuals and special interest groups new to the role of authority will need spokespersons and strategists who can communicate effectively and plan for the future. On the other side, businesses and government will need persons who can develop and maintain relationships with the new groups. This "bridge-building" will be a big component of public affairs in the future as corporations and government must deal with new special interests on the world stage. The same is true for international relations and development.

Public affairs practitioners must be prepared to create new strategies for dealing with these newly developing or expanding constituencies. Communication channels and problem solving methods of the past may not necessarily be successful today or in the future. The successful public affairs professional will be the one who knows the needs and wants of clients and effectively provides them.

Since public affairs persons will often serve in the capacity as those who can break down barriers between groups, they will often find themselves in a strong position to initiate change within an organization. Public affairs practitioners will often find themselves on the front lines of change; in this capacity they will not only provide feedback to the organization, but in some cases, help to change the organization itself.

To do this effectively, public affairs must step up and rightfully take its place at the corporate table and be an equal partner in management. Practitioners must become well-versed in the bottom line/big picture outlook if they hope to become players in the new order of power.

Continuing Battle for Term Limits

Recent court decisions may well have sounded the death knell of term limits. Term limits, a popular type of campaign reform, is considered an effective way to restrain the powers of incumbency and spending by members of Congress. This idea may have reached its zenith during the '94 election as seven states—Alaska, Colorado, Idaho, Maine, Massachusetts, Nebraska and Nevada and two cities—Washington, D.C. and Spokane, Washington, all approved term limit measures. That brings the total to 23 states that have approved term limits in the past five years.

However, the U.S. Supreme Court, in a May 1995 ruling, dealt a major blow to supporters of congressional term limits. In a 5 to 4 decision, the Court invalidated congressional term limit laws. Those laws would have meant mandatory retirement in 1998 for 78 current members of the U.S. House and Senate.

Term limits seem more attractive to the public in times of economic uncertainty, political scandal and other instances when the public as a whole or a large segment feels insecure or powerless to function or participate in society. Leaders of term limit movements quite often have their own political agendas. Term limits provide those on the outside of the political process accelerated access or at least better opportunities to reach office than exist under the current system.

This is probably well illustrated by the elections of 1994. The Republican Contract with America indicated that a Republican Congress would mean the passage of term limits. Many of the candidates who were elected with this issue as part of their platform undoubtedly breathed a sigh of relief when the issue died. A good deal of posturing was required during the process of killing term limits in the 1995 session of Congress, but was necessary for political reasons. It is human nature for those in office to wish to remain in office and for a political party long out of power to wish to remain in power rather than to gamble losing its authority through term limits. This is especially true of the Congressional leaders who would be the first victims of term limits.

Advocates of term limits who are not political may rightfully point out that established elected officials often seem to be insulated from the same rules and laws that affect the public. In many instances this is true or at least perceived by the public as being true. Consistently there have been stories of one Congressman or another who has either skirted the edge of legality and ethical conduct or has actually gone over the edge but who has not met with swift justice. While at one time the private lives and moral ethics of Congressmen were treated as off limits by the press, today it is the road to a Pulitzer for an aspiring journalist. This sometimes excessive coverage only stokes the public's willingness to accept term limits.

Groups that feel they have been abused, ignored or otherwise mistreated by government also can be supporters of term limits. If the group is unable to defeat an incumbent, term limits are attractive in that, given time, he/she will be gone and the group may have a better chance with his/her replacement and may in fact be able to have a hand in replacing the individual with someone sympathetic to their cause.

The same holds true for someone who wishes to run for office. It is a fact of life that it is usually very difficult to beat an incumbent. That is why so many candidates seek office when an incumbent retires. With term limits, one need merely wait for the current term to conclude to increase one's chance for success. It will be interesting to see how many of our current Congressmen who ran on a ticket espousing term limits will step down without term limit mandates.

Those who oppose term limits make a number of points. One of the main arguments against term limits is that over the years there has been a great deal of turnover during elections. To opponents of term limits, the ballot box is the best method of removing from office those who no longer represent their constituencies. They contend term limits throw the baby out with the bathwater.

Opponents also indicate that government has become so complex that you cannot continually turn out experienced officials without damaging government. Quite often government bodies are substantially larger than private concerns. The federal government has no equal on the private side in terms of size and complexity. Opponents emphasize that corporate executives and stockholders would immediately reject a similar suggestion that they limit the tenure of their top employees and mandate constant turnover.

As part of this same argument the opponents of term limits point out that the learning curve in government today, even at the local

government level, is getting longer and longer. To endure the reinventing of the wheel by each new crop of officials would be wasteful
and the results would be more detrimental to governmental operations than the current system.

As noted earlier, the term limits door may well be closed by the
current courts. This does not mean that it will no longer be advocated either through a constitutional change or by future courts.
Issues in government never die. They recycle from time to time.
Term limits as an issue will be viable whenever there is political,
economic or social uncertainty in a large part of the electorate.

Campaign Financing Reform

Campaign financing reform has always been a difficult problem
because it pits the haves against the have-nots in a contest for power.
Given the importance of money and other assets in elections, it is
easy to see that campaign reform is one of the hot buttons of those
in public life.

An incumbent enjoys a distinct advantage over a non-incumbent
unless the non-incumbent has personal or other wealth available.
Most incumbents have built up their fundraising mailing lists; they
have access to lobbyists and special interest groups who generally
support the incumbent; and they usually have the support and assistance of their party leadership which can provide money and other
politically valuable assets to them in their campaigns.

As noted above, the non-incumbent is at a disadvantage unless
he/she has some unusual support. Obviously the best thing for a non-
incumbent to have is personal wealth. This has become more common on the national level than at the local level. Individuals have
committed millions of their own resources to run for Congress, usually the Senate. This situation also exists at the local level on a
smaller scale. It is quite common for someone running for local
office to take out a home mortgage or in other ways go into debt
in order to run for office.

Another difficulty for the non-incumbent is lack of access to
special interest groups. Special interest groups and lobbyists are
aware of the difficulties of unseating an incumbent and are reluc-
tant to oppose him/her without good reasons. Party support may or
may not be worthwhile. In some elections the endorsement of a

political party is the equivalent of being elected. In other instances, party affiliation means little or can even be detrimental.

When an incumbent is asked to vote for campaign financing reform it is often viewed as being asked to vote against his or her best interests. Political "ins" have always had trouble passing campaign reform for this reason. In 1994, despite a 12-year effort to limit special interest money flowing into campaigns, Congress could not muster the necessary votes to approve a reform measure. Former Senate Majority Leader George Mitchell's comment that "Americans recognize the corrosive effect of money on elections," fell largely on deaf ears.[10] This response becomes understandable when one realizes that:

- 80% of all the money raised by congressional candidates in recent years has come from political action committees;

- Congressional campaigns cost more than ever and rely increasingly on big contributors—only one-third of 1% of all Americans gave $200 or more to a congressional candidate in 1992; and

- The residents of one zip code on New York's Upper East Side contributed more money to congressional races in 1992 than did the residents of each of 21 states.[11]

There are a number of campaign reform proposals available at any given time. There are those that represent the views and ideas of the reformers and non-incumbents and there are those of the incumbents. While those of the incumbents are usually less dramatic than those of the reformers and will usually not change the system as much as the reformers, incumbents control the process for change and will resist change unless circumstances dictate otherwise.

The current system of campaign financing is the result of previous efforts at reform. Oftentimes reform works for a while, but human ingenuity and other factors beyond the vision of the reformers impact the process and the system must be revised. Who knew how important television and other media would become in campaigns? Thirty years ago the impact of media campaigns was unfamiliar. Decisions about public access to the media for campaign purposes set the game rules for our current campaigns and also set the requirement for large sums of money. This has effectively fenced out those without substantial funds available to them from the "publicly owned" airwaves.

The impact of the Internet and new information highways that are still developing on the campaign process have yet to be determined. They will obviously be substantial as we weave our communications networks of telephone, television, cable, computers and other components of the information highway together in the coming years.

Those in public affairs will be on the cutting edge of this evolution and will undoubtedly have a major impact on campaigning. The evolution of this new technology will be the best opportunity for campaign finance reform available in the foreseeable future. If it requires money to access the system of the future, not much will change. If the current free access continues and is expanded it will provide us with a unique vehicle for campaign reform.

Conclusion

If there is an underlying theme that ties the above-mentioned thoughts together, it is this: Change in the future will be rapid, constant and inevitable. In our profession we must accept change, anticipate it, embrace it and assist in fashioning it or be left behind.

Challenges and opportunities will abound in the public affairs field as many culturally diverse groups and issues take their place on a crowded main stage. Leaders in all areas of human endeavor will seek new ways to communicate with, influence and understand these groups and their needs. The public affairs community can expect to fill the four following roles.

1. *Navigator* - Clients and employers will expect us to steer them in the right direction on emerging issues. As always, we will serve as the moral conscience for those we serve.

2. *Mediator* - Bridge-building where none currently exists will be a vital part of public affairs. Emerging players and the status quo will both need experienced professionals who can unify both sides.

3. *Futurist* - Public affairs practitioners, generally in the front
   lines of what is happening, will be called upon by management to anticipate and predict emerging issues, opportunities
   or threats to the organization along with preventive measures
   to take.

4. *Communicator* - This may be our most important function:
   communicating better, faster, more effectively than anyone
   else.

The future will be a different place than we're used to. By the
beginning of the next century, New York and Tokyo will be the only
"western" cities among the world's 10 largest. All others will be in
what we today consider Third World countries.[12] What does this
mean? It means that your skills and talents will be pushed to new
limits. We must be prepared to meet that challenge.

Notes

1. James Crumpi, *Public Management*, Vol. 72, No. 1, December 1990.
2. Tom Adams, Adams Media Research, "The Making of a Precedent,"
Entertainment Weekly, February, 10, 1995.
3. Peter Harkness, *Governing*, January 1995, p. 4.
4. "State of America's Cities," Research Report of the National League
of Cities, January 1995.
5. *Ibid.*
6. Jeff Greenfield, "America Lacks a Sense of Shame," Chicago *Sun-
Times*, November 25, 1988, p. 45.
7. Crumpi, p. 278.
8. J. Forinelli, "Needed: A New U.S. Perspective on Global Relations,"
Public Relations Journal, Vol. 46, p. 18-19.
9. Alvin Toffler, *Powershift: Knowledge, Wealth & Violence at the Edge
of the 21st Century* (New York: Bantam Books, 1991).
10. "GOP Stalling Kills Campaign Reform," *Chicago Tribune*, October 1,
1994.
11. Center for Responsive Politics.
12. James E. Kirby, *SMU Magazine*, Fall 1994. Original source: *The World
and South Africa in the 1990s* by Clem Sunter.

CHALLENGES ON THE
HORIZON

Chapter 28

Activist Groups and New Technologies: Influencing the Public Affairs Agenda

Richard Alan Nelson

Even so, this means numerous opportunities for creating new "win-win" situations abound. By monitoring each other's activities, they may actually come to appreciate one another better.

Problems Facing Activist Communicators

Let us assume for the moment that you are a non-business activist attempting to reach out to new audiences as well as mobilize current supporters. If you look at the world from this point of view, you see that your opponents (often working in corporate public affairs positions) generally have better access, particularly in navigating government and media. They are wealthy enough to be able to target key issues, monitor proposed bills which could help or hurt their interests, and enlist expert testimony, secure second party endorsements, and maintain backdoor contacts for their positions. Activists also rarely have the resources their opponents do in turning for assistance to former administration officials now working in highly respected Washington, D.C., and New York-based law firms and public relations consultancies.

These are difficult enough problems for you, but add to them the challenges of trying to impact on a large, diverse, culturally different and seemingly disinterested populace in a nation as important internationally as the United States. The overall effectiveness of activist efforts often prove questionable and the ideological playing field is not an even one. You know activist groups have historically suffered from (largely successful) attempts to ignore and marginalize them by dominant coalitions except where the power elites' commercial or political interests are advanced. You, too, can seek to lobby the American political leadership through formal and informal interpersonal contacts with powerbrokers in Congress, the White House, and the major national media. Your staff (possibly volunteers) may also conduct socio-politico intelligence activities to monitor developments, keep track of potential supporters and opponents, and attempt to build support through brochures, booklets, videos and other communications. Despite some successes, however, in your heart of hearts as an activist you may well feel dissatisfied by the cultural double standards, widespread disinformation, media distortion, racist/religious prejudice, and continuing ignorance that you still encounter.

Implications of Changing Technologies

So you give up, right? No! With true activist pluck, you determine to find another way. For good or evil, the communications genie has been unleashed—giving you new opportunities to score an end run around your opponents.

Just as the printing press changed social institutions forever and radio and television altered the nature of democratic politics in the twentieth century, you know CMC (computer-mediated communication) is already redefining the nature of the politics at the dawn of the twenty-first. The post-World War II concept of the mass market is largely being displaced, along with the mythology of a homogeneous America or non-nationalist Europe. The demise of mass marketing involves a transition to "target," "stratified," "niche," or "tailored" efforts at communicating to specific groupings of individuals. The relatively new concept of "narrowcasting" to highly specialized, homogeneous audiences allows for cost-effective message placement to population sub-groups on an unprecedented scale. Increased use of direct mail, fax, toll-free 800 telephone numbers, on-line computer services, optic two-way capacity, international direct satellite-to-home transmission, and other new technological breakthroughs may well open additional doors and opportunities for information disseminators. Such direct-access media offer a relatively unregulated open platform for airing political views and proposals without challenge from a questioning press or an awakened corporate community.

Widespread private ownership of audio and video cassette players, for example, encouraged American religious broadcaster "Pat" Robertson to distribute free tapes (or "electronic campaign buttons") to targeted voting groups with his message unedited by network newscasters. The result: political professionals were surprised by the unexpected early caucus voter turnouts for Robertson in the 1988 Republican presidential nomination race. Promotion of his "800" phone number during the 1992 primaries by insurgent Democrat Jerry Brown showed others that technology could directly link candidate and campaign. Similarly, the 1992 presidential bids by independent Ross Perot and Democrat standard bearer Bill Clinton revolutionized national campaigning strategies via sophisticated phone banks, town meeting videoconferences, and appearances on *Larry King Live* and other talk shows designed to reach out to potential voters and circumvent the mainstream press. The Republican successes in 1994 depended on the continuing proliferation of such populist talk programs to help stimulate and mobilize popular interest—especially those political issues taken up by rabble-rousing air personalities on radio no longer worried about government speech control regulations largely abolished in that medium. And the defeat of House Speaker Tom Foley (D-Washington) was orchestrated using the Internet, a medium off the radar screen for his campaign managers who were totally blindsided by the extent of computer networking and fundraising activity undertaken by their opponents.

Fortunately or unfortunately, the revolution in information technology is outpacing the ability of the political and business community to control direct people-to-people communication. So far the right has been most active in taking advantage of changes in conventional media, but the new politics is open to all. In contrast with the not-so-distant past, when members of Congress identified hot issues from a handful of constituent letters, numerous interest groups across the political spectrum now have built sophisticated "grassroots" electronic networks that can generate an astonishing volume of calls, letters, and e-mail from folks back home. Interest groups assert that their grass-roots efforts are a healthy means of getting people in touch with their government. Millions of new activists are being organized to call lawmakers and talk shows, make speeches and write to local newspaper editors. All over Capitol Hill, Senate and House offices collectively are receiving as many as 1,000 phone calls and voice mail messages a month, automatically sorted by aides in terms of issue, printed out and placed daily on congressional desks—up to 4.2 million phone calls a month. Accompanying the phone calls are an avalanche of letters, postcards, faxes, Mailgrams, e-mail, and other communiques to lawmakers—running to more than 400 million pieces a year.

Many activist groups argue that the cascade of calls and letters they generate add important balance to public policy debates, although the reverse can also be true as pro-business forces adapt. The U.S. Chamber of Commerce, for instance, is installing a phone bank that will call the chamber's 215,000 members about issues of concern to the organization. The Chamber hopes to form a huge base of its own activist members—grouped by business type and location—who will agree to be contacted by a computer-driven phone bank when a hot issue arises in Congress. Chamber members will be mailed materials in advance that will background them on such issues as health reform. Then when a key vote looms, a computer will start dialing their numbers with a recorded message. Those answering the phone will be able to press 1 to have a Mailgram or letter sent in their name to their representative, press 2 to record a voice-mail message for the lawmaker or press 3 to have a computer connect them immediately with the lawmaker's office. Later, the computer will print out the member's choice so that Chamber officials can gauge the level of cooperation. Other examples include the millions of cards and letters prompted by Jack Bonner and Associates, a Washington-based firm that assists only corporate interests, helped keep Northrop Corporation's B-2 Stealth bomber alive, helped auto makers fight off tougher fuel-economy standards and helped banks defeat a forced reduction in credit-card interest rates. The Stealth bomber campaign in 1991 and 1992 involved calls from 200 trained phone bank operators to members of 5,000 groups—including farm, senior citizens, minority, even religious groups—in more than 100 "politically responsive" congressional districts to write or phone their representatives to support the radar-evading bomber.

That is why new applications of computer technologies, such as Internet and e-mail, which provide very inexpensive vehicles for still unfiltered and uncensored communication, are important factors opening up alternative opportunities for average people and local community groups—as well as intelligent corporate public affairs people—to influence the public policy process. The Internet online computer information services phenomenon, for example, allows for mass interactive conversation via computer—a lively new public space for fostering a genuine participatory democratic politics adapted to the needs of an advanced post-industrial society.[1]

By participating in issue-oriented conversation via computer, millions of individuals now connected with the Internet are creating different "virtual communities" with their own political life (Rheingold, 1993). At the same time, links through the Internet are going free to millions of academics and other influentials who communicate domestically and internationally. These and other activists are currently using the Internet in five key ways, to:

1. *Provide targeted audiences with objective information and propaganda, through*
   a. *web pages and computerized archival sites for downloading of documents, journals, etc.*
   b. *links to other sites with similar interests, creating a network of like-minded individuals*
   c. *news announcements and media releases*
   d. *fact sheets*
   e. *historical data*
   f. *redistribution of items appearing in mainstream and specialized news media*
   g. *uploading of reports, documents, software, etc. for retrieval by interested users*

2. *Use information to mobilize others via*
   a. *networked alternative news and information sources*
   b. *interpretive commentary on events*
   c. *action alerts to special events, urgent issues*
   d. *requests to respond to others with messages/flames/boycotts*
      - *legislators*
      - *government agencies (domestic and foreign)*
      - *corporate sponsors*
      - news media people

  • other activists
e. membership recruitment
f. job notices

3. Engage in fundraising through
  a. sales of organizationally-acceptable materials (books, videos, journals, paraphernalia, etc.)
  b. requests for donations to specific activist causes/funds

4. Conduct research, such as
  a. interactive research collaboration with shared files
  b. answers to problems/requests for help
  c. information searches using NetScape®, Mosaic®, and other easy-to-use computerized "browser" search software with capabilities to
    · transfer files and software programs through mechanisms such as file transfer protocol (ftp) and gopher
    · get information via telnet and other services
    · conduct wide area information searches (wais)
  d. on-line surveys
  e. calls for papers/conferences
  f. educational/teaching aids
    · case studies
    · syllabi
    · finding guides
    · handy tips, and

5. Partake in general discussion (chat e-mail and topic-oriented usenet lists) with friends/colleagues/others with shared interests.[2]

Conclusion

   This community interaction in cyberspace is already drawing the attention of political scientists, public opinion analysts, and journalists who recognize these developments have significant implications for democratic theory (Abramson, Arterton, and Orren, 1988; Ronfeldt, 1992; Margolis, Fisher, and Resnick, 1994; Peck, 1995). Activists at least now have a cornucopia of new opportunities to creatively reach out to their constituencies. The "electronic highway" of literally thousands of bulletin boards, e-mail, and other services already in existence means activists can intelligently by-pass restrictions on distribution of information. The dominance of mainstream media distribution outlets such as Associated Press and the broadcast networks is now able to be outflanked. Other new tele-communications technologies promise to further redefine the infor-mational environment dramatically in ways only dimly perceived. Ironically, these alternative communication processes are at least indirectly subsidized by governmental and private institutions, so the exercise of greater advocacy and democratization is not without controversy. Many social problems will remain, demanding contin-ued efforts to overcome unfortunate stereotypes. Even so, this means numerous opportunities for creating new "win-win" situations abound. By monitoring each others activities, they may actually come to appreciate one another better. But building mutual understanding will require activists and their corporate public affairs counterparts to seriously work together in finding common ground. If efforts to expand conflict resolution are to succeed, this will also necessitate renewed dedication to developing long-term programs of two-way communication that apply strategic management principles.

Notes

1. The global Internet is a loosely organized information system (or "web") of at least 15,000 voluntarily interconnected computer data networks, reaching more than 100 countries and serving over 15 million individual us-ers in government agencies, universities, foundations, think tanks, corpora-tions, and other sites. By 1995, more than 3 million computers, terminals, and other devices were accessible on the Internet, making it the fastest-grow-ing on-line service. Cyberspace differs from broadcasting where those in charge of the studios and distribution networks can dictate content. Unlike conven-tional commercial systems, which depend on individually paying customers, the Internet is run as a cooperative without central control or ownership. Because the Internet has no center, political agenda setting can emerge through the process of interaction by communicators who are both a receiving center and a broadcaster. This freedom and inexpensive cost are opening up new vistas, even though "moderators" and "list owners" on some of the thousands of interest/usergroup communication vehicles on the Internet are now more frequently exercising some forms of editorial control. Advertisers, however, have become increasingly interested in the demographics of Internet users and so a number of commercial services such as CompuServe®, Prodigy®, and America Online® now are connected. New copyrighted but free software programs ("freeware") such as Mosaic® and NetScape® (which also come in

advanced commercial versions) feature colorful graphics and help screens, simplifying access to the ever growing World Wide Web® and a host of local electronic community networks.

2. Important sources for activist information include:

• *The Activist's Oasis*, a web site featuring "practical tools for trouble-makers" with links to activist organizations, activist mailing lists, issues lists, government organizations, and other data. Online web page address inside the <> marks is <http://www.matisse.net/~kathy/activist/activist.html>.

• *Institute for Global Communications* (IGC), an important catalyst sup-porting international communications and information exchange. The IGC Networks—ConflictNet, EcoNet, LaborNet, PeaceNet, and WomensNet—form a computer system dedicated to environmental preservation, peace, human rights, and other "progressive" causes. IGC is also a member of the Associ-ation for Progressive Communications, linking more than 16,000 activists in over 95 countries, helping start news networks such as the Alternex (Brazil) and GlasNet (Russia). Web page <http://www.igc.org/> and e-mail <apcadmin @igc.apc.org>.

• *Inter Press Third World News Agency*, a non-profit cooperative with more than 900 English- and Spanish-language media outlets around the world. Web page <http://www.lead.org/ips/ips.html> and e-mail <ips-info@igc.apc. org>.

• *Online Activism Resource List*, a detailed guide to a variety of groups. Web page <http://www.lib.ox.ac.uk/internet/news/faq/archive/net-community. resources.part1.html>.

• The *Electronic Frontier Foundation*, an anti-censorship, pro-free speech group interested in communication rights and new media technologies. Web page <http://www.eff.org> and e-mail <eff@eff.org>.

• *The Activists Mailing List* <activ-l@mizzou1.missouri.edu or activ-l@mizzou1.bitnet>, a major outlet for various groups, moderated by Rich Winkel <rich@pencil.cs.missouri.edu>.

• *The Network Observer*, edited by Phil Agre, a monthly electronic news-letter about networks and democracy. Web page <http://communication.ucsd .edu/pagre/tno.html> and e-mail <pagre@ucsd.edu>.

• *Ragan's Interactive Public Relations: Marketing Communications and PR in the Age of Cyberspace*, a useful newsletter featuring a variety of up-dates and tips for public relations and public affairs professionals published 24 times a year by Lawrence Ragan Communications, Inc., in Chicago. e-mail <71154.2605@compuserve.com> and fax <312-335-9583>.

Selected References

Abramson, Jeffrey B., F. Christopher Arterton, and Gary R. Orren (1988). *The Electronic Commonwealth: The Impact of New Media Technologies on Democratic Politics*. New York: Basic Books.

Edelman, M. (1988). *Constructing the Political Spectacle*. Chicago: University of Chicago Press.

Hall, Stuart. (1979). "Culture, the Media and the Ideological Effect." Pp. 315-348 in J. Curran, M. Gurevitch, and J. Woollacott, eds. *Mass Communication and Society*. Beverly Hills, Calif.: Sage.

Heath, Robert L. (1990). "Corporate Issues Management: Theoretical Underpinnings and Research Foundations." Pp. 29-66 in Larrisa A. Grunig and James E. Grunig, eds. *Public Relations Research Annual, Volume 2*. Hillsdale, New Jersey: Lawrence Erlbaum Publishers.

Heath, Robert L., and Richard Alan Nelson. (1989). *Issues Management: Corporate Public Policymaking in an Information Society*. Newbury Park, Calif.: Sage.

Margolis, Michael, and Gary A. Mauser (1989). "Public Opinion as a Dependent Variable: An Empirical and Normative Assessment." Pp. 365-379 in Margolis and Mauser, eds. *Manipulating Public Opinion: Essays on Public Opinion as a Dependent Variable*. Pacific Grove, Calif.: Brooks/Cole.

Margolis, Michael, Bonnie Fisher, and David Resnick (1994). "A New Way of Talking Politics: Democracy on the Internet." Paper presented at the Annual Meeting of the American Political Science Association.

Nelson, Richard Alan. (Spring 1990). "Bias Versus Fairness: The Social Utility of Issues Management." *Public Relations Review* 16(1), 25-32.

Nelson, Richard Alan. (1988). "Public Policy Implications of the New Communication Technologies." Pp. 366-385 in Robert L. Heath, ed. *Strategic Issues Management: How Organizations Influence and Respond to Public Interests and Policies*. San Francisco & London: Jossey-Bass Publishers.

Paletz, David L., and John Boiney (1988). "Interest Groups and Public Opinion." Pp. 534-546 in J. Anderson, ed. *Communication Yearbook 11*. Newbury Park, Calif.: Sage.

Peck, Grant. (23 April 1995). "Cyberspace Activists Enjoy Free Rein, World Stage." *Sunday Advocate* (Baton Rouge, Louisiana), p. 19A. Associated Press wire story.

Resnick, David, and Stephen E. Bennett (1993). "Rethinking Political Participation." (Mimeo). Chicago: Midwest Political Science Association.

Rheingold, Howard (1993). *The Virtual Community: Homesteading on the Electronic Frontier*. Reading, Mass.: Addison-Wesley Pub. Co.

Ronfeldt, David (1992). "Cyberocracy is Coming." *Information Society Journal* 8(4), 243-96.

Ryan, Charlotte (1991). *Prime Time Activism: Media Strategies for Grass Roots Organizing*. Boston: South End Press.

Wittenberg, Ernest, and Elizabeth Wittenberg. (1990). *How to Win in Wash-*

ington: Very Practical Advice about Lobbying, the Grassroots and the Media. Cambridge, England: Basil Blackwell.

Wriston, Walter B. (1992). *The Twilight of Sovereignty: How the Information Revolution is Transforming Our World.* New York: Charles Scribner's Sons.

Chapter 29

Ethics and Public Affairs:
An Uneasy Relationship

Kirk O. Hanson

Public affairs and public relations professionals are aware of the critical importance of straightforward communication to the reputation and effectiveness of the organization. Yet the very nature of their work conspires to make ethical behavior difficult for them to achieve. This article examines the unavoidable ethical tensions in the role of public affairs, describes several trends which are making those tensions both easier and more difficult to manage, and suggests principles which could help the public affairs professional guide his or her behavior. Finally, this article presents a set of questions an organization can ask itself to audit the ethics of its public affairs activities.

The public affairs profession has labored for many decades to meet the challenge of and demand for ethics. This concern is not new. What *is* new is how the national and global environment regard, reward and sanction the ethics of the organization and its public affairs professionals. Never before have the public activities and the public communication of organizations been so widely scrutinized. And never before has ethical behavior had such potential to influence an organization's bottom line and its achievement of its fundamental objectives. The ethics of public affairs is today a strategic concern. An organization, whether a business, a non-profit agency or a college, ignores the ethics of its public dealings at its own peril.

The Conflicting Roles of the
Public Affairs Professional

Problem 1:
The Limits of Advocacy

Examining the structure and tasks of the public affairs profession immediately highlights the unavoidable ethical conflicts in this organizational role. Public affairs practitioners stand at the boundary of their own organizations and communicate with governments, the community, and other organizations and interests. They are charged with representing the interests of their own organization but, as citizens themselves and as representatives of organizations that are also citizens, they share a responsibility for the effective functioning of our American system of public decision making and public debate. In short, they are at one moment an advocate for a single interest *and* a trustee for the integrity of the public policy process.

Some would argue that the role of the public affairs professional is analogous to that of the lawyer. Under this view, some conclude public affairs is simply advocacy and one's role is to present the organization's case as persuasively as possible. The public affairs practitioner, these individuals argue, has little or no responsibility for the achievement of the common good, for the integrity of the public policy process, nor for the inclusion of all relevant voices in the public debate.

Others, including myself, consider the public affairs professional not solely an advocate, but also as a citizen—with the right to "petition government" or express the interest of his or her organization—but also with the responsibility to insure that the process of public debate and decision is open and complete. Under this view, all participants must serve as guarantors of the free exchange of ideas, even by for those with limited resources and access. This view, held by the majority of public affairs professionals today, means that the practitioner must continually balance advocacy for his or her own organization with a commitment to the airing of all important voices on any public concern.

Problem 2:
The Challenge of Two-Way Communication

There is a second unavoidable conflict in the role of public affairs. At the same time the practitioner articulates the interests of the organization to the broader world, he or she also articulates and brokers the legitimate interests of outside groups to the managers within the organization. Many interests beyond the shareholders and the board members of the organization are now recognized as "stakeholders," those who are influenced by and therefore have a legitimate stake in the behavior of the organization.

When the public affairs practitioner communicates the interests of the organization to those outside and the interests of those outside to the organization, there are inevitably difficult choices about the weight to give each perspective. Should external concerns be presented to company managers as legitimate or as misguided and marginal? Should the practitioner's task ever be to advocate the stakeholder's concerns over those of his or her own organization? The challenge is to strike the right balance between mindless advocacy of the organization's positions and, conversely, total identification with the outside interest.

The creative practitioner will work to reconcile the interests of the organization with those of the community or other outside interest, perhaps by invoking a longer-term interest or by finding some new common ground. But there will still remain cases where the interests of the company, no matter how long term and creatively drawn, diverge from those of the company's publics.

There will be times too when very important interests of the company diverge from what most observers, and even the practitioner, believe is "the common good." How a public affairs professional handles such cases is the ultimate test of ethics and public responsibility.

Even when the practitioner gets the balance right, there is no relief from the ethical pressures. The managers of the public affairs practitioner's organization may feel she has "gone over to the other side" because she shows any empathy for the other's position. Conversely, the outside interest may feel the public affairs professional is nothing more than a "corporate mouthpiece" because she won't adopt all of the other's concerns.

Problem 3:
The Practitioner as Agent

There is a third conflict central to the role of public affairs. The public affairs person is almost always an agent, either an employee of the organization or a consultant. He or she gives advice but does not make the final decision about the public affairs strategy, the

tactics pursued, nor the honesty and completeness of the communication. Inevitably, conflicts with the organization's management will
arise.

The client is frequently less sophisticated about the long term
value to the organization of more candid, accurate, and complete
communication. The client will want to release only "good news"
and favorable information. The public affairs professional will occasionally have a client who gives direct orders to communicate in
a less than truthful way or to obfuscate some information the practitioner believes should be clearly stated. Occasionally, the practitioner may become aware of some action by his or her organization
which is illegal or just morally abhorrent to his or her values. The
client's instinct may be to bury the information. The practitioner
may know or believe it must be revealed, to satisfy the law or to
protect the organization from greater long-term damage.

The practitioner has divided loyalties in each of these cases: to
the client managers, to the client organization, to the public, and to
his or her own conscience. In each case, the practitioner must choose
an appropriate response to each conflict of this type: exit, voice, or
loyal silence. Fortunately, the public affairs agent selects his or her
clients just as the client hires the agent. The wise public affairs
practitioner can avoid many of the worst conflicts by evaluating the
business and reputation of prospective employers and avoiding the
worst of them. But how much of a match in values is really necessary to justify taking an assignment? Is there a way to predict and
identify which clients will create the most conflicts?

Ethical choices are an unavoidable part of daily public affairs
responsibilities. The editing of a simple press release or the preparation of a "one-pager" on a proposed amendment involve choices
regarding honesty, full disclosure, conflicts between the values of
the practitioner and the interests of the corporation. Thoughtful and
always vigilant choices are necessary to sort out these conflicting
obligations.

The Changing Environment
of Public Affairs Ethics

While establishing that ethical behavior is particularly difficult
for the public affairs professional, we can also identify several trends
that are strengthening the resolve of the ethically sensitive practi-

tioner. These trends help public affairs professionals advance their own ethics and that of their organization.

Today more than ever the integrity of the organization and its public affairs officials is on public display. An increasingly vigilant and global public and global media enhance the connection between organizational integrity and organizational success. More managers at all levels acknowledge the strategic value of a good reputation and its connection to straightforward communication. Organizations—for profit, not-for-profit, and governmental—are recognizing that customers, employees, suppliers, distributors, funders and trustees who *trust* the organization are more likely to do business with it, go to work for it, and contribute to it. This greatly aids the accomplishment of its organizational objectives.

Several trends demonstrate this point.

- *The reaction of funders.* In the wake of the ethical failings at the United Way of America and the NAACP, contributions dried up and funders demanded reforms before they would again place trust in the organizations. These are warning signs for all non-profit and educational organizations.

- *Consumer reaction to corporate scandals.* Recent cases have demonstrated that consumers tend to avoid (boycott may be too strong a word) patronizing businesses that have had major scandals. Exxon, Denny's, Sears, and more recently The Body Shop have experienced sales declines due in part to adverse publicity.

- *Consumer preference for "responsible" companies.* The evidence is less clear that consumers selectively *buy* from companies with good ethical reputations. The publication of *Shopping for a Better World*[1] by the Council on Economic Priorities has given consumers ready access to the social and ethical records of consumer products companies though it is unclear how much impact this book has had. Some argue that a general reputation for responsible management and communication influences consumers' perceptions of the reliability of the product itself.

- *Consumer preference for "ethical" products.* A growing minority of consumers prefer "green" products which contribute to environmental sustainability or to other social objectives such as limiting cruelty to animals or promoting the economic development of poorer areas of the globe. There has also been a growth of "cause-related marketing" wherein many types of products and services are packaged with contributions to worthy causes ("$1 of every purchase goes to . . .")

• *The growth of ethical investing.* While still small relative to the investments held by large institutions, the growing stake and prominence of "ethical investors" and "ethical mutual funds" provides some acknowledgment and perhaps reward for companies that manage ethically. At minimum, the many evaluations and critiques of corporate behavior by "clean funds" and their advisors contribute to the availability of data on corporate ethical behavior.

• *The growth of the global media.* During the last ten years, the media's newfound emphasis on business and on non-profit organizations had a significant impact on organizations. Today the most important development is the growing global character and reach of the media. Little significant corporate or organizational behavior will escape the media's attention, whether it occurs in Oklahoma, Costa Rica or Pakistan. Media scrutiny comes in many forms: the immediacy of 24 hour televised headline news and the detailed and extensive coverage possible in specialized and targeted newsletters and other low-circulation publications. The Internet serves as a 24 hour instantaneous and interactive medium, as Intel found out when it resisted replacing its defective Pentium chips. With so many more ways to deliver information, more information will be collected and disseminated.

• *The global growth of interest groups.* Several studies have documented the increasing number of non-governmental organizations (NGOs) active in other countries and globally. They articulate new types of concerns and broaden the demands on public affairs. These diverse groups encourage and police organizational behavior and public communication in all parts of the globe.

- *The growing availability of data on ethical behavior.* As noted above, there is a growing body of data on organizational behavior. One can use on-line sources to learn the criminal and compliance records of companies, the fund raising expenses of non-profits, the ratings that organizations get from research groups on the environment, diversity, sexual harassment, and community involvement. It is now possible for an aggressive reporter, a creative undergraduate, or even a technically savvy 12-year-old to peruse an organization's records and tap public data bases to examine many dimensions of its performance. The data will grow exponentially and its simple availability will influence more customers and investors to take ethical behavior into account.

- *The growth of "principles" organizations.* Over the past ten years, several new efforts have produced ethical codes or principles for adoption by companies. Stimulated by the perceived success of the Sullivan Principles on corporate operations in South Africa, other principles have been developed for corporate operations in Northern Ireland and South Korea, for corporate environmental efforts, and for chemical industry practices. Such "principles" organizations are attracting the participation of many mainstream companies. Once one's competitor or a large number of other organizations have joined such an effort, it becomes difficult to refuse to participate.

All of these trends change the world of public affairs. They demonstrate clearly that there is much more attention focused on the behavior of organizations and their communication. They also show that the velocity of communication has increased dramatically. As the public affairs professional responds to more communication in real time, his or her command of ethical principles will be more severely tested.

Collectively, these trends provide a much more sensitive and immediate feedback loop to evaluate, reward and punish the truthfulness and completeness of organizational communications. The outsider wanting to examine whether and when a company revealed certain information can search selected archives or data bases and answer the question in a matter of moments. Whereas old press releases and "unfortunate" statements to the public could often be forgotten, they are now archived electronically and saved, ready to demonstrate the inconsistency of an organization's statements—in living color.

These trends also heighten the strategic importance of public affairs to all organizations. As "relationships"—with customers, employees, suppliers, communities, as well as shareholders—become more critical, the contribution public affairs can make to those relationships heightens the strategic importance of public affairs. Public affairs becomes essential to the organization's marketing, to its fund raising, to effective coordination and communication with suppliers and other business partners, to the successful management of litigation, as well as to the traditional relationships with the media and government. And some activities long managed by public affairs—regulatory enforcement, media relations, permit granting—take on a new importance to organizational success.

Managing the Ethics of Public Affairs

Successful management of the ethics of public affairs involves the personal commitment of individuals and an ongoing and persistent dialogue in public affairs departments, firms and professional associations about the difficult choices to be made. Within the Public Affairs Council, past debates on the ethics of the profession have led to the adoption of *Ethical Guidelines*[2] for the Public Affairs professional. This articulate statement exhorts the practitioner to "maintain professional relationships based on honesty and reliable information," "protect the integrity of the public policy process and the political system," and "understand(s) the interrelation of business interests with the larger public interests." The code uses approximately 150 more words to elucidate these three fundamental principles.

Each individual, public affairs department or firm needs to adopt for itself a set of principles which give more adequate direction through the ethical shoals. The language of these principles may still be inadequate to the task, but the thinking and dialogue which accompany the development of a set of principles will help those who seek to follow them. And their continual discussion and reinforcement of the principles will make them living statements.

One way to create such a set of principles is to answer questions which explore the three fundamental conflicts described earlier in this article. If an individual, public affairs department or public affairs firm can answer the following questions, they can write a set of principles:

On The Limits of Advocacy

- Which stakeholders have a right to communication from the organization and on what topics?
- At what point does advocacy communication become dishonest communication?
- When does selective disclosure constitute deception?
- When does selective disclosure of organizational information distort the public policy process? What information must an organization disclose?
- When do public affairs efforts unfairly prevent adequate public debate?
- When should a public affairs professional insist that another voice or interest be heard?
- When is insisting that another voice be heard disloyal to one's own organization?

On Public Affairs as Two-Way Communications

- Who are the legitimate stakeholders of the organization that deserve to be heard by the organization?
- When is stonewalling an outside interest unfair to that stakeholder?
- When should a public affairs professional insist that his or her organization heed the concern of an outside interest?
- When is recommending that the organization satisfy an outside interest disloyalty or an admission of failure?

On Public Affairs Professionals as Agents

- How much of a match between practitioner and client values should there be before accepting an assignment?
- When should a public affairs professional vocally object to a client's decision regarding a public affairs matter?

- When should a public affairs professional refuse to carry out a directive from a client?
- When should a public affairs professional resign an account?

Only active and ongoing dialogue about the meaning of these principles and the proper balance between conflicting roles can adequately prepare the professional for the flood of small and large decisions faced. The dialogue over the ethics of public affairs and new dilemmas which arise needs to occur continually in the public affairs departments, public affairs firms, and public affairs professional associations. Every organization must orient its new employees to these fundamental conflicts of public affairs and the principles the group has developed to address them.

In the absence of a formal enforcement process, a professional association must create a visible and ongoing debate among its members on professional ethics. It fails its members if it does not make ethics a feature in every annual meeting--including debates on key dilemmas, the discussion of difficult cases which have arisen in the previous year, or testimonials from respected members of the profession on how they manage their own ethical behavior.

Auditing Public Affairs Ethics

The adoption of principles to guide public affairs must be accompanied by a periodic assessment or audit of the organization's actual behavior. This will also serve to raise questions or decisions which have not received adequate discussion in the past.

The following list of audit questions has been developed from The Public Affairs Council's *Ethical Guidelines* and from the writings and speeches of many other public affairs professionals who have spoken eloquently on the ethical dilemmas of their profession.

On Communication

1. Are all my (our) communications accurate?
2. Are all my (our) communications complete enough to avoid foreseeable misperceptions?
3. Do all my (our) communications accurately reflect the organization's actual positions on key matters?

4. Have I (we) selectively omitted certain information which should have been communicated?
5. Have I (we) communicated to all groups who have an interest in or a right to know about my organization's plans/position?
6. Is my (our) communication on the same subject to different stakeholders—government, employees, shareholders, suppliers, etc.—consistent?
7. Is my (our) communication always timely?
8. Do I (we) always disclose the identity of my client or employer?
9. Is my (our) communication respectful of the positions of other participants in the public policy process? Do I (we) disparage the interests or motives of others?
10. Have I (we) sought to preempt, disrupt or drown out the communications of other legitimate interests?
11. Have I (we) facilitated the communication of important perspectives which are not represented in the public policy process?
12. Do I (we) respond to inquiries and criticisms openly and without rancor?
13. Do I (we) refuse to use communication as a vehicle for retribution and revenge?

On Two Way Communication

14. Do I (we) meet with and listen to outside groups who are legitimate stakeholders of my organization?
15. Do I (we) present the views of outside groups to my own organization in a balanced way?
16. Do I (we) counsel my own organization to heed outsiders' views when they are the ethical course of action?

On Client Relationships and Employment

17. Do I (we) work only for organizations whose mission and values are consistent with my own?
18. Do I (we) inform all my clients of my ethical commitments and that I would not lie, cheat, steal or misrepresent for them?

19. Do I (we) resist pressures from clients to shade the truth or conceal information that should be disclosed?
20. Have I (we) resigned an account when it was right to do so?

On Legal and Regulatory Responsibilities

21. Do I (we) fulfill all reporting requirements on my work required by law?
22. Do I (we) know, respect and abide by all federal, state and local laws that apply to lobbying and related public affairs activities?
23. Do I (we) know, respect and abide by all laws governing campaign finance and other political activities?

The Future of Public Affairs Ethics

The increasing complexity of the organization's relationships with its stakeholders and its publics can only increase the importance of public affairs in the decades ahead. That complexity and the rapidly evolving communications and information technology will continue to shape the specific tasks which occupy the time of the public affairs professional. But the unavoidable and central conflicts in the role of public affairs outlined in this article will persist—as will the importance of managing the ethics of public affairs.

Notes

1. Council on Economic Priorities, *Shopping for a Better World* (San Francisco: Sierra Club Books, 1994).
2. Public Affairs Council, "Ethical Guidelines," The 1995 Annual Report of the Public Affairs Council (Washington, D.C.): 28.

Chapter 30

International Public Affairs: Managing within the Global Village

D. Jeffrey Lenn

Introduction

The pace of globalization is accelerating rapidly, leading to a fuller integration of national economies. Domestic companies find themselves under siege in their local markets by foreign competitors. Consumers can choose from a dazzling array of products imported from around the world. Governmental officials struggle to keep pace with shifting industry boundaries and new technologies which constantly threaten to make regulation obsolete. Shifts in international financial markets have direct impact on local farmers, manufacturers and retailers. A global village is under construction.

These changes are the result of a combination of economic, political and technological forces. Economic forces are shaping new patterns of market integration so that shifts in the economy of one country are felt immediately in a number of others. The end of the Cold War has unleashed new political forces which have undone well-established alliances and forged new bilateral and multilateral agreements between unlikely partners. Rapid technological advances have provided us with a world of instant communication where seemingly minor, local events capture the imagination of an international audience. Globalization is a fact of life which requires a new orientation of political and business leadership in order to adapt to its demands.

Public Affairs and Globalization

The response to globalization by corporate public affairs departments and public relations firms has too often been reactive. American corporate public affairs executives believe that their capacity to manage effectively in the international arena is "slightly, if not at all, developed" (Post 1993, p. 187). There is a lack of coordination across national boundaries, difficulty in making linkages with other parts of the corporation and inadequate staffing (Kennelly & Gladwin 1995 and Meznar 1995). There are exceptions in individual corporations, but generally the situation can be characterized as slow in adapting to this new environment.

Within public relations firms, the importance of the international dimension is clearly recognized, but there is a serious lack of skill and experience to help corporate clients address these new challenges. Senior practitioners point to a diminution of world leadership among American public relations firms because of their inability to link global with local programs and strategies (Epley 1992). A recent study of Public Relations of Society of America membership indicates that only 22% of the respondents think they are prepared to compete in the global market (Fitzpatrick & Whillock 1993). An exception to this trend is the work by several leading firms on privatization and communication programs in the former Soviet Union and Eastern Europe.[1] Although some firms are making progress toward incorporating the international dimension into their practice, there is still a lag between opportunity and capability.

One reason is the heavy reliance on "the American model" of public affairs. Although it is both the largest and most sophisticated model, its basic assumptions have not been challenged even with the current changes in the international market (Botan 1992). Globalization is bringing to light new issues for business leaders that require fresh approaches. But public affairs executives and professionals, comfortable in their American and European niches, often find it difficult to change old habits and to respond to these new challenges.

The New Shape of International Public Affairs

Globalization demands a fresh approach and greater sophistication among those in the profession, whether employed by the multinational corporation (MNC) or the public relations firm. Successful management in the global village requires a new set of guidelines to form the basis of the strategies, structure and staffing of corporate public affairs offices.[2]

Five Guidelines

1. Recognize the importance of culture in shaping human life and be sensitive to its impact on individual and organizational behavior. The cultural dimension of human relationships is too often their most hidden element. Culture shapes us so subtly that we are often unaware of its impact. Language, customs and societal roles are imprinted early in life to shape individual personalities and value systems.

The public affairs professional must first develop an awareness of his or her own cultural underpinnings in order to achieve multicultural awareness and expertise. The next step in the learning process is to focus on another culture in order to understand differences and similarities with one's own. Finally, a new perspective of tolerance and appreciation is achieved through developing friendships with people from another culture. The most important tool for multicultural awareness is learning another language. Assuming that everyone will understand and speak your language misses an essential point. "We can sell in any language, but people buy in their own language," is an adage used by William Corbett to make the point that public affairs professionals must be multi-lingual (1991, p. 12).

Sensitivity to cultural differences is essential for establishing working relationships in other countries. Experimentation with new behavioral patterns expands personal awareness and develops skill in managing public affairs. "When in Rome, do as the Romans do" is an old adage often suggested as a guideline for adapting to new cultural surroundings. But it is too simplistic to be helpful. What do Romans *actually* do? What expectations do they have of each other? Are these norms applicable to non-Romans? What impact does being Italian, European and Christian have on "Roman behavior?" The complexity of cultural influences on behavior requires a sophisticated sensitivity and flexibility to be able to choose appropriate behavior in each situation.

2. Anchor an international public affairs strategy firmly within the organization and its objectives. Cultural understanding must include an appreciation of the power of an organization in shaping individual behavior. Built deeply into each organization is a set of beliefs and values which gives it a distinctive personality. Honed by its history, purpose, products and services, and past and current management, this culture is a powerful force in determining how employees act. John Sculley, when he was chairman of Apple Computers, found himself constantly surrounded by a more casual culture which didn't easily lend itself to his expectations that the company become more efficient to compete effectively in the changing computer market. Louis Gerstner, in his role as chairman of IBM, has found that a proud and stubborn corporate culture is a strong undertow on his attempts to reposition the company.

International public affairs must also be linked to international corporate objectives to be successful. Just as the strategic capabilities of a corporation must be targeted to industry requirements, public affairs strategies must be aligned with its strategic plan. It is axiomatic that public affairs professionals be attuned to the strategic direction of the corporation and understand their role as assisting management in achieving of their goals. Such an anchoring will provide an integrated approach to dealing with the complex external environment in which the various divisions of the company operate.

3. Create an international public affairs strategy which is both responsive to local conditions and adaptable to the global market. To gain competitive advantage in the increasingly global market, a corporation must develop a "transnational solution" (Barlett and Ghoshal 1989). The MNC must focus on three major objectives—realizing global scale efficiencies, being flexible and responsive to national markets, and promoting worldwide learning and innovation. A transnational strategy successfully links global and local markets through products and services which meet the needs of its various customers and are produced efficiently. This also means structuring the corporation so that strategic decision-making is centralized to assure consistency across the globe while operational decision-making is allocated to country managers to maintain adaptability to local conditions.

Public affairs strategies should mirror this transnational approach of the MNC. Harold Burson, founder of Burson-Marsteller, suggests a two-tiered approach—"centralization for coordination and consistency of policies and messages; but regional implementation for

adaptation to local language, culture and politics" (Epley 1992).
Integrating the local with the global is essential to the success of
various public affairs programs.

4. Focus on key stakeholders in designing an international public affairs strategy. The dynamic external environment of the corporation is complex and often confusing. Stakeholder management is a helpful tool for understanding and interacting with this rapidly changing environment.[3] A stakeholder is any individual or group who can strongly influence, or be influenced by, the corporation. Stakeholder mapping allows management to identify its stakeholders, determine their interests or "stakes," assess their power, and design strategies by which to manage these relationships.

The first step in stakeholder management is differentiating primary from secondary stakeholders to assess their relationship to the company. Primary stakeholders have regular contact with the corporation because of their economic interests. These include customers, suppliers, competitors, employees and shareholders. Governmental agencies and local communities also fall into this category although their interests are not primarily economic. Secondary stakeholders have sporadic contact with the corporation and are therefore not intimately involved with its operation. Activist groups and media both fall into this type of stakeholder group.

Stakeholders change in terms of their proximity, interests and power. A public issue initiated by a small group can bring media attention to the company and propel secondary stakeholders into a primary position. Management is forced to address their demands while at the same time producing products and services for customers, responding to the actions of competitors, conforming to governmental regulations, and encouraging employee productivity and maximizing shareholder wealth. Stakeholder management provides an excellent framework by which to portray the dynamic and complex nature of the external environment.

International public affairs professionals must incorporate the full set of stakeholders with their differing interests and power when designing strategies. A stakeholder focus allows for a more sophisticated response to the varied demands of corporate constituencies. It also gives impetus to an integrated corporate strategy because various parts of the firm are already engaged with different stakeholder groups. For example, marketing, with its orientation toward customer relations, and human resources, with its focus on employ-

ee relations, become partners with public affairs in the process of
stakeholder management.

**5. Utilize strategic partnerships with those who have a variety
of cultural expertise to develop and implement an international
public affairs strategy.** A lack of knowledge about other cultures
requires a commitment to new awareness and learning by the public affairs professional. Multicultural awareness is based on partnerships with those who are knowledgeable and skilled in other
cultures. Over time, these develop into friendships which have powerful impact on individual and corporate ability to adapt to different cultures.

Initiating strong partnerships requires a careful search for expertise both inside and outside the company. Because the major responsibility for public affairs in foreign subsidiaries is often allocated
to line managers, public affairs professionals must start by developing internal alliances in order to understand the specifics of various country operations. Consultants with expertise in individual
countries provide another resource for shaping strategies that are
customized for local markets. Finally, networks of public affairs
professionals can be utilized to help in responding to the specific
demands of various countries and regions.

Whether in recognizing cultural influence, organizational goals,
local conditions, key stakeholders, or strategic partnerships, the
variables just enumerated are, of course, applicable to all public affairs programming. On occasion, they may seem more vital against
a global backdrop; in reality they are always basic public affairs
practice.

The International Imprint
on the Public Affairs Portfolio

The wide range of responsibilities of public affairs professionals
reflects differences in industry, company tradition, size, and management expectations. The MNC focuses its resources on six major
activities—media/press relations, government relations, issue management, community relations, philanthropy, and internal communications (Post 1992; Meznar 1995; Kennelly & Gladwin 1995). Each
activity in the public affairs portfolio requires modification in order to incorporate the international dimension.

Media/Press Relations

An international media/press relations strategy must be built on a full understanding of who owns the media in each country. While the commitment to open societies and a free press has made great strides globally, there are still considerable differences among countries. The role of media in society varies considerably, depending largely on ownership (private or state), even though all mass media have the common responsibility to be communicators to the "masses." (Hiebert 1992). Careful analysis of ownership patterns sets the stage for understanding editorial and advertising policies as well as how business will be covered in each country.

John Reed (1989) suggests that an international media relations program must be based on a sophisticated cultural awareness to be successful. Even the words that designate media vary across national borders. For example, a newspaper does not mean the same thing in the United States and China. A magazine in the U.S. is almost exclusively a print medium while in France it refers primarily to a television program. A reporter may be a sophisticated journalist (Germany, Japan, U.S.), an unsophisticated "hack" for whom reporting is a job to supplement income (Mediterranean, Middle East, African and Southeast Asia countries) or a government writer (China).

The choice of media requires a full appreciation of reader and viewer habits. Business executives utilize different sources to get their news (Reed 1989). In France, they read national business publications; in Italy, regional business papers; and in German areas of Switzerland, German metropolitan and national papers. Recently, several international English language newspapers have become common sources of business news around the world. Many executives now rely on *The Wall Street Journal* in its various regional editions as well as *The Financial Times* and *The International Herald Tribune* for updated information on financial markets and political events. CNN International, founded in 1985, has revolutionized the industry and become a major source of news for business and political leaders throughout the world.

Recognition of the media as a stakeholder rather than an adversary or pawn in a public affairs strategy is important for success in national markets. Establishing "partnerships" with reporters limits the possibility of surprise stories which embarrass the company. Utilizing foreign nationals with linguistic fluency and sensitivity to the nuances of viewer or reader responses as direct links to the media is important. Tracking the changing tastes in readership and viewership by opinion leaders in each country assures that press coverage will connect with target audiences.[4]

Government Relations

The international dimension of public affairs is most obvious in designing a government relations strategy. With the collapse of communism, individual countries are experimenting with new types of governing processes. A full understanding of each public policy process requires sophistication. *Institutions* need to be carefully analyzed to determine the process by which law and regulation are developed and adjudicated. *Politicians* must be profiled to understand their bases of power and ideological biases. *Political parties* should be monitored with attention to changing leadership patterns, their ability to control elected membership and access to financial resources. *Bureaucrats* must be analyzed to determine their views on various issues as well as their relationships with elected officials. *Interest groups* must be identified and analyzed to forecast their positions on public policy issues and the likelihood they will take political action. Finally, *public opinion* about issues and politicians needs to be tracked to detect sentiments which have impact on business.

A key variable in strategy design is public sentiment about the legitimacy of business involvement in the political process. The foreign corporation will always be suspect in its attempts to influence public policy. Clarity about the laws that govern the nature and methods of political involvement are essential for effective government relations. Some countries allow politicians, and even bureaucrats, to be full-time employees of a corporation; others allow elected officials to be paid agents; while others deny such involvement because governmental service is valued as a public trust.

Differing expectations about the role of trade associations in the public policy process have impact on the crafting of a political strategy. "Peak associations," which represent all members of an industry in individual European countries, act as partners with government officials in designing law and regulation. American trade associations often find themselves lobbying hard to even gain access to their own federal governmental officials. Also, membership in national trade associations may be limited to domestic companies,

forcing foreign MNCs to either go it alone or join together informally to represent their interests.

The new European Union (EU) offers a specific example of the
debate about appropriate strategies for attempting to influence government. American companies with offices in Brussels vary in their
approach to EU government agencies. They range from advertising
a position on a public policy issue to more direct attempts to influence policy or regulatory decisions—"holding the pen" to write legislation or regulation (Lenn, Brenner, et al. 1993). "Transparency,"
whether direct attempts to influence the public policy process should
be open or shielded from public view, is a major issue in the EU.
The more traditional European position of totally covert political
action stands in stark contrast to the American standard of disclosure, and even registration of lobbyists.

Coordination of government relations activity across countries is,
of course, important for full effectiveness. Bilateral and multilateral trade agreements are the umbrellas under which MNCs operate
as they seek competitive advantage. Working closely with home government officials to assure fair treatment in host countries requires
careful timing and skillful negotiation. Simultaneous targeting of
home and host countries may be important for assisting entry into
new markets, limiting tariff barriers or stalling crippling regulation.

The performance of Toys R Us in Japan and Germany is an interesting example of how an integrated government relations program can assist in entering new markets (Baron 1993). In Japan,
faced with strong opposition from local communities, small toy retailers and a complex web of wholesalers, management nevertheless decided to pursue its domestic strategy of large discount stores
with a full line of toys. It chose to develop a strategic alliance with
McDonald's, which had hired a Japanese executive to take the lead
in opening its stores throughout Japan. His experience in negotiating with local officials and national government bureaucrats was
effective in getting Toys R Us stores into a number of cities. American management maintained close contact with the Office of the
U.S. Trade Representative throughout the process in the event it
would be necessary to move the issue onto the trade talk agenda.

In Germany, the opposition came from toy stores, toy manufacturers, unions, and center city retailers. Toys R Us hired a well-
known German executive as its subsidiary president because of his
success in restructuring a major German department store chain. He
was able to negotiate with local officials to open the first stores

just outside central shopping districts. In the process, he demonstrated to German producers that overall demand in the toy market would grow and convinced the unions that retail jobs would not be lost.

Issue Management

Issue management in the international arena requires a full appreciation of various national differences in the movement of public policy issues through their life cycles. In pluralistic democratic systems, issues tend to "bubble up" from local communities with interest groups organizing to advocate their various positions through private and public channels. In authoritarian regimes, the issues are prioritized by an elite with limited public discussion about alternative solutions, leading eventually to public policies that are "pushed down" into society. Understanding the political impact of public awareness, and the number of individuals and groups involved in issue resolution, is critical to managing an issue.

New information technology has accelerated the tendency of domestic issues to take on regional and global dimensions. A local dispute can rapidly become "international" with full news coverage and citizen demands that home and host country political leaders take immediate action. The most effective corporate strategy is often one of containment, focused on the goal of keeping the issue local. This limits the number of stakeholders who are aware of the issue, focuses attention on a select group of decision-makers for resolution and concentrates the expertise of corporate management. The alternative, more costly approach is to elevate the issue to the global arena and force other corporations and a number of governments to address it. Of course, sometimes the opposition elevates an issue beyond the national borders of origin.

The Bhopal explosion in India rocked Union Carbide management. They attempted to localize the issue but soon found themselves caught in the middle of a rapidly evolving international issue with two governments, a number of interest groups, a bevy of lawyers and even employees in a number of countries embroiled in the issue. The migration of the issue across borders caught them by surprise and resulted in embarrassing and costly consequences to the corporation.

In a different kind of international issue challenge, Levi-Strauss, when faced with recent public criticism for selling clothing manufactured by children in Southeast Asia, voluntarily began to enforce International Labor Organization child labor standards in Bangladesh. It negotiated agreements with local contractors to continue to pay the children wages and hire them back when they were 14. In the meantime, the company paid the full bill to send them to school. Levi-Strauss management then took the lead in getting other American clothing manufacturers to agree to investigate the employment practices of their Asian suppliers. In the process, the company successfully managed its supplier, employee, competitor and government stakeholders through a strategy which highlighted its commitment to international social responsibility.

In a word, the keystone of a good issues management program, domestic or international is, per the old song, "an-ti-ci-pa-tion."

Community Relations

A strong community relations program is vital to the MNC operating plants. Its physical presence as a new neighbor makes the foreign-owned plant highly visible and, therefore, vulnerable. Successful community relations programs require a number of ingredients (See chapter 14). Choosing nationals as local managers is an important first step in gaining credibility. Developing strong relationships with community leaders signals a long-term commitment. Engaging various stakeholder groups in a two-way communication process establishes links with the entire community. Funding schools, medical facilities and parks demonstrates a commitment to the community interest.

The strategies of Japanese automobile companies, which built manufacturing facilities in Tennessee and Ohio in the 1980s, are good examples of how to design effective community relations programs. Not known for their sophistication in international public affairs, Japanese management showed themselves to be fast learners. Good pay, excellent working conditions, funding for new schools, strong working relationships with mayors and governors, and contributions to local organizations smoothed the entry of these MNCs into several American towns. Heeding the advice of public affairs firms they hired as consultants, management capitalized on this strategy through an extensive communications program which cited the production of quality automobiles by satisfied workers in new partnerships between local communities and large, foreign corporations.

Philanthropy

Charitable giving by business has a venerable tradition, based on the almost universal belief that the wealthy have some responsibility for sharing with the poor. In the U.S. and some European countries this tradition has led to fully developed corporate programs to help organizations dedicated to everything from the arts to job creation. There are, however, important differences throughout the world in the expectations about the need for business philanthropy. In European social democracies, the government provides a number of services for its citizens so that there is a limited set of demands for corporate giving. In Japan and many Asian countries, the corporation is an extended family, founded on a paternalistic philosophy, which is responsible for a full range of employee needs besides that of job security. Consequently, there is little expectation that the corporation will engage in philanthropic endeavors for society as a whole. The American tradition, wedded to beliefs in limited government and the importance of voluntary organizations to meet pressing social needs, is one in which corporate giving is virtually a mandate.

Both American and Japanese corporations have struggled to develop philanthropic programs which conform to the expectations of the various countries in which they operate. American executives, experienced in taking leadership in raising and donating money to charitable organizations, are developing differentiated philanthropy policies for individual countries. Japanese executives, faced with new demands by charitable groups in American communities in which they have built factories, are learning to overcome their cultural bias by instituting selective giving programs. Public affairs professionals must assist management in developing philosophies and programs which fit local conditions.

The general trend in corporate philanthropy appears to be a much tighter relationship between business objectives and selective contributions.

Internal Communications

The diversity of employees within the MNC makes the task of designing an effective internal communications program very challenging. The global reach of operations with linguistic and cultural differences requires a wider range of media by which to communicate with employees. The decision about the "official" language of corporate communication is a fundamental question. The home country language is the preferred choice for the primary language but secondary languages must be chosen with an eye for ease of communication. Multinational business demands multi-linguistic communication vehicles.

Print media is still the most important medium as company newsletters and magazines carry executive messages as well as local news targeted to specific employee audiences. But computer and telecommunications technology is supplementing paper. Live broadcasts from executive offices beam updated information to offices throughout the world. Teleconferencing and the Internet allow managers at various locations to maintain daily contact.

Fostering two-way communication so that employees have an opportunity to respond and provide feedback to executives is a critical element of a corporate internal communications program. Sensitivity to cultural differences is important in encouraging employee feedback. The power of unions in European countries dictates a close working relationship between managers and union leadership in understanding employee concerns. In countries where the family is the major institution in society (often where full families work together in a plant), feedback must be solicited through family heads. In democratic societies, asking individual employees for their ideas through regular meetings, focus groups and opinion surveys is the best option. Public affairs departments must work closely with their human resources counterparts to coordinate efforts in developing these programs.

The International Imprint on the Structure of Public Affairs

Organizing the public affairs function to carry out this portfolio of activities in a global market is a complex process with a number of variables. Corporate public affairs departments have begun to evolve structurally in response to changes in the MNC strategy and structure.[5] The most fundamental choice in structural design, of course, is whether to centralize or decentralize the decision-making process. Along with structural decisions comes the choice of mechanisms to use for the coordination of public affairs strategy across various countries.

Centralization or Decentralization

The choice between a centralized structure with strategy and policy dictated from corporate headquarters and a decentralized structure where local managers have greater discretion is dependent on *five factors*.

1. Corporate Strategy and Structure. The shape of the overall corporate strategy and its accompanying structure is the most important factor in the design of the public affairs structure. It often depends on the mission, and the status of that mission in various countries. A market strategy which focuses on the manufacture and distribution of standardized, low-cost products throughout the world is most often executed through tight control from corporate headquarters. A centralized public affairs department with full authority given to the chief public affairs officer in the home office is the preferred choice to accompany this type of strategy. On the other hand, a market strategy which focuses on distinctive products for individual countries or regions, allows country managers considerable discretion to respond to local demands. The corresponding public affairs structure is one in which staff are assigned to national subsidiaries with the responsibility for designing programs which are responsive to local demands. Many large MNCs have a hybrid market strategy with a confederation organizational structure which dictates a shared approach to decision-making within the worldwide public affairs function.

2. Corporate Size. The larger the corporation and the more extensive its operations, the more likely that it will develop a confederation organizational structure. The public affairs structure should conform to this shared decision-making model because differences in public policy issues and culture require strategies which balance global consistency and local responsiveness. The chief public affairs officer will be responsible for the umbrella strategy while encouraging local staff to adapt it to their individual contexts. The smaller MNC will most often centralize its public affairs decision-making until it expands its operations into a number of countries.

3. Scope of the Public Affairs Function. In the early stages of internationalization, the corporate public affairs function is limited in scope and, perhaps, even managed by the CEO. As the function evolves into one with a broad portfolio of activities, it will begin to expand its staffing both at headquarters and within national subsidiaries. Authority to design programs and address public policy issues will be delegated to these professionals with the assumption that they can balance global and local demands.

4. Quality and Availability of the Public Affairs Staff. The fewer the qualified public affairs professionals available to the corporation, the more likely the function will be centralized. The hiring of more professionals allows for greater decentralization. As they are placed throughout the global network, they are able to take on more responsibility for assisting country managers in their operations.

5. Types of Programs and Issues. Community relations and philanthropy will be delegated to the local level because of the need to be responsive to local demands. Government relations, on the other hand, will more likely be centrally coordinated in order to integrate strategies directed toward home and host countries. Issue management and media relations increasingly require a shared approach in order to respond to the tendency by activist groups and the media to internationalize local issues. Internal communications is also shared between headquarters and national subsidiaries so as to maintain consistency in the corporate message while focusing on differences among employee groups.[6]

Types of Coordinating Strategies

A public affairs strategy has three major objectives: conformity to overall corporate strategy, consistency across various countries and easy accessibility to vital information. There are a number of methods by which to coordinate public affairs across various countries to meet these objectives.

1. Mission Statement and Strategic Plan. These form the basis for linking all operations of the corporation. They serve as the reference points for assessing the legitimacy and effectiveness of public affairs programs and policies.

2. Visitation by Headquarters Public Affairs Executives. Regular visits by top public affairs executives to operations abroad provide opportunities to explain and coordiante corporate strategy and policy as well as to update information about issues in the field.

3. Meetings of the Public Affairs Staff. An annual meeting of key public affairs professionals is an important vehicle for updates on shifts in corporate strategy. It also provides a forum for discussing emerging issues within each country or region to identify points of linkage.

4. Electronic Communication. Regular correspondence by mail, telephone, fax and e-mail is essential for understanding the status of programs and policies. Teleconferencing allows for face-to-face discussions about issues and strategies.

5. Regular Performance Review of Individual Staff. An annual review of individual performance is critical for monitoring staff assigned to subsidiaries. These meetings reinforce the links between individual and corporate objectives.

6. Training Programs. Programs which focus on various aspects of public affairs management nurture individual development as well as instill a sense of professionalism.

7. Cross-Country Staff Assignments. The movement of staff among various subsidiaries and headquarters gives them exposure to the global public affairs operations. It broadens their perspective on the range of issues faced by the corporation in different countries and reinforces the need to balance consistency with adaptability.

Again, these objectives are applicable not only in international public affairs settings, but also in domestic public affairs.

The International Imprint
on the Public Affairs Staff

Managing this complex portfolio of activities in a structure which fits nicely within the corporation requires skilled and knowledgeable professionals. Staffing the public affairs function with high quality full-time employees and part-time consultants is critical to the success of a public affairs strategy.

Selecting and Managing the Corporate Staff

Effective full-time public affairs professionals must be able to manage three sets of conflicting demands.

1. The tension between achieving corporate objectives and satisfying stakeholder demands. Public affairs professionals need a full understanding of the competitive realities of the market. They must have facility with the languages of strategy, marketing and production in order to understand how top management attempts to position the corporation within its competitive environment. They must have a strong grounding in finance in order to understand the impact of international markets on corporate financing and stock prices. Finally, they must appreciate the corporate imperative to survive and grow as measured by the bottom line of profitability.

On the other hand, public affairs professionals need to be able to respond to the demands of various stakeholder groups. Strong ties with stakeholders must be established in order to understand their stake in the corporation, their values and commitments and their resource base. Because stakeholders have limited views, the public affairs staff must be skillful in communicating a fuller picture of the corporation and its needs. They must also become skilled negotiators in order to forge mutually acceptable agreements with stakeholders on specific issues.

2. The tension between global and national demands. The acculturation process of the public affairs professional requires full involvement in the operation of a national subsidiary while maintaining a commitment to the global corporation. This inevitable tension between the global and national is difficult to manage and can lead to an identification with one side or the other. The professional can become so deeply immersed in the local culture that he or she "goes native." Personal identity becomes linked with a particular nationality or culture with only a grudging loyalty to the corporation. On the other hand, the professional can become totally absorbed in the culture of the corporation so that local differences and expectations are discounted as trivial. This tension must be addressed for effectiveness in the job of public affairs.

Management can utilize various methods to assure that this tension is recognized and managed successfully. A series of assignments in different countries forces the professional to recognize the continual balancing of local and global cultures. Incorporating various nationalities into public affairs departments, or as members of short-term project teams, encourages cross-cultural awareness. Corporate training programs focused on expanding cultural sensitivity and expertise can be offered (Burk 1994). Each of these methods reinforce the international character of the MNC as it pursues its strategies in various markets, countries and cultures.

3. The tension between functional expertise and general management capability. A major objective of public affairs professionals is to continually refocus the corporation on its external environment and to assist managers and employees to respond to its demands. Like other functional managers, the public affairs professional has to continue to develop a specialized knowledge base and set of skills. Without attention to personal professional growth, the corporation will lose one of its core competencies. On the other hand, the public affairs professional must see himself or herself as part of the general management team that is dedicated to the sustainability of the corporation as a whole. Success in general management comes from experience and education beyond the narrow confines of public affairs.

This tension is most apparent at the local level where functional managers work closely as a team. Sharp edges must be smoothed through daily contact with others whose perspectives have been honed in marketing, production, finance, engineering, and human resources and public affairs. Public affairs professionals are incorporated in the process of translating the corporate strategy into a national strategy. The specific focus of public affairs is meshed with others to achieve divisional goals.

Choosing and Managing Consultants

International consultants provide a valuable resource for public affairs executives. They can handle specific projects without the additional cost of fringe benefits and office space. They can open channels of communication in other countries because of their contacts and friendships. They can provide insights into cultural nuances which may not be understood by corporate staff. Overall, consultants can become strategic partners to leverage scarce resources for more significant impact.

Consultants must be chosen with care. Small, national consulting firms offer more flexibility and special expertise while large, multinational firms with offices throughout the world can coordinate activities across a number of countries (Epley 1992). The critical objective is getting timely response to local issues while maintaining consistency on a global level. Contracting with a large, full-service firm is one way of meeting this objective. An alternative is to contract for country-specific projects with smaller firms that are tied into the emerging global network of independent public affairs firms.

The chief public affairs executive needs to develop a long-term strategy which couples internal with external expertise. Internal staff bring a full understanding of the broad corporate strategy to bear on addressing issues and designing programs. External consultants bring specific expertise in a country or region as well as experience from working with other firms. The integration of these two sets of professionals guarantees successful implementation of the strategy.

Summary

The advent of globalization poses unprecedented challenges and opportunities for public affairs professionals. Profound changes in markets and societies have generated the need to reassess many basic assumptions about the practice of public affairs. A new philosophy must be developed to lay the foundation for reshaping activities, structures and staffing to become truly international. A new global perspective, freed from the parochialism of national biases, will support corporate management as they cross national borders to compete in new markets.

The encouraging spread of democracy around the world means that power if being diffused. It means that the natural constituencies of public relations/public affairs professionals—whether these constituencies are called stakeholders, publics, audiences, or simply "groups of important people"—are increasingly important to the success of virtually any international enterprise. This means that public affairs professionals who prepare adequately will have a bright future indeed.

Notes

1. Another interesting exception to this trend is the rapid growth of the field of public relations in the Peoples Republic of China. Sam Black (1992) estimates that 100,000 people are employed in the field with another 500,000 taking courses. Two journals have been launched and the China International Public Relations Association has grown rapidly in membership.

2. This chapter will focus on public affairs within the multinational corporation. Here, the term "public affairs" describes the comprehensive process and set of activities by which the corporation attempts to manage its external environment. The study by James Post (1993) confirms this trend toward subsuming a wide variety of activities under the umbrella term of "public affairs" in the corporation. The multinational corporation is important because it is the primary venue for international public affairs whether carried out by internal staff or consultants. The latter are most often based in the public affairs or public relations firms whose primary goal is to assist in planning and implementing corporate public affairs strategy.

3. Larissa Grunig (1992) suggests that public relations has been too limited in its focus on a single public. She introduces the term "publics relations" to describe the various constituencies of the corporation. The concept of stakeholders, although similar, is a more comprehensive term for understanding the groups which are intimately linked with the corporation.

4. Joyce Wouters (1992) provides a comprehensive overview of how to design a media relations program for the international market. Her book identifies major communication media, makes suggestions for selected countries and gives insights into the cultural differences of various audiences.

5. The first major study of 15 MNCs found significant differences in the management of the public affairs function (Dunn, Cahill & Boddewyn 1979). No standard method or structure for coordinating public affairs activities across countries was evident. A follow-up analysis by J. J. Boddewyn (1982) suggested that the issue of centralization vs. decentralization needed resolution for more effective managment of the function. A Conference Board study (Lusterman 1985) confirmed the growth of public affairs within the MNC, but highlighted the fact that there was no consensus on how best to structure and manage across countries. A study of 9 American and 1 Dutch MNCs with public affairs offices in Brussels demonstrated the continuing difficulty in devising processes and structures by which to coordinate government relations and public affairs strategies focused on the new European Union (Lenn, Brenner, et al. 1993). A study of 405 of the largest U.S. MNCs (Meznar 1995) and another one focused on 125 U.S. and non-U.S. MNCs asssociated with the Global Public Affairs Institute (Kennelly & Gladwin 1995) give a more comprehensive picture of international public affairs. Both studies conclude that there is still no consensus on the best way to integrate public affairs strategy into an overall corporate strategy.

6. The study by Martin Meznar in 1995 confirms the centralization of government relations programs. He concludes that "social issue" management

is decentralized to the local level, a somewhat surprising finding in light of the trend toward the internationalization of a number of local issues which require a comprehensive response by corporate management.

References

Andrews, P. (1987). *Public affairs offices in large U.S. corporations: Evaluation, structure, and development.* Ph.D. Dissertation, Boston University.

Baron, D. (1993). *Business and its environment.* Englewood Cliffs, NJ: Prentice-Hall.

Barlett, C. A. & Ghoshal, S. (1989). *Managing across borders: The transnational solution.* Boston: Harvard Business School Press.

Black, S. (1992). Chinese update. *Public relations quarterly,* Fall: 41-42.

Boddewyn, J. J. (1982). International pubic affairs. In J. Walter & T. Murray (Eds.), *Handbook of international business.* New York: John Wiley.

Botan, C. (1992). International public relations: Critique and reformulation. *Public relations review,* 18(2): 149-159.

Burk, J. (1994). Training MNC employees as culturally sensitive boundary spanners. *Public relations quarterly,* Summer: 40-44.

Corbett, W. J. (1991). EC '92: Communicating in the new Europe. *Public relations quarterly,* Winter: 7-13.

Dunn, S. W.; Cahill, M. F. & Boddewyn, J. J. (1979). *How fifteen transnational corporations manage public affairs.* Chicago: Crain Books.

Epley, J. S. (1992). Public relations in the global village: An American perspective. *Public relations review,* 18(2):109-116.

Fitzpatrick, K. R. & Whillock, R.K. (1993). Assessing the impact of globalization on U.S. public relations. *Public relations review,* 19(4): 315-325.

Gomez, A. B. (1992). Not public relations but integrated social communication. *International public relations review,* 15(2): 9-10.

Grunig, L. A. (1992). Strategic public relations constituencies on a global scale. *Public relations review,* 18(2): 127-136.

Hiebert, R. E. (1992). Global public relations in a post-communist world: A new model. *Public relations review,* 18(2), 117-126.

Kennelly, J. J. & Gladwin, T.N. (1995). Patterns and trends in the management of global public affairs. In D. Collins (Ed.), *1995 proceedings of the International Association for Business and Society.* Vienna, Austria: International Association for Business and Society: 26-35.

Lenn, D. J.; Brenner, S. N.; *et al.*(1993). Managing corporate public affairs and government relations: U.S. multinational corporations in Europe. In J. E. Post (Ed.), *Corporate social performance and policy,* Vol. 14, Greenwich, CT: JAI Press: 103-138.

Lusterman, S. (1985). *Managing international public affairs.* New York: The Conference Board.

Meznar, M. B. (1995). Public affairs practices in multinational corporations: A description and preliminary analysis. In D. Collins (Ed.), *1995 proceedings of the International Association for Business and Society.* Vienna, Austria: International Association for Business and Society: 19-25.

Post, J. E. (1993). The state of corporate public affairs in the United States: Results of a national survey. In J. E. Post (Ed.), *Corporate social performance and policy,* Vol. 14, Greenwich, CT: JAI Press: 79-89.

Reed, J. M. (1989). International media relations: Avoid self-blinding. *Public relations quarterly,* Summer: 12-15.

Sharpe, M. L. (1992). The impact of social and cultural conditioning on global public relations. *Public relations review,* 18(2): 103-107.

Wouters, J. (1992). *International public relations.* New York: AMACOM.

About the Editor

Lloyd B. Dennis is a public affairs executive with nearly 30 years experience in developing and managing strategic corporate communications programs for major institutions in both the public and private sectors.

In 1993 he opened a public affairs consulting practice in Los Angeles. From the mid-1980s until the end of 1992, Dennis served as executive director of public affairs at the Los Angeles Department of Water and Power, the nation's largest municipal utility. For the 15 years prior, he was at First Interstate Bank of California, where as senior vice president and director of public affairs he managed all external relations activities, including serving as president of the Bank's Foundation.

Prior to joining First Interstate, Dennis worked as speech writer and public information officer to three Secretaries of the Treasury, in both the Johnson and Nixon Administrations, in the Office of the Assistant Secretary for Public Affairs, U.S. Treasury Department. Prior experience included working for nearly ten years as a journalist with *The New York Times*, in both the New York and Washington offices; *The Baltimore Sun* and *Congressional Quarterly*.

He has published many articles on public affairs, corporate communications and public policy issues; has lectured at numerous business schools; and has conducted a graduate course, "Public Affairs and Business," at the School of Public Administration at the University of Southern California. He holds a Master of Arts degree from the School of International Service, American University, Washington, D.C., and a Bachelor of Arts degree from the School of Communications, Boston University.

About the Editorial Project Director

Gary D. Avery is a political scientist by training and has been active as a communications professional for 32 years. In addition to serving as project manager for this book, he has had extensive experience on Capitol Hill and in the commercial banking industry in both California and Washington, D.C.

Avery's involvement with this project began in 1992 when he was invited by the Public Affairs and Government Section to prepare a feasibility study. Project manager duties commenced one year later.

Avery consults extensively with both private and public sector clients. In addition to editorial services, specialties include government relations and community affairs. A native of Pekin, Illinois, he holds a B. A. With Honors in Government from Valparaiso University, a Master's degree from Arizona State University and has completed all coursework and examinations for a doctorate in Political Science and Public Administration at the University of Maryland. He has lectured on public affairs in the School of Business at California State University, Los Angeles.

About the Contributors

William C. Adams, APR, Fellow PRSA, associate professor in the School of Journalism and Mass Communication, Florida International University. A corporate communications professional for 25 years prior to joining FIU, Adams is co-author of *The Media Guide for Academics*.

Kenneth P. Arnold, APR, manages Ogilvy Adams & Rinehart's work on behalf of the Chlorine Chemistry Council. He has also coordinated press activities involving EPA and FDA regulation of agricultural chemicals and food safety procedures. Prior to joining OA&R he was with the T. Dean Reed Company.

William C. Ashley is president of Ashley & Associates, a consulting center specializing in anticipatory management techniques. He was chief architect of the anticipatory management and strategic trend programs at Sears, McDonalds and United Airlines. He is co-author of *Anticipatory Management: 10 Power Tools for Achieving Excellence into the 21st Century*.

Gary D. Avery is an independent public affairs counselor based in the Washington, D.C. area. Since 1985 he has consulted with large organizations in both the public and private sectors including Southern California Association of Governments, Rockwell International and KCET-PBS for Central and Southern California. Earlier he served as a legislative aide to U.S. Senators Birch Bayh and Walter Mondale and as a Washington representative for Chase Manhattan Bank. Beginning in 1973 he was vice president for government relations at First Interstate Bank of California.

Janet M. Bedrosian, APR, is the congressional/legislative liaison with the External Affairs staff of the U.S. Bureau of Land Management in Sacramento. She was previously with the Bureau's Public Affairs Office in Washington, D.C. as a public information officer and assistant chief for public affairs operations.

Herb B. Berkowitz, vice president for public relations at The Heritage Foundation, is a former magazine journalist.

Sylvia J. Brucchi, APR, director of public affairs for the Pacific Northwest Region of the USDA Forest Service, has spent more than 25 years with the Service encouraging the agency and its constituents to work together in the stewardship of the nation's national forests.

Sara Burton resides in Japan where she teaches Japanese business people. She was formerly the manager-administration of the North American Public Affairs Research Group (NAPARG), School of Business and Economics, Wilfrid Laurier University. She has contributed to several publications in the public affairs benchmarking area.

W. Howard Chase, president of Howard Chase Enterprises, was one of the founders of the Public Relations Society of America. He has worked for Fortune 100 Companies and served as counsel to several Administrations. In addition to lecturing and consulting, Dr. Chase is the author of *Issue Management: Origins of the Future* and founding editor of "Corporate Public Issues and Their Management."

John F. Coy is president of The Consulting Network, a company that specializes in providing management and strategic planning services to major corporations in the areas of corporate social responsibility, community relations, contributions, and workplace philanthropy. He serves as a senior consultant to the Corporate Services division of the Council on Foundations and has written a number of articles and publications on corporate citizenship.

Teresa Yancey Crane is president of Issue Action Publications, Inc., a publishing firm specializing in newsletters, reports and books on corporate public policy and issue management. Crane has covered the field of issue management since 1979, when she began writing for *Corporate Public Issues and Their Management*, the twice-monthly newsletter she now edits and publishes. In 1988, Crane founded the Issue Management Council, a membership organization for corporate issue managers, where she now serves as president.

Michael K. Deaver, executive vice president and director of corporate affairs of Edelman Public Relations, is an analyst of the American political scene. From 1981 to 1985 he was assistant to the President of the United States and deputy chief of the White House Staff. He is widely credited with being the architect of communications for President Reagan, including the Presidential campaigns of 1980 and 1984.

Lloyd B. Dennis is president of his own public affairs consulting firm in Los Angeles. His more than 30 years of public affairs experience includes work in both the public and private sectors. He holds an M.A. and B.A. and has taught "Public Affairs in Business" for several semesters at the School of Public Administration at the University of Southern California. The author's contribution to the chapter "Historical Antecedents: Public Affairs in Full Flower— 1975-1985" is dedicated in memory of a mentor and pioneer in corporate social responsibility, Stephen D. Gavin.

William E. Duke, APR, Fellow PRSA, currently serves as senior consultant to the Western States Petroleum Association and Pacific Visions Communications of Los Angeles, where he provides counsel to the National Association of Counties, American Psychological Association, and the Kennedy Center. Mr. Duke also is Professor Emeritus at the University of Southern California, where he teaches graduate communications and journalism classes. From 1973 to 1990 he held increasingly more responsible public relations/public affairs positions with ARCO in both Washington and Los Angeles. Before joining ARCO he had been a journalist, broadcaster, U.S. Senate and campaign aide, and the first director of public affairs of the Corporation for Public Broadcasting.

Edwin A. Feulner, Jr. is president of The Heritage Foundation and past chairman of the U.S. Advisory Commission on Public Diplomacy, which oversees the U.S. Information Agency and Voice of America.

Craig S. Fleisher, Ph.D., associate professor of Business Policy and Law in the School of Business and Economics, Wilfred Laurier University, is author of *Public Affairs Benchmarking: A Comprehensive Guide* and over 50 articles in journals such as "Long Range Planning," "Total Quality Management" and "Public Relations Review."

Stuart Z. Goldstein is vice president, corporate communications, National Securities Clearing Corporation in New York. He has extensive experience in both corporate communications and public affairs as well as both the public and private sectors. He spent a decade running political campaigns in New Jersey.

Hernando González is associate professor at the School of Journalism and Mass Communication at Florida International University. He consults extensively in international communications. His Ph.D. is from Stanford University.

Kirk O. Hanson is a senior faculty member at the Stanford University Graduate School of Business and chairman of the Santa Clara County Ethics Commission. He was the first president of the Business Enterprise Trust, promoting exemplary behavior in business, and has conducted corporate values and ethics workshops.

Mark A. Hart is a vice president with Public Communications, Inc. in Tampa. His areas of professional expertise include advocacy campaigns, corporate issues and community involvement, and public interest/public policy groups. He is a former account executive with Ogilvy & Mather Public Relations and reporter for the *Chicago Tribune*. This author's contribution was made in memory of Rick F. Orsinger, J.D.

Raymond L. Hoewing is president of the Public Affairs Council, a business-financed association serving public affairs executives. He previously spent several years in line management positions with Inland Steel Company and was active in politics in Illinois. He has taught government affairs at the graduate level at George Washington University.

John M. Holcomb is associate professor of Legal Studies and Business Ethics at the University of Denver. He previously served on the staff of the Public Affairs Council.

James F. Keane, Ph.D., is a lobbyist with Winston Strawn in Chicago. He recently served as senior fellow at the University of Illinois' Institute of Government and Public Affairs. Keane is a former member of the Illinois House of Representatives where he served as Deputy Majority Leader. He is a co-editor of *Illinois Local Government: A Handbook.*

Kenneth D. Kearns, APR, a partner in San Francisco-based Kearns & West, is a public relations counselor working to expand the use of effective public relations to improve decision making at all levels of society. He specializes in energy, the environment and telecommunications.

Gary Koch, APR, is communications/education coordinator for the Illinois Municipal League and adjunct assistant professor of communications at Lincoln Land Community College and Springfield College. He is co-editor of *Illinois Local Government: A Handbook.*

William J. Koch, APR, Fellow PRSA, is director of communications and public relations for Ohio-based Laidlaw Passenger Services Group. He previously served as executive vice president and CEO for Meeker Public Relations. He is co-author of *No Surprises: The Crisis Communications Management System.*

Margery Kraus is president and CEO of APCO Associates, a Washington, D.C. firm providing public affairs and public relations services. She also manages the global public affairs practice of the GCI Group, APCO's parent company, and a division of Grey Advertising.

Nick L. Laird, J.D., is president of Laird & Associates, a public affairs, issues management firm that offers consulting assistance on creating and managing profit center programs. His background in industry and public service includes serving as Administrative and Legislative Assistant to two Congressmen; Washington representative for Shell Oil Company; and Executive Director of the Electric Reliability Coalition.

D. Jeffrey Lenn, Ph.D., is associate professor of Strategic Management and Public Policy in the School of Business and Public Management at The George Washington University. His research and teaching focus on business-government relations, corporate political strategy and strategic management. He has consulted with a number of corporations as well as many governmental agencies and associations.

James E. Lukaszewski, APR, Fellow PRSA, is a public relations counselor, assistant adjunct professor of communications at New York University's Management Institute and civilian advisor to the U.S. Marine Corps. He is a former deputy commissioner of the Minnesota Department of Economic Development and author of the series *Executive Action Crisis Management, Executive Action Crisis Management Workbook* and *Executive Action Emergency Media Relations Guide*.

Charles S. Mack is president and CEO of the Business-Industry Political Action Committee (BIPAC). In over 30 years of corporate, association and political experience at both state and national levels, he has been president of the New York State Food Merchants Association and director of public affairs for CPC International Inc. He is the author of *Lobbying and Government Relations: A Guide for Executives* and *The Executive's Handbook of Trade and Business Associations*.

Richard R. Mau is senior vice president of communications for Rockwell International Corporation. He was previously vice president of public and financial relations for Raytheon Company and prior to that, vice president of corporate and government relations at Sperry Corporation.

Patrick A. McGee, APR, is vice president of the Public Affairs Practice Group at Langdon Starr, Inc. in Toronto. A public relations consultant and chair of the Board of Directors of the Canadians for Health Research Society, he began his career as a journalist and subsequently worked in both corporate public relations and as a government advisor in the Province of Alberta.

Richard Alan Nelson, Ph.D., APR, is associate dean for graduate studies and research and professor, Manship School of Mass Communication, Louisiana State University, Baton Rouge, Louisiana. He is co-author of *Issues Management: Corporate Public Policymak-*

ing in an Information Society, (1989), and author of the forthcoming *A Chronology and Glossary of Propaganda in the United States.* Nelson is listed in the Heritage Foundation's annual guide to public policy experts.

Robert A. Neuman is president of Neuman and Company. A former senior consultant to the 1992 Clinton/Gore campaign at the Democratic National Convention, he was a vice president with Ogilvy & Mather Public Affairs from 1989 to 1991. He was for many years a senior advisor to Congressman Morris Udall and was co-author of Udall's *Too Funny to be President* in 1988.

Kathleen O'Neil is a vice president at Roper Starch Worldwide Inc., the nation's oldest opinion polling firm. She is an expert in public opinion research. She has directed surveys of many different target populations, using a wide variety of methodologics. Her clients have included Fortune 500 companies, government agencies, trade associations, major newspapers and magazines, and non-profit organizations. Ms. O'Neil has a B.A. from Boston College and a master's degree in communications from Cornell University.

John L. Paluszek, APR, Fellow PRSA, has been president of Ketchum Public Affairs since 1984. He managed the public relations firm Paluszek & Leslie Associates, Inc. prior to its acquisition by Ketchum Communications. A pioneer in linking public relations to social responsibility, Paluszek founded Corporate Social Action, Inc. in 1972. In 1992 he received the PRSA Gold Anvil award for lifetime achievement in public reations. He is author of *Will the Corporation Survive?* and *An American Journey.*

Ronald E. Rhody, APR, Fellow PRSA, is the chief executive of Rhody and Company, Inc., a public relations and communications consulting firm formed to help organizations successfully manage their way through periods of significant change. Prior to forming RCI, he was executive vice president and director, Corporate Communications and External Affairs, for Bank-America Corporation and Bank of America NT&SA and a member of the corporation's Senior Management Council. He began his career in print and broadcast journalism and in state government in his native Kentucky.

Anna L. West, APR, is a partner in San-Francisco-based Kearns & West, specializing in developing collaborative solutions among traditional adversaries in energy, the environment and telecommunications.

Barbara Whitney is president of Barbara Whitney & Associates, an executive recruiting firm she founded in 1986. She also serves as a consultant to the Public Affairs Council where she has been director of career counseling since 1981. She has also worked in business management and for national research and recruiting firms.